Donne's Prebend Sermons

Donne's Prebend Sermons

Edited, with an Introduction
and Commentary, by
Janel M. Mueller

Harvard University Press
Cambridge, Massachusetts
1971

© Copyright 1971 by the President and Fellows of Harvard College
All rights reserved
Distributed in Great Britain by Oxford University Press, London
Library of Congress Catalog Card Number 77–143229
SBN 674–21485–4
Printed in the United States of America

To Herschel Baker

Preface

An edition of Donne's Prebend sermons that follows so closely in the wake of George Potter's and Evelyn Simpson's monumental, ten-volume *Sermons of John Donne* requires some explanation. What I have done here is conceived both as an outgrowth of their edition and as an independent introduction to Donne's preaching. I shall explain my two purposes in turn.

The Potter-Simpson edition performed the invaluable service of furnishing accessible and reliable texts of Donne's one hundred and fifty known sermons, listing variant readings in the seventeenth-century manuscripts and editions (as well as the liberties taken in Henry Alford's nineteenth-century edition), raising general biographical, historical, and literary concerns in the Introductions, and, in the Appendices to the last volume, laying groundwork for the source study and annotation which had to be foregone because of the massiveness of the basic undertaking. My debt to Potter and Mrs. Simpson is evident. My own Introduction particularizes and enlarges upon the concerns of their Introductions, especially in attempting to indicate what in the Prebend sermons reflects Donne in particular and what the program of the *via media* in general. In my Introduction I have also benefited from the work of R. C. Bald, Helen Gardner, Dennis Quinn, Ruth Wallerstein, and Joan Webber. Although this edition of mine was finished by the time that Winfried Schleiner's excellent study of the imagery of Donne's sermons appeared, I have been happy to discover how far we concur regarding the substance and emphases of Donne's preaching.

While the textual implications of my critical apparatus are, as might be expected, minor—the last section of the Introduction describes my divergences from Potter and Mrs. Simpson—the rest of the commentary is offered as a modest contribution to knowledge of Donne's preaching methods and as a corrective to unexamined assumptions.

In preparing this edition I have verified each instance of Donne's use of Scripture in the Prebend sermons and annotated his various practices in citing the English, Latin, and Hebrew versions which he evidently consulted. For a list of these versions I am greatly indebted to Don Cameron Allen's informative analysis of the citations in the *LXXX Sermons* of 1640 ("Dean Donne Sets His Text," *Journal of English Literary History*, X (1943), 208–229). My findings as a whole, which are tabulated in Appendix B, establish Donne as an equal master with Lancelot Andrewes, the acknowledged leader of conservative Anglican preachers in the earlier seventeenth century, in demonstrating the integrality of the Word of God in human discourse by means of the profuse citation and allusion which are so marked a feature—if not, as more radical preachers then thought, a fault—of the sermons of this school. In particular, my findings with regard to Donne's use of Scripture reveal a much more energetic and wide-ranging use of English and Latin versions than is commonly supposed. This, however, is a use geared not simply to philological niceties but to possibilities of illustrating—which for Donne meant imaging—the meaning of a text. In fact, Donne's employment of different versions of the Bible in the imagistic development of his exegesis shows especially clearly in the Prebend sermons. I have tried to document the process as fully as possible, since it is an integral factor in his particular method of preaching and a primary link between Donne and homiletic tradition as well.

In addition, I have traced to their sources most of Donne's references to the Church Fathers, the Scholastics, and other commentators and writers in the Prebend sermons. Nearly all of this research breaks new ground. Because of Alford's inadequate edition and Donne's own practice of citing passages accurately but giving inexact indications of his sources, there is at present almost no confirmation of the showy but demonstrably genuine erudition which his preaching shared with the school of Andrewes. In default of a broad study of the extent to which sixteenth- and seventeenth-century Anglicans implemented their appeal to the Creeds, Councils, and Fathers of the first five Christian centuries and to the supporting weight of the majority view in subsequent tradition, Donne's chief contemporaries and successors remain yet quite satisfactorily annotated in the Library of Anglo-Catholic

Theology, and his forbears superbly served by the volumes of the Parker Society. In Donne's case exceptionally, then, evidence of his kinds of sources, and the use he made of them, is lacking. (Mary Paton Ramsay's still important pioneer study, *Les Doctrines médiévales chez Donne* [London, 1917], deals almost exclusively with neo-Platonic elements.) In view of the critical and scholarly attention lavished on Donne's poetry and the lengths to which primary materials have been traced both in Milton's prose and poetry, the current state of affairs is all the more remarkable. I have begun on a remedy by collecting evidence that Donne was as deeply read in the entire history of theology and exegesis as Izaak Walton, his first biographer, claimed. Beyond this fact, Donne's predilections emerge as being strongly toward the central Anglican synthesis for which St. Augustine and St. Thomas Aquinas are chiefly the basis of support. But Donne's more particular and nearly exclusive bias toward Latin texts and versions when invoking authorities seems to be the stamp of his earliest education, on which his later study of Greek and Hebrew had little effect. Likewise, the greater frequency with which Donne cites Roman rather than Reformed authors of the sixteenth and seventeenth centuries may be a trace of the route by which he personally found his place in the Church of England. Yet, Donne's Anglicanism is anything but idiosyncratic. In documenting the solidity of his doctrinal and exegetical positions I have been fortunate in Charles H. and Katherine George's compilation of the gamut of much opinion in *The Protestant Mind of the English Reformation, 1570–1640* (Princeton, N.J.: Princeton University Press, 1961). But where my commentary treats Donne's own thought and work, or the larger English background, I have gleaned from a variety of sources in attempting to set the Prebend sermons within a relevant and revealing context. My attempt has been preceded in a large and general way by R. C. Bald's welcome new, full-scale biography of Donne, which admirably furnishes contextual references for every phase but necessarily focuses more on the man than on his works.

As an independent introduction to Donne's preaching, this edition of the Prebend sermons has many competitors for attention. There have been many recent collections which aim at familiarizing the generally informed reader with the homiletic achievement of a well-known poet. While it is easy to see that the bulk of Donne's sermons is too formidable ever to gain a large audience, it is not easy to agree on selecting among them. Why have I chosen the Prebend sermons? First, because anthologizers of Donne's prose have for the most part excerpted passages from his preaching, advancing appreciation at the cost of considerable misconception. This cost is too high, as the gatherings of entire individual sermons—for example, Mrs. Simpson's and Edmund Fuller's—have demonstrated. It need not be argued that a sermon of Donne's, like any other work, is best read and certainly best understood whole. But I do wish to claim that the advantage of wholeness extends to an entire series in the case of the five Prebend sermons, and that as a unit they rank high among Donne's best and most representative productions. (The unit, as originally designed, was preserved in its first printing in *LXXX Sermons*—and in Alford's otherwise highhanded edition—but is broken in the chronological ordering of Potter and Mrs. Simpson.) This edition attempts to eschew the vices of other volumes of selections from Donne's sermons—such as, all too often, excising Donne's Latin phrases and copious doubling—but to practice their virtues of manageability and informativeness.

What I hope from my presentation of the Prebend sermons is that Donne will stand revealed at the height of his powers and productivity in his ministry, in full mastery of the means of interpretation and discourse which he took over from homiletic tradition but made his own through years of experiment. Beyond this, I hope Donne will register as the truly distinctive figure he was. I am not now thinking only of his prodigious wit and eloquence—for Donne in our century receives his literary due—but of his impressive conception of what the Christian ministry required of him and his fidelity to this conception, whatever inward struggle it involved. If, as Douglas Bush has claimed, Donne's broadmindedness toward differing religious and political points of view has been overestimated, the facts show, none the less, that Donne exercised salutary and rare restraint in the mounting quarrel between Crown and people in his day and that there was a professional price for giving his preaching all of the enduring moral rather than topical thrust he could achieve. In the rash of preferments to the episcopate in the first years of Charles I's reign, Donne was not made a bishop although far less distinguished and deserving men among the conservative Anglican party were. And, despite his great personal reputation as a preacher, only six of Donne's sermons were published in his lifetime while torrents of graceless and timeserving prose ran through the presses of London and Oxford. Yet if the revitalizing of traditional homiletic purposes and the establishment of a distinctly Anglican approach to the interpretation of Scripture in preaching were insufficient to recommend Donne's sermons to the printers of his day, it is now increasingly recognized that Donne's sermons, together with Richard Hooker's *Of the Laws of Ecclesiastical Polity,* are our most valuable written legacy from the great constructive phase of English Protestantism. If this edition in any way furthers recognition of Donne's role in this achievement, it will have justified itself beyond the explanations of this Preface.

I gratefully acknowledge permission from the University of California Press to reproduce the Prebend sermons from the Potter-Simpson edition.

My thanks are also due for the use of rare book collections at Alma College, Los Gatos, California; the University of Chicago; the University of Illinois at Urbana; Loyola University at Chicago; The Newberry Library; and Seabury-Western Theological Seminary; and my use of the microfilm services of the Bibliothèque Nationale and the British Museum. I owe much to Professor Coert Rylaarsdam of the Divinity School of the University of Chicago for his assistance with Donne's Hebrew; and to Professors Paul Droulers and Garcia Villoslada of the Pontifical Gregorian University in Rome, and Professor Alan H. Nelson of the University of Chicago for help in research.

Several of my colleagues at the University of Chicago have given me moral support and my manuscript a careful reading; I owe thanks to David Bevington, John G. Cawelti, Arthur Friedman, Michael J. Murrin, William A. Ringler, Jr., and Edward W. Rosenheim, Jr. It is, moreover, a pleasure to acknowledge a debt of longer standing—the guidance in working on Donne's sermons which I received as a graduate student from Herschel Baker, Douglas Bush, and Kenneth B. Murdock of Harvard University. Herschel Baker has also kindly read and made suggestions regarding the present study. My last and greatest indebtedness is to my husband Ian, who, in this venture as in all other things, has been my twin compass.

J.M.M.

Contents

Introduction

Introduction

THE BIOGRAPHICAL CONTEXT

Unlike Saul of Tarsus who in a blinding flash from heaven was called to become St. Paul, the rake Jack became the exemplary Doctor Donne through a long, agonizing, and equivocal process. There was never a more equivocal moment than just before Donne's taking of holy orders when he announced his intention of printing his poems and made a last desperate attempt to secure civil employment by importuning the Earl of Somerset. But the will of God and of King James, who refused to envisage Donne as anything but a preacher, held fast. Was Stuart divine prerogative ever more conclusively proven upon a subject? At last Donne, whose perceptions were always acute (it is he who remarked in a letter on the change from Jack to Doctor Donne), exercised his penchant for analogical thinking and discerned God's hand in that of his monarch, to which he submitted.[1] Still the change from resolute courtier to committed divine would continue.

The whole process was as it was because Donne, more like his other self-chosen spiritual progenitor, St. Augustine, was a man of extraordinary sexual passion, ambition, self-consciousness, and verbal endowments, added to acute intelligence. Both were impelled to worldly experience and enjoyment beyond the impulsions of most men, and both adopted a Christian world-view that placed strong emphasis on the working of God's providence in the particulars of events and objects, on the wilfulness of human nature, and on the power of rhetoric (especially figurative language that rendered concrete the movement of thought and emotion) to bring the soul to an awareness of divine

1. R. C. Bald in fact demonstrates that Donne could have had some secular appointment in 1614 but acceded instead to the King's preference that he take holy orders. See *John Donne: A Life* (New York and Oxford: Oxford University Press, 1970), pp. 291–294.

grace. The writings of these two men register throughout the personal implications of this world-view, but they are found most intensely and sustainedly in the narrative portion of St. Augustine's *Confessions* and in certain of Donne's divine poems, such as the Holy Sonnets and hymns, together with his *Devotions upon Emergent Occasions.* When Donne survived instead of succumbing—as he and his doctors expected —to relapsing fever, this work changed direction away from a last spiritual testament and became a pledge of renewal and final confirmation in his calling. It sets the pace and note of the subsequent productive period in his ministry: the glorious noon of his late-dawning day.

After an absence of several months occasioned by his fever, Donne returned to the pulpit of St. Paul's Cathedral in London at Easter 1624. Having been gravely ill he now spoke like a man brought back from the dead. He expatiated in his sermon on the figurative senses of his text, the "resurrections" of this life, which he construed (drawing upon St. Augustine) as deliverances from sin and suffering. But this Easter sermon is not merely an academic or ingenious verbal exercise; Donne's textual exposition is, in fact, a fuller version of the thoughts about recovery which he had recorded some weeks earlier in the twenty-first Expostulation and Prayer of the *Devotions,* written while he was still in his sickbed. He felt that he had been granted a personal Easter.

Like the dark wood where Dante found himself in middle life, Donne's illness midway in his ministry led to a new clearsightedness of the soul. His conviction that his life was restored so that he could preach resulted in many more extant sermons from the three years after his recovery than from any other three-year period of his ministry. All of these sermons are full-length discourses displaying the openness of form, the imagistic richness, and the breathless and manifold movement of suspended syntax to a swift close which have come to be associated with the maturation of Donne's pulpit style.[2] In contrast, as if to corroborate his absorption in his sermons, the letters and poems drop off noticeably after mid-1624. In March 1625 Donne sent his "Hymne

2. See especially chs. 2–6 of Joan Webber's *Contrary Music: The Prose Style of John Donne* (Madison, Wis.: University of Wisconsin Press, 1963) and ch. 4 of Winfried Schleiner's *The Imagery of John Donne's Sermons* (Providence, R.I.: Brown University Press, 1970).

to the Saints, and to Marquesse Hamylton" to Sir Robert Ker, confessing in his covering letter that the elegy had been troublesome to write. He also spelled out his preference for preaching:

> I presume you rather try what you can doe in me, than what I can doe in verse. . . . If you had commanded mee to have waited on his body to Scotland and preached there, I would have embraced the obligation with more alacrity.[3]

But the most compelling evidence of the special enthusiasm of Donne's middle years at St. Paul's, from mid-1624 to mid-1627, is found in the sermons themselves. Like the Cathedral's patron saint and like his favorite non-Biblical authority, St. Augustine, Donne had always made much of himself—particularly his past—in his preaching, in order to make much more of the grace of God through protestations of his own unworthiness. But after Donne's illness the focus shifts largely from the man to the work. "Who but my selfe can conceive the sweetnesse of that salutation, when the Spirit of God sayes to me in a morning, Go forth to day and preach," exclaimed Donne at Whitehall in April 1626.

> What a Coronation is our taking of Orders, by which God makes us a Royall Priesthood? And what an inthronization is the comming up into a Pulpit, where God invests his servants with his Ordinance, as with a Cloud, and then presses that Cloud with a *Vae si non,* woe be unto thee, if thou do not preach, and then enables him to preach peace, mercy, consolation, to the whole Congregation.[4]

Vae si non, an excerpt from the Vulgate rendering of a passage in St. Paul's first letter to the Corinthians where the urgency of preaching

---

3. Sir Edmund Gosse, *The Life and Letters of John Donne* (New York: Dodd, Mead and Co., 1899), II, 215.

4. *The Sermons of John Donne,* ed. Evelyn M. Simpson and George R. Potter, 10 vols. (Los Angeles and Berkeley, Calif.: University of California Press, 1953–1962), VII. 4. 570–572, 591–597. This edition is used for all quotations from the sermons; its system of volume, sermon, and line numbering is also adopted except in quotations from the Prebend sermons. Its critical apparatus is referred to in ordinary fashion by volume and page.

the Gospel and saving souls is described, echoes like a refrain through Donne's sermons and conveys the paramount sense of vocation which he felt in this period. But it was, doubtless, not unrelated to his increasing reputation as a preacher. Donne had long since overcome the reservations about "very pleasant poeticall deanes" expressed by John Chamberlain (but probably shared by other Londoners) at the time of Donne's appointment to the Deanery of St. Paul's in 1621.[5] It is clear that his fame solidified in the years from 1624 to 1627, mainly though not only at the Cathedral. The passage just quoted, for instance, is from a sermon delivered in his turn among the Chaplains-in-Ordinary to King Charles. Although King James had originally made the appointment as part of his promise to advance Donne if he took orders —a promise that reached to extracting his Doctor in Divinity degree from Cambridge University and conferring the Deanery of St. Paul's —Donne still remained more of a protégé than a power in his own right under the old King. Lancelot Andrewes was the *"Stella praedicantium"* of the reign, the oddest and most enduring of James I's string of favorites. But Donne's prestige as a court preacher increased with a change in monarchs. From the time of Andrewes' death in 1626, early in the new King's reign, until his own in 1631 Donne held an unrivaled position, for which there is no indication in his sermons or elsewhere of his paying the price of accommodation that William Laud was later to pay.[6] Donne was summoned to preach the first sermon King Charles heard, beginning a series of frequent court appearances; there are more court sermons from Donne's six years under Charles than from his ten under James. Moreover, Izaak Walton's *Life* testifies rapturously regarding the fruits, in these same years, of Donne's labors in the London parish of St. Dunstan's-in-the-West. He had been granted the living in the spring of 1624, just after his recovery. Among his eight extant sermons known to have been preached at St. Dun-

5. Letter of 17 November 1621 to Sir Dudley Carleton, *The Letters of John Chamberlain,* ed. Norman E. McClure (Philadelphia: American Philosophical Society, 1939), II, 408.

6. In his chapter entitled "Dean," Bald discusses several aspects of Donne's probity as a churchman in what must be remembered was always an Erastian context. The worst to be said of Donne is only that he was not energetically reformist. See *John Donne: A Life,* pp. 389–430.

stan's, six date from this period of phenomenal productivity and a seventh almost certainly belongs to it.[7]

Viewed as part of his dedication to preaching, Donne's Prebend sermons become representative of his middle years at St. Paul's simply by virtue of their conception. Donne set out to affirm a continuity between his routine liturgical duties and his preaching; the result was a series of five sermons in every way comparable to those which he delivered at Christmas, Easter, and Whitsunday when the Dean was required by statute to preach in the Cathedral. Since the great festivals of the church year were his particular responsibility, Donne always prepared a major discourse. But it is at once remarkable and thoroughly indicative of this period of his life that he should discover a similar incentive in his far more modest role as one of the thirty Prebendaries of St. Paul's.

The nature of the office of Prebendary is specified by the Statutes of St. Paul's Cathedral which regulate, among many other matters, the number, order, and rank of the clergy (or Chapter) and assign their tasks. Presided over by the Bishop of London, the Cathedral Chapter consisted of thirty regular canons, or Prebendaries, including the Dean. An ancient statute, believed to transmit apostolic practice, required that each canon recite daily a portion of the Psalter, *"pro salute vivorum et requie defunctorum Ecclesiae Beati Pauli benefactorum."*[8] The force of the prescription (and of the income from leased land by which Prebends were endowed) to insure the continuance of this daily recita-

---

7. This is "An Anniversary Sermon preached at S. Dunstans, upon the commemoration of a Parishioner, a Benefactor to that Parish" (*Sermons,* vol. X, no. 8). Baird W. Whitlock has suggested that this sermon is the one for which the Churchwardens' Accounts of St. Dunstan's record payment to Donne on 29 June 1624 ("Donne at St. Dunstan's—I," *London Times Literary Supplement* [16 September 1955], p. 548). Mrs. Simpson accepts Whitlock's suggestion (Introduction, *Sermons,* X, 25).

8. ("For the health of the living and the repose of the departed benefactors of St. Paul's Cathedral"), *Registrum Statutorum et Consuetudinum Ecclesiae Sancti Pauli Londinensis,* ed. W. Sparrow Simpson (London, 1873), p. xxi. Simpson calls attention to the fact that the great compilation of Cathedral statutes made by Dean Lisieux in 1450 includes a number of much earlier date. R. C. Bald discusses the functioning of the Prebendal system of the Cathedral with reference to Donne's own time (*John Donne: A Life,* pp. 389–399).

tion can be seen even at the present day. Along the row of thirty Prebendal stalls in the Cathedral choir, the first words of the individual portions are still posted over each stall as an aid to the memory. Donne was Prebendary of Chiswick; his Psalms were the sixty-second through the sixty-sixth,[9] in the numbering of the Authorized (King James) Version.

Donne says in his Prebend sermons that his decision to preach on a text from each of his five Psalms grew out of his desire to show and share their spiritual benefits. But a factor in this decision may have been an incident related by Walton that took place during Donne's near-fatal illness in the winter of 1623–24. As he lay in his sickbed, his life in doubt, he was visited by the well-meaning and worldly-wise cleric Dr. Henry King, who urged Donne to consider that it was time both to make a will providing for his seven children and to renew leases on the property endowing several Prebends, Donne's own included. King offered to take charge of renegotiating the leases so that Donne's Prebend—that was to say, under the circumstances, his estate —would be worth substantially more. Donne's answer was that he would not take money he had not earned, but in a characteristic manner he recast the personal question of profit or renunciation as a question of God's will. If he, Donne, were providentially restored to useful service in his calling, then he would gladly, as Walton reports his words, "take the reward which the bountiful benefactors of this church have designed me; for God knows my children and relations will need it." Perhaps, then, when Donne first contracted with his congregation in May 1625 to preach his Prebend sermons, this was part of a larger bargain.

Equally, however, there was another kind of connection. The idea recalls two of the distinguished preaching Fathers of the Greek Church, Origen and St. Chrysostom, and their homilies on texts from the daily lessons in the liturgy. Common to all such projects is the recognition that the service of worship and the message of the preacher alike derived directly out of the Word of God. The execution was intended to demonstrate, explicitly in Donne's case, the integrality of the Christian ministry and the vitality of its ancient traditional functions of prayer and preaching.

9. Simpson, *Registrum Statutorum*, p. 25.

No book of the Bible was more amenable to Donne's purpose of exhibiting—in an Anglican perspective—the vitality of Christian tradition than his favorite, the Psalms. Donne's affection for this book, to which he alluded on several occasions in his sermons, was not merely a poetic response to verse forms which controlled intense personal religious feeling and evoked associations of divine harmony and order. Donne also valued the wealth of typological significance that had been amassed by many commentators through the Christian centuries, beginning with the Fathers and especially with St. Augustine's *Enarrationes in Psalmos*. The recorded fact that Christ descended from the house and lineage of David prompted discovery of many Messianic prefigurements (types) in the Psalmist's life and words. Although typological interpretation was made of other books, notably Isaiah, Ezekiel, and Canticles, Donne bespeaks the enormous influence of Augustinian tradition in remarking in the first Prebend sermon that "No booke of the Old Testament is so like a Gospel, so particular in all things concerning Christ, as the Psalmes" (ll.18–19). In a similar vein and in several different contexts in his sermons he reverted to St. Basil's observation that the Psalms encompass all that is taught in the other books of the Bible.[10]

Such assertions as these arise out of the ancient creative and redemptive implications of the Word in Christian thought. They were very congenial to Donne, for whom working with the soul's two hands—

---

10. *Sermons*, IV.3.61–65; IV.12.130–133; V.14.773–776; VI.15.3–6. To these citations Donne always appends the condition (not found in St. Basil) that if all other books of the Bible were to perish, the Psalms would suffice for the defense and propagation of the Christian faith. What St. Basil actually says translates as follows: "Prophets, however, teach some things, historical writers others, the Law something else, and proverbial counsel yet another kind of thing. But the Book of the Psalms brings together what is most serviceable in all the others" (Exordium of his *Homily on Psalm 1, Patrologiae cursus completus . . . Series graeca*, ed. J. P. Migne *et al*. [Paris, 1857–1904], vol. XXIX, col. 212). Interestingly, St. Ambrose, a near contemporary of St. Basil's, makes exactly the same assertion (*In Psalmum 1 Enarratio, Patrologiae cursus completus . . . Series latina*, ed. J. P. Migne *et al*. [Paris, 1844–1903], vol. XIV, col. 967; this series is cited hereafter as *PL*). Although Donne was fluent in Latin, he gives no sign of familiarity with the passage in St. Ambrose. Moreover, it is unlikely that he knew enough Greek to read St. Basil in the original, so his intermediate source is probably responsible for intensifying St. Basil's hyperbole.

the right, Faith, and the left, Reason—meant seizing on analogies and correspondences from the world and experience which confirmed the truths of religion anew. While Donne's analogies and correspondences are themselves rarely new, their immediacy comes from his sensitive handling of figures of speech in accordance with the figurative senses of Scripture.[11] However, in Donne's embattled age traditional methods of interpreting Scripture continued to sustain the onslaught mounted at the time of the Reformation. More recent Biblical studies emphasized factualism and historicism as antidotes to the extremes of allegory as it had developed through the Fathers and Schoolmen.[12] Donne was well aware of conflicting approaches in exegesis as in other religious concerns, if not in his early twenties at which time Walton dates Donne's mastery of "the body of divinity as it was then controverted betwixt the Reformed and the Roman Church," then at least by his late thirties when he was in a position to advise on the manuscript version of *A Catholike Appeale* by the Anglican apologist Thomas Morton[13] and to produce his own *Pseudo-Martyr*. In the latter work, dating from 1610, Donne's knowledge and expertise still stand revealed, as they were to King James, in the minute sifting of the (insubstantial) grounds on which the Pope claimed to bind the consciences of English Catholics.

Nevertheless, by the beginning of the seventeenth century in England a movement was underway within native Protestantism which sought to recede from enmeshment in divisive issues and, instead, to hold to primitive and catholic Christian teaching as set forth in the Creeds, Church Councils, and writings of the early Fathers. The van of this movement was Richard Hooker's exposition *Of the Laws of Ecclesiastical Polity,* whose first five books appeared in 1595. Momen-

11. Winfried Schleiner offers substantial evidence of the traditionalism of the analogies and correspondences in Donne's preaching (*The Imagery of John Donne's Sermons,* pp. 68–200). There is also much traditionalism in the metaphors of works relating to identifiable actual experiences: for example, "Goodfriday, 1613. Riding Westward," the "Hymne to Christ, at the Authors last Going into Germany," and the *Devotions*.

12. On the persistent hostility of historicism to the main current of exegesis in the Church Fathers, see Helen Gardner, "The Drunkenness of Noah," *The Business of Criticism* (Oxford: Oxford University Press, 1959), pp. 79–100.

13. For details, see Bald, *John Donne: A Life,* pp. 202–212.

tum increased with the royal preferment given to Andrewes and finally reached overbearing heights in the power and policies of William Laud. Yet during the years of his ministry Donne found in the spacious traditionalism of the Anglo-Catholic movement, which he helped to establish, a way through and beyond continual religious wrangling that satisfied his reason and faith alike. This way, the celebrated *via media*,[14] undoubtedly recommended itself at the outset as the best available escape from Donne's living dilemma: whether to yield to the instinct for self-preservation and the desire for a position of influence in society or to maintain the family heritage (since Thomas More, Donne's maternal great-granduncle) of Romanism and martyrdom.[15] At last, however, Donne came to complete conviction in the Church of England, imbuing himself so deeply in its principles that ultimately he came to make his own, singular contribution in his preaching, which demonstrated the soundness of Anglican principles regarding the interpretation of Scripture. These next require careful notice, for they are essential to an understanding of what Donne in the second Prebend sermon called "the Idea of my Sermons."

THE SENSE OF THE PLACE

Donne never ceased showing how "sermon" derived from *"sermo"*; for him preaching meant, always and above all, preaching the Word of God, the Scriptures, the only sure source of divine truth available to human minds. In one regard he carried out as literally as possible the great imperative of Christ the Word Incarnate to his apostles, the first ministers of the Church—if "literally" is taken as faithful adherence to the words of the original. This is in the profusion of Biblical citations and allusions in his discourse,[16] a habit which Donne shared with the

14. See the studies of Sir H. J. C. Grierson, "John Donne and the *Via Media*," *Modern Language Review*, XLIII (1948), 305–314; and William R. Mueller, *John Donne, Preacher* (Princeton, N.J.: Princeton University Press, 1962), pp. 148–162.

15. Chs. 2–4 of Bald's *John Donne: A Life* contain an admirable discussion of the pressures—if not persecutions—felt by Donne's relatives and other English Catholics of the time.

16. See Appendix B for a table of Scriptural occurrences in the Prebend sermons.

school of preachers who imitated the manner of Lancelot Andrewes. Like Andrewes, Donne was given to introducing tags and phrases from the Vulgate as a kind of oral punctuation setting off the subsequent citation of the whole verse in an English rendering, almost as if to signal where the preacher's words ended and the Word of God began. For in this and other ways the vital distinction made explicit in the fourth Prebend sermon is always maintained. "All the Sermon is not Gods word, but all the Sermon is Gods Ordinance, and the Text is certainely his word" (ll.720–721). Also, Donne's frequency of citation makes preaching conduce to faith by showing how God keeps his promises. The evidence is that God is the God of his Word; thus far conviction in the faith resembles conviction at the bar. Donne the jurist persists in Donne the preacher.

But unlike Andrewes Donne does not go to great pains in consulting the Hebrew and Greek texts and the numerous translations available in his day to establish an authoritative and authentic reading of a verse. (Donne's philological research has, in fact, the opposite objective: to open many possibilities of nuance and meaning, not to settle upon one.) As he saw the matter, the problem in misunderstanding or missing the sense of Scripture was less likely to be one of scholarship than of sin. A sermon, which was to convey the sense of Scripture, was supremely serious business because the salvation of souls was at stake; and Donne has many reproaches for those who, in preaching or in being preached to, trivialize or frustrate the purpose of saving souls. He reprehends preachers who cater to popular taste with racy topicality, making affairs of the time their text, or with a great show of learning, wit, or eloquence serve up "a Pye of plums." He reprehends auditories for such tastes and for taking umbrage in the thought that they are part of a crowd rather than realizing that God through the preacher is addressing each of them. Above all, however, as his ministry wore on Donne came to recognize (and in this to know himself and his age well) that the major obstacle to the sense of Scripture was human curiosity, the love of speculation—whether expressed in the allegorical excesses of patristic and medieval exegesis or the inveterate theologizing upon God's eternal decrees which occupied the Puritanically inclined London preachers and populace:

That which Christ hath plainly delivered, is the exercise of my Faith; that which other men have curiously disputed, is the exercise of my understanding. . . . It is the Text that saves us; the interlineary glosses, and the marginal notes, and the *variae lectiones,* controversies and perplexities, undo us. . . . It is the hand of man that induces obscurities; the hand of God hath written so, as a man may runne, and read; walk in the duties of his calling here, and attend the salvation of his soul too.[17]

Human nature being what it was, preaching was still very much needed—as Christ knew, who ordained it for his Church—even though God's Word itself was clear enough to be grasped by any man. The danger which preaching counteracts is that of losing oneself in intellectual vagaries instead of coming to the total response of being which is faith. So obvious was this to Donne that he says it outright only once in his sermons, in the latter part of his ministry and in an aside: "A Sermon intends *Exhortation* principally and *Edification,* and a holy stirring of religious affections, and then *matters of Doctrine,* and points of *Divinity,* occasionally, secondarily, as the words of the text may invite them."[18]

But if Donne does not bother much with definitions of the sermon, he is led by his awareness of the waywardness and error of human reasoning into a continual, Anglican insistence that the individual expositor test his determination of the meaning of a text by, and conform it to, the sense of the place accepted by the Church. If a preacher does not submit himself to the Church, his words are not of the nature of a divine ordinance but only personal opinion. Donne is very far from radical theories of latter-day "prophesying"; rather, he is more assiduous than any other preacher of his time in pointing out mistakes and discrepancies in commentators of every persuasion. He likes to refer

17. *Sermons,* III.9.55–88. Schleiner (*The Imagery of Donne's Sermons,* p. 59) also remarks on Donne's particular censuring of the sin of curiosity.

18. *Sermons,* VIII.3.10–13; cf. II.15.352–353. Contrast with Donne the lack of any distinction between a lecture and a sermon in Luther and Calvin, as pointed out by Dennis Quinn, "Donne's Christian Eloquence," *Journal of English Literary History,* XXVII (1960), 279.

in his preaching to St. Augustine's impassioned acknowledgment in the twelfth book of the *Confessions* that, even if Moses were to appear and were implored to explain what he said in Genesis, he would do so in Hebrew and would be hard to understand. As Donne remarks in the first Prebend sermon, "The best men are but Problematicall, Onely the Holy Ghost is Dogmaticall" (ll. 336–337).

What, however, was to be understood by submitting to the Church? This was the poet-divine who wrote "Show me deare Christ, thy spouse, so bright and cleare. . . ." The answer given in the sermons transcends the geographical and sectarian conceptions of the sonnet. To Donne as a public spokesman for the *via media,* the Church is the high road traveled by Christians of all places and times, a concourse of fundamental beliefs and doctrines in which deviations show themselves as the exceptions they are. In Donne's recasting of the notable dictum of St. Vincent of Lérins, a fifth-century Father (who is also cited in the fifth Prebend sermon), individual interpretations of Scripture must be consonant with "that which all Churches alwayes have thought and taught to be necessary to salvation."[19] The requirement is not merely in the interest of human community but in keeping with the divine authority invested solely in the Church. The peril and perplexity of Donne's private search for the meaning of the Word in the little world of his sick self led first to the urgent tone of the *Devotions* and then, in the sermons postdating his recovery, to a special emphasis on the means of salvation—preaching and the sacraments—which are the Church's ordinances alone. The Church viewed as the broad mainstream of Christian teaching and tradition was the necessary guarantor and assessor of any man's attempt to find religious truth.

In implementing and demonstrating the proper interpretation of Scripture, Donne's sermons contain many references to the principles which had been standard since the time of St. Augustine and were professed in his day by Roman and Reformed controversialists alike:

19. *Sermons,* III.9.112–113. The pronouncement, standardized as the Vincentian Canon by which the Church is to discriminate between authoritative and unauthoritative traditions, occurs in bk. I, ch. 2, of St. Vincent's *Commonitorium*: "In ipsa item Catholica Ecclesia magnopere curandum est ut id teneamus quod ubique, quod semper, quod ab omnibus creditum est. Hoc est etenim vere proprieque catholicum" (*PL,* L, 640).

to acknowledge that the Word of God encompasses all meaning—so that any passage may mean a number of things—but to distinguish clearly between its literal sense and its possible spiritual or figurative senses. A crucial test for the literal sense was to insure that it could stand within and maintain the integrity of its context. The literal sense was basic; the spiritual or figurative senses presupposed it and could not be allowed to displace it as the primary meaning of a text. The literal sense was also the only ground of Christian doctrine, being in its directness of the nature of proof. St. Augustine said, *"Figura nihil probat";* and the Church from his day to Donne's concurred.

Donne pursues consideration of the senses of Scripture in three frequently quoted passages which bear directly on an understanding of his preaching methods and of his place in the development and traditions of Biblical interpretation. In these three passages, one in the *Essays in Divinity* written shortly before his ordination in 1615, one in his Christmas sermon of 1621, and one in his Easter sermon of 1624, he insists on the supremacy of "the literall sense." This Donne defined, echoing Aquinas in the tenth article of the first question of the *Summa Theologica,* which in turn owes much to St. Augustine, as the principal intention of the Holy Ghost in a particular place.[20] St. Thomas himself observes (citing the twelfth book of the *Confessions*) that a multiplicity of meanings is not unfitting within even the literal sense of Scripture since its author is the all-knowing God.[21] Then he gives some examples of the multiplicity of the literal sense of Scripture. In conventional writings the literal sense is a factual or historical statement, dealing with things, persons, and events having ordinary objective existence. But according to St. Gregory the Great—whose elaboration of the influential Augustinian discussion of "words," "things," and "signs"[22] is

20. St. Thomas Aquinas, *Summa Theologica. Literally Translated by Fathers of the English Dominican Province* (New York: Benziger Bros., 1947), pars I^a, q. 1, art. 10: "The literal sense is that which the author intends, and . . . the author of Holy Writ is God." Helen Gardner remarks on Donne's use of Aquinas in *The Business of Criticism,* pp. 136–137.

21. Cf. St. Augustine's *De doctrina Christiana,* bk. III, ch. 27; English translation by John J. Gavigan under the title *Christian Doctrine* in *The Fathers of the Church,* vol. IV (New York: Cima Publishing Co., 1947).

22. See *De doctrina Christiana,* bk. I, chs. 2–3; bk. II, chs. 1–6, 16; bk. III, chs. 5–10.

quoted by St. Thomas—the literal sense of the Bible is peculiar in that, when its words refer to things, the things refer to other things. The peculiarity is due to God's use of physical reality to intimate and reflect spiritual reality in his Word. Thus there is an inseparable "parabolical" or metaphorical sense within the literal sense. Other aspects which Aquinas subsumes in the literal sense are what St. Augustine calls the aetiological and analogical senses—respectively, finding the reason in the specific circumstances or cultural context of a verse why it says what it does, and showing by culling and comparing texts that the truth of one place of Scripture does not contradict the truth of another.[23]

Despite all this latitude in the literal sense of Scripture, St. Thomas insists that the distinction between it and the spiritual senses is a real one which cannot be defined or synthesized away. He proceeds to comment on the different spiritual senses and the steps toward a deepening understanding of religious truth which they represent, however differently they may be termed or classified. The first of the spiritual senses is the moral, which signifies what things one ought to do—especially by means of the examples of Biblical personages or of the pattern of the life of perfection as led by Christ. The second is the allegorical, in which the things of the Old Testament signify—that is, intimate—the New. The third is the anagogical, in which things of this world signify what relates to the eternal glory of heaven. Aquinas is careful to say that this schematization is not definitive, merely illustrative. He calls attention to the legitimate alternative classification made by Hugh of St. Victor, in which the historical, allegorical, and tropological (which would be the moral sense) are distinguished and the anagogical is made a subclass of the allegorical. But in all events the primacy of the literal sense, the progression of the spiritual senses, and the distinction between the two are to be borne in mind by the expositor of Scripture.

Donne makes the same insistence on the distinction between the literal and the spiritual or figurative senses, but in the *Essays* he gives the subject his own pessimistic coloring, focusing rather upon conflicting human opinions than on the plenitude of the mind of God as

23. Aquinas cites St. Augustine's *De utilitate credendi*, ch. 3 (*PL*, XLII, 68–70).

expressed in his Word: "The word of God is not the word of God in any other sense then literall, and that also is not the literall, which the letter seems to present, for so to diverse understandings there might be diverse literall senses; but it is called literall, to distinguish it from the Morall, Allegoricall, and the other senses. . . ."[24] In the luminous, affirmative Christmas sermon of 1621, his first as Dean of St. Paul's, Donne, however, gives a more traditional (Augustinian and Thomistic) cast to the distinction:

> And therefore though it be ever lawfull, and often times very usefull, for the raising and exaltation of our devotion, and to present the plenty, and abundance of the *holy Ghost* in the *Scriptures* . . . to induce the *diverse senses* that the Scriptures doe admit, yet this may not be admitted, if there may be danger thereby, to neglect or weaken the *literall sense* it selfe.[25]

Finally in the Easter sermon, his first after the illness that gave rise to the profusely metaphorical *Devotions* where correlations are pursued between texts of Scripture and aspects of personal experience, Donne reiterates the distinction between the literal and spiritual or figurative senses only, seemingly, to make it of no effect. He asserts of the Holy Ghost that "his principall intention in many places, is to expresse things by allegories, by figures; so that in many places of Scripture, a figurative sense is the literall sense."[26]

This sequence of pronouncements has occasioned a good deal of difficulty in attempts both to relate Donne to an exegetical tradition which he explicitly invokes and to discover statements of principle about what he does with a text. It has seemed that Donne could be rescued either from the imputation of doubletalk or of confusion, but not the two together. On the one hand, the phrasing of his definition of the literal sense and his terms (moral, allegorical) for the others clearly bespeak a source in the *Summa Theologica*, but Aquinas cannot possibly be an authority for the identity of the literal and figurative senses "in many places of Scripture" as asserted by Donne, for this

24. *Essays in Divinity*, ed. Evelyn M. Simpson (Oxford: Clarendon Press, 1952), pp. 39–40.

25. *Sermons*, III.17.176–182.

26. *Sermons*, VI.2.10–13.

is the opposite of what Aquinas maintains. (Although recent and not-so-recent work on *Biathanatos* shows that Donne could shrewdly twist his authorities when he had a mind to, it is only fair to be wary of attributing the practice to him as a preacher.) On the other hand, it is possible to exonerate Donne and to shift the responsibility by pointing out that neither St. Augustine nor St. Thomas—nor, for that matter, any other writer—makes a satisfactory distinction between the metaphors, parables, and other figures of speech that are included in the literal sense of Scripture and the types, allegories, and other kinds of symbolic significance that are designated as spiritual senses. To be sure, St. Augustine does say that the figurative dimensions of the literal sense are in the speaker's mind, so that the meaning of the text is, literally, the meaning of the metaphor, while other kinds of figurative significance are in the mind of the reader, hearer, or interpreter. But this distinction is blurred in turn by his assertion that the Holy Ghost's advance knowledge of the different ways men would understand the Bible was taken into account in the forms of expression used and by his acknowledgment that the same text can be literal to one person and figurative to another, yet the opinions of both can be warranted.[27] Thus the partially conflicting traditional aims of placing Christian doctrine on the unassailable ground of the literal sense and of maintaining the primacy of spiritual significance in every word of the Bible, which caused the formulation of the multiple senses, have been invoked to account for the awkwardness of relating precept to practice in Donne's preaching.[28]

Although there is much truth in the claim that Donne shares in the view of Scripture and its interpretation which became traditional after St. Augustine, it is not a sufficient explanation of Donne's particular

27. Regarding the respective points, see *De doctrina Christiana,* bk. III, chs. 59, 27, 17.

28. Helen Gardner was the first to try to reconcile Donne's precepts and practice with the literalism of the age (*The Business of Criticism,* p. 136). Dennis Quinn subsequently appealed to the difficulties in the tradition ("John Donne's Principles of Biblical Exegesis," *Journal of English and Germanic Philology,* LXI [1962], 322–325). But the best account to date is Schleiner's (*The Imagery of Donne's Sermons,* pp. 185–200), which emphasizes the connection between the development of Donne's figures and the determination of the multiple senses of Scripture.

method to invoke the more general inconsistencies found in the tradition. Throughout the sermons his practice is to give little more than preliminary attention to the literal sense understood as the historical or factual content of a text; the emphasis is overwhelmingly on what the multiple senses term the moral sense—the applicability of the text to the state of a man's soul and what he ought to do. Even where, as rarely, Donne uses the progression of the multiple senses as the organizing principle of a sermon,[29] the proportions enlarge least of all the literal sense and most of all the moral and, shading into it, the allegorical. This distribution is not unique to Donne; it is frequent in Andrewes, whose influential recourse to traditional homiletics determined the peculiar character of much earlier seventeenth-century Anglican preaching and manifestly had an impact on Donne. But although the dynamic of the multiple senses informed the preaching of the school of Andrewes, the principles are almost without exception left implicit. Andrewes himself remarks only once that "Our books tell us, the Scripture will bear four senses . . . and a kind of ascent there is in them," proceeding to distinguish the literal (dealing with Moses), the analogical (relating David to Moses), the moral (concerning sins as enemies), and the prophetical (concurring with "the testimony of Jesus, which is the spirit of all prophecy").[30]

Donne's great explicitness about principles of Biblical interpretation is, however, the exception; by using the terminology of the multiple senses he invites reference to them. This in turn reveals that his increasingly frequent and effective practice of pursuing the spiritual significance of Scripture by enlarging on—or, as he called it, "dilating"—figures of speech or common nouns in his texts does not stay within the confines of the traditional literal sense.[31] On the other hand he

29. In two series of sermons on Penitential Psalms, one perhaps preached in the spring of 1618 (*Sermons,* II, nos. 1–6), the other probably in the spring of 1623 (*Sermons,* V, nos. 15–19; VI, no. 1).

30. *Ninety-six Sermons* (Oxford, 1841), III, 226–227.

31. See Dennis Quinn's conclusion from within the Thomistic frame of reference: "It is most historical and most accurate to think of Donne's sermons as spiritual or, specifically, tropological exegesis" ("John Donne's Principles of Biblical Exegesis," p. 326). Cf. Schleiner, *The Imagery of Donne's Sermons,* p. 196: Donne's "is as outspoken a plea for the use and usefulness of scriptural allegory as one could expect from a Protestant pulpit."

demonstrates his affinities with a post-Augustinian age, the newer emphases on historicism and textual investigation, by attacking the excesses and absurdities of allegorical interpretation from the time of the Fathers to his own. These oddities and apparent discrepancies in Donne can nevertheless be made intelligible within the nearer context of native English Protestantism of the sixteenth century. The salient features of an Anglican method of Biblical interpretation emerge already in the remarkable pioneering work of William Tyndale but were destined to be bypassed for other more pressing concerns and to lie dormant until the dawning of a constructivist era in the last decade of the century. Hence Donne's role is as much that of founder as inheritor, as will be seen from what follows.

When even before the onset of the Reformation in England the question of vernacular editions of Scripture became a burning issue (Tyndale, though self-exiled, was brought to death at the stake), the issue centered on what was to be the Protestant claim that God's Word was written for and to every man. Tyndale's convictions led him to act upon this claim; and in his Prefaces to books of the Bible which he translated into English and in *The Obedience of a Christian Man* (1528), he described the nature of Scripture and how it was to be understood. The roots of Tyndale's conception of the Biblical message were Augustinian. In a forthright manner he repeats in his Prefaces directed to the ordinary reader the wonderful "process"—by which he means "progression"—of the whole. The Old Testament contains in detail God's Law, which the sinful soul hates because it knows itself condemned and guilty; the New Testament contains the Gospel (the "evangelion," the good news) of the sinful soul's salvation by Christ, the sinless Son of God. The impact of this narrative progression, according to Tyndale, is a spiritual progression which extends and completes the Biblical one, bringing it full circle from Gospel to Law again and raising the soul from sin to salvation. At first the soul, moved to hatred of the Law, receives with a joy and relief bordering on incredulity the account of Christ's blood, his death, his meekness and patience in suffering wrongs. But in feeling how merciful and loving God in Christ is, the soul begins to love in return and "to consent to the law of God, how that it is good and ought so to be, and that God is righteous which made it; and desire to fulfil the law, even as a sick man desireth to be whole."[32] Thereafter, to the soul brought to faith in Christ through love, the combined message of the Old and New Testaments is "to learn to keep his laws spiritually, that is to say, of love for his sake, and . . . also suffer the curing of our infirmities."[33]

The methodological implications of Tyndale's emphasis on the spiritual and moral significance of the Bible are indicated in the section headed "The Four Senses of Scripture" in *The Obedience of a Christian Man*. What begins as a pointed animadversion against the Church of Rome—editions read variously "chopological" and "tropological"—evolves into a most seminal and original contribution to English hermeneutics. With a few strokes Tyndale reduces the multiple senses successively until at last even the basic traditional literal-nonliteral distinction vanishes into the unity of form (a figurative means of speaking) and content (what is being said):

> They divide the scripture into four senses, the literal, tropological, allegorical, and anagogical. The literal sense is become nothing at all: for the pope hath taken it clean away. . . . He hath partly locked it up with the false and counterfeited keys of his traditions, ceremonies, and feigned lies; and partly driveth men from it with violence of sword. . . . The tropological sense pertaineth to good manners (say they), and teacheth what we ought to do. The allegory is appropriate to faith; and the anagogical to hope, and things above. Tropological and anagogical are terms of their own feigning, and altogether unnecessary. For they are but allegories, both two of them; and this word allegory comprehendeth them both, and is enough. For tropological ["chopological"] is but an allegory of manners; and anagogical, an allegory of hope. And allegory is as much to say as strange speaking, or borrowed speech: as when we say of a wanton child, "This sheep hath magots in his

---

32. Tyndale's first Prologue to the New Testament, published separately as "A Pathway into the Holy Scripture" and reprinted in *Doctrinal Treatises and Introductions to Different Portions of the Holy Scriptures,* Parker Society XLIII (1848), 19. The process is also detailed in the Epistle to the Reader of the New Testament, pp. 389–391; the Prologue to Genesis, pp. 398–405; the Prologue to the Prophet Jonas, pp. 463–464; and the Prologue upon the Gospel of St. Matthew, p. 469–476.

33. *Ibid.,* p. 476.

tail, he must be anointed with birchen salve;" which speech I borrow of the shepherds.

Thou shalt understand, therefore, that the scripture hath but one sense, which is the literal sense. And that literal sense is the root and ground of all . . . , whereunto if thou cleave, thou canst never err or go out of the way. And if thou leave the literal sense, thou canst not but go out of the way. Neverthelater, the scripture useth proverbs, similitudes, riddles, or allegories, as all other speeches do; but that which the proverb, similitude, riddle, or allegory signifieth, is ever the literal sense. . . .[34]

Of greatest importance here is the conception of Scripture as a continuum of meaning (the literal sense) and the rejection of mystical and mystifying assumptions about the properties of the Holy Ghost's language. Its forms of expression are human forms of expression so that human beings can understand; recondite and ingenious constructions placed on Biblical texts result, says Tyndale, in "sophistry" and "blindness," not the truth that moves the soul from hatred to love. He repudiates the contention that St. Paul's dictum about the killing letter and the life-giving spirit was intended to denigrate the literal sense. For this becomes a unified, all-encompassing, and universally intelligible meaning, as Tyndale proceeds to define it:

God is a Spirit, and all his words are spiritual. His literal sense is spiritual, and all his words are spiritual. . . . All the scripture is either the promises and testament of God in Christ, and stories pertaining thereto, to strength thy faith; either the law and stories pertaining thereto, to fear thee from evil doing. There is no story nor gest, seem it never so simple or so vile unto the world, but that thou shalt find therein spirit and life and edifying in the literal sense: for it is God's scripture, written for thy learning and comfort. . . . Finally, all God's words are spiritual, if thou . . . see the right meaning of the text, and whereunto the scripture pertaineth, and the final end and cause thereof.[35]

This bold recasting of the sense of Scripture so as to reduce the intri-

34. *Ibid.*, pp. 303–304.
35. *Ibid.*, pp. 309, 310.

cate traditional superstructure to the literal sense exudes a humanistic confidence in man's perceptions and understanding. Tyndale mentions only the most basic rules of traditional exegesis: that "allegory proveth nothing, neither can do" and that the literal sense is found "by the process of the text, or by a like text of another place." Questions of influence aside, a minimum of rules and a sanguine attitude continue to characterize what Anglican pronouncements there are on the interpretation of the Bible in the rest of the sixteenth century. But while the tone and approach are the same as Tyndale's, there is a decided shift of emphasis. As "Search the Scriptures" (John 5.39) became the rallying cry of the Reformation and met compliance in all quarters including Rome, the dominant view of the Church of England came to be that interpretation of the Bible was not itself an issue: Roman assertions of infallibility and the disputatiousness of "hot gospellers" regarding purported difficulties were equally misguided. Hugh Latimer stands virtually alone in his repeated insistence on "the necessary office of preaching, the office of salvation,"[36] which required some amount of textual interpretation and comment. Part of what makes his Sermon of the Plough (1548) so memorable, beyond its vigorous and colloquial idiom, is the anomaly of an entire discourse devoted to the unremitting duties of a preacher of the Word depicted as "a plougher and sower of seed in God's field, that is, the faithful congregation."[37]

The sixteenth century in England was not, by and large, an age of sermons or of interpretations of Scripture for any but controversial and polemical purposes. These required a rigid and narrow literalism. Under such circumstances it was constantly reiterated, from Coverdale and Cranmer onward through the middle decades, that the message of Scripture is for all, can be understood by all, and should be available to all in their own language for their own perusal.[38] The nature and

36. See Latimer's *Sermons*, Parker Society XXVII (1844), 291–292, 349, 358, 418–419, 470–471, 504. For this period there is a singularly high proportion of sermons among Latimer's literary remains.

37. *Ibid.*, pp. 59–78.

38. See, e.g., "Myles Coverdale unto the Christian Reader" (Prologue to his 1535 translation of the Bible) in *Remains*, Parker Society XIV (1846), 11–22; Thomas Cranmer, "A Prologue or Preface to the Bible" (1541?) in *Works*, Parker Society XVI (1846), 14; cf. 21, 118–125; William Fulke, *A Defense of the sincere and true Translations of the holie Scriptures into the English tong . . .* (1583), Parker Society XVII (1843), 77.

reception of such sermons as were preached are illustrated by two outstanding and yet very representative productions of John Jewel's: the Paul's Cross sermon before his consecration as Bishop of Salisbury in 1559 and the encomium on the riches of God's Word freely offered to all, published as "A Treatise of Holy Scripture" (1570). The latter met with no particular notable response; but the former sermon, which contained the famous open challenge to anyone—especially Papists—to show where the English Church deviated from the Bible, the Fathers, or the General Councils "for the space of six hundred years after Christ,"[39] elicited attacks that kept Jewel's pen in his hand making good the challenge for the rest of his life. Along with distinguished contemporaries in an emerging Establishment he worked unceasingly to set curbstones at the right (Roman) and left (Anabaptist) edge of the *via media,* enabling Hooker finally in the 1590s to trace the whole route.

But before there could be discoursing *Of the Laws of Ecclesiastical Polity* defense had to be made of the English Church polity against the pretensions of Rome to infallibility and supreme authority, both spiritual and temporal, on the one hand, and against the move to vest authority in the individual congregation—or minister or layman—on the other. Although the earliest signs of home-grown dissent centered upon the issue of clerical dress, they rapidly spread and solidified into far-reaching questions of the form and function of church government in England. If the Vestiarian Controversy was to smolder unresolved through more than a half-century of efforts to deal with it—efforts ranging from Archbishop Parker's moderately conformist *Advertisements* (1563) to King James's exacerbated and exacerbating declarations at the Hampton Court Conference (1604)—it is less wonder that the anti-episcopal, revisionist sentiments of the widely espoused *First* and *Second Admonitions to the Parliament* (1572–1573) were not de-

---

39. The later written copy reads: "If any learned man of all our adversaries, or if all the learned men that be alive, be able to bring any one sufficient sentence out of any old catholic doctor, or father, or out of any old general council, or out of the holy scriptures of God, or any one example of the primitive church . . . for the space of six hundred years after Christ . . . I promised then that I would give over and subscribe unto him" (John Jewel, *Works,* Parker Society XXIII [1845], 20–21).

flected even by Hooker but were absorbed by turns and degrees into the revolutionary fervor which precipitated the Civil War and produced the Commonwealth. Yet internal disagreements were by no means the only problem of the Church of England, and, in the eyes of most of her sixteenth-century defenders, not even the most pressing one. The emphasis of this period was on defining Anglo-Catholicism over against the dogmas and doctrines of the Continent. The sacrament of the Eucharist had to be disabused of the dogma of Transubstantiation and such practices as private communion, communion in only one kind, reservation, and "idolatrous" worship without reducing it to a Zwinglian commemoration of the Passion of Christ. The upshot of the first controversial age of Anglicanism was, not unnaturally, a spate of apologetical works and a corresponding desire for domestic peace and quiet which viewed preaching as at best a mixed blessing. A mere two Books of Homilies for reading and rereading from the pulpits of the land was the authorized allotment under the Elizabethan Settlement. This spate of apologetical works, moreover, generated great heat and considerable light in some regards. For example, sixteenth-century Anglican apologists rehabilitated in an admirable fashion the Thomistic distinction between matters indifferent and matters fundamental to Christian faith—a distinction which, in their eyes, the opprobrious Council of Trent had made of no effect. But in other regards the formulation of basic principles was delayed. This was especially the case with noncontroversial interpretation of Scripture, which was held to be the true function of preaching.

Thus John Whitgift spoke for the majority of his fellow Anglican apologists in reproving Thomas Cartwright. The sense of Scripture, Whitgift maintained, is so evident that public reading alone is more effectual for instruction and edification than most sermons, which are commonly marred by the preacher's vainglory, sedition, and error.[40] Only gradually as the century wore on were there acknowledgments that difficulties pertaining to the Bible lay not only in the weakness of the speaker and hearers, but to some degree in the text itself. What is the evolving view of the sixteenth-century Church of England on the

40. John Whitgift, *The Defense of the Answer to the Admonition, against the Reply of Thomas Cartwright* (1574), in *Works,* Parker Society XLIX (1853), 30–31, 36, 54–55.

interpretation of Scripture? The various reflections—all of them inci-
dental rather than systematic—ran in a strongly Augustinian vein.

The point of departure continued to be warnings against the presumption, overcuriosity, and misjudgment to which men's minds were
ever prone. But the expositor's natural liabilities could be offset by
recognition of the coherence and consistency of all facets of divine
revelation, consummately exhibited in the Bible. This Augustinian
view of the Bible as a clear and complete compendium of fundamental
beliefs and morals, to which the medieval Church added the weight of
concurring testimony from the Fathers and Councils, became conven-
tionalized as the rule or proportion or analogy of faith. Sixteenth-
century Anglicans, following the lead of Luther, took pains to restore
the primary Augustinian emphasis on the completeness and unity of
the body of Scripture, independent of other authority, when they invoked the analogy of faith as a guide to interpretation.[41] This emphasis was ultimately absorbed and transformed by Hooker—who, however, did not use the term—in his majestic tribute to the rational perfection of God's means or laws, foremost among them Scripture, for
making himself known to man.[42] Other principles besides systematic
agreement invoked by sixteenth-century Anglicans include the Augustinian specification that, if an understanding of Scripture is true, it will
conduce to the twofold love of God and neighbor.[43] Another, extrapo-
lated from the rules for identifying figurative expressions given in the
third book of *De doctrina Christiana,* is a careful attending to the
context, conditions, and circumstances of any Biblical utterance. In his
Prologue to "the Christian reader" Coverdale says: "It shall greatly
help thee to understand scripture, if thou mark not only what is spoken

41. See, e.g., Henry Bullinger's pronouncement that the "exposition of the
Scriptures is to agree fitly and in every point proportionally with our faith"
(*Fifty Sermons, Divided into Five Decades* [1577], Parker Society VII [1849],
75, 77, 78) and William Fulke's reference to expounding "by conference of other
plainer texts of Scripture, according to the analogy of faith" (*Defense of Translations,* p. 37). Cf. Cranmer, *Works,* p. 17, and the remarks attributed to Latimer
in Nicholas Ridley's *Works,* Parker Society XL (1841), 113.

42. The argument builds through much of the first half of the *Ecclesiastical
Polity,* but especially focuses in I.xiii–xiv; II.viii.5–7; III.iii.3, iv.1.

43. Bullinger specifically cites bk. I, ch. 36 of *De doctrina Christiana* where the
principle is set forth (*Fifty Sermons,* p. 77).

or written, but of whom, and unto whom, with what words, at what time, where, to what intent, with what circumstance, considering what goeth before, and what followeth after."[44]

These pronouncements delivered by sixteenth-century Anglicans as personal precautions constitute by implication—and in actuality where their sermons have survived—a method of preaching. The Augustinian procedures for discovering the meaning of a text, which these men uniformly espoused, dictated a detailed plan of discourse traceable everywhere in the efflorescence of preaching under the influence of Lancelot Andrewes. But the full-scale declaration of the policy of the Church of England in interpreting Scripture, long conspicuously lacking, also appeared at the end of the century under the usual polemical pressures. This was William Whitaker's *Disputatio de Sacra Scriptura; contra huius temporis papistas, inprimis, Robertum Bellarminum Iesuitam . . . & Thomam Stapletonum . . .*, which had its first edition in 1588. (The English translation for the Parker Society was made from the edition of 1610 and renders the title as *A Disputation on Holy Scripture, against the papists, especially Bellarmine and Stapleton*.)

In this treatise, after retreading familiar ground on the sufficiency, consistency, and absolute authority of the Bible, Whitaker accords St. Augustine customary precedence as he broaches for the first time since Tyndale—and more precisely and learnedly than he—the complex traditional question of

the number of the senses of scripture, which the fathers determine to be various; that is, the historical, which they have styled also the grammatical or literal sense, the aetiological, the analogical and the allegorical. Upon this fourfold interpretation of scripture consult Augustine, *de Utilitate Credendi*, c. 3: where he says that it is the historic sense, when we are told what was done, and what not done; that scripture is expounded aetiologically, when it is shewn

44. *Remains*, p. 15; cf. Bullinger: "Moreover, it is requisite in expounding the scriptures, and searching out the true sense of God's word, that we mark upon what occasion everything is spoken, what goeth before, what followeth after, at what season, in what order, and of what person anything is spoken" (*Fifty Sermons*, pp. 77–78). Schleiner (*The Imagery of Donne's Sermons*, p. 165) locates the ultimate origins of these grammatical categories and *claves* in formal rhetoric, which was practically unchanged from St. Augustine's time to Donne's.

why any thing was done or said; analogically, when the agreement of both Testaments is explained; allegorically, when we are taught that some things which are written are not to be taken in the letter, but understood figuratively. Others, however, enumerate other kinds of mystical senses, as the tropological, the allegorical, and anagogic; of which we read a great deal in Origen and the rest.[45]

For the most part this passage derives (without acknowledgment) from the same passage in the *Summa* that serves as the source of Donne's definition of the literal sense. Whitaker then proceeds to attribute to the Jesuits—although, as has been seen, the line of thinking goes back to St. Augustine and St. Thomas—the explicit limitation of the multiple senses to two: the historical or literal, defined as the meaning which the words immediately present, and the mystic or spiritual, defined as reference to something other than what the words designate. This something other may be tropological or anagogical or allegorical.

Next, purporting to speak officially for the Church of England, Whitaker takes the important step which Tyndale had taken earlier and disclaims both the possibility of separate (coexistent or graded) meanings and the severance of the letter from the spirit. "We concede," says Whitaker,

> such things as allegory, anagoge, and tropology in scripture; but meanwhile we deny that there are many and various senses. We affirm that there is but one true, proper and genuine sense of scripture, arising from the words rightly understood, which we call the literal: and we contend that allegories, tropologies, and anagoges are not various senses, but various collections from one sense, or various applications and accommodations of that one meaning.[46]

The effect of Tyndale's and Whitaker's claim comes to be felt especially in the preaching of Donne and the school of Andrewes. These

45. Whitaker, *A Disputation on Holy Scripture*, Parker Society XLVI (1849), 403. The English translation for this edition was made by the Rev. William Fitzgerald.

46. *Ibid.*, p. 404. Cf. William Perkins, *The Arte of Prophecying* (1592), in *The Workes* (London, 1612), III, 737: "*There is one onely sense, and the same is the literall.* An allegorie is onely a certaine manner of uttering the same sense. The Anagoge and Tropologie are waies, whereby the sense may be applied."

men establish a spectrum of literality in which the opposing and un-resolvable issues of objective and subjective meaning are absorbed into a focus on the constant factor of divine inspiration in Scripture where differences are not different senses but different purposes in interpreting a text. The most important of these with regard to Donne's preaching is Whitaker's commendation of tropology, what in the traditional scheme is the moral sense: "In this treatment of texts, and such educings of various admonitions and exhortations, the greatest part of the minister's function lies. But all such things flow and are concluded from the very words themselves. This, therefore, is not a new or various meaning, foreign to the words themselves, but absolutely one and the same with the literal sense." Thus, finally, Whitaker can present an all-embracing literal sense not as an Anglican novelty, but indeed a point of agreement with Thomistic implications now first properly understood. To this end he cites Aquinas: "Since the literal sense is that which the author intends, and the author of holy scripture is God, who comprehends all things together in his mind; there is nothing improper in saying that, *even according to the literal sense,* there are several meanings of scripture in one text."[47]

Here, then, within "this Park" of the Church of England—the soul's "Pasture" for which Donne thanked God in his *Essays*—is to be found a developed theory of the literal sense which explicitly commends and comprehends the paramount moral emphasis of his preaching. When the cosmopolitan Donne is rightly seen in his native context, his recasting of Aquinas emerges not as misunderstanding or obscuration but, rather, as the articulation of a specifically Anglican position. In fact, the Anglican perspective of Donne's sermons extends beyond the principles of Biblical interpretation to the procedures by which the principles are to be put into effect. It is worth noting Whitaker's catalogue of these procedures for its pertinence to what Donne may be observed doing with Scripture in his sermons.

In Whitaker's *Disputation* a broadside attack on the doctrine of papal infallibility as applied to determining the meaning of the Holy Ghost in Scripture occupies six chapters between the definition of the literal sense and the further elaboration of positive procedures—the

47. *A Disputation on Holy Scripture,* pp. 407, 408. Emphasis mine.

proper means of finding the true sense of a text. (This train of thought, with an excursus into anti-Jesuit polemics, is equally characteristic of Donne.) Whitaker develops the Anglican approach as follows. Since the meaning of the Holy Ghost is the true sense of Scripture, heartfelt prayer and meditation (observe the occasion and tenor of Donne's *Essays*) are prerequisites to Bible study. So too is knowledge of the original languages, Hebrew and Greek, by which misconceptions gained from translations are avoided. (Walton tells of Donne's deferring his ordination for three years while "he applied himself to an incessant study of textual divinity and to the attainment of a greater perfection in the learned languages, Greek and Hebrew.") In dealing with the text itself, says Whitaker (anticipating the opening remarks in Donne's Easter sermon of 1624), the expositor is to consider which words "are proper, and which figurative and modified."

> For, when words are taken figuratively, they should not be expounded strictly. "It is," says Augustine, in his books of Christian Doctrine, "a wretched bondage of the soul, when signs are taken for things"; that is, when what is spoken figuratively is expounded as if spoken strictly.[48]

"Fourthly . . . we ought to consider the scope, end, matter, circumstances (that is, as Augustine says, the persons, place and time), the antecedents and consequents of each passage. . . ." Then "one place must be compared and collated with another; the obscurer places with the plainer or less obscure;" yet "not only similar places are to be compared with similar, but dissimilar passages are also to be compared together."[49] Beyond such procedures, the expositor is to avail himself of the commentaries, expositions, and opinions of others who are more skilled and learned, as even St. Jerome, St. Augustine, and other Fathers did. (In earlier seventeenth-century Anglican preaching these procedures were taken so seriously that they were made not merely preparatives for the pulpit but the program of the sermon itself.) But the expositor's sense and those of the authorities he consults must ultimately be found to

48. *Ibid.*, p. 470. ("Ea demum est miserabilis animae servitus, signa pro rebus accipere"—*De doctrina Christiana*, bk. III, ch. 5.)

49. *A Disputation on Holy Scripture*, pp. 470–472.

accord with the analogy of faith, which we read of, Rom. xii.6. Now the analogy of faith is nothing else but the constant sense of the general tenour of scripture in those clear passages of scripture, where the meaning labours under no obscurity; such as the articles of faith in the Creed, and the contents of the Lord's Prayer, the Decalogue, and the whole Catechism: for every part of the Catechism may be confirmed by plain passages of scripture. Whatever exposition is repugnant to this analogy must be false.[50]

Donne's own insistence—in the second Prebend sermon and elsewhere in his preaching—focuses on the analogy of faith understood as Whitaker defines it, but his contribution to Anglican principles of Biblical interpretation is to make explicit the adjustment from writing controversy to preaching sermons, the shift from questions of logic to questions of living. In this shift his and his age's great mentor still served as guide, as this passage from a sermon delivered late in Donne's ministry clearly attests: "First then, undertaking the consideration of the literall sense . . . we joyne with S. *Augustine.* . . . So far I will goe, saies he, so far will we, in his modesty and humility accompany him, as still to propose, *Quod luce veritatis, quod fruge utilitatis excellit,* such a sense as agrees with other Truths, that are evident in other places of Scripture, and such a sense as may conduce most to edification."[51] In observing that the elements of a right exposition of Scripture come to a convergence of *veritas* and *utilitas,* Donne reveals one of the profoundest correspondences between his thinking and that of St. Augustine: the inseparability of the moral life from the awareness of truth. Thus in a stately passage in a sermon from his middle years at St. Paul's Donne addressed the individual hearer. If one could not remember all the appeals made to faith by citations of places of Scripture and all the appeals made to reason and judgment by sentences from the Fathers and Schoolmen, "yet if thou remember that which concerned thy sin, and thy soul, if thou meditate upon that, apply that,

50. *Ibid.,* p. 472. Cf. William Perkins, *The Workes,* III, 740: "If the native (or naturall) signification of the words doe manifestly disagree with either the analogie of faith or very perspicuous places of Scripture: then the other meaning which is given of the place propounded, is naturall & proper, if it agree with contrary and like places. . . ."

51. *Sermons,* IX.3.64–131.

thou hast brought away all the Sermon, all that was intended by the Holy Ghost to be preached to thee."[52]

According to Donne, the intention of the Holy Ghost, the literal sense of Scripture and the sermon, were brought home to the soul through the knowledge of one's own nature, which Tyndale also saw as the effect of God's Word, and which readied the soul to respond to divine grace. Thus, along with the principles of Biblical interpretation governing the dispensing end of preaching, Donne emphasized at the receiving end the Augustinian practice of self-scrutiny, exhorting his hearers to discover inwardly their likeness, however defaced, to God, in whose image man was made. For only through knowing one's own nature could one come to realize one's destiny as projected in the two Testaments—the progression from Law to Gospel, in Pauline terms the putting off of the old man and the putting on of the new, the regeneration whereby human existence passed from sin and death to the perfect and everlasting life envisioned in the beginning by its divine Creator. Some attention must now be given in turn to the view of human nature which in Donne's preaching is a necessary adjunct to his view of the sense of Scripture.

THE APPEAL TO THE SOUL

From conceiving of the soul as the image of God St. Augustine came to develop his seminal theories of psychology and epistemology, which are most fully and systematically treated in books IX through XV of *De Trinitate*. What Donne says about the soul manifests the continuing influence of *De Trinitate* on his preaching.[53] The crux of the work is St. Augustine's interpretation of Genesis 1.26, where man is said to have been made in the divine image. This is taken to mean that the workings of the human consciousness reflect the relations of the Persons of the Trinity, and St. Augustine traces the reflections in what he considered to be the two essential activities of the soul—know-

52. Sermons, VII.13.131–139.

53. Schleiner examines the sealing imagery by which Donne most often represents the image of God in the soul, showing its traditional roots (*The Imagery of Donne's Sermons,* pp. 109–119). But he makes a seemingly unwarranted identification of the image of God with the Logos, rather than the Trinity.

ing and loving. Both require a subject, an object, and an interplay between them; that is, knowledge comes into being only when there is a knower, something to be known, and the cognizance by the one of the other, and love can exist only when there is a lover, a beloved, and the affection between them. According to St. Augustine, knowledge and love are illustrations of the operative unity of Father, Son, and Holy Ghost; but, beyond that, they are the means to bring man to a saving knowledge of God. The exercise of the soul's powers, in self-scrutiny and the study of Scripture, leads first to perception of the true being and purpose of man and then to a restoration of its divine likeness defaced by sin. Knowledge of God is the means to love of God. Thus creation and redemption constitute a correspondence in process between man and God.

These mutual implications between psychology and theology arise out of St. Augustine's endeavor in *De Trinitate* to make the divine nature intelligible through a series of analogies. The most appealing one for later writers, including Donne, associated each of the Persons of the Trinity with its respective human faculty. Among the soul's three powers, understanding was linked with the Father, will with the Son, and memory with the Holy Ghost. First the memory, charged with recollections of God's goodness, impressed itself on the understanding (or, as an alternative possibility, impelled the will to right action). In either case, the memory alone prompted the rest of the soul to the attainment of knowledge and goodness by which its divine image was restored. The Augustinian analogy between the Trinity and the faculties of man became the basis of two widely disseminated treatises on spiritual growth and regeneration, St. Bernard's *Tractatus de gradibus humilitatis et superbiae* and the *Itinerarium mentis in Deum* long attributed to St. Bonaventure. Later, in the sixteenth and seventeenth centuries, the whole tradition was taken over into numerous manuals of meditation, of which the most influential was the *Exercitia spiritualis* of St. Ignatius Loyola.

No present-day student of Donne's religious poetry is unacquainted with the affinities between his work and Ignatian meditation,[54] which,

54. See Louis L. Martz, "John Donne in Meditation: *The Anniversaries*," *Journal of English Literary History*, XIV (1947), 247–273, and *The Poetry of Meditation* (New Haven, Conn.: Yale University Press, 1954), pp. 43–56, 107–

however, are not so much a question of direct transmission to the sardonic author of *Ignatius His Conclave* as of reaffirmation of the Augustinian and Bernardine spiritual dynamic in which the whole age shared. In fact, Donne's labeling of St. Bernard "the Father of Meditation" and his frequent use of the term "meditation" to describe his own sermons connect most closely with the *Sermones in Cantica,* where eloquent demonstration is made anew of the Augustinian reciprocal relation between knowing and loving God. For Donne the preacher this was the importance of the theory of psychology underlying systematic meditation: that it showed the way to rousing and working upon the reason and will of man. Whatever the particulars by which he came to the recognition, he did recognize—as in the example of St. Bernard—the shared objectives of preaching and of meditation: spiritual renewal and growth. As he adapted the methods of meditation to his poetry, he adapted the psychology of meditation to his sermons. "Accustome thy selfe," he exhorted his hearers, "to meditations upon the Trinity, in all occasions, and finde impressions of the Trinity, in the three faculties of thine owne soule."[55]

When Donne speaks in this manner the Augustinian cast of his thinking emerges—the subjectivity of the process by which man comes to know and love God. However, other passages in the sermons supplement this subjective emphasis with the more objective Thomistic account of human psychology given in questions 75 to 83 of the first part of the *Summa Theologica.* Aquinas viewed man as a uniquely rational creature in an intelligible universe. Because he is free and finite, man is fallible. Yet he alone of the creatures is able to become aware of and respond to the existence and perfection of God and to receive grace, whereby essential goodness is imparted to human nature. To the extent that Donne adopted the Thomistic view of man he shared in the indebtedness of the most noted exponents of Anglican thought in his age, taking his place beside Richard Hooker, Robert

---

112, 135–149; Helen Gardner, who independently affirmed meditative influences upon Donne in her edition of *The Divine Poems* (Oxford: Clarendon Press, 1952), pp. l–lv; cf. Thomas F. Van Laan, "John Donne's *Devotions* and the Jesuit Spiritual Exercises," *Studies in Philology,* LX (1963), 191–202.

55. *Sermons,* III.5.750–752.

Sanderson, and Jeremy Taylor.[56] Yet St. Augustine's characteristic pessimism remained the strongest element in Donne's analyses of human behavior. (Without arguing, for example, whether the pessimism of the *Anniversaries* is personal or impersonal, it is at least clear that the often-noted medievalism of outlook in these two poems is really Augustinianism.) With St. Augustine Donne the preacher deplores the difficulty of working upon the understanding, for it requires "long and cleer instruction," while the will, in addition to needing "an instructed understanding," is "in it self the blindest and boldest faculty." Thus, reaching the conclusion reached in book X of the *Confessions*, Donne concludes: "Here then the holy-Ghost takes the neerest way to bring a man to God, by awaking his memory."[57] Elsewhere in the sermons he declares that "the Memory is oftner the Holy Ghosts Pulpit that he preaches in, then the Understanding,"[58] indicating the direct implication from Scripture to preaching:

> Of our perverseness in both faculties, *understanding,* and *will,* God may complain, but as much of our *memory;* for, for the rectifying of the *will,* the *understanding* must be rectified; and that implies great difficulty: But the *memory* is so familiar, and so present, and so ready a faculty, as will always answer, if we will but speak to it, and ask it, *what God hath done for us, or for others.* The art of *salvation,* is but the art of *memory.*[59]

In his emphasis upon the memory as the preacher's means of access to the soul and to the more refractory faculties of reason and will, Donne is singular among Anglican preachers of his day. He had, moreover, a singularly broad conception of the powers of the memory. It differs considerably from the quite ordinary notion which Andrewes, for example, expressed in his sermons on Luke 16.25 and 17.32, two texts which refer to the memory. Andrewes regarded the memory as a receptacle for learned precepts and truths and as a recorder for past experience. Its usefulness for the preacher lay in its capacity to retain

56. See H. R. McAdoo, *The Structure of Caroline Moral Theology* (London: Longmans, Green, and Co., 1949).
57. *Sermons,* II.11.13–17.
58. *Sermons,* VIII.11.303–305.
59. *Sermons,* II.2.46–52.

counsel that augmented the lessons of life. Donne, however, followed the Platonizing lead of St. Augustine in investing the memory with the additional power of reflecting upon the acquired and innate knowledge of the mind. What is remembered becomes "a second, a ruminated, a reflected knowledge," designated by the terms "recognition" and "acknowledgment."[60] The whole impetus in Donne's sermons, as in the analysis of memory in the *Confessions,* is to move beyond the truth of the all too strongly felt Pauline lament—"For the good that I would I do not: but the evil which I would not, that I do" (Romans 7.19)—to a discovery of regenerative potential in some human faculty. This discovery is made in the memory, "the stomach of the soul," which takes in and assimilates God's blessings. But Donne goes a step further than St. Augustine in his own metaphor, which represents the memory as not only passively reflecting but actively projecting the goodness and mercy of God:

> And therefore . . . we may be bold to call it the Gallery of the soul, hang'd with so many, and so lively pictures of the goodness and mercies of thy God to thee, as that every one of them shall be a catachism to thee, to instruct thee in all thy duties to him for those mercies: And as a well made, and well plac'd picture, looks alwayes upon him that looks upon it; so shall thy God look upon thee, whose memory is thus contemplating him, and shine upon thine understanding, and rectifie thy will too.[61]

Considering the great importance of this faculty in Donne's view of human nature, it is not surprising that he regarded the ministry of the Church, by which divine grace is made available, as primarily appealing to the memory.[62] This perspective had a number of other ramifications, among which was Donne's wholehearted participation in the Anglican recourse to primitive and catholic Christian belief and practice, the Creeds, Councils, and Fathers—the corporate "memory" of the continuing body of Christ. Another was Donne's love of church

---

60. *Sermons,* IV.12.113–120; cf. IX.2.605–615.

61. *Sermons,* II.11.85–96. As Joan Webber remarks (*Contrary Music,* p. 208 n. 28), Donne errs in ascribing to St. Bernard the characterization of the memory as the stomach of the soul; the phrase occurs in bk. X, ch. 14 of St. Augustine's *Confessions.*

62. *Sermons,* II.12.327–332; cf. VIII.11.607–610.

music, liturgy, and ceremony, which stimulated the sensory responses of the memory and made the soul more tractable—as George Herbert also perceived—to divine things. Donne publicly defended "Ritual, and Ceremoniall things" in an outdoor sermon to the London populace at St. Paul's Cross on May 6, 1627, but a more personal endorsement is reported in Walton's *Life of Donne*. Donne had the "Hymn to God the Father" which he wrote in his sickness of 1623–24 set "to a most grave and solemn tune" and "often sung to the organ by the choristers of St. Paul's Church in his own hearing, especially at the evening service," whereupon he was known to remark:

> "The words of this hymn have restored to me the same thoughts of joy that possessed my soul in my sickness when I composed it. And, Oh the power of church-music! that harmony added to this hymn has raised the affections of my heart and quickened my graces of zeal and gratitude. . . ."

And Donne was certain that in such stirrings he felt what others felt, for in confronting God this uncommon divine felt himself a most common man. While his preaching is the fullest expression of his genius, it is also the fullest testimony of his adherence to homiletic precedent in seeing the abundantly figurative language of Scripture as the means by which the Holy Ghost works upon the human memory and furnishes a model of expression for the preacher. Donne's traditionalist notions of Scriptural discourse and of the sermon patterned on them will be discussed in the following section.

THE MODE OF DISCOURSE

In Donne's age, an age which scrutinized and stressed the text of Scripture far beyond the confines of the pulpit, it was universally assumed that the qualities of Biblical expression set a model for the sermon to follow. This was not a new but rather an age-old assumption. It had guided St. Augustine's contention in book IV of *De doctrina Christiana* that, as the words of the Bible contained all wisdom and eloquence, the preacher was to draw as he needed on the full resources of humane learning in the service of divine truth. Until the Reformation the Augustinian conception of Scripture and the sermon carried all others before it; and its force continued to be felt in the preaching manuals of the sixteenth and seventeenth centuries which prescribed patterns of sermon construction derived more or less strictly from the classical oration: invention or division of the text into its several parts, disposition or amplification of the parts with a view to opening up their meaning, and finally a general or specific application of the text to the auditory. But despite a still widespread conformity (also the product of school and university training) to classical patterns, a body of conflicting opinions about the nature of Scripture and the sermon was growing in strength and vociferousness by the beginning of the seventeenth century.

The radical Puritan John Downame spoke for many in asserting that "the holie Ghost in penning the Scriptures hath used great simplicitie and wonderful plainnesse."[63] In his preaching manual *The Arte of Prophecying* (1592) the prestigious William Perkins took the doctrinaire Calvinist position that the sermon was not to profane its exposition of God's Word by mingling it with human art or learning. The spreading Puritan practice of preaching extemporaneously rather than from memory with the assistance of brief notes (as more traditionally inclined Anglicans like Andrewes and his school, and Donne himself, did) was justified by pointing to Christ's calling of rude, unlettered men to be his disciples, whom he then made the apostles and first ministers of the Church. It was hard to counter such a judgment of the apostles, and those who, like Donne, decried extemporaneous preaching did so on the grounds that it was presumptuous to proceed as if circumstances were identical with those of the early Church, when most people were entirely ignorant of the Gospel and the apostles were under the special inspiration of the Holy Ghost. The intervening centuries of Christianity had established careful and workable procedures governing the office—or, as Donne usually called it, the "Ordinance"—of preaching.[64]

But this newly current judgment of the apostles had not been alto-

---

63. Quoted by Douglas Bush, *English Literature in the Earlier Seventeenth Century,* 2nd ed. (Oxford: Clarendon Press, 1962), p. 328.

64. Schleiner connects rejection of extemporaneous preaching with the rhetorical principle of decorum (*The Imagery of Donne's Sermons,* pp. 51–55), but adds that "the issue for Donne . . . is also quite clearly a matter of church discipline. He sees a functional link between careful preparation and theological conformity" (pp. 53–54).

gether unanticipated even by St. Augustine, who admitted in the fourth book of *De doctrina Christiana* that when he first confronted Latin versions of the Bible with his background in classical rhetoric he was appalled by what seemed to be blatant crudity and ignorance. Only as he came to thorough study and understanding of the Bible did he reach the view, lyrically expressed in chapter 7, that it had issued from the mind of God both wisely and eloquently, with wisdom and eloquence so sublimely conjoined that the one was at no point separate from the other. This recounting is of utmost importance for what it reveals of St. Augustine's conception of Scriptural—and, indeed, all —language as the physical embodiment of mental and spiritual reality. His continual insistence is on the inherent rationale and dynamic of Scriptural language as the sensible manifestation to human minds of the thought and intent of God. Thus the latter half of the fourth book is devoted to showing that the question is not whether to use adorned or unadorned phrases or whether, among the conventional levels of style, the high or the moderate or the low should be used in this or that instance. For everything in Christianity is of the greatest importance, pertaining to nothing less than what God has done for man and what man must do in return. The point is that everything in Scripture reflects or expresses in some way the ultimate divine purpose and that this must be the endeavor of the preacher too.

It will be evident that the Augustinian theory of sacred discourse (Scripture and sermon) has broad and profound implications in itself, but it also functioned as part of the total Christian world-view that held from the time of the Church Fathers until the seventeenth century. The Christian world-view presupposed that everything which God made, did, and said was a species of self-revelation, manifesting aspects of the divine mind and being. Implicit and explicit in this world-view was the acknowledgment that for man, in his earthly life at least, God remained ultimately and essentially unknowable; thus these manifestations were of all the more value and significance. Among them the physical universe was treated, as the great commonplace developed, as the Book of the Creatures, and the peculiar natures of all animate and inanimate things were taken as evidence of the existence, power, wisdom, and goodness of the Creator. The Scriptures, however, were God's highest and most complete revelation to man, brought to fulfillment in the person of Christ. Even and espe-

cially in this culminating revelation the human need to experience
through the senses and to understand by degrees is met in the concreteness, detail, and specificity of Biblical narrative—the progression from
the Law and the Prophets to the Gospel, and, above all, the central
event of the Incarnation. Thus what in St. Augustine and in Donne
begins as commendation of the manifold richness of the Holy Ghost's
language in Scripture comes to be a complex and all-embracing world-
view in which every word and object and event, rightly seen and understood, symbolizes the greatness and goodness of God.

And accordingly the inevitable and universal modulation into plain
style in preaching and in all forms of expression by the end of the
seventeenth century had ramifications reaching far beyond rejection
of the highly artificial mode of patristic preaching revived by the school
of Andrewes and Donne and far beyond an ordinary revolution in
rhetorical taste. It is now a platitude but also, nevertheless, a portentous
fact that the complex and all-embracing symbolic world-view of Christian tradition lapsed with the disappearance of a style which Dr. John-
son with characteristic penetration first labeled "metaphysical"—for
"metaphysical" it was at its heart and at its best. This is not the place
to rehearse these ramifications, since they took place after Donne's
death. But it is most pertinent to emphasize here that Donne held the
traditional symbolic view of reality and its reflection in language with
an intensity and imagination unparalleled in any other preacher of his
age, exhibiting its vitality in a grandeur of expression with which he
uniquely among the exponents of the *via media* perpetuated the manner of the great preaching Fathers in expounding the order, plenitude,
and purposiveness of God's works and Word.

In discussing Donne's mode of preaching it is convenient to begin,
as book IV of *De doctrina Christiana* begins, with the explicit commendation of the qualities of Biblical expression, for this is a very
pronounced feature of his sermons and one of his most obvious points
of adherence to Augustinian conceptions. The soaring strain inspired
by his source is sounded early in Donne's ministry:

There are not so eloquent books in the world, as the Scriptures:
Accept those names of Tropes and Figures, which the Gram-
marians and Rhetoricians put upon us, and we may be bold to say,

that in all their Authors, Greek and Latin, we cannot find so high, and so lively examples, of those Tropes, and those Figures, as we may in the Scriptures: whatsoever hath justly delighted any man in any mans writings, is exceeded in the Scriptures. The style of the Scriptures is a diligent, and an artificial style; and a great part thereof in a musical, in a metrical, in a measured composition, in verse.[65]

What matters to Donne here and in numerous other passages throughout his sermons is the affective power of the Holy Ghost's eloquence ("whatsoever hath justly delighted any man") in patterns of sound, and figures of speech and thought that arouse the attention and impress upon it what is being said. This was, of course, also St. Augustine's motive in synthesizing the techniques of classical oratory with the message of Christianity: to infuse the Word of Life into the lives of men by instructing, pleasing, and persuading them with it. Donne acknowledges directly in another context that the Holy Ghost always speaks in such forms and phrases in the Bible as may best work upon them to whom he speaks.[66] A similar remark comes from Andrewes, who said that God "attireth His speech in the habit, uttereth it in the phrase, figure, and accent . . . as may seem most fit and forcible to prevail with us."[67] And, indeed, in many of the more superficial and imitable techniques by which traditional preaching had enforced correspondences between sound and sense, image and idea, Andrewes and Donne resemble each other. They both learned from Tertullian's example to use antithesis and paradox and wordplay to convey the mysteries of Christian faith, from St. Bernard's balancing and rhyming of words and phrases to express in concinnities the divine harmony of the universe, and from patristic and medieval predecessors generally to pursue the spiritual significance in every syllable of Scripture.

Yet it was Donne alone who evolved an eloquent style to mirror not only the inferred intent of the Holy Ghost in a text but the movement of his own mind in undertaking to penetrate its meaning. His sermons

65. *Sermons*, II.7.241–249. Cf. Schleiner's interesting use of this passage to demonstrate Donne's sense of rhetorical decorum (*Ibid.*, pp. 20–21).
66. *Sermons*, II.14.644–645.
67. *Ninety-six Sermons*, I, 341.

consist of capacious units, paragraphs and sentences which hold in suspension and in tension many lesser elements—these often registering
insistent perceptions or hovering uncertainties—but coalescing in
wholes charged with psychological energy and immediacy, inspiring
wonder at the workings of this instrument which is the divine image
and so, finally, a response to its Creator. The kinetic and evocative
power of Donne's preaching, moreover, is directly related to the intensity of his insight into St. Augustine's conceptions of the soul,
Scripture, and the sermon. In particular, Donne's eloquence arises out
of his realization that the Holy Ghost was "a Metaphoricall, and Figurative expresser of himselfe" insofar as he was "a direct worker upon
the soule and conscience of man."[68]

The abundance of imagery in the Bible—which embraced all kinds
of concreteness and detail because "things" were not simply "things"
but also "signs"—operated to fill the soul's gallery, the memory, with
pictures that vivified the apprehension of meaning. Even more than
the objects of the external world, the words of Scripture were means of
revelation. Certain materials had traditionally provided substance since
they were introduced by Origen, the first great exegete of the Church,
and then became second nature in many of the Latin Fathers, whose
fixing upon the very letter of Scripture yielded anything but literalism.
These included the use of so-called natural history which recounted the
often fabulous characteristics of regions and the fish and fowl, beasts
and men within them, of number symbolism which probed the significance of repeated numbers (like three, seven, ten, and forty) in
Scripture, and of etymology of Hebrew names and words and analysis
of solecisms. All of these and especially the last—attentiveness to the
spiritual overtones of linguistic peculiarities—have a place in Donne's
preaching. Yet his employment of them does not have the schematizing
and abstracting effect of much traditional allegorizing of Scripture
because he remains alert to the actualities of his text and context, seeking always to highlight them as they are and not to blur them in a
grand design.

In Donne's preaching the stress is on the figuring, imaging, signifying force of Biblical language in order to make it memorable in

68. *Sermons,* IX.14.559–561.

the special Augustinian sense and thus to activate the reason and will to holy ends. For this undertaking his poetic genius, with its constant enforcement of analogies not readily apparent to ordinary minds, was admirably suited. The sustained energy of Donne's preaching comes from his dwelling and enlarging upon images in his texts or in supplemental Biblical citations, his construing of common nouns as figures of speech, and his extracting of latent metaphors where none are apparent. In all this Donne always gives the credit to the Holy Ghost; yet it is much too simple to transfer the credit to the poetic genius of Donne. The complicated fact is that Donne relied greatly on the rich homiletic tradition begun with the Church Fathers and expanded during the Middle Ages,[69] which in his age his verbal sensibilities and vital responses found so uniquely congenial and true. When the credit is shared there is no danger of minimizing either the conventionality or the originality of Donne the preacher. In the latter regard, at the close of one sermon he characteristically professes himself loath to leave off his exposition of the latitude and elegance of one of the metaphors of Scripture. Donne thus exhibits a very different kind of consciousness and commitment than Andrewes, who remarks revealingly at an early point in an Easter sermon: "Symbolical Divinity is good, but might we see [this truth] in the rational too? We may see it in the cause, in the substance, and let the ceremony go."[70] Such a dismissal could never have occurred to Donne. For it was precisely through steeping itself in the symbolic force of Scripture as traditionally interpreted— the continuum and correspondence of physical object and spiritual truth—that the sermon made its impress upon the soul.

The sense of Scripture which the soul received from Donne's preaching is, as has been noted, predominantly moral. He saw his task as transmitting the urgent recognition of God's judgment and mercy which radiates from the Bible, and, correspondingly, to find unacceptable any principles or practices of interpretation which divorced spiritual from literal meaning. No one exemplifies better than Donne how the term "tropology" came successively to designate the use of tropes and a discoursing on matters of conscience and conduct. For in going

69. For the most complete demonstration to date, see Schleiner, *The Imagery of Donne's Sermons*, pp. 68–156.

70. *Ninety-six Sermons*, II, 214.

into detail and depth in pursuing the significance of his text, he never lost sight of the overall divine intent which makes the Bible unique among books. Sin and salvation were the subjects on which Scripture spoke to the soul.

The dominance of broad and basic considerations in Donne's view of Scripture had a formative effect on his sermons. So intent was he on its unity that he regularly chose texts which he could treat as summaries or abridgments of larger wholes—the chapters or books where they are found. In this fashion he was able to demonstrate afresh the spiritual significance arising directly out of the contextual emphasis of the literal sense. Already in the *Essays in Divinity,* Donne's proto-sermons, the two projected disquisitions, or "books", on the first verse of Genesis and the first verse of Exodus come to involve exegetical, historical, theological, and devotional concerns arising from Genesis and Exodus in their entirety. Likewise in the first Prebend sermon he not only finds trust explicitly mentioned once but also "spread over all the verses of the Psalme before" (ll. 99–100), and in the second Prebend sermon he pays tribute to the sixty-third Psalm as one of those that "spread themselves over all occasions, Catholique, universall Psalmes, that apply themselves to all necessities" (ll. 11–13). A related habit in Donne's handling of texts was his refusal to compartmentalize "sense" and "use"—the conventional terms for, respectively, the basic meaning and the optional implications. According to the preaching manuals of Donne's day, the two were to be separated very carefully: "sense" was to be given its full due in the section of "amplification" following the division of the text into parts; and "use" was to be dealt with, if there were time and inclination, in a section of "application" just prior to the conclusion of the sermon.[71] But Donne often announced his intention of making "the right use of the right sense" of his text, and it is rarely possible to find a dividing line between amplification and application in his preaching. That the one should subsume the other is, of course, a further consequence of his Anglican view that there is a continuum and not a hierarchy of meaning in Scripture.

71. Dennis Quinn remarks on the unemphatic, and subordinate, place given to application by such characteristic Reformed theorists as William Perkins and Andreas Hyperius ("Donne's Christian Eloquence," p. 279; "John Donne's Principles of Biblical Exegesis," p. 328).

Donne's unremitting concern with the unity of the Bible and its application to the soul stemmed from his native passion for essentials. These always remained for him embedded in circumstantiality, in the here and now; the Incarnation as the climax of God's revelation to man loomed large in his consciousness. Application was, therefore, not merely a sermon subdivision; but, as he told his hearers, "a continuall application of all that Christ Jesus said, and did, and suffered, to thee"[72] was the central function of the Church's ministry and the sole objective of the Christian life. But how was application to be achieved? It consisted in going beyond "an Historicall assent" to the Word of God—the attitude that these things happened, but what are they to me?—and experiencing the record of human salvation as the means of one's own. It consisted in the absorption of personal fears and joys into the suspense and fulfillment of the Biblical narrative, in becoming aware through the preaching of the Word, of the Word Christ himself:

> the subject of the Word of God, of all the Scriptures, of all that was shadowed in the Types, and figur'd in the Ceremonies, and prepared in the preventions of the Law, of all that was foretold by the Prophets, of all that the Soule of man rejoyced in, and congratulated with the Spirit of God, in the *Psalms,* and in the *Canticles,* and in the cheerefull parts of spirituall joy and exultation, which we have in the Scriptures; Christ is the foundation of all those Scriptures, Christ is the burden of all those Songs; Christ was *in sermone* then, then he was in the Word.[73]

Like St. Augustine and St. Bernard before him, Donne responded especially fervently to the potential in Biblical typology, which disclosed the wholeness of the two Testaments through tracing the integration of particular elements into the total pattern. In typology God's will not only for Abraham or Moses or Job but for all men in Christ emerged in its complete coherence. The impetus of typology properly used was congenial to Donne. In his preaching he showed respect for the actuality and individuality of Biblical personalities—his favorites

72. *Sermons*, VII.8.635–637.
73. *Sermons*, I.8.94–102.

being St. Paul and the Psalmist David—and he never denigrated the type in the splendor of what was typified. For as Christ united Godhead and manhood, so, in a lesser but analogous fashion, men's lives in and beyond the pages of the Bible demonstrated the conjunction of human nature and divine purpose. Donne testified in his *Devotions* that the more he understood this in the Scriptures, the more he understood his own experience.

Thus "the true searching of the Scriptures" is "to finde all the *histories* to be *examples* to me, all the *prophecies* to induce a Saviour for *me,* all the *Gospell* to apply Christ Jesus to *me,*" and the next step is to "turne to thine owne *history,* thine *owne life.*"[74] Having come to be a Christian is to see the Jews' prophecy made history to oneself, the Jews' hope and reversion made possession and inheritance, the Jews' faith made matter of fact, and "all that was promised and represented in the Law, performed and recorded in the Gospel, and applied in the Church." The Christian comes from types and figures "to him that is *Logos* it self, the Word; to apprehend and apply Christ himself."[75] This is to come to no cosmic principle of Greek philosophy but, indeed, to the traditional devotional end of conformity to Christ (often evoked graphically in Donne's sermons), which is, "That thou art willing to live according to his Gospell, and ready to dye for him, that dyed for thee."[76]

For Donne the manifestation and application of Christ were, finally, "the Sermon of the Sermon."[77] The vital purpose of the discourse of the Holy Ghost and the preacher was to actuate the Word of life in the lives of men. Donne did not shrink from the clear special implications with regard to the preacher's own life. As St. Augustine in the concluding chapters of *De doctrina Christiana* acknowledges that he who preaches must above all practice because his example is a powerful sermon to others, so Donne near the close of the third Prebend sermon voiced his conviction that "the subsequent life is the best printing, and the most useful and profitable publishing of a Sermon" (ll. 665–666). That he continued to act to the last upon this conviction is well

74. *Sermons,* III.17.700–711.
75. *Sermons,* VIII.15.589–592, 601–606.
76. *Sermons,* VII.10.231–233.
77. *Sermons,* VII.11.512.

attested by the circumstances surrounding the delivery of *Death's Duell*, Dr. Donne's "own funeral sermon," and by his commissioning to be drawn from the life, for his personal *memento mori* while he yet lived, a portrait of himself in his shroud. (The top folds of the shroud in the sculpture that was subsequently made suggest a—heavenly?— crown.)

The last recorded events seem very strange. Donne went far beyond the Scripturalism of St. Augustine, who had large sheets inscribed with the Penitential Psalms hung around his deathbed for his contemplation. In considering these events, however, it is well to recall the stress which Anglican principles of interpretation placed upon context—where these events, like the texts of the Bible, derive and reveal their meaning. Seen in context, the strangeness is not just the effect of the Dean of St. Paul's idiosyncrasy. It is equally the effect of ordinary people's estrangement from the extraordinary seriousness which makes for saintliness. Because seriousness in relating the Word of God to one's own works and world is extraordinary, saintliness is always unlooked for. It is particularly unlooked for here, where the evidence lies exposed to other possible interpretations, in such a thoroughly human being as Donne.[78]

THE PREBEND SERMONS

Since his Readership in Divinity at Lincoln's Inn in the early years of his ministry, Donne's custom in preaching a series of sermons was to make each one independent and complete in itself. He had to do this when he preached the Prebend sermons at intervals of from three to nine months over more than two years—a far broader span of time than that of any other series he delivered. Yet it is equally clear that the Prebend sermons constitute a larger whole. As a whole, the series displays the sweep of Donne's thought, absorbed in the nature and condition of man as presented and especially imaged in his texts. The movement of thought proceeds out from an analysis of man as Donne

---

78. But see R. C. Bald's sympathetic treatment of Donne's last days and, in particular, his suggestion that "the frail figure standing . . . on the urn" is intended to image the fundamental Christian doctrine of the resurrection of the body (*John Donne: A Life*, p. 535).

found him and ends with a return, at long last, to the here and now from which Donne began. Like a vast parabola anchored at its two extremities in the actualities of this life, the Prebend sermons extend to anticipate at their height the joy and glory of the life to come. Coherence and continuity are maintained at every point in the series through the intent double vision imposed by the perspective on Scripture which made every earthly thing, as Donne put it, "a Type or Earnest" of heaven. Given the entirely arbitrary character of his Prebendal assignment, it is no inconsiderable measure of the mastery and flexibility which Donne's preaching had by this time attained that he could discover in texts from his five Psalms a comprehensive expression of the foremost concerns of his mind and ministry.

The First Prebend Sermon

The first Prebend sermon, delivered at St. Paul's on May 8, 1625, opens with a prolonged introduction, or *exordium,* which sets the meditative tone and pace of the entire series. "We consider," Donne begins. He proceeds to place the entire Psalter in its traditional high place of regard in the Church: for its moral and spiritual sustenance, including its Christological implications, and for its liturgical utility—latterly reaffirmed by his Prebendal commission, which he explains. The point is how admirably the Psalter ministers to all private and public religious needs, of which the series of sermons is to be a demonstration. Thus he makes the initial step of taking cognizance of man's state in terms of his text, Psalm 62.9, "Surely men of low degree are vanity, and men of high degree are a lie; to bee laid in the balance, they are altogether lighter then vanity." The dark tones of the verse inevitably foreshadow the substance of his treatment of human nature. But Donne did not simply deliver a diatribe along the lines of, for instance, St. Ambrose's exposition of the same text, which warned of the severe judgment to fall on all wicked speech and works and exhorted the baptized to be mindful of their promise to renounce the world and to despise its blandishments and vices.[79] Instead the equally traditional moral and spiritual orientation of the first Prebend sermon assumes a distinctive literary cast as a result of Donne's characteristic preoccupation with the wealth of connotation in the language of the Bible.

79. *PL,* XIV, 1236–1237.

The division of the text according to two basic complementary considerations, "The maner, and the matter" (in which sound follows sense), and then into further pairs of propositions and counterpropositions, reflects the single Biblical image, "to bee laid in the balance." Donne indicates that the sermon will develop analogously by weighing this against that: specifically, in the first section, the suggestion of a comparative offsetting somewhat the strong wording of the text in itself, for if man were altogether nothing he could not be weighed at all; in the second section, text against context, where again literal concerns show themselves as spiritual ones in the recognition that man weighed against God is indeed nothing; and in the third section, a fixing upon the fulcrum—all stability comes, as the entire sixty-second Psalm confesses, from trust in the "blessed, and gracious, and powerfull God" whom it names "by so many names of assurance and confidence."

Each section of the first Prebend sermon reinforces by pursuing and proliferating the image of balancing and weighing which, characteristically, is not static but kinetic, and productive of alternations of idea and mood. In the first section, the consideration of man in himself and among his fellow men, the first evidence comes from the words of Scripture. The elevated references which the Holy Ghost makes to man in many different places are corroborated on the one hand by the great act of man's Creation and on the other by the great act of man's Redemption. But the evidence of Scripture is balanced by the evidence gained from observing human life. Like countless writers of the Renaissance, Donne finds man to be the crown of all creation, the sole bearer of the image of God, and also, in his various roles—civil set off against ecclesiastical—of priest, prince, magistrate, and judge, to share in the responsibilities and benefits of society.[80] Thus, man in God's eyes and in his own is far from being nothing.

Over against the affirmative progression of the first section Donne traces back through man's illusory confidence in his own capabilities in the second section. This, he says significantly, is "our best use of the words, (as our translation exhibits them)": not directly to elaborate on "Surely" as an intimation of the sureness of God, but to contrast to

80. Admittedly, the subject is conventional enough, but it may have been suggested by the Epistle for the third Sunday after Trinity (May 8 in 1625). I Peter 2.11–17 admonishes those living in Christian liberty to continue nevertheless in obedience to existing forms of civil authority.

the absolute declarative statements which the Holy Ghost alone can make the absurdities of the Roman claim to infallibility and the Puritan assurance about salvation. In this negative section the one positive note is the remark on the spiritual overtones of the use of the word "Amen" in the Gospel of St. John. Here polemics takes a form frequent in Donne: an attack on doctrine is made by way of an attack on abuses of language.[81] The interworkings of amplification and application in his preaching also stand revealed in the protracted consideration of the force of the comparison in the text. This is made with all the sharpness and boldness of an erstwhile satirist in what is acknowledged to be a kind of satire. Donne begins by comparing the rich and the poor of his day—a vexed subject not strictly dealt with, as he admits, in the text, but one from which "good doctrines of edification" arise—and then goes on to explain the wording of the text proper. "Men of high degree" are those in prominent positions in the Church and State, and "men of low degree" are the common people at large, of whom Donne like his younger contemporary Sir Thomas Browne held no exalted conception. Under the ingenious construction given by Donne to the Hebrew poetic device of repetition with slight variation, "men of high degree" are called "a lie" because they do not keep their promises, "men of low degree" are called "vanity" because of their fickle and inconstant nature, and both together are called "lighter than vanity" because hope in them (as Donne had proved by long and bitter personal experience) is entirely futile.

At this point Donne pauses to reflect on the middle estate between high and low, suggesting in passing the roots of contemporary preaching in the tradition of classical rhetoric.[82] This passage is a brief testimony, as Milton's undergraduate Prolusions written not many years later are a more extensive one, to the influence of the ancients on all kinds of training and thinking in the Renaissance. Donne's tone, however, is colored by the lengthening shadows of the age and the cast of his own religiosity. He asserts that the middle state, unlike the extremes of fortune, fosters a self-reliance which poses the greatest possible danger to the ultimate fate of the soul. The function of these reflections,

81. Cf., e.g., *Sermons*, VII.2.423–751; VII.13.17–39.

82. On this point as related to Donne's preaching, see Schleiner, *The Imagery of Donne's Sermons*, pp. 13–62.

in the imagistic development of the whole sermon, is to show that the fulcrum—the still center—does not lie within man.

A long summary sentence beginning "Put all together" bobs back and forth between its parenthetical inserts and makes the transition from the instability of man's nature and state to the surety of faith in God and the larger message of the sixty-second Psalm. The third and final part of the first Prebend sermon is less a conclusion than an on-going exercise of Donne's priestly office, the office he had placed first among man's relations to man. Here he seemingly undertakes to emulate St. Athanasius, who is cited at the beginning of this sermon for his pre-eminence among early writers of the Church in applying the Psalms to human needs. The result is a settling of the intricate weights and balances of the whole discourse in a blend of catechism and benediction as the Dean of St. Paul's uses his singularly intense awareness of the power of language to administer reassurance through the names of strength—*Refuge, Defence, Rock, Salvation*—ascribed to God in the other verses of the Psalm. He draws to a quiet close in a passage of simple speech that is an effective implied contrast to the flattery and false promises of men to men: "Any of these notions is enough to any man, but God is all these, and all else, that all soules can thinke, to every man." With a final pairing off of two successive verses from the prophet Micah on the dangers of trusting man and the security of trusting God, the first Prebend sermon ends.

The Second Prebend Sermon

Donne's second Prebend sermon was preached at St. Paul's on January 29, 1626, two weeks after a somber sermon at St. Dunstan's which, by dwelling on the fleshly and spiritual corruption of man, reflected what must have been his personal reaction to returning to London after the wasting and seemingly interminable outbreak of the plague in 1625. The opening of the second Prebend sermon, however, declares in praise of the Psalter that it ministers to every man "in every emergency and occasion," and reiterates what Donne had said in the opening of the first Prebend sermon about the spiritual—especially typological and liturgical—applicability of the book as a whole. The celebrated poise and mastery of image and idea in this discourse emerge early, in the setting and dividing of the text, Psalm 63.7, "Because thou has been my helpe, therefore in the shadow of thy wings will I rejoyce."[83] Donne traces a contraction of the whole Psalter into this Psalm and the whole Psalm into this verse only to turn and discover in the words of his text, as if they had substantial reality, "the whole compasse of Time, Past, Present, and Future; and these three parts of Time, shall be at this time, the three parts of this Exercise." The first part, the present time, relates to the moment of utterance and hence the situation of the Psalmist as shown in the context: the title and the rest of the verses of the Psalm. The present is a time of distress. The second part, the past, and the third part, the future, are drawn from the convergence of two different verb tenses in the text; the past and the future are, in contrast to the present, linked in an expression of assurance. In Donne's grammar of the soul the sequence of tenses and the assured tone of the text intimate God's continuing presence, imaged as a circle, which becomes the referent of every subsequent consideration in the second Prebend sermon.

But the first part, the consideration of the present, harks back to the first Prebend sermon in its use of images of weights and balances to figure forth David's situation and to generalize upon it to the condition of all men. In the treatment of the first topic, a comparison of temporal and spiritual afflictions, Donne's use of Biblical quotations to confirm the universality and inevitability of temporal afflictions is reminiscent of the world-weary strain in his preaching six years earlier, when he returned from serving as chaplain of Viscount Doncaster's embassy to the Continent in the troubled months preceding the start of the Thirty Years' War.[84] There is almost quantitative, physical

83. For an exhaustive discussion in support of the view that Donne's images and syntax tend to qualify the positive thrust of this discourse, see William J. J. Rooney, "John Donne's Second Prebend Sermon—A Stylistic Analysis," *Texas Studies in Literature and Language,* IV (1962), 24–34.

84. Walton's report that Donne returned to England "with his sorrows [over his wife's death] moderated" is at odds with the surviving specimens of his preaching—the two-part sermon on the dangers and evils of riches, preached at Whitehall on April 2, 1620 (*Sermons,* III, no. 1); the melancholy discourse on Job's sufferings, delivered on January 7, 1621 before the Countess of Bedford (III, no. 8); and the sermon on the mainly deleterious effects of worldly prosperity, preached at Whitehall on April 8, 1621 (III, no. 10). For an account of the frustrations of the Doncaster embassy and the turmoil on the Continent, see Bald, *John Donne: A Life,* pp. 338–365.

weight in the amassed Biblical citations and examples which illustrate that "All our life is a continuall burden, yet we must not groane; A continuall squeasing, yet we must not pant. . . ." The development of this section is entirely dependent on the association of images—from the crushing weight of temporal afflictions (through "stone" as a measure of weight?) to the "spirituall stoniness, and obduration" of heart which Donne depicts as the supreme affliction (with an assist from a Jesuit commentator's allegorizing of Pliny). The cumulative sense of the famous paragraph on the wrath of God is, as in the first Prebend sermon, to squelch all possibility of an inner equilibrium of one's own creation, to eliminate all approaches to a middle and safe ground in one's own "moral constancy." Predictably, the ultimate counterpoise to the burden of this life is located in "the blessed Metaphore, that the Holy Ghost hath put into the mouth of the Apostle, *Pondus Gloriae. . . . An exceeding waight of eternall glory,*" but it will be time in the third Prebend sermon to enlarge upon this figure of speech. Here the emphasis is rather on the fulcrum provided by the ministry of the Church in this life, as extracted by Donne from the context of his text—David's expressions of longing after the altars of the Lord during his sojourn in the desert. Again, by way of typology, amplification merges with application; David's situation shows the benefits of public worship and the gravity of any kind of exclusion, among which Donne's moral intent emphasizes the personal indifference that leads one to exclude himself.

In the second part of the sermon the inclination to objectify the words of a text is especially evident. The phrase "Because thou hast been" is construed successively as an "idea" and a "pattern" or "example"; "my helpe" is construed as "my helper" (with an additional balancing of God's not leaving man to himself against God's not leaving out man). The implication of this lyrical and often quoted section, which attests to Donne's conviction within the *via media,* is to confirm the rightness of typological readings of Scripture and life: as God's prophecies become histories in the two Testaments—a frequent Augustinian reflection—so the histories of the Bible become prophecies of what God will do for the soul in the present. There are no overt organizing images in this section, but its content subtly enhances connotations of balancing (this was done in the past; this will be done in the future) and of circularity (God's help is never ending).

The third part of the sermon develops the phrase "in the shadow of thy wings will I rejoyce." After a roundabout approach through some characteristic considerations of the power taken to inhere in names, Donne conducts an extremely interesting and exact examination of the figure "the shadow of thy wings." He refuses to fall into blurry, comfortable associations of parental protection and sustenance, but points out that all of the occurrences of "wings" in the Psalms are used not of safety and actual deliverance but only of temporary respite, "refreshing," "respiration"—that is, a moment to catch one's breath. Here the connection with the soul's breathlessness under the burden of life is manifest while remaining implicit. This, then, is the use of Donne's scholarship: to satisfy the spirit, not merely the mind. Here, also, "rejoyce" becomes substantial in the substantive *Gaudium,* joy.

An interlude of reflection on the present need for joy and on the disheartenment of the times is at once timeless and timely—for Donne is surely alluding to the emotional and physical exhaustion attendant on the worst plague epidemic in his lifetime, which killed tens of thousands of people in London and environs in less than a year. Thus he proposes at this low-spirited time, in this as yet earthbound sermon, to "raise your hearts, and dilate your hearts, to a holy Joy, to a joy in the Holy Ghost." He performs on this proposal in a dazzling, rapid sequence of images which expand and soar aloft before the inward eye of the soul. The point of departure is a map in two hemispheres (God's circle projected as a globe), which in turn becomes the basis of a compound analogy: the joy and glory of heaven are as the Eastern and Western hemispheres of earth, and as the Old World has been familiar but the New, America, long withheld from man's knowledge, so the glory of heaven is withheld in this life but the joy of heaven afforded in the awareness of God's care for man in this world. Donne's discourse modulates into direct address exhorting the soul to discovery of joy in envisioning the rejoicing of angels and martyrs over the conversion of a single soul. "Conceive," he says (and the pun is not in levity, but in utter earnest), conceive of joy here as the Holy Ghost is described in the opening verses of Genesis—brooding with outspread wings over the newly formed world (again God's circle of past, present, and future blessings), produced all things that were produced. Now the perspective is airborne, at the eye level of the divine Dove, and Donne projects the imagined panorama of the joy of this world flowing into the joy of heaven, "as a River flowes into the Sea." But this much-protracted culminating paragraph will mount still higher in coming to a close and bearing up the hearers with a sense of joy through visualizing the soul's entrance into beatitude. The repetition and suspension used in the vast circular development of the final periodic sentence give Donne's diction the involved and charged quality also conspicuous in Andrewes' efforts to express this experience.[85] However, Donne's translation of human life into the fullness of joy is incomparably advanced beyond Andrewes' in a magnificently apt metaphor of the ultimate translation, used years earlier in the *Second Anniversary*—the translation of the soul after death from earth to heaven. The whole is a prime example of "the art of salvation" as "the art of memory," the appeal to the vision of the inward eye.

The Third Prebend Sermon

In the same register and a harmonizing key Donne preached his third Prebend sermon at the service of Evening Prayer in the Cathedral on November 5, 1626. The occasion, the anniversary of the Gunpowder Plot, is of interest because there is virtually no topicality in the sermon (in direct contrast to Andrewes' long series of sermons for yearly commemorations of the Gunpowder Plot and the Gowries' Conspiracy). The choice of date and circumstance (a secondary, not the main service of the day where, perhaps, there would have been a compelling obligation to talk about the Jesuit threat) seems to reflect Donne's continuing purpose of finding the enduringly spiritual in the here and now. And 1626 was a wonderful year in his experience; he wrote in his private account-book: "This year God hath blessed me and mine with *multiplicatae sunt super nos misericordiae tuae*."[86] In the third Prebend ser-

---

85. Andrewes portrays joyfulness as the end result of the spiritualization of experience in the conclusion of his Christmas sermon of 1613 (*Ninety-six Sermons*, I, 134).

86. Izaak Walton came into possession of the private account-book which Donne kept while he was Dean. Walton's excerpts from the prayers at the end of yearly entries are dated only in the 1640 edition of the *Life of Donne*. See David Novarr, *The Making of Walton's "Lives"* (Ithaca, N.Y.: Cornell University Press, 1958), pp. 88–89.

mon he would speak specifically of man's participation in God's glory, expounding Psalm 64.10, "And all the upright in heart shall glory."

After the customary review of his Prebendal obligations in his introduction, Donne explicitly links the third Prebend sermon with the second by reintroducing the image of the two hemispheres of joy and glory. He modifies somewhat his earlier assertion that the glory of heaven is reserved for the life to come. Here in this life there could be some heavenly luster—"a beame" or "a tincture," evoking images of the sun and of the alchemical transmutation of baser metals into gold which surface again later in the discourse. Just as before, Donne plots out the next area of exploration for which the text of Scripture will be the means of spiritual discovery: "So, in these words which I have read to you now, our voyage lies about the Hemispheare of Glory, for, (*All the upright in heart shall Glory.*)"

The point of embarkation is taken over from the second Prebend sermon: the continuity of this life with the next through the Christian's continuous spiritual translation of earthly experience. "The glory of God shining through godly men, this glory which we speake of, is the evidence, and the reflexion of the glory from above." But in the third Prebend sermon the realization of divine truth is the product of an unremitting scrutiny of the etymology and grammar of Donne's text, the effort to translate earthly life into heavenly terms imposing this concentration on the details of the Holy Ghost's language with, of course, their latent images. Thus, as Donne divides his text (and discourse), he maps or diagrams the sentence. The two parts are the subject and the predicate; the first part of the sermon treats the subject, the upright in heart, "the persons proposed by God."

Entrance into the first part is by way of one province of the literal sense—as Aquinas classified St. Augustine's distinctions—aetiology, why the text is phrased as it is. The search for reasons, and the reasons themselves, are figured in a witty turn on the medieval commonplace of the Book of the World.[87] Donne projects the world as a vast library. God, for his part, is depicted as a reader of his own works (each man's life is a book); he reads for enjoyment (delight in virtue) but also for

87. See Schleiner, *The Imagery of Donne's Sermons,* pp. 94–103, for a discussion of the derivation of this *topos* and its uses by Donne.

general information ("to know what we do"). If such is God's study, man—in Donne's dilation of the figure—is wrong to be inquisitive about the "Booke of life," "the Records of Heaven" in which the inscrutable eternal divine purposes are recorded. The preacher squarely rebukes the contemporary curiosity over damnation—whether in the form of the Puritan doctrine of reprobation or the Roman doctrine of limbos and purgatory ("multiplied Hells"). The line of the *via media* is shown to be God's way, and God's way is shown in his way of speaking in this text: he makes a positive, not a negative emphasis and intimates that what men are now they shall become then. The aetiology of the text, according to Donne, is to affirm personal moral responsibility and practical moral concerns.

The rest of the first part consists of a remarkable literal and spiritual exposition of the phrase "upright in heart." Donne reverts to the Hebrew *Iashar* and its concordance definitions—*"Rectitudinem,* and *Planiciem"*—and, thus equipped, proceeds to amplify and apply the inherent metaphors. Upright men are direct men; but insofar as they are men of this world, their ways are of this world—that is, as the words objectify in images, the path traced by even the straightest steps is an arc, a part of a circle. Even the best earthly path can never be a straight line. Yet, insofar as upright men are men of God, they can always go to him "in a direct line, a straight, a perpendicular line; For God is verticall to me, over my head now, and verticall now to them, that are in the East, and West-Indies; To our Antipodes, to them that are under our feet, God is verticall, over their heads, then when he is over ours." Apart from the beauty of rhythm and sound, the virtuosity of this section inheres in Donne's recognition of the fundamental likeness of geometrical and ethical concepts, both of which are entirely real to men even though they relate to an ideal which this world can only approximate.

Also, however, the secondary connotations fit and enrich. The East and West Indies foreshadow the Church Militant and the Church Triumphant, the joint company of the faithful which Donne proceeds to treat in the second part of the sermon. But first there is a typological excursus, again rising out of a literalist concern with context, but geared to the usual combination of amplification and application. Here there is some sense of the obliquity against which the upright in heart must guard themselves in this life. As David was constant and yet circumspect in the exercise of his religion, the faithful of the Church of England are to be wary of the "hypocriticall conformity" of Romanist sympathizers; they are not to trust themselves "at a superstitious Service" for whatever reason. In this brief passage only does one glimpse the straws in the current wind—the Jesuit scare, still fresh since 1605, and the increasing frequency of Catholic conversions among the ladies and gentlemen of the court of Charles I.[88] This topicality modulates, at the very end of the first part, in a reprise of the preceding imagistic development as Donne expounds the word "all." What does "all" mean? To fill a space with fulness of being: as God is omnipresent, at once the "Center" and "circumference" of life.

The second part of the third Prebend sermon develops directly out of the Hebrew primary root of the verb in Donne's text and the moral and spiritual connotations of its reflexive and passive form. Donne's purported ostentation with regard to his purportedly meager Hebrew has been so much emphasized that a word should be said in his defense. Although his remarks about Hebrew etymology and grammar here are absolutely exact, he chooses to make himself intelligible by quoting the renderings of several Latin and all but one of the principal English translations of the Bible in his day, which illustrate the several nuances of the original approximated by each translator in turn. To be sure, this was the utility of a variety of translations according to St. Augustine (in chapter 12 of the second book of *De doctrina Christiana*), but Donne very unpretentiously puts this old rule to good effect. The whole section defines and copiously illustrates how *Halal,* the Hebrew primary root, developed from an original meaning of "to be bright, to be clear" used both of sounds and colors to a later, more abstract meaning of "to praise, to glory." In particular, the reflexive imperfect verb form in the text, *Iithhalelu,* is imaged and expanded upon with a wide and superbly chosen range of citations (Aristotle and Philo Judaeus appear in company with the Bible and Donne's favorite Church Fathers) to show how the giving and receiving of glory and praise make complex but complete moral and verbal sense.

88. This is an interesting demonstration of how typology, and tropology generally, could adapt from explication to application by being carried down to the preacher's own time. The practice is widespread in seventeenth-century preaching. Cf. Schleiner, *The Imagery of Donne's Sermons,* pp. 199–200.

The final section, beginning at the marginal heading *Futurum,* gets underway with a last pair of philological observations. There is no present tense in Hebrew, just an imperfect and a perfect (as the earth is imperfect and heaven is perfect); there are no superlatives in Hebrew (but their force is achieved, Donne says often elsewhere in his preaching, by adding the name of God to a noun). The spiritual overtones of such solecisms are then explored as Donne seeks to extend the range of the verb in his text beyond all earthly discourse. Since the imperfect tense covers all uncompleted action, that is, all but past action, it binds up what is now and what shall be in an intimation of the inexpressible glory of heaven "where there shall be an everlasting present, and an everlasting future, there *the upright in heart shall be praised,* and that for ever." Voices, like tenses, are transcended in the plenitude of heavenly glory which Donne endeavors to represent through alternating the active and passive senses of the verb in his text. The outcome is a brief, brilliant Hallelujah passage rivaling Andrewes' well-known inventions on the name Immanuel.[89] Then, in the manner of an antiphon, the massive conclusion beginning at the marginal heading *Aeternum* gathers up the whole wealth of imagistic connotation generated previously in the sermon—the clearness and brightness of virtue, the voyage from one hemisphere to another (in the soul's translation from the Church Militant to the Church Triumphant), the witty variation on the commonplace Book of the Creatures (Donne's life is a printing and publishing of his sermons)—and finally projects the totality of meaning in the text as an evocation of what cannot be directly expressed, the redounding splendor of life with God.

The Fourth Prebend Sermon

From the rhetorical and conceptual magnificence of the second and third Prebend sermons where the illimitable meaning of a text is ex-

89. *Ninety-six Sermons,* I, 143–146. A closer analogue to Donne (in content, that is) occurs in Andrewes' Christmas sermon of 1619, an exposition of Luke 2.14, "Glory to God in the highest": "Now let God above have the glory of this day. . . . But we have nothing to render Him for all His goodness, for his ἐνδοκία, but δόξα . . . . And it is the humble man that gives God the true glory, that sings this song right, when all is done. The glory that comes to God is δόξα δι ἐνδοκίαν, the first word for the last. With glory it begins, with good-will it ends; and with good-will it begins, and with glory ends" (*ibid.,* I, 224, 229).

plored, Donne turned to an increasingly specific emphasis on the Church as sole repository and source of spiritual ministration. He delivered his fourth Prebend sermon at St. Paul's on January 28, 1627, quite likely in the evening.[90] His text was Psalm 65.5: "By terrible things in righteousnesse wilt thou answer us, O God of our salvation; who art the confidence of all the ends of the earth, and of them that are a far off, upon the sea." What is to develop into a protracted discourse begins in ringing, confident tones with a combined *praecognitio textus* (advance survey of the text) and *divisio* (division of the text, and the sermon, into parts). Donne launches into a witty elaboration of an analogy between miracles of a physical nature (Thomistically defined) and conversion of souls—in particular, between Christ's Feeding of the Five Thousand and the spiritual nourishment furnished in the Psalms. This text, indeed, is a course of three meals, consisting of the knowledge of God afforded in Nature (breakfast), in the Jewish Law (dinner), and in the Christian Church (supper—in which the sacrament of the Lord's Supper is a foretaste of the heavenly supper of the Lamb referred to in the book of Revelation). Or, better, says Donne, as his preaching mirrors the movement of his mind, the text is a table Grace, a humble acknowledgment and blessing of God for these three ways of coming to know and worship him. Thus the three parts of the fourth Prebend sermon are set: "What God hath done in Nature, what in the Law, what in the Gospel."

The Nature-Law-Gospel progression is commonplace in Donne's work; in fact, it might be called the fundamental category of his religious thought. The progression underlies the argument of *Biathanatos* and the *Essays in Divinity*. Its close affinities with typology, which for Donne linked the three stages, are obvious. But the stages of revelation first play a formative role in the sermons after Donne's appointment to the Deanery of St. Paul's. During his first years as Dean, from late 1621 to late 1623, he frequently dwelt in his preaching on the latitude in a single verse of Scripture, finding in a few words not only the illustrative function of natural phenomena but also the promissory force of the Old Testament and the confirmatory force of the New.

90. In the third part of the sermon Donne says: "You have said in your prayers here, (*Lord, from whom all good counsails doe proceed*) And God answers you from hence. . . ." The italicized phrase is from the Order for Evening Prayer in the *Book of Common Prayer*.

To insight of this kind a verse from the Prophet Job could prove as amenable as one from the Gospel of St. John.[91] But no matter what book is used, it is often difficult to guess from the face of things how Donne's text could yield him intimations of the knowledge of God to be found in Nature, in the Law, and in the Gospel. Hence a careful look at the exposition of the fourth Prebend sermon has some general value for an understanding of his interpretive methods.

Donne educes from the phrases "the confidence of all the ends of the earth, and of them that are a far off, upon the sea" the awareness of all men in their natural state that they are the handiwork and reflection of a divine Creator. It should be noted that this is not merely the work of an ingenius intelligence; the gloss on this text in the Geneva Bible, with which Donne was certainly familiar, gives warrant for such a construction. Thus the first level of meaning is distinguished on the habitual Augustinian assumption of a metaphorical extension of reference. Donne's other constant interests in the broader significance of his texts and in the spiritual overtones of Biblical language become the complementary means of discovering the second level of meaning. Although this verse lacks explicit mention of the Jewish Law its consideration is invited because, according to Donne, a sense of the Law "inanimates the whole Psalme, and is transfused thorow every part thereof; and so, it falls upon this verse too." But the meaning of the verse does not end here. For the phrase "O God of our salvation" uses a Hebrew word—*Iashang* in Donne's transliteration—which derives from the same primary root as "Saviour," one of the most familiar names of Christ. Etymology, then, is given typological force to produce the textual basis for the examination of the nature and solemnity of "Gods proceeding with us in the Christian Church," which occupies by far the greatest portion of the fourth Prebend sermon.

The last words of the text constitute the first topic—the knowledge of God in Nature. This part of the sermon is profusely metaphorical and more diffuse than controlled. But Donne's espousal of Augustinian psychology and its theological implications is interestingly in evidence. He begins by sketching rapidly the building up of the physical uni-

91. See, e.g., the sermon on Job 36.25 preached at Hanworth on August 25, 1622, before the Earls of Carlisle, Northumberland, and Buckingham (*Sermons,* IV, no. 6), and the third sermon on John 1.8, preached at St. Paul's on October 13, 1622 (IV, no. 8).

verse by God (the "Inne" or "Lodge" of this world) for the habitation of man, but this part is not to develop into a variant on the standard cosmological argument for man's knowledge of God. God is not merely a "Builder," he is also a "Housekeeper" who sustains all men with natural knowledge of himself—a plain and common fare rather than the "most precious and costly dishes" like Christ's Body and Blood served in the Christian Church, whose manner of preparation no man knows. Donne contends, in direct opposition to the argument from natural philosophy which many English theologians would make before the end of the century, that our knowledge of God comes basically from our consciousness of possessing a reasonable and immortal soul capable of grace and glory, not from our perception of the design of the fabric of the universe. What is particularly interesting in the fourth Prebend sermon is that the Augustinian access to knowledge of God through self-knowledge proceeds through a Thomistic conception of the human soul, in which rationality and immortality as aspects of the divine image are the chief emphases. At all events this compound conception of the soul is then imaged as the movement of the sun in its Ptolemaic sphere, for in an analogous fashion the grace of God moves upon the natural human faculties and enlightens them to fundamental moral awareness—fear of God's judgment, hope of his blessing. An imaginative reprise of the geometrical imagery from the third Prebend sermon, here adapted to universal human reachings out to the divine, concludes the figuring forth of man in the state of Nature as conceived by Donne:

> Here is a new Mathematiques; without change of Elevation, or parallax, I that live in this Climate, and stand under this Meridian, looke up and fixe my self upon God, And they that are under my feete, looke up to that place, which is above them, And as divers, as contrary as our places are, we all fixe at once upon one God, and meet in one Center; but we doe not so upon one Sunne, nor upon one constellation, or configuration in the Heavens; when we see it, those Antipodes doe not; but they, and we see God at once.

A single paragraph comprises the second part, devoted to the knowledge of God afforded in the Jewish Law. This treatment is so cursory that it was overlooked, by Donne himself possibly, in assigning marginal headings to the parts of the sermon. The Jewish Law was a topic on which Donne at other times could expand considerably, tracing parallels between the ritual prescriptions of the Old Testament and the sacramental institutions of the New (the stuff and substance of the traditional allegorical sense as defined by Aquinas). But here Donne is content to pass to the Christian Church after a bare statement of the principle that "The law did not onely shew, what was sin, but gave some light of remedy against sin, and restitution after sin, by those sacrifices, which, though they were ineffectual in themselves, yet involved, and represented Christ, who was their salvation." It is not unreasonable to infer here a measure of uneasiness at the prospect of making a detailed discussion of the Jewish Law on such a flimsy textual basis. The second section is, and is only, a necessary connective in the total structure of the sermon.

The third part of the fourth Prebend sermon occupies five hundred lines (out of eight hundred in the whole sermon) with an extended treatment of the knowledge of God afforded in the Christian Church. Despite passages of conceptual brilliance and intensely imaginative metaphorical expression, this is by and large a kind of disciplinary session which emits a strong patristic savor, especially of St. Cyprian's numerous tracts on conduct at worship. The tone is set in Donne's elucidation—based on the best Latin translation of the Old Testament available in his day, that of Immanuel Tremellius and Franciscus Junius—of the difficult phrase "answer by terrible things in righteousnesse." He takes this as an imperative to "come alwayes to all Acts, and Exercises of Religion, with reverence, with feare, and trembling, and make a difference, between Religious, and Civill Actions." One of the most affective techniques in the sermon, and especially in the third part, is Donne's illustration of the meaning of the text by repeating it at the end of paragraphs as an insistent summons that cannot be disregarded. This strategic placement enforces the essential thrust of the exposition in the lengthy third part.

The first of a long sequence of Christian actions required by God is, in Donne's conception, constant watchfulness over "our manners, and conversation"—a further manifestation of the primary moral emphasis in his preaching. Mounting severity marks his subsequent detailing of acts of "holy amazement" and "reverential feare" by which the divine presence should be acknowledged in divine service.[92] Consider, Donne says, how often fundamental doctrines suffer distortion; how repeatedly the sanctity of the edifice is profaned by business and gossip—as St. Paul's Cathedral certainly was in his time.[93] In like manner he warns his congregation against abuses of prayer, disrespect for sermons, and unworthy reception of the sacraments. The third part concludes with an awesome evocation of the moment of death, a frequent scene in Donne's preaching,[94] and a demonstration of what he means by conformity with Christ. In this connection Donne draws upon the universal embrace of the Church to serve, as the opened sense of his texts served in the second and third Prebend sermons, as a bridge from this life to the life to come. Yet the parting consideration is not joy and glory, but the awe and fear of God which continues in heaven as on earth: "As the Militant Church is the porch of the Triumphant, so our reverence here, may have some proportion to that reverence which is exhibited there."

The Fifth Prebend Sermon

The fifth Prebend sermon, like the others in the series, was delivered at St. Paul's, but it alone bears no date in its heading, which was presumably attached to the manuscript copy by Donne himself and

92. Severity on this subject is a distinct feature of conservative Anglican preaching during Laud's ascendancy, but it is also found earlier. See Andrewes' castigation of irreverence (*Ninety-six Sermons,* I, 399–407) and John Cosin's vindication of ritual and ceremony in his sermon at the Bishop of Carlisle's consecration on December 3, 1626 (*Works* [Oxford, 1843], I, 101–103). See also the note to ll. 644–674 of the fourth Prebend sermon.

93. An instance of Donne's disciplinary fervor is provided in the Repertory Books of the London Court of Aldermen and was brought to light by Baird W. Whitlock, "The Dean and the Yeoman," *Notes & Queries,* n.s. I (1954), 374–375. The entry, dated March 12, 1630, concerns a Christopher Ruddy who refused to kneel properly during worship at St. Paul's although "thrice admonished by the virgers from the Dean then present." Ruddy had to endure a period of imprisonment in Newgate as a consequence. See also Bald, *John Donne: A Life,* pp. 402–405.

94. See Joan Webber's discussion of Donne's deathbed scenes in *Contrary Music,* pp. 111–114.

printed in its first-person form in *LXXX Sermons*.[95] The strongest
evidence points to a date in May or June of 1627.[96] The text of the
sermon is Psalm 66.3, "Say unto God, how terrible art thou in thy
works! Through the greatnesse of thy power shall thine enemies submit themselves unto thee." In the contentious survey of Roman textual
tradition and interpretation relating to this Psalm with which Donne
begins the sermon, he registers his awareness that the sixty-sixth Psalm
was regularly interpreted (on the basis of its Septuagint title) as a
prophecy of God's most potent demonstration of sovereignty—the
Resurrection. St. Augustine, for example, had made this interpretation
the basis of a jubilant exposition of this Psalm.[97] But the mood of the
fifth Prebend sermon is anxious and circumspect, not expansive in the
way needed to enforce a Christological interpretation. Still Donne is
able to infer from the divergent tenses of his text a prompting to typology, as he did from the grammatically similar text of the second Prebend sermon. Thus the two parts of the sermon emerge as Retrospect
and Prospect or (in St. Augustine's terminology, which also is used
here) History and Prophecy: what God has done argues what he will
do. But after this broad and characteristic division, the exposition splin-
ters into many different subdivisions, which constitute an almost
dogged attempt to make the text give up its meaning.

The meaning it exhibits through most of the sermon is a contemporary relevance, and the contracted range and chastened tone of the
fifth Prebend sermon are produced by Donne's undertaking to fit
God's Word to God's world, specifically, to the turbulent and troubled
England of the day. In refusing to countenance patristic precedent and
make a Christological interpretation of his text, Donne, however, was
not breaking new ground. He was merely opting for a younger over
an older tradition. The younger tradition is illustrated by a sermon on
the text of the fifth Prebend sermon by a German Reformed theolo-

---

95. The fullest account of the complications involved in the printing of the
sermons is Robert Krueger's "The Publication of John Donne's Sermons," *Review of English Studies,* XV (1964), 151–160.

96. The evidence is reviewed in Appendix A, "The Date of the Fifth Prebend
Sermon."

97. *Enarrationes in Psalmos,* LXV (PL, XXXVI, 785–801).

gian, Victorinus Strigel, which construes the verse as an assurance to the true people of God that "the power of the Turkish tyrantes" and "the furies of the Pope and his Champions" shall presently be made of no avail.[98] Such contemporary application was an almost inevitable outgrowth of the insistence on literality, narrowly understood, made in the exegesis introduced at the time of the Reformation. Even "use" or "application" assumed a factual and historical nature, although the connection of the Davidic age and the present is hard to explain except as a vestige of typology. At any rate, the declared concern with history found in the newer mode of Biblical interpretation is also found in the fifth Prebend sermon. Narrowness and unrelieved topicality are prevented, however, by Donne's constant purpose of ministering to the soul.

There is a high degree of audience sensitivity throughout this discourse, despite its air of great preoccupation with current political events. After explaining his many subdivisions of the text Donne ruefully acknowledges that he has given, rather, a "Paraphrase," so that the time remaining will allow only for "Repetition," not "Dilatation." But all that is necessary, he says, is to fix the text in his auditory's memory. He does this in a refrainlike repetition of the text at the end of paragraphs, as in the preceding sermon. Once again the technique enhances what he sees as the meaning of the verse: a constantly applicable principle for life in dark and uncertain times. Other aspects of the fifth Prebend sermon serve, more particularly, as inducements to hearers and readers of the whole series to remember preceding Prebend sermons. The attack on the Roman Church for not really settling the conscience recalls passages in the first and third; the sublime consideration of the divine Ideas in the second Prebend sermon passes in brief review; the warnings against excessive curiosity about God's eternal decrees and his intention of damning men without reference to their personal moral state (attested by Puritans, but always repudiated by Donne) make another appearance here; and the catalogue of the names of God in the first Prebend sermon recurs for a short interval

---

98. Victorinus Strigel, *A fourth Proceeding in the Harmony of King Davids Harp. That is to say; A Godly and learned Exposition of six Psalmes . . . beginning with the 62. and ending with the 67. Psalme,* tr. Richard Robinson (London, 1596), p. 36.

in the fifth. Above all, the provisional consolation administered at the end of this discourse recalls what Donne made of "the shadow of thy wings" in the second Prebend sermon. In several major respects this sermon is a prosaic counterpart to that one, and substitutes for its visionary flight solidly terrestrial pastoral counsel. At least, this is the effect of Donne's typology in the present case.

In the first part of the sermon David's authorship of the Psalm induces an extended consideration of the kingdom of Israel. Like Andrewes in a number of court sermons and Hooker in the eighth book of the *Laws of Ecclesiastical Polity,* Donne discovers in the English monarchy, where the King is Head both of State and Church, the closest existing analogue to the form of government represented in the Old Testament. The sermon proceeds to an affirmation of the Stuart theory of divine right and from thence to an insistence on the duty of the King to advance religion abroad as well as maintain it at home.[99] The latter is an evident allusion to Charles I's involved and inconclusive military projects against France and Spain, especially, it would seem, Buckingham's planned expedition against the Isle of Rhé, for which funding was extracted grudgingly from most Londoners. An admonition to all, but particularly those in authority like the "men of high degree" of the first Prebend sermon, binds up the exposition of the "History" of the text. The preservation of Church and State requires universal assistance. After casting aspersions on the secret machinations of English Papists and the divisive practices of English Puritans, Donne applies the first half of his text to his hearers: speaking of God's works means that they are to draw explicit connections between the Bible and the events of the age. But, wisely, he does not descend to examples—a practice which produced many servile sermons

99. Cf. Hooker, *Laws of Ecclesiastical Polity,* VIII.viii.5, where the conditions under which the King is brought to exercise ecclesiastical authority are detailed, and the declaration of principle in VIII.ii.3: "When therefore Christian kings are said to have spiritual dominion or supreme power in ecclesiastical affairs and causes, the meaning is, that within their own precincts and territories they have authority and power to command even in matters of Christian religion, and that there is no higher nor greater that can in those causes over-command them, where they are placed to reign as kings." See also Andrewes, *Ninety-six Sermons,* V, 245: "This also, that God may be our Lord, that is, that our religion may be safe, doth certainly very much depend on the Prince."

on the Laudian side and many splenetic sermons on the other side among preachers of his and succeeding times.

A topical implication remains discernible, however, as Donne proceeds to the prospective sense of his text. In an updating of the Scholastic definition, he characterizes as God's enemies those who are "in their nature irreconcilable" with the divine purpose, exclusive of "all personall, and all nationall hatred" between men of faith who understand this purpose differently. Such temperate counsel—for the seventeenth century—is consistent with Donne's own views, but he purports to educe it here from a significant stylistic peculiarity of the New Testament, where "*Hostis* . . . is not read," but "*Inimicus,* that is, *non amicus,* unfriendly, is read there often, very very often." On the strength of Biblical precedents Donne proceeds to exhort his hearers to recognize, on their own behalf, "a holy league, Defensive, and Offensive; God shall not onely protect us from others, but he shall fight for us against them; our enemies are his enemies." Carried along, perhaps, by his verbal absorption in the names of God (Donne accepts the belief of Origen and many of the Latin Fathers that the nature of a being is radically revealed in its name), he begins to envision how "just Lawes" and "Armies" will enforce conformity in England. But suddenly he draws himself up short: "I direct not your thoughts upon publique Considerations; It is not my end; It is not my way."

Upon abandoning his long tenacious hopes of becoming a courtier and statesman, Donne had found his way and end in the ministry of the Word. His enterprise, as he simply and eloquently tells his congregation here, was "to bring you home to yourselves," there to make them aware of inner enemies (of God and themselves)—temptations and personal weaknesses. Hence at the close of the fifth Prebend sermon his habitual concern reasserts itself; a metaphorical construing of his text produces a moral emphasis. Yet Donne returns almost compulsively to topical matters in his final words, as if the anxiety of the times made him speak in spite of himself to offer some sort of immediate consolation. It is at best a conditional kind, again a temporary refreshing, a moment to catch one's breath, and no "resurrection":

So hast thou reason too to call it Peace in the Church, and peace in the State, when Gods enemies, though they be not rooted out, though they be not disposed to a hearty Allegeance, and just Obedience, yet they must be subject, they must submit themselves whether they wil or no, and though they wil wish no good, yet they shall be able to doe no harme. For, the Holy Ghost declares this to be an exercise of power, of Gods power, of the greatnesse of Gods power, that his enemies submit themselves, though with a fained obedience.

Thus, with a regrounding in the very actualities of experience, the Prebend sermons complete the cycle of double perspective which Donne equated with the insight of the inspired writers of Scripture and sought in his own *Devotions,* that is, the seeing of the spiritual in the temporal. He, a poet always, always preserved the tenuous but essential balance of emphasis in the use of analogy and metaphor. Although he desired to read God's hand in the world as clearly as he read it in the Bible, he had no mystical bent leading him to lose sight of the world. So far, in fact, was his spiritual view of life from renunciation of the world that his insistence on practical morality—on certain kinds of religious actions and attitudes—increased throughout his ministry.

However, possibly because he held so firmly to an Augustinian conception of man's nature, Donne never mistook any earthly kingdom for the heavenly one, nor human policies for the divine will. Even as he preached his Prebend sermons, evidence of this tragic mistake to which the age was prone accumulated in the ravages of the Thirty Years' War on the Continent. In another fifteen years the same mistake was to precipitate civil war in England, where Laud, Manwaring, and other Anglican divines backed the imposition of uniformity and the absolutism of Charles I. Although Donne aligned himself on most issues with the Laudian party (as is evident in his conception of reverence at worship in the fourth Prebend sermon and of the King's authority in the fifth) and was as personally ambitious as any man of the time, he declined as priest and preacher to claim authority in political questions or to obtrude upon them theological sanctions. The learned author of *Pseudo-Martyr* might well have courted Charles' favors by giving himself pretensions. All the while fellow divines were deciding to do just this. Laud lectured Parliament on its responsibilities and the limits of its powers with imperturbable assurance in his sermons at the opening sessions of 1626 and 1628. Moreover, in 1627, the year of the fourth and fifth Prebend sermons, Sibthorpe's and Manwaring's infamous sermons were published. The latter asserted that the penalty of disobeying the King in whatever matter was eternal damnation.

Yet the fifth Prebend sermon does not take the easy alternative of skirting civil matters altogether. It appeals to Old Testament precedent regarding the governance of Church and State by kingly supremacy. It asks for King Charles, in a time of general ill-will and suspicion, the trust and good will of his subjects. And it joins with the four other Prebend sermons in an affirmation of divine providence in human affairs. But the fifth Prebend sermon refrains from the presumption of passing God's own judgment on the events at hand, reverting instead to the certainties of the history in Scripture to gather courage, comfort, and, above all, resignation in present circumstances.

With the advantage of hindsight it is possible to mark in the telling appraisal of the troubles of this life and the attendant resignation at the close of the fifth Prebend sermon something of an elegiac cast as Donne moved into the last years of his ministry. There still follow many masterful discourses, including his most celebrated, *Death's Duel,* another exposition of a text from the Psalms. Actually, however, he had reached the peak of his productivity by the time he completed his great series of Prebend sermons.[100] Yet while the series exhibits the extraordinary energy of Donne's middle years at St. Paul's, the greatness of the Prebend sermons is not ultimately reducible to biographical facts. For the integrality of image and idea and the plenitude of meaning derived from the language of a text reflect what in him was an ever-quickening response to the ageless inspiration of the Word. Its qualities produce the literary intensity of Donne's preaching and, even more, he would have it understood, whatever significance his sermons possess as literature.

The Text of the Prebend Sermons

The Prebend Sermons were first printed in *LXXX Sermons Preached by That Learned and Reverend Divine, Iohn Donne, Dr in Divinitie.*

---

100. Bald rightly warns against inferences about Donne's physical and mental state because there is so little evidence from 1628 onwards (*John Donne: A Life,* p. 508). However, Bald bears out the sense of a final phase in grouping the years 1628–1631 in his chapter entitled "Last Days."

. . . (London, 1640), the earliest of three posthumous folio collections of the sermons which Donne's son John saw through the press. A scanning of *LXXX Sermons* and of the few textual corrections recorded by Potter and Mrs. Simpson for the sermons reprinted from this edition suffices to confirm the judgment that this is "a magnificent volume, beautifully printed."[101] But *LXXX Sermons* carries a weight of conviction reaching beyond accuracy and attractiveness. The phrasing of the headings for the Prebend sermons and a number of others seems to come from Donne's own hand, leading to the plausible inference that this volume was printed from the copy which he spoke of writing out during his last, long illness.[102] Presumably the marginal references were also worked up by Donne at this time. If so, the Biblical ones are of particular interest because they exhibit an apparently conscious policy of avoiding the excessive scruples of Puritan contemporaries who, according to Donne,

> call everything a falsification, if the place be not rightly cyphard, or the word exactly cited; and magnifie one another for great Text men, though they understand no Text, because they cite Book, and Chapter, and Verse, and Words aright.[103]

The text of the Prebend sermons in this edition has been reproduced by photo offset from the Potter-Simpson edition, which basically gives the text of *LXXX Sermons*. The infrequent emendations of readings in the body of the sermons and the marginal Biblical references which Potter and Mrs. Simpson made are all specifically acknowledged in my notes. But my notes also register my excising of Potter's and Mrs. Simpson's added marginal references to texts of Scripture, which they enclosed in brackets. I excise their additions and restore the reading of *LXXX Sermons* on two separate grounds: (1) there is good cause

---

101. Potter and Simpson, General Introductions, *Sermons,* I, 1.

102. See the manifestly autobiographical heading in *Sermons,* II, 269: "At the Haghe Decemb. 19. 1619. I Preached upon this Text. Since in my sicknesse at Abrey-hatche in Essex, 1630, revising my short notes of that Sermon, I digested them into these two." Donne also wrote out some sermons for his son John during an enforced retreat from plague-stricken London in 1625 (Introduction, *Sermons,* VI, 34).

103. *Sermons,* IX.8.616–619.

to believe that *LXXX Sermons* perpetuates Donne's own deliberate textual policy and should not be tampered with at will; (2) the Potter-Simpson additions, as they stand, are misleading in their inadequacy as indications of the degree of Scripturalism in Donne's discourse. (While I have increased considerably the number of identified Biblical references in the Prebend sermons, as my Appendix B will show, I am also far from claiming that my tabulations are exhaustive.) Finally, my notes record and adjust the very few accidental departures of the Potter-Simpson text of the Prebend sermons from that of *LXXX Sermons*.

On the whole, of course, my efforts reaffirm the reliability of Potter's and Mrs. Simpson's work. The measure of the textual contribution which I have endeavored to make will be taken in the notes to Prebend I.323; III.225–226 mg.; IV.267 mg., 330–336 and mg.; V.516–529, 686, and in my discussion of the probable date of the fifth Prebend sermon in Appendix A.

Prebend Sermons

Preached at St. Paul's

The first of the Prebend of *Cheswicks* five Psalmes; which five are appointed for that Prebend; as there are five other, for every other of our thirty Prebendaries.
Preached at S. Pauls, May 8, 1625.

Psal. 62.9. *Surely men of low degree are vanity, and men of high degree are a lie; To bee laid in the balance, they are altogether lighter then vanity.*

W E consider the dignity of the Book of Psalmes, either in the whole body together, or in the particular limmes and distribution thereof. Of the whole Body, it may be enough

Basil.

to tell you that which S. *Basil* saith, That if all the other bookes of Scripture could perish, there remained enough in the booke of Psalmes for the supply of all: And therefore he cals it *Amuletum ad profligandum dæmonem;* Any Psalme is Exorcisme enough to expell any Devill, Charme enough to remove any tentation, Enchantment enough to ease, nay to sweeten any tribulation. It is abundantly enough that [10] our Saviour Christ himselfe cites the Psalmes, not onely as Canonicall Scripture, but as a particular, and entire, and noble limme of that

Luk. 24.44

Body; *All must be fulfilled of me,* (saith he) *which is written in the Law, in the Prophets, and in the Psalmes.* The Law alone was the Sadduces Scripture, they received no more: The Law and the Prophets were (especially) the Scribes Scripture, they interpreted that: The Christians Scripture, in the Old Testament, is especially the Psalmes. For (except the Prophecy of *Esay* be admitted into the comparison) no booke of the Old Testament is so like a Gospel, so particular in all things concerning Christ, as the Psalmes.

72

²⁰ So hath the Booke of Psalmes an especiall dignity in the intire Body, all together. It hath so also in divers distributions thereof into parts. For even amongst the Jewes themselves, those fifteen Psalmes which follow immediatly and successively after the 119. Psalme, were especially distinguished, and dignified by the name of *Graduall Psalmes;* Whether because they were sung upon the Degrees and staires ascending to the Altar, Or because hee that read them in the Temple, ascended into a higher and more eminent place to reade them, Or because the word *Graduall* implies a degree of excellency in the Psalmes themselves, I dispute not; But a difference those fifteen
³⁰ Psalmes ever had above the rest, in the Jewish and in the Christian Church too. So also hath there beene a particular dignity ascribed to those seven Psalmes, which we have ever called the *Penitentiall Psalmes;* Of which S. *Augustine* had so much respect, as that he commanded them to be written in a great Letter, and hung about the curtaines of his Death-bed within, that hee might give up the ghost in contemplation, and meditation of those seven Psalmes. And it hath beene traditionally received, and recommended by good Authors, that that *Hymne,* which Christ and his Apostles are said to have sung after the Institution and celebration of the Sacrament, was a *Hymne* com-
⁴⁰ posed of those six Psalmes, which we call the *Allelujah Psalmes,* immediatly preceding the hundred and nineteenth.

So then, in the whole Body, and in some particular limmes of the Body, the Church of God hath had an especiall consideration of the booke of Psalmes. This Church in which we all stand now, and in which my selfe, by particular obligation serve, hath done so too. In this Church, by ancient Constitutions, it is ordained, That the whole booke of Psalmes should every day, day by day bee rehearsed by us, who make the Body of this Church, in the eares of Almighty God. And therefore every Prebendary of this Church, is by those Constitu-
⁵⁰ tions bound every day to praise God in those five Psalmes which are appointed for his Prebend. And of those five Psalmes which belong to mee, this, out of which I have read you this Text, is the first. And, by Gods grace, (upon like occasions) I shall here handle some part of every one of the other foure Psalmes, for some testimony, that those my five Psalmes returne often into my meditation, which I also assure

August.

Matt. 26.30

Psalmus integer

my selfe of the rest of my brethren, who are under the same obligation in this Church.

For this whole Psalme, which is under our present consideration, as *Athanasius* amongst all the Fathers, was most curious, and most ⁶⁰ particular, and exquisite, in observing the purpose, and use of every particular Psalm, (for to that purpose, he goes through them all, in this maner; If thou wilt encourage men to a love, and pursuit of goodnesse, say the first Psalme, and 31. and 140, &c. If thou wilt convince the Jewes, say the second Psalme; If thou wilt praise God for things past, say this, and this, And this, and this if thou wilt pray for future things) so for this Psalme, which we have in hand, he observes in it a summary abridgement of all; For of this Psalme he sayes in generall, *Adversus insidiantes,* Against all attempts upon thy body, thy state, thy soule, thy fame, tentations, tribulations, machinations, defama-⁷⁰ tions, say this Psalme. As he saith before, that in the booke of Psalmes, every man may discerne *motus animi sui,* his owne sinfull inclinations expressed, and arme himselfe against himselfe; so in this Psalme, he may arme himselfe against all other adversaries of any kinde. And therefore as the same Father entitles one Sermon of his, *Contra omnes hæreses,* A Sermon for the convincing of all Heresies, in which short Sermon he meddles not much with particular heresies, but onely establishes the truth of Christs Person in both natures, which is indeed enough against all Heresies, and in which (that is the consubstantiality of Christ with the Father, God of God) this Father *Athanasius,* hath ⁸⁰ enlarged himselfe more then the rest (insomuch, that those heretiques which grow so fast, in these our dayes, The Socinians, (who deny the Godhead of Christ) are more vexed with that Father, then with any other, and call him for *Athanasius, Sathanasius*) As he cals that Sermon, a sermon against all Heresies, so he presents this Psalme against all Tentations, and Tribulations; Not that therein *David* puts himselfe to waigh particular tentations, and tribulations, but that he puts every man, in every triall, to put himselfe wholly upon God, and to know, that if man cannot helpe him in this world, nothing can; And, for man, *Surely men of low degree are vanity, and men of high degree* ⁹⁰ *are a lie; To be laid in the balance, they are altogether lighter then vanity.*

Divisio

We consider in the words, The maner, and the matter, How it is

spoken, And what is said. For the first, the maner, this is not absolutely spoken, but comparatively, not peremptorily, but respectively,
not simply, but with relation. The Holy Ghost, in *Davids* mouth, doth
not say, That man can give no assistance to man; That man may looke
for no helpe from man; But, that God is alwayes so present, and so
all-sufficient, that wee need not doubt of him, nor rely upon any other,
otherwise then as an instrument of his. For that which he had spread
100 over all the verses of the Psalme before, he summes up in the verse immediatly before the Text, *Trust in God at all times, for hee is a*
refuge for us; and then, hee strengthens that with this, What would
yee prefer before God, or joyne with God? man? what man? *Surely*
men of low degree are vanity, and men of high degree are a lie; To
be laid in the balance, they are altogether lighter then vanity.

Which words being our second part, open to us these steps: First,
that other Doctrins, morall or civill Instructions may be delivered to
us possibly, and probably, and likely, and credibly, and under the like
termes, and modifications, but this in our Text, is Assuredly, un-
110 doubtedly, undeniably, irrefragably, *Surely men of low degree, &c.* For
howsoever when they two are compared together, with one another, it
may admit discourse and disputation, whether men of high degree, or
of low degree doe most violate the lawes of God; that is, whether
prosperity or adversity make men most obnoxious to sin, yet, when
they come to bee compared, not with one another, but both with God,
this asseveration, this *surely* reaches to both; *Surely, The man of low*
degree is vanity, and, as *Surely, The man of high degree is a lie.* And
though this may seeme to leave some roome, for men of middle ranks,
and fortunes, and places, That there is a mediocrity, that might give an
120 assurance, and an establishment, yet there is no such thing in this case,
for (as *surely* still) *to be laid in the balance, they are all,* (not all of
low, and all of high degree, all rich, and all poore, but) All, of all conditions, *altogether lighter then vanity.*

Now, all this doth not destroy, not extinguish, not annihilate that
affection in man, of hope, and trust, and confidence in any thing; but
it rectifies that hope, and trust, and confidence, and directs it upon the
right object: Trust not in flesh, but in spirituall things, That wee
neither bend our hopes downeward, to infernall spirits, to seeke help
in Witches; nor mis-carry it upward, to seeke it in Saints, or Angels,

¹³⁰ but fix it in him, who is nearer us then our owne soules, our blessed, and gracious, and powerfull God, who in this one Psalme is presented unto us, by so many names of assurance and confidence, *My expectation, my salvation, my rocke, my defence, my glory, my strength, my refuge,* and the rest.

I Part
*Quid homo
erga Deum*

First then these words, *Surely men of low degree, and men of high degree are vanity,* are not absolutely, simply, unconditionally spoken; Man is not nothing: Nay, it is so farre from that, as that there is nothing but man. As, though there may bee many other creatures

Gen. 3.20 living, which were not derived from *Eve,* and yet *Eve* is called *Mater* ¹⁴⁰ *viventium,* The Mother of all that live, because the life of none but man, is considered; so there bee so many other Creatures, and Christ

Marke 16.15 sends his Apostles to preach, *Omni Creaturæ,* to every creature, yet he meanes none but Man. All that God did in making all other creatures, in all the other dayes, was but a laying in of Materials; The setting up of the work was in the making of Man. God had a picture of himselfe

Colos. 1.15 from all eternity; from all eternity, the Sonne of God was the *Image of the invisible God;* But then God would have one picture, which should bee the picture of Father, Sonne, and Holy Ghost too, and so made man to the Image of the whole Trinity. As the Apostle argues,

Heb. 1.5 ¹⁵⁰ *Cui dixit, To whom did God ever say, This day have I begotten thee,* but to Christ? so we say, for the dignity of man, *Cui dixit,* of what creature did God ever say, *Faciamus,* Let us, us make it, All, all, the Persons together, and to imploy, and exercise, not onely Power, but Counsaile in the making of that Creature? Nay, when man was at worst, he was at a high price; man being fallen, yet then, in that undervalue, he cost God his own and onely Son, before he could have him. Neither became the Son of God capable of redeeming man, by any lesse, or any other way, then by becomming man. The Redeemer must be better then he whom he is to redeeme; and yet, he must abase ¹⁶⁰ himselfe to as low a nature as his; to his nature; else he could not redeeme him. God was aliened from man, and yet God must become man, to recover man.

Gen. 1.28 God joyned man in Commission with himselfe, upon his Creation, in the *Replete* and *Dominamini,* when he gave Man power to possesse the Earth, and subdue the Creature; And God hath made man so equall to himselfe, as not onely to have a soule endlesse and immortall,

as God himselfe, (though not endlesse and immortall as himselfe, yet endlesse and immortall as himselfe too, though not immortall the same way, (for Gods immortality is of himselfe) yet as certainly, and
170 as infallibly Immortall as he) but God hath not onely given man such an immortall soule, but a body that shall put on Incorruption and Immortality too, which he hath given to none of the Angels. In so much, that howsoever it be, whether an Angel may wish it selfe an Archangel, or an Archangel wish it selfe a Cherubin; yet man cannot deliberately wish himselfe an Angel, because he should lose by that wish, and lacke that glory, which he shall have in his body. *We shall*   Marke 12.25
be like the Angels, sayes Christ; In that wherein we can be like them, we shall be like them, in the exalting and refining of the faculties of our soules; But they shall never attaine to be like us in our glorified
180 bodies. Neither hath God onely reserved this treasure and dignity of man to the next world, but even here he hath made him *filium Dei,*   Luke 6.35
The Sonne of God, and *Semen Dei,* The seed of God, and *Consortem*   I Joh. 3.9
divinæ naturæ, Partaker of the divine Nature, and *Deos ipsos,* Gods   2 Pet. 1.4
themselves, for *Ille dixit Dii estis,* he hath said we are Gods. So that, as though the glory of heaven were too much for God alone, God hath called up man thither, in the ascension of his Sonne, to partake thereof; and as though one God were not enough for the administration of this world, God hath multiplied gods here upon Earth, and imparted, communicated, not onely his power to every Magistrate, but the
190 Divine nature to every sanctified man. *David* asks that question with a holy wonder, *Quid est homo? What is man that God is so mindfull of him?* But I may have his leave, and the holy Ghosts, to say, since God is so mindfull of him, since God hath set his minde upon him, What is not man? Man is all.

Since we consider men in the place that they hold, and value them according to those places, and aske not how they got thither, when we see Man made The Love of the Father, The Price of the Sonne, The Temple of the Holy Ghost, the Signet upon Gods hand, The Apple of Gods eye, Absolutely, unconditionally we cannot annihilate man, not
200 evacuate, not evaporate, not extenuate man to the levity, to the vanity, to the nullity of this Text (*Surely men altogether, high and low, are lighter then vanity.*) For, man is not onely a contributary Creature, but a totall Creature; He does not onely make one, but he is all; He is

Quid homo erga hominem

not a piece of the world, but the world it selfe; and next to the glory of God, the reason why there is a world.

But we must not determine this consideration here, That man is something, a great thing, a noble Creature, if we refer him to his end, to his interest in God, to his revetsion in heaven; But when we consider man in his way, man amongst men, man is not nothing, not un-
210 able to assist man, not unfit to be relyed upon by man; for, even in that respect also, God hath made *Hominem homini Deum,* He hath made one man able to doe the offices of God to another, in procuring his regeneration here, and advancing his salvation hereafter; As he says,

Obad. 21   *Saviours shall come up on Mount Sion;* which is the Church. Neither hath God determined that power of assisting others, in the Character of Priesthood onely, (that the Priest should be a god, that is, doe the offices and the work of God to the people, by delivering salvation unto them) but he hath also made the Prince, and the secular Magistrate, a god, that is able to doe the offices, and the works of God, not onely to
220 the people, but to the Priest himselfe, to sustaine him, yea, and to countenance, and favour, and protect him too, in the execution and exercise of his priestly office; As we see in the first plantation of those two great Cedars, The Secular, and the Ecclesiasticall Power, (which, that they might alwayes agree like brethren, God planted at first in those two brethren, *Moses* and *Aaron*) There, though *Moses* were the temporall, and *Aaron* the spirituall Magistrate, yet God sayes to *Moses,*

Exod. 7.1   *I have made thee a God to Pharaoh,* (but not onely to *Pharaoh*) but *Aaron thy brother shall be thy Prophet;* for, (as he had said before)

Exod. 4.16 *Thou shalt be to him in stead of a God.* So usefull, so necessary is man
230 to man, as that the Priest, who is of God, incorporated in God, subsists

Isidor   also by man; for, *Principes hujus seculi rationem reddituri sunt,* The Princes of this world must give God an account, *Propter Ecclesiam, quam à Christo tuendam susceperunt,* for that Church, which Christ hath committed to their protection. In spirituall difficulties, and for spirituall duties, God sends us to the Priest; but to such a *Priest* as is a

Heb. 4.15   man; and (as our comfort is expressed) *A Priest which was touched with the feeling of our infirmities, and was in all points tempted like as we are:* for the businesses of this world, Rights, and Titles, and

Deut. 16.18 Proprieties, and Possessions, God sends us still to the Judge; (*Iudges*
240 *and officers shalt thou make in all thy gates*) Judges to try between

man and man; And the sword in battaile tryes between State and State, Prince and Prince; And therefore God commands and directs the levying of men to that purpose, in many places of the history of his people; particularly God appoints *Gideon* to take a certaine proportion of the army, a certaine number of Souldiers. And in another place, there goes out a presse for Souldiers from *Moses* mouth; He presses them upon their holy allegeance to God, when he sayes, *Who is on the Lords side, let him come unto me.* So, in infirmities, in sicknesses of the body, we aske with the Prophet, *Is there no balme in* ²⁵⁰ *Gilead? Is there no Physitian there?* God does not reprove *Asa* for seeking of helpe of the Physitians; but the increpation lyes onely upon this, *That he sought to the Physitian, and not to the Lord.* God sends man to the Priest, to the Prince, to the Judge, to the Physitian, to the Souldier, and so, (in other places) to the Merchant, and to cunning Artificers, (as in the building of the Temple) that all that man needs might be communicated to man by man.

    So that still, simply, absolutely, unconditionally, we cannot say, Surely men, men altogether, high or low, or meane, all are lesse then vanity. And surely they that pervert and detort such words as these, ²⁶⁰ to such a use, and argue from thence, Man is nothing, no more then a worme or a fly, and therefore what needs this solemne consideration of mans actions, it is all one what he does, for all his actions, and himselfe too are nothing; They doe this but to justifie or excuse their own lazinesse in this world, in passing on their time, without taking any Calling, embracing any profession, contributing any thing to the spirituall edification, or temporall sustentation of other men. But take the words, as the Holy Ghost intends them, comparatively, what man compared with God, or what man considered without God, can doe any thing for others, or for himselfe? When the Apostle sayes, *That* ²⁷⁰ *all the world is but dung,* when the Prophet sayes, *That all the Nations of the world are lesse then nothing,* when the Apostle sayes even of himselfe, *that he is nothing,* all this is nothing in comparison of that expression in the same Apostle, *That even the preaching of the Gospel is foolishnesse,* That that which is the *savour of life unto life,* Gods owne Ordinance, *Preaching,* is but *foolishnesse;* Let it be a *Paul* that plants, and an *Apollo* that waters, if God give not increase, all is but frivolousnesse, but foolishnesse; And therefore boldly, confidently,

Judg. 7.

Exod. 32.26

Jer. 8.22
2 Chro. 16.12

Phil. 3.8
Esay 40.17

2 Cor. 12.11
I Cor. 1.21

uncontroulably we may proceed to the propositions of our Text, which constitute our second part, Man, any man, every man, all men, col-
²⁸⁰ lectively, distributively, considered so, (comparatively with God, or privatively without God) is but a *lie,* but *vanity, lesse then vanity.*

2 Part

Surely

To make our best use of the words, (as our translation exhibits them) we make our entrance, with this word of confidence, and infallibility, which onely becomes the holy Ghost, in his asseverations, and in which he establishes the propositions following; Surely, surely men of low degree, and as surely, men of high, and, surely still all men together, are lighter then vanity. Men deliver their assertions otherwise modified, and under other qualifications. They obtrude to us miraculous doctrines of Transubstantiation, and the like, upon a possibility
²⁹⁰ onely; It may be done, say they, It is possible, God can doe it. But that is far from the assurednesse of the Holy Ghost, Surely it is so; for

Chrysost.

Asylum hæreticorum, est omnipotentia Dei, is excellently said, and by more then one of the Fathers, The omnipotence of God is the Sanctuary of Heretiques, Thither they fly, to countenance any such error; This God can doe, why should you not beleeve it? Men proceed in their asseverations farther then so, from this possibility to a probability; It will abide argument, it hath been disputed in the Schoole, and therefore is probable; why should not you beleeve it? And so they offer us the doctrine of the immaculate conception of the blessed
³⁰⁰ Virgin without Originall sinne; But this probability reaches not to this assurednesse of our text, *surely.* They will goe farther then this probability, to a verisimilitude, it is more then meerly possible, more then fairly probable, it is likely to be so; some of the ancient Fathers have thought so; and then, why should not you beleeve it? and so they offer us prayer for the dead. Farther then this verisimilitude they goe too; They goe to a *Piè creditur,* It may be piously beleeved, and it is fit to beleeve it, because it may assist and exalt devotion to thinke so; And then why should you not beleeve it? And so they offer us the worship of Images and Reliques. But still, all this comes short of our assured-
³¹⁰ nesse, *Surely,* undoubtedly, undisputably it is so.

And when the Romane Church would needs counterfeit the language of the Holy Ghost, and pronounce this surenesse upon so many new Articles in the Councell of Trent, it hath not prospered well with them; for we all know, they have repented that forwardnesse since,

and wished they had not determined so many particulars to be matter
of faith; because after such a determination by a Councell, they have
bound themselves not to recede from those doctrines, how unmaintenable
soever they be in themselves, or how inconvenient soever they fall
out to be to them. And therefore we see, that in all the solicitations that
320 can be used, even by Princes, to whom they are most affected, they will
not come now to pronounce so surely, to determine so positively upon
divers points that rest yet in perplexity amongst them. Which hath
raysed so many commotions in the kingdom of Spaine, and put
more then one of their later Kings, to send divers Ambassages to
Rome, to solicite a cleare declaration in that point, but could never, nor
can yet attaine it, that is, The immaculate conception of the blessed
Virgin without Originall sinne. So also, for the obligation that the
lawes of secular Magistrats lay upon the Conscience, so also for the
Concurrence of Grace, and Free-will, and divers others; in which they
330 will not be drawne to this, Surely, to determine and declare of either
side; for, indeed that is the language of the Holy Ghost.

It hath been observed amongst Philosophers, that *Plato* speaks probably,
and *Aristotle* positively; *Platoes* way is, It may be thus, and
Aristotles, It must be thus. The like hath been noted amongst Divines,
between *Calvin,* and *Melanchton; Calvin* will say, *Videtur,* It seemes
to be thus, *Melanchton,* It can be no otherwise but thus. But the best
men are but Problematicall, Onely the Holy Ghost is Dogmaticall;
Onely he subscribes this *surely,* and onely he seales with Infallibility.
Our dealings are appointed to be in yea, yea, and nay, nay, and no
340 farther; But *all the promises of God are yea, and Amen,* that is, surely,
verily; for that is his Name; These things saith *The Amen,* He that is
Amen. And it is not (I hope) an impertinent note, That that Euangelist
S. *Iohn,* who considers the Divinity of Christ, more then the
other Euangelists doe, does evermore, constantly, without any change,
double that which was Christs ordinary asseveration, *Amen.* As oft as
the other Euangelists mention it in Christs mouth, still they expresse
it with one *Amen, verily I say;* S. *Iohn* alwayes, *Amen, Amen, verily,
verily,* it is thus and thus. The nearer we come to the consideration of
God, the farther we are removed from all contingencies, and all in-
350 clination to Error, and the more is this *Amen, verily, surely,* multiplied
and established unto us.

2 Cor. 1.20
Rev. 3.14

It is in doctrines and opinions, as it is in designes and purposes; *Goe to,* (sayes the Prophet, by way of reprehension) *Goe to, you that say, we will goe to such a City, and trade thus and thus there, &c.* So, goe to, you that pronounce upon every invention, and Tradition of your own, a *Quicunque vult salvus esse,* Whosoever will be saved, must beleeve this, and clogge every problematicall proposition with an *Anathema,* Cursed be he, Excommunicated he that thinks the contrary to this; Goe to, you that make matters of faith of the passions of men.
360 So also, goe to, you that proceed and continue in your sinnes, and say, Surely I shall have time enough to repent hereafter. Goe to, you that in a spirituall and irreligious melancholy and diffidence in Gods mercy, say, Surely the Lord hath locked up his mercy from me, surely I shall never see that Sunne more, never receive, never feele beame of his mercy more, but passe through this darknesse into a worse. This word, *surely,* in such cases, in such senses, is not your mothers tongue, not the language of the Christian Church. She teaches you, to condition all in Christ; In him you are enabled to doe all things, and without him nothing. But absolutely, unconditionally, this *surely* is appropriated to
370 the propositions, to the assertions of God himselfe; And some of those follow in this text.

Comparatio Divitis & Pauperis

Now that which the Holy Ghost presents here upon this assurednesse, is, *That men of low degree are vanity, and that men of high degree are a lie;* These are both sure, and alike sure. It is true that it constitutes a Probleme, that it admits a Discourse, it will abide a debatement, whether men of high degree, or of low degree be worst; whether riches or poverty, (both considered in a great measure, very rich, and very poore) Prosperity or Adversity occasion most sinnes. Though God call upon us in every leafe of the Scripture, to pity the
380 poore, and relieve the poore, and ground his last Judgement upon our

Mat. 25.34

works of mercy, ·(*Because you have fed and clothed the poore, inherit the kingdome*) yet, as the rich and the poore stand before us now, (as it were in Judgement) as we inquire and heare evidence, which state is most obnoxious, and open to most sinnes, we embrace, and apply to

Exod. 23.3
Levit. 19.15

our selves that law, *Thou shalt not countenance a poore man in his cause;* And (as it is repeated) *Thou shalt not respect the person of the poore in Iudgement.*

There is then a poverty, which, without all question, is the direct

way to heaven; but that is spirituall; *Blessed are the poore in spirit.*   Mat. 5.3
390 This poverty is humility, it is not beggary. A rich man may have it, and
a beggar may be without it. The Wiseman found not this poverty, (not
humility) in every poore man. He found three sorts of men, whom his
soule hated; And one of the three, *was a poore man that is proud.* And   Ecclus. 25.2
when the Prophet said of Jerusalem in her afflictions, *Paupercula es &*
ebria, Thou are poore, and miserable, and yet drunke, though (as he   Esay 51.21
addes there) *it were not with wine,* (which is now, in our dayes an
ordinary refuge of men of all sorts, in all sadnesses and crosses to relieve themselves upon wine and strong drinke, which are indeed strong
illusions) yet, though Jerusalems drunkennesse were not with wine, it
400 was worse; It was a staggering, a vertiginousnesse, an ignorance, a
blindnesse, a not discerning the wayes to God; which is the worst
drunkennesse, and fals often upon the poore and afflicted, That their
poverty and affliction staggers them, and damps them in their recourse
to God, so far, as that they know not, *That they are miserable, and*   Revel. 3.17
wretched, and poore, and blinde, and naked. The Holy Ghost alwaies
makes the danger of the poore great, as well as of the rich. *The rich*   Pro. 10.15
mans wealth is his strong City. There is his fault, his confidence in that;
But *Pavor pauperum, The destruction of the poore is his poverty;*
There is his fault, Desperation under it. *Solomon* presents them, as
410 equally dangerous, *Give me neither poverty, nor riches.* So does *Booz*   Pro. 30.8
to *Ruth, Blessed be thou of the Lord, my daughter, in as much as thou*   Ruth 3.10
followedst not young men, whether poore, or rich. That which *Booz*
intended there, Incontinency, and all vices that arise immediately out
of the corruption of nature, and are not induced by other circumstances,
have as much inclination from poverty, as from riches. May we not
say, more? I doubt we may. He must be a very sanctified man, whom
extreame poverty, and other afflictions, doe not decline towards a jealousie, and a suspicion, and a distrusting of God; And then, the sins
that bend towards desperation, are so much more dangerous, then
420 those that bend towards presumption, that he that presumes, hath still
mercy in his contemplation, He does not thinke, that he needs no
mercy, but that mercy is easily had; He beleeves there is mercy, he
doubts not of that; But the despairing man imagines a cruelty, an
unmercifulnesse in God, and destroyes the very nature of God himselfe. Riches is the Metaphor, in which, the Holy Ghost hath delighted

Rom. 2.4
11.33
Ephes. 3.8
ver. 16

to expresse God and Heaven to us; *Despise not the riches of his good-nesse,* sayes the Apostle; And againe, *O the depth of the riches of his wisdome;* And so, after, *The unsearchable riches of Christ;* And for the consummation of all, *The riches of his Glory.* Gods goodnesse ⁴³⁰ towards us in generall, our Religion in the way, his Grace here, his Glory hereafter, are all represented to us in Riches. With poverty God ordinarily accompanies his comminations; he threatens feeblenesse, and warre, and captivity, and poverty every where, but he never threatens men with riches.

Ordinary poverty, (that is a difficulty, with all their labors and industry, to sustaine their family, and the necessary duties of their place) is a shrewd, and a slippery tentation. But for that street-beggery, which is become a Calling, (for Parents bring up their children to it, nay they doe almost take prentises to it, some expert beggers teach others what ⁴⁴⁰ they shall say, how they shall looke, how they shall lie, how they shall cry) for these, whom our lawes call Incorrigible, I must say of them

Matt. 15.26

(in a just accommodation of our Saviours words, *It is not meet to take the childrens bread, and to cast it to dogs*) It is not meet, that this vermin should devoure any of that, which belongs to them who are truely poore. Neither is there any measure, any proportion of riches, that exposes man naturally to so much sin, as this kinde of beggery doth. Rich men forget, or neglect the duties of their Baptisme; but of these, how many are there, that were never baptized? Rich men sleepe out Sermons, but these never come to Church: Rich men are negligent ⁴⁵⁰ in the practise, but these are ignorant in all knowledge.

It would require a longer disquisition, then I can afford to it now, whether Riches, or Poverty (considered in lesser proportions, ordinary riches, ordinary poverty) open us to more, and worse sins; But consider them in the highest and in the lowest, abundant riches, beggerly poverty, and it will scarce admit doubt, but that the incorrigible vagabond is farther from all wayes of goodnesse, then the corruptest rich man is. And therefore labour wee all earnestly in the wayes of some lawfull calling, that we may have our portion of this world by good meanes. For first, the advantages of doing good to others in a reall ⁴⁶⁰ reliefe of their wants, is in the rich onely, whereas the best way of a good poore man, to doe good to others, is but an exemplary patience, to catechize others by his suffering; And then, all degrees of poverty are dangerous and slippery, even to a murmuring against God, or an invading of the possessions, and goods of other men, but especially the lowest, the desperate degree of beggery, and then especially, when we cannot say it is inflicted by the hand of God, but contracted by our owne lazinesse, or our owne wastfulnesse.

This is a problematicall, a disputable case, Whether riches or poverty occasion most sins. And because on both sides there arise good doc-
470 trines of edification, I have thus far willingly stopped upon that disputable consideration. But now, that which wee receive here, upon *Davids,* upon the Holy Ghosts security, Surely it is thus, It is surely so, is this, That we shall be deceived, if we put our trust in men; for, what sort of men would we trust? *Surely men of low degree are vanity.* And this, if it be taken of particular men, needs no proving, no illustrating, no remembring. Every man sees and acknowledges, that to rely upon a man of no power, of no place, no blood, no fortune, no friends, no favour, is a vanity, *Surely men of low degree are vanity.* The first younger brother that was borne in the world, because he
480 was lesse then another, is called by the very name of *vanity;* The eldest brother *Cain* signifies *possession,* but *Abel* is *vanity.*

But take it of a whole body of such men, Men of low degree, and it is so too; the Applause of the people is vanity, Popularity is vanity. At how deare a rate doth that man buy the peoples affections, that payes his owne head for their hats? How cheaply doth he sell his Princes favour, that hath nothing for it, but the peoples breath? And what age doth not see some examples of so ill merchants of their owne honours and lives too? How many men, upon confidence of that flattering gale of winde, the breath and applause of the people, have taken
490 in their anchors, (that is, departed from their true, and safe hold, The right of the Law, and the favour of the Prince) and as soone as they hoysed their sailes, (that is, entred into any by-action) have found the wind in their teeth, that is, Those people whom they trusted in, armed against them. And as it is in Civill, and Secular, so it is in Ecclesiasticall, and Spirituall things too. How many men, by a popular hunting after the applause of the people, in their manner of preaching, and humouring them in their distempers, have made themselves incapable of preferment in the Church where they tooke their Orders, and preached themselves into a necessity of running away into for-

Men of low
degree

⁵⁰⁰ raine parts, that are receptacles of seditious and schismaticall Sepa-
ratists, and have been put there, to learne some trade, and become
Artificers for their sustentation? The same people that welcommed
Christ, from the Mount of Olives, into Jerusalem, upon Sunday, with

Matt. 21.9   their *Hosannaes to the Sonne of David,* upon Friday mocked him in
Jerusalem, with their *Haile King of the Iewes,* and blew him out of
Jerusalem to Golgotha, with the pestilent breath, with the tempestu-
ous whirlwind of their *Crucifige's.* And of them, who have called the

Matt. 10.25   Master Beelzebub, what shall any servant looke for? *Surely men of
low degree are vanity.*

High degree   ⁵¹⁰   And then, under the same oath, and asseveration, *Surely,* as surely
as the other, *men of high degree are a lie.* Doth *David* meane these
men, whom he calls a *lie,* to be any lesse then those whom hee called
vanity? Lesse then vanity, then emptinesse, then nothing, nothing
can be; And low, and high are to this purpose, and in this consideration, (compared with God, or considered without God) equally nothing. He that hath the largest patrimony, and space of earth, in the
earth, must heare me say, That all that was nothing; And if he ask,
But what was this whole Kingdom, what all Europe, what all the
World? It was all, not so much as another nothing, but all one and
⁵²⁰ the same nothing as thy dung-hill was. But yet the Holy Ghost hath
beene pleased to vary the phrase here, and to call *Men of high degree,*
not *vanity,* but *a lie,* because the poore, men of low degree, in their
condition promise no assistance, feed not men with hopes, and therefore cannot be said to *lie,* but in the condition of men of high degree,
who are of power, there is a tacit promise, a naturall and inherent assurance of protection, and assistance, flowing from them. For, the
Magistrate cannot say, That he never promised me Justice, never
promised mee Protection; for in his assuming that place, he made me
that promise. I cannot say, that I never promised my Parish, my
⁵³⁰ service; for in my Induction, I made them that promise, and if I
performe it not, I am a lie; for so this word *Chasab* (which we translate *a lie*) is frequently used in the Scriptures, for that which is defec-

Esay 58.11   tive in the duty it should performe; *Thou shalt bee a spring of water,*
(sayes God in *Esay*) *Cujus aquæ non mentiuntur, whose waters never
lie,* that is, never dry, never faile.

So then, when men of high degree doe not performe the duties of
their places, then they are a lie of their owne making; And when I

over-magnifie them in their place, flatter them, humor them, ascribe more to them, expect more from them, rely more upon them, then I
540 should, then they are a lie of my making. But whether the lie be theirs, That they feare greater men then themselves, and so prevaricate in their duties; Or the lie be mine, that canonize them and make them my God, they, and I shall be disappointed; for, *Surely men of high degree are a lie.* But we are upon a Sermon, not upon a Satyr, therefore we passe from this.

And, for all this, there may seeme to be roome left for the Middle-state, for a mediocrity; when it is not so low as to be made the subject of oppression, nor so high as to be made the object of ambition, when it is neither exposed to scorne and contempt, nor to envy, and under-
550 mining, may we not then trust upon, not rest in such a condition? Indeed, this mediocrity seemes (and justly) the safest condition; for this, and this onely enjoyes it selfe: The lazy man gets not up to it; The stirring man stayes not at it, but is gone beyond it. From our first Themes at Schoole, to our Texts in the Pulpit, we continue our praysing and perswading of this mediocrity. A man may have too much of any thing; *Anima saturata, A full soule will tread hony under his feete;* He may take in knowledge till he be ignorant; Let the Prophet *Ieremy* give the Rule, *Stultus factus est omnis homo à scientia, Every man becomes a foole by knowledge,* by over-weening,
560 and over-valuing his knowledge; And let *Adam* be the example of this Rule, His eyes were opened by eating the fruit, and he knew so much, as he was ashamed of it; Let the Apostle be the Physitian, the moderator, *Sapere ad sobrietatem,* not to dive into secrets, and un-revealed mysteries. There is enough of this doctrine involved in the fable, *Acteon* saw more then he should have seene, and perished. There is abundantly enough expressed in the Oracle of Truth, *Vzza* was over-zealous in an office that appertained not to him, in assisting the Arke, and suffered for that.

We may quickly exceed a mediocrity, even in the praise of Medi-
570 ocrity. But all our diligence will scarce finde it out. What is medi-ocrity? Or where is it? In the Hierarchy of the Roman Church they never thought of this mediocrity; They go very high, and very low, but there is no meane station; I meane no denomination of any Order from meannesse, from mediocrity. In one degree you finde em-broydered shooes, for Kings to kisse, and in another degree bare feet;

Mediocrity

Prov. 27.7

Ier. 10.14

Rom. 12.3

2 Sam. 6.6

we finde an Order of the *Society of Iesus;* and that is very high, for, Society implies community, partnership; And we finde low descents, *Minorits,* men lesse then others, and *Minims,* least of all men; and lower then all them, *Nullans,* men that call themselves, *Nothing;* And
580 truly, this Order, best of all others hath answered and justified the name, for, very soone, they came to nothing. Wee finde all extreames amongst them, even in their names, but none denominated from this mediocrity.

But to passe from names to the thing; indeed what is Mediocrity? where is it? Is it the same thing as Competency? But what is competency? or where is that? Is it that which is sufficient for thy present degree? perchance thy present degree is not sufficient for thee; Thy charge perchance, perchance thy parts and abilities, or thy birth and education may require a better degree. God produced plants in Para-
590 dise therefore, that they might grow; God hath planted us in this world, that we might grow; and he that does not endeavour that by all lawfull meanes, is inexcusable, as well as he that pursues unlawfull. But, if I come to imagine such a mediocrity, such a competency, such a sufficiency in my selfe, as that I may rest in that, that I thinke I may ride out all stormes, all dis-favours, that I have enough of mine owne, wealth, health, or morall constancy, if any of these decay, this is a verier vanity, then trusting in men of low degree, and a verier lye, then men of high degree; for, this is to trust to our selves; this is a
Habbak. 1.16   *sacrificing* to our owne *nets,* our owne industry, our owne wisdome,
600 our owne fortune; And of all the Idolatries of the Heathen, who made Gods of every thing they saw or imagined, of every thing, in, and betweene Heaven and hell, we reade of no man that sacrificed to himselfe. Indeed no man flatters me so dangerously, as I flatter my selfe, no man wounds me so desperately, as I wound myselfe; And therefore, since this which we call Mediocrity, and Competency is conditioned so, that it is enough to subsist alone, without relation to others, dependency upon others, feare from others, induces a confidence, a relying upon my selfe; As, that which we imagine to be the middle region of the ayre, is the coldest of all, So this imagined mediocrity,
610 that induces a confidence in our selves, is the weakest rest, the coldest comfort of all, and makes me a lye to my selfe. Therefore may the Prophet well spread, and safely extend his asseveration, his *Surely,* upon all, high, and low, and meane; *Surely to be laid in the balance, they are altogether lighter then vanity.*

Here then, upon a full enumeration of all parts, the Prophet concludes upon all. If therefore thou have the favour of great ones, the applause of the people, confidence in thy selfe, in an instant, the power of those great ones may be overthrowne, or their favour to thee withdrawne from thee, (and so, that bladder is pricked, upon which thou
620 swommest) The applause of the people may be hushed and silenced, (either they would not, or they dare not magnifie thee) And, thine owne constancy may be turned into a dejection of spirit, and consternation of all thy faculties. Put all together, (which fals out seldome, that any man can do so) but if he can do that, (which is the best state of man, that can be imagined in this world, that he hath all these together, the favour of High and low, and of himselfe, that is, his owne testimony in his conscience, (though perchance an erring, a mistaking conscience) yet, the Prophet had delivered the same assurance before (even of that state of man, which is rather imagined,
630 then ever possest) *Surely every man, at his best state, is altogether vanity;* And here, he adds, *lighter then vanity.* Vanity is nothing, but there is a condition worse then nothing. Confidence in the things, or persons of this world, but most of all, a confidence in our selves, will bring us at last to that state, wherein we would faine be nothing, and cannot. But yet, we have a balance in our text; And all these are but put together in one balance. In the other scale there is something put to, in comparison whereof all this world is so light. God does not leave our great and noble faculty, and affection of hope, and trust, and confidence, without something to direct it selfe upon, and rectifie it
640 selfe in. He does not; for, for that he proposes himselfe; The words immediately before the text, are, *God is a refuge;* and in comparison of him, *To be laid in the balance, Surely they are altogether lighter then vanity.*

So then, it is not enough not to trust in the flesh (for, for that, *Cursed be man, that trusted in man, or maketh flesh his arme;* Their flesh cannot secure thee, neither is thine owne *flesh brasse,* that thou canst endure the vexations of this world, neither can *flesh* and *blood* reveale unto thee the things of the next world) It is not enough not to trust in flesh, but thou must trust in that that is Spirit. And when thou
650 art to direct thy trust upon him, who is spirit, the spirit of power, and of consolation, stop not, stray not, divert not upon evill spirits, to seeke advancement, or to seeke knowledge from them, nor upon good

Lighter then
vanity

Psal. 39.5

Deus omnia
Ier. 17.5
Iob 6.12
Mat. 16.17

spirits, the glorious saints of GOD in Heaven, to seeke salvation
from them, nor upon thine owne spirit, in an over-valuation of thy
purity, or thy merits. For, there is a pestilent pride in an imaginary
humility, and an infectious foulenesse in an imaginary purity; but
turne onely to the onely invisible and immortall God, who turnes to
thee, in so many names and notions of power, and consolation, in
this one Psalme. In the last verse but one of this Psalme, *David* sayes,
660 *God hath spoken once, and twice have I heard him.* God hath said
enough at once; but twice, in this Psalme, hath he repeated this, in
the second, and in the sixt verse, *He onely is my Rocke, and my Sal-*
vation, and my Defence, And, (as it is inlarged in the seventh verse)
my Refuge, and my Glory. If my *Refuge,* what enemy can pursue
me? If my *Defence,* what tentation shall wound me? If my *Rock,*
what storme shall shake me? If my *Salvation,* what melancholy shall
deject me? If my *Glory,* what calumny shall defame me?

I must not stay you now, to infuse into you, the severall consolations
of these severall names, and notions of God towards you. But, goe
670 your severall wayes home, and every soule take with him that name,
which may minister most comfort unto him. Let him that is pursued
with any particular tentation, invest God, as God is a *Refuge,* a Sanctuary. Let him that is buffeted with the messenger of Satan, battered
with his owne concupiscence, receive God, as God is his *Defence* and
target. Let him that is shaked with perplexities in his understanding,
or scruples in his conscience, lay hold upon God, as God is his *Rock,*
and his anchor. Let him that hath any diffident jealousie or suspition
of the free and full mercy of God, apprehend God, as God is his
Salvation; And him that walks in the ingloriousnesse and contempt
680 of this world, contemplate God, as God is his *Glory.* Any of these
notions is enough to any man, but God is all these, and all else, that
all soules can thinke, to every man. Wee shut up both these Considerations, (man should not, (that is not all) God should be relied upon)
with that of the Prophet, *Trust ye not in a friend, put not your confi-*
dence in a guide, keepe the doores of thy mouth from her that lies in
thy bosome; (there is the exclusion of trust in man) and then he adds
in the seventh verse, because it stands thus betweene man and man,
I will looke unto the Lord, I will looke to the God of my Salvation, my
God will heare me.

Mic. ult. 5

The second of my Prebend Sermons upon my five Psalmes.
Preached at S. Pauls, Ianuary 29. 1625.

Psal. 63.7. *Because thou hast been my helpe, Therefore in the shadow of thy wings will I rejoyce.*

THe Psalmes are the Manna of the Church. As Manna tasted to every man like that that he liked best, so doe the Psalmes minister Instruction, and satisfaction, to every man, in every emergency and occasion. *David* was not onely a cleare Prophet of Christ himselfe, but a Prophet of every particular Christian; He foretels what I, what any shall doe, and suffer, and say. And as the whole booke of Psalmes is *Oleum effusum,* (as the Spouse speaks of the name of Christ) an Oyntment powred out upon all sorts of sores, A Searcloth that souples all bruises, A Balme that searches all wounds; so are there some certaine Psalmes, that are Imperiall Psalmes, that command over all affections, and spread themselves over all occasions, Catholique, universall Psalmes, that apply themselves to all necessities. This is one of those; for, of those Constitutions which are called Apostolicall, one is, That the Church should meet every day, to sing this Psalme. And accordingly, S. *Chrysostome* testifies, That it was decreed, and ordained by the Primitive Fathers, that no day should passe without the publique singing of this Psalme. Under both these obligations, (those ancient Constitutions, called the Apostles, and those ancient Decrees made by the primitive Fathers) belongs to me, who have my part in the service of Gods Church, the especiall medi-

Wisd. 16.20

Cant. 1.2

Constitut. Apostol.

Chrysost.

tation, and recommendation of this Psalme. And under a third obligation too, That it is one of those five psalmes, the daily rehearsing whereof, is injoyned to me, by the Constitutions of this Church, as five other are to every other person of our body. As the whole booke is Manna, so these five Psalmes are my Gomer, which I am to fill and empty every day of this Manna.

Divisio

Hieron.

Now as the spirit and soule of the whole booke of Psalmes is contracted into this psalme, so is the spirit and soule of this whole psalme contracted into this verse. The key of the psalme, (as S. *Hierome* calls ³⁰ the Titles of the psalmes) tells us, that *David* uttered this psalme, *when he was in the wildernesse of Iudah;* There we see the present occasion that moved him; And we see what was passed between God and him before, in the first clause of our Text; (*Because thou hast been my helpe*) And then we see what was to come, by the rest, (*Therefore in the shadow of thy wings will I rejoyce.*) So that we have here the whole compasse of Time, Past, Present, and Future; and these three parts of Time, shall be at this time, the three parts of this Exercise; first, what *Davids* distresse put him upon for the present; and that lyes in the Context; secondly, how *David* built his assurance upon ⁴⁰ that which was past; (*Because thou hast been my help*) And thirdly, what he established to himselfe for the future, (*Therefore in the shadow of thy wings will I rejoyce.*) First, His distresse in the Wildernesse, his present estate carried him upon the memory of that which God had done for him before, And the Remembrance of that carried him upon that, of which he assured himselfe after. Fixe upon God any where, and you shall finde him a Circle; He is with you now, when you fix upon him; He was with you before, for he brought you to this fixation; and he will be with you hereafter, for

Heb. 13.8

He is yesterday, and to day, and the same for ever.

⁵⁰ For *Davids* present condition, who was now in a banishment, in a persecution in the Wildernesse of Judah, (which is our first part) we shall onely insist upon that, (which is indeed spread over all the psalme to the Text, and ratified in the Text) That in all those temporall calamities *David* was onely sensible of his spirituall losse; It grieved him not that he was kept from *Sauls* Court, but that he was kept from Gods Church. For when he sayes, by way of lamentation,

Ver. 1

That he was in a dry and thirsty land, where no water was, he ex-

presses what penury, what barrennesse, what drought and what thirst
he meant; *To see thy power, and thy glory, so as I have seene thee in*
⁶⁰ *the Sanctuary.* For there, *my soule shall be satisfied as with marrow,*
and with fatnesse, and there, *my mouth shall praise thee with joyfull*
lips. And in some few considerations conducing to this, That spirituall losses are incomparably heavier then temporall, and that therefore, The Restitution to our spirituall happinesse, or the continuation
of it, is rather to be made the subject of our prayers to God, in all
pressures and distresses, then of temporall, we shall determine that
first part. And for the particular branches of both the other parts,
(The Remembring of Gods benefits past, And the building of an
assurance for the future, upon that Remembrance) it may be fitter
⁷⁰ to open them to you, anon when we come to handle them, then now.
Proceed we now to our first part, The comparing of temporall and
spirituall afflictions.

    In the way of this Comparison, falls first the Consideration of the
universality of afflictions in generall, and the inevitablenesse thereof.
It is a blessed Metaphore, that the Holy Ghost hath put into the mouth
of the Apostle, *Pondus Gloriæ,* That our *afflictions* are but *light,* because there is an *exceeding,* and an *eternall waight of glory* attending them. If it were not for that exceeding waight of glory, no other
waight in this world could turne the scale, or waigh downe those
⁸⁰ infinite waights of afflictions that oppresse us here. There is not onely
Pestis valde gravis, (the pestilence grows heavy upon the Land) but
there is *Musca valde gravis,* God calls in but the fly, to vexe Egypt,
and even the fly is a heavy burden unto them. It is not onely *Iob* that
complains, *That he was a burden to himselfe,* but even *Absaloms*
haire was a burden to him, till it was polled. It is not onely *Ieremy*
that complains, *Aggravavit compedes,* That God had made their fetters and their chains heavy to them, but the workmen in harvest
complaine, That God had made a faire day heavy unto them, ·(*We*
have borne the heat, and the burden of the day.) *Sand is heavy,* sayes
⁹⁰ *Solomon;* And how many suffer so? under a sand-hill of crosses, daily,
hourely afflictions, that are heavy by their number, if not by their
single waight? And *a stone is heavy;* (sayes he in the same place)
And how many suffer so? How many, without any former prepara-
tory crosse, or comminatory, or commonitory crosse, even in the midst

Ver. 2
Ver. 5
Ver. 5

1 Part.
Afflictio
universalis
2 Cor. 4.17

Exod. 9.3
8.24
Job 7.20
2 Sam. 14.26
Lament. 3.7

Mat. 20.12
Pro. 27.3

of prosperity, and security, fall under some one stone, some grind-stone, some mil-stone, some one insupportable crosse that ruines them? But then, (sayes *Solomon* there) *A fooles anger is heavier then both;* And how many children, and servants, and wives suffer under the anger, and morosity, and peevishnesse, and jealousie of foolish 100 Masters, and Parents, and Husbands, though they must not say so? *David* and *Solomon* have cryed out, That all this world is *vanity,* and *levity;* And (God knowes) all is waight, and burden, and heavinesse, and oppression; And if there were not a waight of future glory to counterpoyse it, we should all sinke into nothing.

I aske not *Mary Magdalen,* whether lightnesse were not a burden; (for sin is certainly, sensibly a burden) But I aske *Susanna* whether even chast beauty were not a burden to her; And I aske *Ioseph* whether personall comelinesse were not a burden to him. I aske not *Dives,* who perished in the next world, the question; but I aske them 110 who are made examples of *Solomons* Rule, of that *sore evill,* (as he calls it) *Riches kept to the owners thereof for their hurt,* whether Riches be not a burden.

Eccles. 5.13

All our life is a continuall burden, yet we must not groane; A con-tinuall squeasing, yet we must not pant; And as in the tendernesse of our childhood, we suffer, and yet are whipt if we cry, so we are com-plained of, if we complaine, and made delinquents if we call the times ill. And that which addes waight to waight, and multiplies the sad-nesse of this consideration, is this, That still the best men have had most laid upon them. As soone as I heare God say, that he hath found 120 *an upright man, that feares God, and eschews evill,* in the next lines I finde a Commission to Satan, to bring in Sabeans and Chaldeans upon his cattell, and servants, and fire and tempest upon his children, and loathsome diseases upon himselfe. As soone as I heare God say, That he hath found *a man according to his own heart,* I see his sonnes ravish his daughters, and then murder one another, and then rebell against the Father, and put him into straites for his life. As soone as I heare God testifie of Christ at his Baptisme, *This is my beloved Sonne in whom I am well pleased,* I finde that Sonne of his *led up by the Spirit, to be tempted of the Devill.* And after I heare God ratifie 130 the same testimony againe, at his Transfiguration, (*This is my beloved Sonne, in whom I am well pleased*) I finde that beloved Sonne of his,

Mat. 3.17

Matt. 4.1

Matt. 17.5

deserted, abandoned, and given over to Scribes, and Pharisees, and Publicans, and Herodians, and Priests, and Souldiers, and people, and Judges, and witnesses, and executioners, and he that was called the beloved Sonne of God, and made partaker of the glory of heaven, in this world, in his Transfiguration, is made now the Sewer of all the corruption, of all the sinnes of this world, as no Sonne of God, but a meere man, as no man, but a contemptible worme. As though the greatest weaknesse in this world, were man, and the greatest fault in
140 man were to be good, man is more miserable then other creatures, and good men more miserable then any other men.

But then there is *Pondus Gloriæ, An exceeding waight of eternall glory,* and that turnes the scale; for as it makes all worldly prosperity as dung, so it makes all worldly adversity as feathers. And so it had need; for in the scale against it, there are not onely put temporall afflictions, but spirituall too; And to these two kinds, we may accommodate those words, *He that fals upon this stone,* (upon temporall afflictions) may be bruised, broken, *But he upon whom that stone falls,* (spirituall afflictions) *is in danger to be ground to powder.* And then,
150 the great, and yet ordinary danger is, That these spirituall afflictions grow out of temporall; Murmuring, and diffidence in God, and obduration, out of worldly calamities; And so against nature, the fruit is greater and heavier then the Tree, spirituall heavier then temporall afflictions.

They who write of Naturall story, propose that Plant for the greatest wonder in nature, which being no firmer then a bull-rush, or a reed, produces and beares for the fruit thereof no other but an intire, and very hard stone. That temporall affliction should produce spirituall stoninesse, and obduration, is unnaturall, yet ordinary. Therefore doth
160 God propose it, as one of those greatest blessings, which he multiplies upon his people, *I will take away your stony hearts, and give you hearts of flesh;* And, Lord let mee have a fleshly heart in any sense, rather then a stony heart. Wee finde mention amongst the observers of rarities in Nature, of hairy hearts, hearts of men, that have beene overgrowne with haire; but of petrified hearts, hearts of men growne into stone, we read not; for this petrefaction of the heart, this stupefaction of a man, is the last blow of Gods hand upon the heart of man in this world. Those great afflictions which are powred out of the Vials

Afflictio spiritualis

Matt. 21.44

Plin. l. 27.11
Litho-
spermus

Ezek. 11.19
and 36.26
Plin. and
Plutar.

Revel. 16

of the seven Angels upon the world, are still accompanied with that
¹⁷⁰ heavy effect, that that affliction hardned them. *They were scorched*
with heats and plagues, by the fourth Angel, and it followes, *They*

ver. 9

blasphemed the name of God, and repented not, to give him glory.
Darknesse was induced upon them by the fift Angel, and it followes,

ver. 11

They blasphemed the God of heaven, and repented not of their deeds.
And from the seventh Angel there fell hailestones of the waight of

ver. 21

talents, (perchance foure pound waight) upon men; And yet these
men had so much life left, as to *blaspheme God,* out of that respect,
which alone should have brought them to glorifie God, *Because the*
plague thereof was exceeding great. And when a great plague brings
¹⁸⁰ them to blaspheme, how great shall that second plague be, that comes
upon them for blaspheming?

Let me wither and weare out mine age in a discomfortable, in an
unwholesome, in a penurious prison, and so pay my debts with my
bones, and recompence the wastfulnesse of my youth, with the beggery of mine age; Let me wither in a spittle under sharpe, and foule,
and infamous diseases, and so recompence the wantonnesse of my
youth, with that loathsomnesse in mine age; yet, if God with-draw
not his spirituall blessings, his Grace, his Patience, If I can call my
suffering his Doing, my passion his Action, All this that is temporall,
¹⁹⁰ is but a caterpiller got into one corner of my garden, but a mill-dew
fallen upon one acre of my Corne; The body of all, the substance of
all is safe, as long as the soule is safe. But when I shall trust to that,
which wee call a good spirit, and God shall deject, and empoverish,
and evacuate that spirit, when I shall rely upon a morall constancy,
and God shall shake, and enfeeble, and enervate, destroy and de-
molish that constancy; when I shall think to refresh my selfe in the
serenity and sweet ayre of a good conscience, and God shall call up
the damps and vapours of hell it selfe, and spread a cloud of diffidence,
and an impenetrable crust of desperation upon my conscience; when
²⁰⁰ health shall flie from me, and I shall lay hold upon riches to succour
me, and comfort me in my sicknesse, and riches shall flie from me, and
I shall snatch after favour, and good opinion, to comfort me in my
poverty; when even this good opinion shall leave me, and calumnies
and misinformations shall prevaile against me; when I shall need
peace, because there is none but thou, O Lord, that should stand for

me, and then shall finde, that all the wounds that I have, come from
thy hand, all the arrowes that stick in me, from thy quiver; when I
shall see, that because I have given my selfe to my corrupt nature,
thou hast changed thine; and because I am all evill towards thee,
²¹⁰ therefore thou hast given over being good towards me; When it comes
to this height, that the fever is not in the humors, but in the spirits,
that mine enemy is not an imaginary enemy, fortune, nor a transitory
enemy, malice in great persons, but a reall, and an irresistible, and an
inexorable, and an everlasting enemy, The Lord of Hosts himselfe,
The Almighty God himselfe, the Almighty God himselfe onely
knowes the waight of this affliction, and except hee put in that *pondus
gloriæ,* that exceeding waight of an eternall glory, with his owne hand,
into the other scale, we are waighed downe, we are swallowed up,
irreparably, irrevocably, irrecoverably, irremediably.

²²⁰   This is the fearefull depth, this is spirituall misery, to be thus fallen
from God. But was this *Davids* case? was he fallen thus farre, into a
diffidence in God? No. But the danger, the precipice, the slippery slid-
ing into that bottomlesse depth, is, to be excluded from the meanes
of comming to God, or staying with God; And this is that that *David*
laments here, That by being banished, and driven into the wildernesse
of Judah, hee had not accesse to the Sanctuary of the Lord, to sacrifice
his part in the praise, and to receive his part in the prayers of the
Congregation; for Angels passe not to ends, but by wayes and meanes,
nor men to the glory of the triumphant Church, but by participation
²³⁰ of the Communion of the Militant. To this note *David* sets his Harpe,
in many, many Psalms: Sometimes, that God had suffered his enemies
to possesse his Tabernacle, (*Hee forsooke the Tabernacle of Shiloh,*   Psal. 78.60
*Hee delivered his strength into captivity, and his glory into the ene-
mies hands*) But most commonly he complaines, that God disabled
him from comming to the Sanctuary. In which one thing he had
summed up all his desires, all his prayers, (*One thing have I desired*   Psal. 27.4
*of the Lord, that will I looke after; That I may dwell in the house
of the Lord, all the dayes of my life, to behold the beauty of the Lord,
and to enquire in his Temple*) His vehement desire of this, he ex-
²⁴⁰ presses againe, (*My soule thirsteth for God, for the living God; when*   Psal. 42.2
shall I come and appeare before God?) He expresses a holy jealousie,
a religious envy, even to the sparrows and swallows, (yea, *the sparrow*   Psal. 84.3

hath found a house, and the swallow a nest for her selfe, and where she may lay her yong, Even thine Altars, O Lord of Hosts, my King and my God.) Thou art my King, and my God, and yet excludest me

Luk. 12.7

from that, which thou affordest to sparrows, *And are not we of more value then many sparrows?*

And as though *David* felt some false ease, some half-tentation, some whispering that way, That God is *in the wildernesse of Iudah,* in

Psal. 84.3   250 every place, as well as in his *Sanctuary,* there is in the Originall in that place, a patheticall, a vehement, a broken expressing expressed, *O thine Altars;* It is true, (sayes *David*) thou art here in the wildernesse, and I may see thee here, and serve thee here, but, *O thine Altars, O Lord of hosts, my King and my God.* When *David* could not come

Psal. 5.7   in person to that place, yet he bent towards the Temple, (*In thy feare will I worship towards thy holy Temple.*) Which was also *Daniels*

Dan. 6.10   devotion; when he prayed, *his Chamber windowes were open towards*

Esa. 38.2   *Ierusalem;* And so is *Hezekias* turning to the wall to weepe, and to pray in his sick bed, understood to be to that purpose, to conforme,

260 and compose himselfe towards the Temple. In the place consecrated

Deut. 31.11   for that use, God by *Moses* fixes the service, and fixes the Reward; And towards that place, (when they could not come to it) doth *Solomon* direct their devotion in the Consecration of the Temple, (*when they are in the warres, when they are in Captivity, and pray*

1 King. 8.44   *towards this house, doe thou heare them.*) For, as in private prayer, when (according to Christs command) we are shut in our chamber, there is exercised *Modestia fidei,* The modesty and bashfulnesse of our faith, not pressing upon God in his house: so in the publique prayers of the Congregation, there is exercised the fervor, and holy courage

Tertull.   270 of our faith, for *Agmine facto obsidemus Deum,* It is a Mustering of our forces, and a besieging of God. Therefore does *David* so much magnifie their blessednesse, that are in this house of God; (*Blessed are they that dwell in thy house, for they will be still praising thee*) Those that looke towards it, may praise thee sometimes, but those men who dwell in the Church, and whose whole service lyes in the Church, have certainly an advantage of all other men (who are necessarily withdrawne by worldly businesses) in making themselves acceptable to almighty God, if they doe their duties, and observe their Church-services aright.

²⁸⁰ Man being therefore thus subject naturally to manifold calamities, and spirituall calamities being incomparably heavier then temporall, and the greatest danger of falling into such spirituall calamities being in our absence from Gods Church, where onely the outward meanes of happinesse are ministred unto us, certainely there is much tendernesse and deliberation to be used, before the Church doores be shut against any man. If I would not direct a prayer to God, to excommunicate any man from the Triumphant Church, (which were to damne him) I would not oyle the key, I would not make the way too slippery for excommunications in the Militant Church; For, that is to endan-²⁹⁰ ger him. I know how distastfull a sin to God, contumacy, and contempt, and disobedience to Order and Authority is; And I know, (and all men, that choose not ignorance, may know) that our Excommunications (though calumniators impute them to small things, because, many times, the first complaint is of some small matter) never issue but upon contumacies, contempts, disobediences to the Church. But they are reall contumacies, not interpretative, apparant contumacies, not presumptive, that excommunicate a man in Heaven; And much circumspection is required, and (I am far from doubting it) exercised in those cases upon earth; for, though every Excommunica-³⁰⁰ tion upon earth be not sealed in Heaven, though it damne not the man, yet it dammes up that mans way, by shutting him out of that Church, through which he must goe to the other; which being so great a danger, let every man take heed of Excommunicating himselfe. The imperswasible Recusant does so; The negligent Libertin does so; The fantastique Separatist does so; The halfe-present man, he, whose body is here, and minde away, does so; And he, whose body is but halfe here, his limbes are here upon a cushion, but his eyes, his eares are not here, does so: All these are selfe-Excommunicators, and keepe themselves from hence. Onely he enjoyes that blessing, the ³¹⁰ want whereof *David* deplores, that is here intirely, and is glad he is here, and glad to finde this kinde of service here, that he does, and wishes no other.

And so we have done with our first Part, *Davids* aspect, his present condition, and his danger of falling into spirituall miseries, because his persecution, and banishment amounted to an Excommunication, to an excluding of him from the service of God, in the Church. And

Excommunicatio

we passe, in our Order proposed at first, to the second, his retrospect, the Consideration, what God had done for him before, *Because thou hast beene my helpe.*

2 Part   ³²⁰ Through this second part, we shall passe by these three steps. First, That it behoves us, in all our purposes, and actions, to propose to our selves a copy to write by, a patterne to worke by, a rule, or an example to proceed by, Because it hath beene thus heretofore, sayes *David,* I will resolve upon this course for the future. And secondly, That the copy, the patterne, the precedent which we are to propose to our selves, is, The observation of Gods former wayes and proceedings upon us, Because God hath already gone this way, this way I will awaite his going still. And then, thirdly and lastly, in this second part, The way that God had formerly gone with *David,* which was, That he ³³⁰ had been his helpe, (*Because thou hast beene my helpe.*)

Idea   First then, from the meanest artificer, through the wisest Philosopher, to God himselfe, all that is well done, or wisely undertaken, is undertaken and done according to pre-conceptions, fore-imaginations, designes, and patterns proposed to our selves beforehand. A Carpenter builds not a house, but that he first sets up a frame in his owne minde, what kinde of house he will build. The little great Philosopher *Epictetus,* would undertake no action, but he would first propose to himselfe, what *Socrates,* or *Plato,* what a wise man would do in that case, and according to that, he would proceed. Of God himselfe, it is safely ³⁴⁰ resolved in the Schoole, that he never did any thing in any part of time, of which he had not an eternall pre-conception, an eternall Idea, in himselfe before. Of which Ideaes, that is, pre-conceptions, pre-

August.   determinations in God, S. *Augustine* pronounces, *Tanta vis in Ideis constituitur,* There is so much truth, and so much power in these Ideaes, as that without acknowledging them, no man can acknowledge God, for he does not allow God Counsaile, and Wisdome, and deliberation in his Actions, but sets God on worke, before he have thought what he will doe. And therefore he, and others of the Fathers

Ioh. 1.3, 4   read that place, (which we read otherwise) *Quod factum est, in ipso* ³⁵⁰ *vita erat;* that is, in all their Expositions, whatsoever is made, in time, was alive in God, before it was made, that is, in that eternall Idea, and patterne which was in him. So also doe divers of those Fathers read

Heb. 11.3   those words to the Hebrews, (which we read, *The things that are seene, are not made of things that doe appeare*) *Ex invisibilibus visi-bilia facta sunt, Things formerly invisible, were made visible;* that is, we see them not till now, till they are made, but they had an invisible being, in that Idea, in that pre-notion, in that purpose of God before, for ever before. Of all things in Heaven, and earth, but of himselfe, God had an Idea, a patterne in himselfe, before he made it.

360 And therefore let him be our patterne for that, to worke after pat-ternes; To propose to our selves Rules and Examples for all our ac-tions; and the more, the more immediately, the more directly our actions concerne the service of God. If I aske God, by what Idea he made me, God produces his *Faciamus hominem ad Imaginem nostram,* That there was a concurrence of the whole Trinity, to make me in *Adam,* according to that Image which they were, and according to that Idea, which they had pre-determined. If I pretend to serve God, and he aske me for my Idea, How I meane to serve him, shall I bee able to produce none? If he aske me an Idea of my Religion, and my
370 opinions, shall I not be able to say, It is that which thy word, and thy Catholique Church hath imprinted in me? If he aske me an Idea of my prayers, shall I not be able to say, It is that which my particular necessities, that which the forme prescribed by thy Son, that which the care, and piety of the Church, in conceiving fit prayers, hath im-printed in me? If he aske me an Idea of my Sermons, shall I not be able to say, It is that which the Analogy of Faith, the edification of the Congregation, the zeale of thy worke, the meditations of my heart have imprinted in me? But if I come to pray or to preach without this kind of Idea, if I come to extemporall prayer, and extemporall preach-
380 ing, I shall come to an extemporall faith, and extemporall religion; and then I must looke for an extemporall Heaven, a Heaven to be made for me; for to that Heaven which belongs to the Catholique Church, I shall never come, except I go by the way of the Catholique Church, by former Idea's, former examples, former patterns, To be-leeve according to ancient beliefes, to pray according to ancient formes, to preach according to former meditations. God does nothing, man does nothing well, without these Idea's, these retrospects, this re-course to pre-conceptions, pre-deliberations.

Something then I must propose to my selfe, to be the rule, and the   *Via Domini*
390 reason of my present and future actions; which was our first branch

in this second Part; And then the second is, That I can propose nothing more availably, then the contemplation of the history of Gods former proceeding with me; which is *Davids* way here, Because this was Gods way before, I will looke for God in this way still. That language in which God spake to man, the Hebrew, hath no present tense; They forme not their verbs as our Westerne Languages do, in the present, *I heare,* or *I see,* or *I reade,* But they begin at that which is past, *I have seene* and *heard,* and *read.* God carries us in his Language, in his speaking, upon that which is past, upon that which he hath
⁴⁰⁰ done already; I cannot have better security for present, nor future,

August. then Gods former mercies exhibited to me. *Quis non gaudeat,* sayes S. *Augustine,* Who does not triumph with joy, when hee considers what God hath done? *Quis non & ea, quæ nondum venerunt, ventura sperat, propter illa, quæ jam tanta impleta sunt?* Who can doubt of the performance of all, that sees the greatest part of a Prophesie performed? If I have found that true that God hath said, of the person of Antichrist, why should I doubt of that which he sayes of the ruine of Antichrist? *Credamus modicum quod restat,* sayes the same Father, It is much that wee have seene done, and it is but little that God hath
⁴¹⁰ reserved to our faith, to beleeve that it shall be done.

There is no State, no Church, no Man, that hath not this tie upon God, that hath not God in these bands, That God by having done much for them already, hath bound himselfe to doe more. Men proceed in their former wayes, sometimes, lest they should confesse an error, and acknowledge that they had beene in a wrong way. God is obnoxious to no error, and therefore he does still, as he did before. Every one of you can say now to God, Lord, Thou broughtest me hither, therefore enable me to heare; Lord, Thou doest that, therefore make me understand; And that, therefore let me beleeve; And that
⁴²⁰ too, therefore strengthen me to the practise; And all that, therefore continue me to a perseverance. Carry it up to the first sense and apprehension that ever thou hadst of Gods working upon thee, either in thy selfe, when thou camest first to the use of reason, or in others in thy behalfe, in thy baptisme, yet when thou thinkest thou art at the first, God had done something for thee before all that; before that, hee had elected thee, in that election which S. *Augustine* speaks of,

August. *Habet electos, quos creaturus est eligendos,* God hath elected certaine

men, whom he intends to create, that he may elect them; that is, that
he may declare his Election upon them. God had thee, before he
430 made thee; He loved thee first, and then created thee, that thou loving
him, he might continue his love to thee. The surest way, and the
nearest way to lay hold upon God, is the consideration of that which
he had done already. So *David* does; And that which he takes knowledge of, in particular, in Gods former proceedings towards him, is,
Because God had been his helpe, which is our last branch in this part,
Because thou hast beene my helpe.

From this one word, That God hath been my *Helpe,* I make account that we have both these notions; first, That God hath not left
me to my selfe, He hath come to my succour, He hath helped me;
440 And then, That God hath not left out my selfe; He hath been my
Helpe, but he hath left some thing for me to doe with him, and by
his helpe. My security for the future, in this consideration of that
which is past, lyes not onely in this, That God hath delivered me, but
in this also, that he hath delivered me by way of a Helpe, and Helpe
alwayes presumes an endevour and co-operation in him that is
helped. God did not elect me as a helper, nor create me, nor redeeme
me, nor convert me, by way of helping me; for he alone did all, and
he had no use at all of me. God infuses his first grace, the first way,
meerly as a Giver; intirely, all himselfe; but his subsequent graces,
450 as a helper; therefore we call them Auxiliant graces, Helping graces;
and we alwayes receive them, when we endevour to make use of his
former grace. *Lord, I beleeve,* (sayes the Man in the Gospel to Christ)
Helpe mine unbeliefe. If there had not been unbeliefe, weaknesse,
unperfectnesse in that faith, there had needed no helpe; but if there
had not been a Beliefe, a faith, it had not been capable of helpe and
assistance, but it must have been an intire act, without any concurrence on the mans part.

So that if I have truly the testimony of a rectified Conscience, That
God hath helped me, it is in both respects; first, That he hath never
460 forsaken me, and then, That he hath never suffered me to forsake my
selfe; He hath blessed me with that grace, that I trust in no helpe but
his, and with this grace too, That I cannot looke for his helpe, except
I helpe my selfe also. God did not helpe heaven and earth to proceed
out of nothing in the Creation, for they had no possibility of any

Quia
auxilium

Mar. 9.24

disposition towards it; for they had no beeing: But God did helpe the earth to produce grasse, and herbes; for, for that, God had infused a seminall disposition into the earth, which, for all that, it could not have perfected without his farther helpe. As in the making of Woman, there is the very word of our Text, *Gnazar,* God made him a *Helper,* 470 one that was to doe much for him, but not without him. So that then, if I will make Gods former working upon me, an argument of his future gracious purposes, as I must acknowledge that God hath done much for me, so I must finde, that I have done what I could, by the benefit of that grace with him; for God promises to be but a helper.

Psal. 51.15

Lord open thou my lips, sayes *David;* that is Gods worke intirely; And then, *My mouth, My mouth shall shew forth thy praise;* there enters *David* into the worke with God. And then, sayes God to him,

Psal. 81.10

Dilata os tuum, Open thy mouth, (It is now made *Thy mouth,* and therefore doe thou open it) *and I will fill it;* All inchoations and 480 consummations, beginnings and perfectings are of God, of God alone; but in the way there is a concurrence on our part, (by a successive continuation of Gods grace) in which God proceeds as a Helper; and I put him to more then that, if I doe nothing. But if I pray for his helpe, and apprehend and husband his graces well, when they come, then he is truly, properly my helper; and upon that security, that testimony of a rectified Conscience, I can proceed to *Davids* confidence for the future, *Because thou hast been my Helpe, therefore in the shadow of thy wings will I rejoyce;* which is our third, and last generall part.

Divisio.

3 Part

490 In this last part, which is, (after *Davids* aspect, and consideration of his present condition, which was, in the effect, an Exclusion from Gods Temple, And his retrospect, his consideration of Gods former mercies to him, That he had been his Helpe) his prospect, his confidence for the future, we shall stay a little upon these two steps; first, That that which he promises himselfe, is not an immunity from all powerfull enemies, nor a sword of revenge upon those enemies; It is not that he shall have no adversary, nor that that adversary shall be able to doe him no harme, but that he should have a refreshing, a respiration, *In velamento alarum,* under the shadow of Gods wings. 500 And then, (in the second place) That this way which God shall be pleased to take, this manner, this measure of refreshing, which God

shall vouchsafe to afford, (though it amount not to a full deliverance)
must produce a joy, a rejoycing in us; we must not onely not decline
to a murmuring, that we have no more, no nor rest upon a patience
for that which remains, but we must ascend to a holy joy, as if all
were done and accomplished, *In the shadow of thy wings will I
rejoyce.*

First then, lest any man in his dejection of spirit, or of fortune,
should stray into a jealousie or suspition of Gods power to deliver
510 him, As God hath spangled the firmament with starres, so hath he
his Scriptures with names, and Metaphors, and denotations of power.
Sometimes he shines out in the name of a *Sword,* and of a *Target,*
and of a *Wall,* and of a *Tower,* and of a *Rocke,* and of a *Hill;* And
sometimes in that glorious and manifold constellation of all together,
Dominus exercituum, The Lord of Hosts. God, as God, is never represented to us, with Defensive Armes; He needs them not. When
the Poets present their great Heroes, and their Worthies, they alwayes
insist upon their Armes, they spend much of their invention upon
the description of their Armes; both because the greatest valour and
520 strength needs Armes, (*Goliah* himselfe was armed) and because to
expose ones selfe to danger unarmed, is not valour, but rashnesse. But
God is invulnerable in himselfe, and is never represented armed; you
finde no shirts of mayle, no Helmets, no Cuirasses in Gods Armory.
In that one place of *Esay,* where it may seeme to be otherwise, where
God is said *to have put on righteousnesse as a breastplate, and a Helmet of Salvation upon his head;* in that prophecy God is Christ, and
is therefore in that place, called *the Redeemer.* Christ needed defensive armes, God does not. Gods word does; His Scriptures doe; And
therefore S. *Hierome* hath armed them, and set before every booke
530 his *Prologum galeatum,* that prologue that armes and defends every
booke from calumny. But though God need not, nor receive not defensive armes for himselfe, yet God is to us a Helmet, a Breastplate,
a strong tower, a rocke, every thing that may give us assurance and
defence; and as often as he will, he can refresh that Proclamation,
Nolite tangere Christos meos, Our enemies shall not so much as
touch us.

But here, by occasion of his Metaphore in this Text, (*Sub umbra
alarum, In the shadow of thy wings*) we doe not so much consider

*Vmbra
Alarum*

Esay. 59.17

Psal. 105.15

an absolute immunity, That we shall not be touched, as a refreshing
540 and consolation, when we are touched, though we be pinched and
wounded. The Names of God, which are most frequent in the Scriptures, are these three, *Elohim,* and *Adonai,* and *Iehovah;* and to assure
us of his Power to deliver us, two of these three are Names of Power.
Elohim is *Deus fortis,* The mighty, The powerfull God: And (which
deserves a particular consideration) *Elohim* is a plurall Name; It is
not *Deus fortis,* but *Dii fortes,* powerfull Gods. God is all kinde of
Gods; All kinds, which either Idolaters and Gentils can imagine, (as
Riches, or Justice, or Wisdome, or Valour, or such) and all kinds
which God himself hath called gods, (as Princes, and Magistrates,
550 and Prelates, and all that assist and helpe one another) God is *Elohim,*
All these Gods, and all these in their height and best of their power;
for *Elohim,* is *Dii fortes,* Gods in the plurall, and those plurall gods
in their exaltation.

The second Name of God, is a Name of power too, *Adonai.* For,
Adonai is *Dominus,* The Lord, such a Lord, as is Lord and Proprietary
of all his creatures, and all creatures are his creatures; And then,
Dominium est potestas tum utendi, tum abutendi, sayes the law; To
be absolute Lord of any thing, gives that Lord a power to doe what
he will with that thing. God, as he is *Adonai, The Lord,* may give
560 and take, quicken and kill, build and throw downe, where and whom
he will. So then two of Gods three Names are Names of absolute
power, to imprint, and re-imprint an assurance in us, that hee can
absolutely deliver us, and fully revenge us, if he will. But then, his
third Name, and that Name which hee chooses to himselfe, and in
the signification of which Name, hee employes *Moses,* for the reliefe
of his people under Pharaoh, that Name *Iehovah,* is not a Name of
Power, but onely of Essence, of Being, of Subsistence, and yet in the
vertue of that Name, God relieved his people. And if, in my afflictions,
God vouchsafe to visit mee in that Name, to preserve me in my being,
570 in my subsistence in him, that I be not shaked out of him, disinherited
in him, excommunicate from him, devested of him, annihilated
towards him, let him, at his good pleasure, reserve his *Elohim,* and
his *Adonai,* the exercises and declarations of his mighty Power, to
those great publike causes, that more concerne his Glory, then any
thing that can befall me; But if he impart his *Iehovah,* enlarge him-

selfe so far towards me, as that I may live, and move, & have my
beeing in him, though I be not instantly delivered, nor mine enemies
absolutely destroyed, yet this is as much as I should promise my selfe,
this is as much as the Holy Ghost intends in this Metaphor, *Sub*
580 *umbra alarum, Vnder the shadow of thy wings,* that is a Refreshing,
a Respiration, a Conservation, a Consolation in all afflictions that are
inflicted upon me.

Yet, is not this Metaphor of *Wings* without a denotation of Power.
As no Act of Gods, though it seeme to imply but spirituall comfort,
is without a denotation of power, (for it is the power of God that
comforts me; To overcome that sadnesse of soule, and that dejection
of spirit, which the Adversary by temporall afflictions would induce
upon me, is an act of his Power) So this Metaphor, *The shadow of*
his wings, (which in this place expresses no more, then consolation
590 and refreshing in misery, and not a powerfull deliverance out of it)
is so often in the Scriptures made a denotation of Power too, as that
we can doubt of no act of power, if we have this shadow of his wings.
For, in this Metaphor of *Wings,* doth the Holy Ghost expresse the
Maritime power, the power of some Nations at Sea, in Navies, (*Woe* Esay. 18.1
to the land shadowing with wings;) that is, that hovers over the world,
and intimidates it with her sailes and ships. In this Metaphor doth
God remember his people, of his powerfull deliverance of them, (*You* Exod. 19.4
have seene what I did unto the Egyptians, and how I bare you on
Eagles wings, and brought you to my selfe.) In this Metaphor doth
600 God threaten his and their enemies, what hee can doe, (*The noise of*
the wings of his Cherubims, are as the noise of great waters, and of an Ezek. 1.24
Army.) So also, what hee will doe, (*Hee shall spread his wings over* Ier. 49.22
Bozrah, and at that day shall the hearts of the mighty men of Edom,
be as the heart of a woman in her pangs.) So that, if I have the
shadow of his wings, I have the earnest of the power of them too; If I
have refreshing, and respiration from them, I am able to say, (as Dan. 3.17
those three Confessors did to *Nebuchadnezzar*) *My God is able to*
deliver me, I am sure he hath power; *And my God will deliver me,*
when it conduces to his glory, I know he will; *But, if he doe not, bee*
610 *it knowne unto thee, O King, we will not serve thy Gods;* Be it
knowne unto thee, O Satan, how long soever God deferre my deliverance, I will not seeke false comforts, the miserable comforts of

this world. I will not, for I need not; for I can subsist under this shadow of these Wings, though I have no more.

Exod. 25.20

The Mercy-seat it selfe was covered with the Cherubims Wings; and who would have more then Mercy? and a Mercy-seat; that is, established, resident Mercy, permanent and perpetuall Mercy; present and familiar Mercy; a Mercy-seat. Our Saviour Christ intends as much as would have served their turne, if they had laid hold upon it,

Matt. 23.37

⁶²⁰ when hee sayes, *That hee would have gathered Ierusalem, as a henne gathers her chickens under her wings.* And though the other Prophets doe (as ye have heard) mingle the signification of Power, and actuall deliverance, in this Metaphor of Wings, yet our Prophet, whom wee have now in especiall consideration, *David,* never doth so; but in every place where hee uses this Metaphor of Wings (which are in five or sixe severall Psalmes) still hee rests and determines in that sense, which is his meaning here; That though God doe not actually deliver us, nor actually destroy our enemies, yet if hee refresh us in the shadow of his Wings, if he maintaine our subsistence (which is a ⁶³⁰ religious Constancy) in him, this should not onely establish our patience, (for that is but halfe the worke) but it should also produce a joy, and rise to an exultation, which is our last circumstance, *Therefore in the shadow of thy wings, I will rejoice.*

Gaudium

I would always raise your hearts, and dilate your hearts, to a holy Joy, to a joy in the Holy Ghost. There may be a just feare, that men doe not grieve enough for their sinnes; but there may bee a just jealousie, and suspition too, that they may fall into inordinate griefe, and diffidence of Gods mercy; And God hath reserved us to such times, as being the later times, give us even the dregs and lees of ⁶⁴⁰ misery to drinke. For, God hath not onely let loose into the world a new spirituall disease; which is, an equality, and an indifferency, which religion our children, or our servants, or our companions professe; (I would not keepe company with a man that thought me a knave, or a traitor; with him that thought I loved not my Prince, or were a faithlesse man, not to be beleeved, I would not associate my selfe; And yet I will make him my bosome companion, that thinks I doe not love God, that thinks I cannot be saved) but God hath accompanied, and complicated almost all our bodily diseases of these times, with an extraordinary sadnesse, a predominant melancholy,

⁶⁵⁰ a faintnesse of heart, a chearlesnesse, a joylesnesse of spirit, and therefore I returne often to this endeavor of raising your hearts, dilating
your hearts with a holy Joy, Joy in the holy Ghost, for *Vnder the
shadow of his wings,* you may, you should, *rejoyce.*

If you looke upon this world in a Map, you find two Hemisphears,
two half worlds. If you crush heaven into a Map, you may find two
Hemisphears too, two half heavens; Halfe will be Joy, and halfe will
be Glory; for in these two, the joy of heaven, and the glory of heaven,
is all heaven often represented unto us. And as of those two Hemisphears of the world, the first hath been knowne long before, but the
⁶⁶⁰ other, (that of America, which is the richer in treasure) God reserved
for later Discoveries; So though he reserve that Hemisphear of heaven,
which is the Glory thereof, to the Resurrection, yet the other Hemisphear, the Joy of heaven, God opens to our Discovery, and delivers
for our habitation even whilst we dwell in this world. As God hath
cast upon the unrepentant sinner two deaths, a temporall, and a
spirituall death, so hath he breathed into us two lives; for so, as the
word for death is doubled, *Morte morieris, Thou shalt die the death,*   Gen. 2.17
so is the word for life expressed in the plurall, *Chaiim, vitarum, God
breathed into his nostrils the breath of lives,* of divers lives. Though
⁶⁷⁰ our naturall life were no life, but rather a continuall dying, yet we
have two lives besides that, an eternall life reserved for heaven, but
yet a heavenly life too, a spirituall life, even in this world; And as
God doth thus inflict two deaths, and infuse two lives, so doth he also
passe two Judgements upon man, or rather repeats the same Judgement twice. For, that which Christ shall say to thy soule then at the
last Judgement, *Enter into thy Masters joy,* Hee sayes to thy conscience   Matt. 25.23
now, *Enter into thy Masters joy.* The everlastingnesse of the joy is
the blessednesse of the next life, but the entring, the inchoation is
afforded here. For that which Christ shall say then to us, *Venite*   Verse 34
⁶⁸⁰ *benedicti, Come ye blessed,* are words intended to persons that are
comming, that are upon the way, though not at home; Here in this
world he bids us *Come,* there in the next, he shall bid us *Welcome.*
The Angels of heaven have joy in thy conversion, and canst thou bee   Luk. 15.10
without that joy in thy selfe? If thou desire revenge upon thine
enemies, as they are Gods enemies, That God would bee pleased to
remove, and root out all such as oppose him, that Affection apper-

taines to Glory; Let that alone till thou come to the Hemisphear of

Revel. 6.10 Glory; There joyne with those Martyrs under the Altar, *Vsquequo Domine,* How long O Lord, dost thou deferre Judgement? and thou
690 shalt have thine answere there for that. Whilst thou art here, here joyne with *David,* and the other Saints of God, in that holy increpation

Psal. 42.5 of a dangerous sadnesse, *Why art thou cast downe O my soule? why art thou disquieted in mee?* That soule that is dissected and anatomized to God, in a sincere confession, washed in the teares of true contrition, embalmed in the blood of reconciliation, the blood of Christ Jesus, can assigne no reason, can give no just answer to that Interrogatory, *Why art thou cast downe O my soule? why art thou disquieted in me?* No man is so little, as that he can be lost under these wings, no man so great, as that they cannot reach to him;

August. 700 *Semper ille major est, quantumcumque creverimus,* To what temporall, to what spirituall greatnesse soever wee grow, still pray wee him to shadow us under his Wings; for the poore need those wings against oppression, and the rich against envy. The Holy Ghost, who is a Dove, shadowed the whole world under his wings; *Incubabat aquis,* He hovered over the waters, he sate upon the waters, and he hatched all that was produced, and all that was produced so, was good. Be thou a Mother where the Holy Ghost would be a Father; Conceive by him; and be content that he produce joy in thy heart here. First thinke, that as a man must have some land, or els he cannot be in
710 wardship, so a man must have some of the love of God, or els he could not fall under Gods correction; God would not give him his physick, God would not study his cure, if he cared not for him. And then thinke also, that if God afford thee the shadow of his wings, that is, Consolation, respiration, refreshing, though not a present, and plenary deliverance, in thy afflictions, not to thanke God, is a murmuring, and not to rejoyce in Gods wayes, is an unthankfulnesse. Howling is the noyse of hell, singing the voyce of heaven; Sadnesse the damp of Hell, Rejoycing the serenity of Heaven. And he that hath not this joy here, lacks one of the best pieces of his evidence for the
720 joyes of heaven; and hath neglected or refused that Earnest, by which God uses to binde his bargaine, that true joy in this world shall flow into the joy of Heaven, as a River flowes into the Sea; This joy shall not be put out in death, and a new joy kindled in me in Heaven; But

as my soule, as soone as it is out of my body, is in Heaven, and does not stay for the possession of Heaven, nor for the fruition of the sight of God, till it be ascended through ayre, and fire, and Moone, and Sun, and Planets, and Firmament, to that place which we conceive to be Heaven, but without the thousandth part of a minutes stop, as soone as it issues, is in a glorious light, which is Heaven, (for all the way to
730 Heaven is Heaven; And as those Angels, which came from Heaven hither, bring Heaven with them, and are in Heaven here, So that soule that goes to Heaven, meets Heaven here; and as those Angels doe not devest Heaven by comming, so these soules invest Heaven, in their going.) As my soule shall not goe towards Heaven, but goe by Heaven to Heaven, to the Heaven of Heavens, So the true joy of a good soule in this world is the very joy of Heaven; and we goe thither, not that being without joy, we might have joy infused into us, but that as Christ sayes, *Our joy might be full,* perfected, sealed with an ever- lastingnesse; for, as he promises, *That no man shall take our joy from*
740 *us,* so neither shall Death it selfe take it away, nor so much as inter- rupt it, or discontinue it, But as in the face of Death, when he layes hold upon me, and in the face of the Devill, when he attempts me, I shall see the face of God, (for, every thing shall be a glasse, to reflect God upon me) so in the agonies of Death, in the anguish of that dis- solution, in the sorrowes of that valediction, in the irreversiblenesse of that transmigration, I shall have a joy, which shall no more evap- orate, then my soule shall evaporate, A joy, that shall passe up, and put on a more glorious garment above, and be joy super-invested in glory. *Amen.*

Iohn 16.24
22

The third of my Prebend Sermons upon my five Psalmes:
Preached at S. Pauls, November 5. 1626. In Vesperis.

Psal. 64.10. *And all the upright in heart shall glory.*

IHave had occasion to tell you more then once before, that our Predecessors, in the institution of the Service of this Church, have declared such a reverence and such a devotion to this particular Booke of Scripture, The Psalmes, as that by distributing the hundred and fifty Psalmes (of which number the body of this booke consists) into thirty portions, (of which number the body of our Church consists) and assigning to every one of those thirty persons, his five Psalmes, to bee said by him every day, every day God receives from us (howsoever wee be divided from one another in place) the Sacri-
10 fice of Praise, in the whole Booke of Psalmes. And, though we may be absent from this Quire, yet wheresoever dispersed, we make up a Quire in this Service, of saying over all the Psalmes every day. This sixty fourth Psalme, is the third of my five. And when, (according to the obligation which I had laid upon my selfe, to handle in this place some portion of every one of these my five Psalmes) in handling of those words, of the Psalme immediately before this, in the seventh verse, (*Because thou hast beene my helpe, therefore in the shadow of thy Wings I will rejoyce*) I told you, that the next world, Heaven, was (as this world is) divided into two Hemispheares, and
20 that the two Hemispheares of Heaven, were Joy and Glory, (for, in those two notions of Joy and Glory, is Heaven often represented

unto us) as in those words which we handled then, wee sailed about
the first Hemispheare, That of Joy, (*In the shadow of thy Wings
will I rejoyce*) So, in these which I have read to you now, our voyage
lies about the Hemispheare of Glory, for, (*All the upright in heart
shall Glory.*) As we said then of Joy, we say of Glory now; There
is an inchoative joy here, though the consummative joy be reserved
for Heaven; so is there also such a taste, such an inchoation of glory
in this life. And as no man shall come to the joyes of Heaven, that
30 hath no joy in this world, (for, there is no peace of conscience without this joy) so no man shall come to the glory of Heaven, that hath
not a holy ambition of this glory in this world; for, this glory which
we speake of, is the evidence, and the reflexion of the glory from
above; for, the glory of God shines through godly men, and wee
receive a beame and a tincture of that glory of God, when we have
the approbation, and testimony, and good opinion, and good words
of good men; which is the Glory of our Text, as far as this world is
capable of glory. *All the upright in heart shall glory,* that is, They
shall be celebrated and encouraged with the glory and praise of good
40 men here, and they shall be rewarded with everlasting glory in
Heaven.

Divisio   In these words we propose to you but two parts; First, the disposition of the Persons, *Omnes recti corde, All the upright in heart,* and
then, The retribution upon these Persons, *Gloriabuntur, They shall
Glory,* or, (as it is in the Vulgat, and well) *Laudabuntur,* They shall
be celebrated, they shall be praised. In the first, The qualification of
the persons, wee shall passe by these steps; First, that God in his
punishments and rewardings proposes to himselfe Persons, Persons
already made, and qualified. God does not begin at a retribution, nor
50 begin at a condemnation, before he have Persons, Persons fit to be
rewarded, Persons fit to be condemned. God did not first make a
Heaven and a Hell, and after thinke of making man, that he might
have some persons to put in them; but, first for his Glory he made
Man, and for those, who by a good use of his grace preserved their
state, Heaven, and for those, who by their owne fault fell, he made
Hell. First, he proposed Persons, Persons in being; And then, for
the Persons (as his delight is for the most part to doe) in this Text
he expresses it; which is, rather to insist upon the Rewards, which

the Good shall receive, then upon the condemnation and judgements
⁶⁰ of the wicked. If he could chuse, that is, If his owne Glory, and the
edification of his Children would beare it, he would not speake at
all of judgements, or of those persons that draw necessary judgements
upon themselves, but he would exercise our contemplation wholly
upon his mercy, and upon Persons qualified and prepared for his
gracious retributions. So he does here; He speaks not at all of per-
verse, and froward, and sinister, and oblique men, men incapable
of his retributions, but onely of Persons disposed, ordained, prepared
for them.

And, in the qualification of these Persons, he proposes first a recti-
⁷⁰ tude, a directnesse, an uprightnesse; declinations downeward, deviations upon the wrong hand, squint-eyed men, splay-footed men, left-
handed men, (in a spirituall sense) he meddles not withall. They
must be direct, and upright; And then, *upright in heart;* for, to be
good to ill ends, (as, in many cases, a man may be) God accepts not,
regards not. But, let him be a person thus qualified, *Vpright;* upright because he loves uprightnesse, *Vpright in heart;* And then, he is
infallibly imbraced, and enwrapped in that generall rule, and proposition, that admits no exception, *Omnes recti corde,* All the upright
in heart shall be partakers of this retribution: And in these branches
⁸⁰ we shall determine our first Part; first, That God proposes to himselfe Persons; Persons thus and thus qualified; he begins at them.
Secondly, That God had rather dwell himselfe, and propose to us
the consideration of good persons, then bad, of his mercies, then his
judgements, for he mentions no other here, but persons capable of
his retributions; And then, the goodnesse that God considers, is
rectitude, and rectitude in the roote, in the heart; And from that
roote growes that spreading universality, that infallibility, *Omnes,*
All such are sure of the Reward.

And then, in our second Part, in the Reward it selfe, though it be
⁹⁰ delivered here in the whole barre, in the Ingot, in the Wedge, in
Bulloyn, in one single word, *Gloriabuntur, Laudabuntur, They shall
Glory,* yet it admits this Mintage, and coyning, and issuing in lesser
pieces, That first we consider the thing it selfe, The metall in which
God rewards us, Glory, Praise; And then, since Gods promise is
fastened upon that, (We shall be praised) As we may lawfully seeke

the praise of good men, so must wee also willingly afford praise to good men, and to good actions. And then, since we finde this retribution fixed in the future, (We shall be praised, we shall be in glory) there arises this Consolation, That though we have it not yet, yet we shall have it, Though wee be in dishonour, and contempt, and under a cloud, of which we see no end our selves, yet there is a determined future in God, which shall be made present, we shall overcome this contempt, and *Gloriabimur,* and *Laudabimur,* we shall Glory, we shall be celebrated; In which future, the consolation is thus much farther exalted, that it is an everlasting future; the glory, and praise, the approbation, and acclamation, which we shall receive from good men, here, shall flow out and continue, to the *Hosannaes* in Heaven, in the mouth of Saints, and Angels, and to the *Euge bone serve, Well done, good and faithfull Servant,* in the mouth of God himselfe.

First then, God proposes to himselfe, (in his Rewards and Retributions) Persons; Persons disposed and qualified. Not disposed by nature, without use of grace; that is flat and full Pelagianisme; Not disposed by preventing grace, without use of subsequent grace, by Antecedent and anticipant, without concomitant and auxiliant grace; that is Semi-pelagianisme. But persons obsequious to his grace, when it comes, and persons industrious and ambitious of more and more grace, and husbanding his grace well all the way, such persons God proposes to himselfe. God does not onely reade his own works, nor is he onely delighted with that which he hath writ himselfe, with his own eternall Decrees in heaven, but he loves also to reade our books too, our histories which we compose in our lives and actions, and as *his delight is to be with the sonnes of men,* so his study is in this Library, to know what we doe. S. *Paul* says, *That God made him a Minister of the Gospel, to preach to the Gentils, to the intent that the Angels might know the manifold wisdome of God by the Church;* That is, by that that was done in the Church. The Angels saw God; Did they not see these things in God? No; for, *These things were hid in God,* sayes the Apostle there; And the Angels see no more in God, then God reveales unto them; and these things of the Church, God reserved to a future, and to an experimentall knowledge, to be knowne then when they were done in the Church. So there are Decrees in God, but they are hid in God; To this purpose

Margin notes:

Mat. 25.21

1 Part.
*Personæ
qualifi-
catæ*

Pro. 8.31

Ephes. 3.7

and entendment, and in this sense, hid from God himselfe, that God
accepts or condemnes Man *Secundum allegata & Probata,* according
to the Evidence that arises from us, and not according to those Records that are hid in himselfe. Our actions and his Records agree; we
doe those things which he hath Decreed; but onely our doing them,
and not his Decreeing them, hath the nature of evidence. God does
not Reward, nor Condemne out of his Decrees, but out of our ac-
140 tions. God sent downe his Commissioners the Angels to Sodome, to
inquire, and to informe him how things went. God goes down
himselfe to inquire, and informe himselfe, how it stood with *Adam*
and *Eve.* Not that God was ever ignorant of any thing concerning
us, but that God would prevent that dangerous imagination in every
man, That God should first meane to destroy him, and then to make
him, that he might destroy him, without having any evidence against
him. For God made man *Ad imaginem suam,* To his owne Image.
If he had made him under an inevitable, and irresistible necessity of
damnation, he had made him *Ad Imaginem Diabolicam,* to the
150 Image of the Devill, and not to his own. God goes not out as a
Fowler, that for his pleasure and recreation, or for his commodity,
or commendation, would kill, and therefore seeks out game that he
may kill it; It is not God *that seeks whom he may devoure:* But God
sees the Vulture tearing his Chickens, or other birds picking his
Corne, or pecking his fruit, and then when they are in that mischievous action, God takes his bowe and shoots them for that. When
God condemns a man, he proposes not that man to himselfe, as he
meant to make him, and as he did make him, but as by his sinnes
he hath made himselfe. At the first Creation, God looked upon
160 nothing; there was nothing; But ever since there have been Creatures, God hath looked upon the Creature: and as *Adam* gave every
Creature the Name, according as he saw the Nature thereof to be;
so God gives every man reward or punishment, the name of a Saint
or a Devill, in his purpose, as he sees him a good or a bad user of
his graces. When I shall come to the sight of the Booke of life, and
the Records of Heaven, amongst the Reprobate, I shall never see the
name of *Cain* alone, but *Cain* with his addition, *Cain that killed his
brother;* Nor *Iudas* name alone; but *Iudas* with his addition, *Iudas
that betrayed his Master.* God does not begin with a *morte morien-*

Gen. 18.16
Gen. 3.9

I Pet. 5.8

Levit. 26.16

¹⁷⁰ *dum,* some body must die, and therefore I will make some body to kill; But God came to a *morte morieris,* yet thou art alive, and mayest live, but if thou wilt rebell, thou must die. God did not call up feavers, and pestilence, and consumptions, and fire, and famine, and warre, and then make man, that he might throw him into their mouths, but when man threw downe himselfe, God let him fall into their mouths. Had I never sinned in wantonnesse, I should never have had consumption; nor feaver, if I had not sinned in Riot; nor death, if I had not transgressed against the Lord of life. If God be pleased to looke upon me, at the last day, as I am renewed in Christ, ¹⁸⁰ I am safe. But if God should looke upon me, (as he made me) in *Adam,* I could not be un-acceptable in his sight, except he looked farther, and saw me in mine own, or in *Adams* sin. I would never wish my selfe better, then God wished me at first; no, nor then God wishes me now, as manifold a sinner as he sees me now, if yet I would conforme my will to his. God looks upon persons; persons so conditioned as they were, which was our first branch, in this first part; and our second is, That he delights to propose to himselfe Persons that are capable of his rewards; for he mentions no others in this place, *All that are upright in heart.*

Insistit in bonis

¹⁹⁰ The first thing that *Moses* names to have been made, was Heaven, (*In the beginning God made Heaven and Earth*) And infinite millions of generations before this Heaven was made, there was a Heaven, an eternall emanation of beams of glory, from the presence of God. But *Moses* tells us of no Hell made at the Creation; And before the Creation, such a Hell, as there was a Heaven, there could not be; for, the presence of God made Heaven; and God was equally present every where. And they who have multiplied Hells unto us, and made more Hells then God hath made, more by their two Limboes, (one for Fathers, another for Children) and one Purga- ²⁰⁰ tory, have yet made their new Hells, more of the nature of Heaven then of Hell. For, in one of their Limboes, (that of the Fathers) and in their Purgatory, there is in them, who are there, an infallible assurance of Heaven, They that are there, are infallibly assured to come to Heaven; And an assurance of salvation will hardly consist with Hell; He that is sure to come to Heaven, can hardly be said to be in Hell.

God was loath and late in making places of torment; He is loath
to speake of Judgements, or of those that extort Judgements from
him. How plentifully, how abundantly is the word *Beatus, Blessed,*
210 multiplied in the Booke of Psalmes? Blessed, and Blessed in every
Psalme, in every Verse; The Booke seems to be made out of that
word, *Blessed,* And the foundation raysed upon that word, *Blessed,*
for it is the first word of the Booke. But in all the Booke, there is not
one *Væ,* not one *woe,* so denounced; Not one *woe,* upon any soule
in that Booke. And when this *Væ,* this *woe* is denounced in some
other of the Prophets, it is very often *Vox dolentis,* and not *Incre-
pantis,* That *Væ,* that *woe,* is a voyce of compassion in him that
speaks it, and not of destruction to them to whom it is spoken. God,
in the person of *Ieremy,* weeps in contemplation of the calamities
220 threatned, *Oh that my head were waters, and mine eyes a fountaine*   Jerem. 9.1
of teares, that I might weepe day and night for the slaine of the
Daughter of my people. It is God that was their Father, and it is
God, their God that slew them; but yet, that God, their Father
weepes over the slaughter. So in the person of *Esay,* God weeps
againe, *I will bewaile thee with weeping, and I will water thee with*   Esay. 16.9
teares. And without putting on the person of any man, God himselfe avowes his sighing, when he comes to name Judgements, *Heu,*   Esay. 1.24
vindicabor, Alas, I will revenge me of mine enemies; And he sighs,
when he comes but to name their sinnes, *Heu abominationes,*   Ezek. 6.11
230 *Alas, for all the evill abominations of the house of Israel.* As though
God had contracted an Irregularity, by having to doe in a cause of
blood, He sighs, he weeps when he must draw blood from them.
God delights to institute his discourses, and to take, and to make his
Examples, from men that stand in state of grace, and are capable of
his Mercies, and his Retributions, as here in this Text, he names onely
those, who are *Recti corde, The upright in heart,* They shall be considered, rewarded.

The disposition that God proposes here in those persons, whom he   *Recti*
considers, is Rectitude, Uprightnesse, and Directnesse. God hath
240 given Man that forme in nature, much more in grace, that he should
be upright, and looke up, and contemplate Heaven, and God there.
And therefore to bend downwards upon the earth, to fix our breast,
our heart to the earth, to lick the dust of the earth with the Serpent,

to inhere upon the profits and pleasures of the earth, and to make that which God intended for our way, and our rise to heaven, (the blessings of this world) the way to hell; this is a manifest Declination from this Uprightnesse, from this Rectitude. Nay, to goe so far towards the love of the earth, as to be in love with the grave, to be impatient of the calamities of this life, and murmur at Gods detain-
250 ing us in this prison, to sinke into a sordid melancholy, or irreligious dejection of spirit; this is also a Declination from this Rectitude, this Uprightnesse. So is it too, to decline towards the left hand, to Modifications, and Temporisings in matter or forme of Religion, and to thinke all indifferent, all one; or to decline towards the right hand, in an over-vehement zeale, To pardon no errors, to abate nothing of heresie, if a man beleeve not all, and just all that we beleeve; To abate nothing of Reprobation, if a man live not just as we live; this is also a Diversion, a Deviation, a Deflection, a Defection from this Rectitude, this Uprightnesse. For, the word of this Text, *Iashar,*
260 signifies *Rectitudinem,* and *Planiciem;* It signifies a direct way; for, the Devils way was Circular, Compassing the Earth; But the Angels way to heaven upon *Iacobs* ladder, was a straight, a direct way. And then it signifies, as a direct and straight, so a plaine, a smooth, an even way, a way that hath been beaten into a path before, a way that the Fathers, and the Church have walked in before, and not a discovery made by our curiosity, or our confidence, in venturing from our selves, or embracing from others, new doctrines and opinions.

Recti
Corde

The persons then, whom God proposes here to be partakers of his Retributions, are first *Recti,* (that is, both Direct men, and Plaine
270 men) and then *recti corde,* this qualification, this straightnesse, and smoothenesse must be in the heart; All the upright in heart shall have it. Upon this earth, a man cannot possibly make one step in a straight, and a direct line. The earth it selfe being round, every step wee make upon it, must necessarily bee a segment, an arch of a circle. But yet though no piece of a circle be a straight line, yet if we take any piece, nay if wee take the whole circle, there is no corner, no angle in any piece, in any intire circle. A perfect rectitude we cannot have in any wayes in this world; In every Calling there are some inevitable tentations. But, though wee cannot make up our circle of a straight line,
280 (that is impossible to humane frailty) yet wee may passe on, without

angles, and corners, that is, without disguises in our Religion, and
without the love of craft, and falsehood, and circumvention in our
civill actions. A Compasse is a necessary thing in a Ship, and the
helpe of that Compasse brings the Ship home safe, and yet that Compasse hath some variations, it doth not looke directly North; Neither
is that starre which we call the North-pole, or by which we know the
North-pole, the very Pole it selfe; but we call it so, and we make our
uses of it, and our conclusions by it, as if it were so, because it is the
neerest starre to that Pole. He that comes as neere uprightnesse, as
290 infirmities admit, is an upright man, though he have some obliquities.
To God himselfe we may alwayes go in a direct line, a straight, a
perpendicular line; For God is verticall to me, over my head now,
and verticall now to them, that are in the East, and West-Indies; To
our Antipodes, to them that are under our feet, God is verticall, over
their heads, then when he is over ours.

To come to God there is a straight line for every man every where:
But this we doe not, if we come not with our heart. *Præbe mihi fili*   Pro. 23.26
cor tuum, saith God, *My sonne give me thy heart.* Was hee his sonne,
and had hee not his heart? That may very well bee. There is a filia-
300 tion without the heart; not such a filiation, as shall ever make him
partaker of the inheritance, but yet a filiation. The associating our
selves to the sonnes of God, in an outward profession of Religion,
makes us so farre the sonnes of God, as that the judgement of man
cannot, and the judgement of God doth not distinguish them. Because, then when the sonnes of God stood in his presence, Satan stood   Iob 1.6
amongst the sons of God; God doth not disavow him, God doth not
excommunicate him, God makes his use of him, and yet God knew
his heart was farre from him. So, when God was in Councell with
his Angels, about *Ahabs* going up to Ramoth Gilead, A spirit came   1 King. 22.22
310 forth and offered his service, and God refuses not his service, but
employes him, though hee knew his heart to be farre from him. So,
no doubt, many times, they to whom God hath committed supreme
government, and they who receive beames of this power by subordina-
tion, and delegation from them, they see Satan amongst the sonnes
of God, hypocrites and impiously disposed men come into these
places of holy convocation, and they suffer them, nay they employ
them, nay they preferre them, and yet they know their hearts are

farre from them; but as long as they stand amongst the sonnes of
God, that is, appeare and conforme themselves in the outward acts of
320 Religion, they are not disavowed, they are not ejected: by us here,
they are not. But howsoever wee date our Excommunications against
them, but from an overt act, and apparant disobedience, yet in the
Records of heaven, they shall meet an Excommunication, and a conviction of Recusancy, that shall beare date from that day, when they
came first to Church, with that purpose to delude the Congregation,
to elude the lawes in that behalfe provided, to advance their treacher-
ous designes by such disguises, or upon what other collaterall and
indirect occasion soever, men come to this place: for, though they bee
in the right way, when they are here, at Church, yet because they are
330 not upright in heart, therefore that right way brings not them to the
right end.

And that is it which *David* lookes upon in God, and desires that

2 Sam. 7.21   God should looke upon in him; *(According to thine owne heart,* saith
David to God, *hast thou done all these great things unto us)* (For,
sometimes God doth give temporall blessings to men, upon whom he
hath not set his heart) And then in the 27. Verse he sayes, (*Therefore
hath thy servant found in his heart, to pray this prayer unto thee*) If
he had onely found it in the Liturgy, and in the manner of the
Service of that Church, to which hee came with an ill will, and
340 against his heart, he would not have prayed that prayer, nay he would
not have come to that Church. For, though *David* place a great joy in

Psal. 35.18   that, (*That he can come to praise God in the Congregation, and in*
40.10   *the great Congregation*) And though *David* seeme even to determine
Gods presence in the Church, (for he multiplies that expostulation,
that adprecation many times, *When shall I come, in conspectum
tuum, into thy presence?* And, *Restore me, O Lord, conspectui tuo,
to thy presence,* Hee was not right, not in the right way, if he came
not to Church) yet there is a case in which *David* glories in, though

Psal. 119.11   (as hee saith there) *In corde meo abscondi eloquium tuum, Thy word*
350 *have I hidden,* locked up, *in my heart.* Though in another, in many

Psal. 40.10   other places, he rejoyce in that, (*I have not hid thy righteousnesse in
my heart, I have not concealed thy truth from the great Congrega-
tion*) yet here he glories in his *Abscondi,* I have hid it. Which, (as
both S. *Hilary,* and S. *Ambrose* referre it to a discreet and seasonable

suppressing of the mysteries of Religion, and not to cast pearles before swine) may also inferre this Instruction; That a man were better serve God at home, (though not in so right a way, if he thinke it right) then to come hither against his heart, and conscience. Not, but that there is better meanes of receiving good here, then at home in private prayer, (though made the right way) But his end in comming is not to make this meanes his way to that good; And therefore his very being here, (though hee be thereby in the right way) because it comes not from an upright heart, as it is a greater danger to us, who are deluded by their hypocriticall conformity, so is it a greater sinne to them, who come so against their conscience. *David* prayes thus, *Incola sum, ne abscondas, I am a stranger, hide not thy commandements from mee,* (Let me not be a stranger at Church, at thy Service.) And so it behooves us to pray too, That those Doores, and those Books may alwayes bee open unto us; But yet I will say with *David* too, *Abscondam eloquium,* where I am a stranger, and in a place of strange, and superstitious worship, I will hide my religion so farre, as not to communicate with others, in a service against my heart; It is not safe for us to trust our selves at a superstitious Service, though curiosity, or company, or dependency upon others draw us thither; neither is it safe to trust all that come hither, if their hearts be not here. For the Retribution of our Text, that is, Thanks and Praise, belongs onely to them, who are Right, and Right of heart, and to them it is made due, and infallible, by this promise from God, and made universall, *Omnes, All the upright in heart shall glory.*

How often God admits into his owne Name, this addition of Universality, *Omne, All,* as though he would be knowne by that especially. He is Omnipotent, There he can doe All; He is Omniscient, There he can know All; Hee is Omnipresent, There he can direct All. Neither doth God extend himselfe to all, that he may gather from all, but that he may gather all, and all might meet in him, and enjoy him. So, God is all Center, as that hee looks to all, and so, all circumference, as that hee embraces all. The Sunne works upon things that he sees not, (as Mynes in the wombe of the earth) and so works the lesse perfectly. God sees all, and works upon all, and desires perfection in all. There is no one word so often in the Bible, as this, *Omne, All.* Neither hath God spread the word more liberally

Psal. 119.19

Omnes

upon all the lines of this Booke, then he hath his gracious purposes upon all the soules of men. And therefore, to withdraw Gods generall goodnesse out of his generall propositions, That he would have all repent, That he came to save all, is to contract and abridge God himselfe, in his most extensive Attribute, or Denotation, that is, his Mercy: And as there is a curse laid upon them, that take away any part, any proposition out of this Booke, so may there be a curse, or an ill affection, and countenance and suspicion from God, that presses

⁴⁰⁰ any of his general propositions to a narrower, and lesse gracious sense then God meant in it. It were as easily beleeved, that God lookes towards no man, as that there should be any man (in whom he sees, that is, considers no sin) that he lookes not towards. I could as easily doubt of the universall providence of God, as of the universall mercy of God, if man continued not in rebellion, and in opposition. If I can say, by way of confession, and accusing my selfe, Lord, my wayes have not beene right, nor my heart right, there is yet mercy for mee. But, to them who have studied and accustomed themselves to this uprightnesse of heart, there is mercy in that exaltation, mercy in the

⁴¹⁰ nature of a Reward, of a Retribution; And this Retribution expressed here, in this word *Glory,* constitutes our second Part, *All the upright in heart shall Glory.*

2 Part.   This Retribution is expressed in the Originall, in the word *Halal;*
Laus   And *Halal,* to those Translators that made up our Booke of Common Prayer, presented the signification of *Gladnesse,* for so it is there, *They shall be glad;* So it did to the Translators that came after, for there it is, *They shall rejoyce;* And to our last Translators it seemed to signifie *Glory, They shall Glory,* say they. But the first Translation of all into our Language (which was long before any of these three)

⁴²⁰ cals it *Praise,* and puts it in the Passive, *All men of rightfull heart shall be praised.* He followed S. *Hierom,* who reads it so, and interprets it so, in the Passive, *Laudabuntur, They shall be praised.* And so truly *Iithhalelu,* in the Original, beares it, nay requires it; which is not of a praise that they shall give to God, but of a praise, that they shall receive for having served God with an upright heart; not that they shall praise God in doing so, but that godly men shall praise them for having done so. All this will grow naturally out of the roote; for, the roote of this word, is *Lucere, Splendere,* To shine out in the

eyes of men, and to create in them a holy and a reverentiall admira-
430 tion, as it was *Iohn Baptists* praise, That he was *A burning, and a
shining Lampe.* Properly it is, by a good and a holy exemplary life, to
occasion others to set a right value upon Holinesse, and to give a due
respect to holy men. For so, where we read, *Their Maidens were not*   Psal. 78.63
given in Marriage, we finde this word of our Text, *Their Maidens
were not praised,* that is, there was not a due respect held of them, nor
a just value set upon them.

So that, this retribution intended for the upright in heart, as in the
growth and extension of the word, it reaches to Joy, and Glory, and
Eminency, and Respect, so in the roote, it signifies Praise; And it is
440 given them by God, as a Reward, That they shall be *Praised;* now,
Praise (sayes the Philosopher) is *Sermo elucidans magnitudinem
virtutis;* It is the good word of good men, a good testimony given by
good men of good actions. And this difference we use to assigne betweene Praise, and Honour, *Laus est in ordine ad finem, Honor
eorum qui jam in fine;* Praise is an encouragement to them that are
in the way, and so far, a Reward, a Reward of good beginnings;
Honour is reserved to the end, to crowne their constancy, and perseverance. And therefore, where men are rewarded with great honours
at the beginning, in hope they will deserve it, they are paid before-
450 hand. Thanks, and Grace, and good countenance, and Praise, are
interlocutory encouragements, Honours are finall Rewards. But, since
Praise is a part of Gods retribution, a part of his promise in our text,
They shall be praised, we are thereby not onely allowed, but bound to
seeke this praise from good men, and to give this praise to good men;
for, in this Coine God hath promised, that the upright in heart shall
be paid, *They shall be praised.*

To seeke praise from good men, by good meanes, is but the same   *Laus à bonis*
thing which is recommended to us by *Solomon, A good name is   quærenda*
rather to be chosen, then great riches, and loving favour, then silver and Prov. 22.1
460 *Gold.* For, *Habent & mores colores suos, habent & odores;* Our good   Bernar.
works have a colour, and they have a savor; we see their Candor,
their sincerity in our owne consciences, there is their colour; (for, in
our owne consciences our works appeare in their true colours; no
man can be an hypocrite to himselfe, nor seriously, deliberately deceive himselfe) And, when others give allowance of our works, and

are edified by them, there is their savour, their odor, their perfume,
their fragrancy. And therefore S. *Hierom,* and S. *Augustin* differ
little in their manner of expressing this, *Non paratum habeas illud è*
trivio, Serve not thy selfe with that triviall, and vulgar saying, As
⁴⁷⁰ long as my conscience testifies well to me, I care not what men say

of me; And so sayes that other Father, They that rest in the testimony
of their owne consciences, and contemne the opinion of other men,
Imprudenter agunt, & crudeliter, They deale weakly, and improvi-
dently for themselves, in that they assist not their consciences, with
more witnesses, And they deale cruelly towards others, in that they
provide not for their edification, by the knowledge and manifestation
of their good works. For, (as he adds well there) *Qui à criminibus*
vitam custodit, bene facit, He that is innocent in his owne heart, does
well for himselfe, but *Qui famam custodit, & in alios misericors est,*
⁴⁸⁰ He that is known to live well, he that hath the praise of good men, to
bee a good man, is mercifull, in an exemplary life, to others, and
promoves their salvation. For, when that Father gives a measure, how
much praise a man may receive, and a rule, how he may receive it,
when he hath first said, *Nec totum, nec nihil accipiatur,* Receive not
all, but yet refuse not all praise, he adds this, That that which is to
be received, is not to be received for our owne sakes, *sed propter illos,*
quibus consulere non potest, si nimia dejectione vilescat, but for their
sakes, who would undervalue goodnesse it selfe, if good men did too
much undervalue themselves, or thought themselves never the better
⁴⁹⁰ for their goodnesse. And therefore S. *Bernard* applies that in the

Proverbs to this case; *Hast thou found Honey? eate that which is*
sufficient. Mellis nomine, favor humanæ laudis, sayes he, By Honey,
favour, and praise, and thankfulnesse is meant; *Meritóque non ab*
omni, sed ab immoderato edulio prohibemur, We are not forbid to
taste, nor to eate, but to surfet of this Honey, of this praise of men.
S. *Augustine* found this love of praise in himselfe, and could forbid it
no man, *Laudari à bene viventibus, si dicam, nolo, mentior,* If I
should say, that I desired not the praise of good men, I should belie
my selfe. He carries it higher then thus: He does not doubt, but that
⁵⁰⁰ the Apostles themselves had a holy joy, and complacency, when their
Preaching was acceptable, and thereby effectuall upon the Congregation. Such a love of praise is rooted in Nature; and Grace destroyes

not Nature; Grace extinguishes not, but moderates this love of praise in us, nor takes away the matter, but onely exhibits the measure. Certainly, he that hath not some desire of praise, will bee negligent in doing praise-worthy things; and negligent in another duty intended here too, that is, To praise good men, which is also another particular branch in this Part.

The hundred forty fift Psalme is, in the Title thereof, called *A*
510 *Psalme of Praise;* And the Rabbins call him *Filium futuri Seculi,* A child of the next World, that sayes that Psalme thrice a day. We will interpret it, by way of Accommodation, thus, that he is a child of the next World, that directs his Praise every day, upon three objects, upon God, upon himselfe, upon other men. Of God, there can be no question; And for our selves, it is truly the most proper, and most literall signification of this word in our Text, *Iithhalelu,* That they shall praise themselves, that is, They shall have the testimony of a rectified conscience, that they have deserved the praise of good men, in having done laudible service to God. And then, for others, That which God
520 promises to Israel in their restauration, belongs to all the Israel of the Lord, to all the faithfull, *I will get thee praise, and fame in every land, and I will make thee a name, and a praise amongst all the people of the earth.* This, God will doe; procure them a name, a glory: By whom? When God bindes himselfe, he takes us into the band with him, and when God makes himselfe the debtor, he makes us stewards; when he promises them praise, he meanes that we should give them that praise. Be all waies of flatterings, and humourings of great persons precluded with a Protestation, with a detestation; Be *Philo Iudæus* his comparison received, His *Coquus,* and his *Medicus,*
530 One provides sweetnesse for the present taste, but he is but a Cooke, The other is a Physitian, and though by bitter things, provides for thy future health; And such is the hony of Flatterers, and such is the wormewood of better Counsellors. I will not shake a Proverbe, not the *Ad Corvos,* That wee were better admit the Crowes, that picke out our eyes, after we are dead, then Flatterers that blinde us, whilst we live; I cast justly upon others, I take willingly upon my selfe, the name of wicked, (if I blesse the covetous whom the Lord abhorreth) or any other whom he hath declared to be odious to him. But making my object goodnesse in that man, and taking that goodnesse in that

Laus danda aliis

Zephan. 3.19

⁵⁴⁰ man, to be a Candle, set up by God in that Candlesticke, God having engaged himselfe, that that good man shall be praised, I will be a Subsidy man so far, so far pay Gods debts, as to celebrate with condigne praise the goodnesse of that man; for, in that, I doe, as I should desire to be done to, And in that, I pay a debt to that man, And in that I succour their weaknesse, who, (as S. *Gregory* sayes) when they heare another praised, *Si non amore virtutis, at delectatione laudis accenduntur,* At first for the love of Praise, but after, for the love of goodnesse it selfe, are drawne to bee good. For, when the Apostle had directed the Philippians upon things that were *True,* and *honest,* and ⁵⁵⁰ *just,* and *pure,* and *lovely,* and *of a good report,* he ends all thus, *If there be any vertue, and if there be any praise, thinke on these things.* In those two sayes S. *Augustine,* he divides all, Vertue, and Praise; Vertue in our selves, that may deserve Praise; Praise towards others, that may advance and propagate Vertue. This is the retribution which God promises to all the upright in heart, *Gloriabuntur, Laudabuntur,* They shall Glory, they shall have, they shall give praise. And then it is so far from diminishing this Glory, as that it infinitely exalts our consolation, that God places this Retribution in the future, *Gloriabuntur,* If they doe not yet, yet certainly they shall glory, And if they ⁵⁶⁰ doe now, that glory shall not goe out, still they shall, they shall for ever glory.

In the Hebrew there is no Present tense; In that language wherein God spake, it could not be said, *The upright in heart, Are praised;* Many times they are not. But God speaks in the future; first, that he may still keepe his Children in an expectation and dependance upon him, (you shall be, though you be not yet) And then, to establish them in an infallibility, because he hath said it, (I know you are not yet, but comfort your selves, I have said it, and it shall be.) As the Hebrew hath no Superlatives, because God would keepe his Children ⁵⁷⁰ within compasse, and in moderate desires, to content themselves with his measures, though they be not great, and though they be not heaped; so, considering what pressures, and contempts, and terrors, the upright in heart are subject to, it is a blessed reliefe, That they have a future proposed unto them, That they shall be praised, That they shall be redeemed out of contempt. This makes even the Expectation it selfe as sweet to them, as the fruition would be. This makes

Gregor.

Phil. 4.8

Futurum

them, that when *David* sayes, *Expecta viriliter,* Waite upon the Lord   Psal. 27.14
with a good courage; Waite, I say, upon the Lord; they doe not
answer with the impatience of the Martyrs under the Altar, *Vsque-*   Rev. 6.10
580 *quo,* How long, Lord, wilt thou defer it? But they answer in *Davids*
owne words, *Expectans expectavi,* I have waited long, And, *Ex-*   Psal. 40.1
pectabo nomen tuum, still I will waite upon thy Name; I will waite   Psal. 52.9
till the Lord come; His kingdome come in the mean time, His kingdome of Grace, and Patience; and for his Ease, and his Deliverance,
and his Praise, and his Glory to me, let that come, when he may be
most glorified in the comming thereof. Nay, not onely the Expectation, (that is, that that is expected) shall be comfortable, because it
shall be infallible, but that very present state that he is in, shall be
comfortable, according to the first of our three Translations, *They*
590 *that are true of heart, shall be glad thereof;* Glad of that; Glad that
they are true of heart, though their future retribution were never so
far removed; Nay, though there were no future retribution in the
case, yet they shall finde comfort enough in their present Integrity.
Nay, not onely their present state of Integrity, but their present state
of misery, shall be comfortable to them; for this very word of our
Text, *Halal,* that is here translated *Ioy,* and *Glory,* and *Praise,* in
divers places of Scripture, (as Hebrew words have often such a
transplantation) signifies *Ingloriousnesse,* and *contempt,* and *dejec-*   Psal. 75.4
tion of spirit; So that Ingloriousnesse, and contempt, and dejection of   Esa. 44.25
600 spirit, may be a part of the retribution; God may make Inglorious-   Job 12.17
nesse, and Contempt, and Dejection of spirit, a greater blessing and
benefit, then Joy, and Glory, and Praise would have been; and so re-
serve all this Glory and Praising to that time, that *David* intends, *The*   Psal. 112.6
righteous shall be in everlasting remembrance. Though they live and
die contemptibly, they shall be in an honorable remembrance, even
amongst men, as long as men last, and even when time shall be no
more, and men no more, they shall have it *in futuro æterno;* where
there shall be an everlasting present, and an everlasting future, there
the upright in heart shall be praised, and that for ever, which is our
610 conclusion of all.

    If this word of our Text, *Halal,* shall signifie *Ioy,* (as the Service   *Æternum*
Booke, and the Geneva translation render it) that may be somewhat
towards enough, which we had occasion to say of the Joyes of heaven,

in our Exercise upon the precedent Psalme, when we sayled thorough that Hemispheare of Heaven, by the breath of the Holy Ghost, in handling those words, *Vnder the shadow of thy wings I will rejoyce.* So that, of this signification of the word, *Gaudebunt in æterno,* They shall rejoyce for ever, we adde nothing now. If the word shall sig-nifie *Glory,* (as our last translation renders it) consider with me, That ⁶²⁰ when that Glory which I shall receive in Heaven, shall be of that exaltation, as that my body shall invest the glory of a soule, (my body shall be like a soule, like a spirit, like an Angel of light, in all en-dowments that glory it selfe can make that body capable of, that body remaining still a true body) when my body shall be like a soule, there

2 Pet. 1.4   will be nothing left for my soule to be like but God himselfe; *I shall*
1 Cor. 6.17   *be partaker of the Divine nature, and the same Spirit with him.* Since the glory that I shall receive in body, and in soule, shall be such, so exalted, what shall that glory of God be, which I shall see by the light of this glory shed upon me there? In this place, and at this time the ⁶³⁰ glory of God is; but we lack that light to see it by. When my soule and body are glorified in heaven, by that light of glory in me, I shall see the glory of God. But then, what must that glory of the Essence of God be, which I shall see thorough the light of Gods own glory? I must have the light of glory upon me, to see the glory of God, and

Rom. 11.33   then by his glory I shall see his Essence. When S. *Paul* cryes out upon the bottomlesse depth of the riches of his Attributes, (*O the depth of the riches, both of the wisedome and knowledge of God!*) How glorious, how bottomlesse is the riches of his Essence? If I cannot look upon him in his glasse, in the body of the Sunne, how shall I

1 Cor. 13.12   ⁶⁴⁰ looke upon him *face to face?* And if I be dazeled to see him as he
1 Joh. 3.2   works, how shall I see him, *Sicuti est, as he is,* and in his Essence? But it may be some ease to our spirits, (which cannot endure the search of this glory of heaven, which shall shew us the very Essence of God) to take this word of our Text, as our first translation of all tooke it, for one beame of this glory, that is *Praise;* Consider we there-fore this everlasting future onely so, How the upright in heart shall be praised in heaven.

First, The Militant Church shall transmit me to the Triumphant, with her recommendation, That I lived in the obedience of the ⁶⁵⁰ Church of God, That I dyed in the faith of the Sonne of God, That

I departed and went away from them, in the company and conduct
of the Spirit of God, into whose hands they heard me, they saw me
recommend my spirit, And that I left my body, which was *the*   I Cor. 6.19
Temple of the Holy Ghost, to them, and that they have placed it in
Gods treasury, in his consecrated earth, to attend the Resurrection,
which they shall beseech him to hasten for my sake, and to make it
joyfull and glorious to me, and them, when it comes. So the Militant
Church shall transmit me to the Triumphant, with this praise, this
testimony, this recommendation. And then, if I have done any good
⁶⁶⁰ to any of Gods servants, (or to any that hath not been Gods servant,
for Gods sake) If I have but fed a hungry man, If I have but clothed
a naked childe, If I have but comforted a sad soule, or instructed an
ignorant soule, If I have but preached a Sermon, and then printed
that Sermon, that is, first preached it, and then lived according to it,
(for the subsequent life is the best printing, and the most usefull and
profitable publishing of a Sermon) All those things that I have done
for Gods glory, shall follow me, shall accompany me, shall be in
heaven before me, and meet me with their testimony, That as I did
not serve God for nothing, (God gave me his blessings with a large
⁶⁷⁰ hand, and in overflowing measures) so I did not nothing for the
service of God; Though it be as it ought to be, nothing in mine own
eyes, nothing in respect of my duty, yet to them who have received
any good by it, it must not seeme nothing; for then they are unthank-
full to God, who gave it, by whose hand soever.

This shall be my praise to Heaven, my recommendation thither;
And then, my praise in Heaven, shall be my preferment in Heaven.
That those blessed Angels, that rejoyced at my Conversion before,
shall praise my perseverance in that profession, and admit me to a
part in all their Hymns and Hosannaes, and Hallelujahs; which
⁶⁸⁰ *Hallelujah* is a word produced from the very word of this Text,
Halal; My *Hallelujah* shall be my *Halal,* my praising of God shall be
my praise. And from this testimony I shall come to the accomplish-
ment of all, to receive from my Saviours own mouth, that glorious,
that victorious, that harmonious praise, that Dissolving, and that
Recollecting testimony, that shall melt my bowels, and yet fix me,
powre me out, and yet gather me into his bosome, that *Euge bone*
serve, Well done, good and faithfull servant, enter into thy Masters   Mat. 25.21

joy. And when he hath sealed me with his *Euge,* and accepted my service, who shall stamp a *Væ quod non,* upon me? who shall say, ⁶⁹⁰ Woe be unto thee, that thou didst not preach, this or that day, in this or that place? When he shall have styled me *Bone & fidelis, Good and faithfull servant,* who shall upbraid me with a late undertaking this Calling, or a slack pursuing, or a lazy intermitting the function thereof? When he shall have *entred me into my Masters joy,* what fortune, what sin can cast any Cloud of sadnesse upon me? This is that that makes Heaven, Heaven, That this Retribution, which is future now, shall be present then, and when it is then present, it shall be future againe, and present and future for ever, ever enjoyed, and expected ever. *The upright in heart* shall have, whatsoever all Trans-⁷⁰⁰ lations can enlarge and extend themselves unto; They shall *Rejoyce,* they shall *Glory,* they shall *Praise,* and they shall bee *praised,* and all these in an everlasting future, for ever. Which everlastingnesse is such a Terme, as God himselfe cannot enlarge; As God cannot make himselfe a better God then he is, because hee is infinitely good, infinite goodnesse, already; so God himselfe cannot make our Terme in heaven longer then it is; for it is infinite everlastingnesse, infinite eternity. That that wee are to beg of him is, that as that state shall never end, so he will be pleased to hasten the beginning thereof, that so we may be numbred with his Saints in Glory everlasting. ⁷¹⁰ Amen.

The fourth of my Prebend Sermons
upon my five Psalmes:
Preached at S. Pauls, 28. Ianuary, 1626.

Psal. 65.5. *By terrible things in righteousness wilt thou answer us,*
O God of our salvation; who art the confidence of all the ends of the
earth, and of them that are a far off, upon the Sea.

GOd makes nothing of nothing now; God eased himselfe of that incomprehensible worke, and ended it in the first Sabbath. But God makes great things of little still; And in that kinde hee works most upon the Sabbath; when by the foolishnesse of Preaching hee infatuates the wisedome of the world, and by the word, in the mouth of a weake man, he enfeebles the power of sinne, and Satan in the world, and by but so much breath as blows out an houre-glasse, gathers three thousand soules at a Sermon, and five thousand soules at a Sermon, as upon *Peters* preaching, in the second, and in the fourth of the Acts. And this worke of his, to make much of little, and to doe much by little, is most properly a Miracle. For, the Creation, (which was a production of all out of nothing) was not properly a miracle: A miracle is a thing done against nature; when something in the course of nature resists that worke, then that worke is a miracle; But in the Creation, there was no reluctation, no resistance, no nature, nothing to resist. But to doe great works by small meanes,

to bring men to heaven by Preaching in the Church, this is a miracle.
When Christ intended a miraculous feeding of a great multitude, he
askt, *Quot panes habetis?* First hee would know, how many loaves
20 they had; and when hee found that they had some, though they were
but five, he multiplied them, to a sufficiency for five thousand persons.
This Psalme is one of my five loaves, which I bring; One of those five
Psalms, which by the Institution of our Ancestors in this Church, are
made mine, appropriated especially to my daily meditation, as there
are five other Psalmes to every other person of our Church. And, by
so poore meanes as this, (my speaking) his Blessing upon his Ordinance may multiply to the advancement, and furtherance of all your
salvations. He multiplies now, farther then in those loaves; not onely
to feed you all, (as he did all that multitude) but to feed you all three
30 meales.

In this Psalme (and especially in this Text) God satisfies you with
this threefold knowledge: First, what he hath done for man, in the
light and law of nature; Then, how much more he had done for his
chosen people, the Jewes, in affording them a law; And lastly, what
he had reserved for man after, in the establishing of the Christian
Church. The first, (in this Metaphore, and miracle of feeding) works
as a break-fast; for though there bee not a full meale, there is something to stay the stomach, in the light of nature. The second, that
which God did for the Jewes in their Law, and Sacrifices, and Types,
40 and Ceremonies, is as that Dinner, which was spoken of in the
Gospel, which was plentifully prepared, but prepared for some certaine guests, that were bidden, and no more; Better meanes then were
in nature, they had in the law, but yet onely appropriated to them
that were bidden, to that Nation, and no more. But in the third
meale, Gods plentifull refection in the Christian Church, and meanes
of salvation there; first, Christ comes in the visitation of his Spirit,
(*Behold I come, and knock, and will sup with him*) (Hee sups with
us, in the private visitation of his Spirit) And then, (as it is added
there) hee invites us to sup with him, hee calls us home to his house,
50 and there makes us partakers of his blessed Sacraments; And by those
meanes we are brought at last to that blessednesse, which he pro-
claimes, (*Blessed are all they which are called to the marriage Supper
of the Lambe*) in the Kingdome of heaven. For all these three meales,

Mark 6.38

Revel. 3.20

Revel. 19.9

wee say Grace in this Text, (*By terrible things, in righteousnesse, wilt thou answer us, O God of our salvation*) for all these wayes of comming to the knowledge and worship of God, we blesse God in this Text, (*Thou art the confidence of all the ends of the Earth, and of them that are a farre off, upon the Sea.*)

The consideration of the meanes of salvation, afforded by God to ⁶⁰ the Jewes in their law, inanimates the whole Psalme, and is transfused thorow every part thereof; and so, it falls upon this Verse too, as it doth upon all the rest; And then, for that, that God had done before in nature, and for all, is in the later part of this Verse, (*Who art the confidence of all the ends of the Earth, and of them that are a farre off, upon the Sea*) And lastly, that that hee hath reserved for the Christian Church, God hath centred, and embowelled in the wombe and bosome of the Text, in that compellation, (*O God of our salvation*) for there the word *salvation,* is rooted in *Iashang,* which *Iashang* is the very Name of *Iesus,* the foundation, and the whole building of ⁷⁰ the Christian Church. So then our three parts will bee these; What God hath done in Nature, what in the Law, what in the Gospel. And, when in our Order wee shall come to that last part, which is that, that we drive all to, (*The advantage which wee have in the Gospel, above Nature, and the Law*) wee shall then propose, and stop upon the Holy Ghosts manner of expressing it in this place, (*By terrible things in righteousnesse wilt thou answer us, O God of our salvation*) But first, look we a little into the other two, Nature, and Law.

First then, the last words settle us upon our first consideration, What God hath done for man in Nature, *Hee is the confidence of* ⁸⁰ *all the ends of the earth, and of them that are a far off, upon the Sea,* that is, of all the world, all places, all persons in the world; All, at all times, every where, have Declarations enow of his power, Demonstrations enow of his Goodnesse, to confide in him, to rely upon him. The Holy Ghost seemes to have delighted in the Metaphore of *Building.* I know no figurative speech so often iterated in the Scriptures, as the name of a *House;* Heaven and Earth are called by that name, and wee, who being upon earth, have our conversation in heaven, are called so too, (*Christ hath a House, which House wee are*) And as God builds his House, (*The Lord builds up Ierusalem,* saith *David*) ⁹⁰ so hee furnishes it, he plants Vineyards, Gardens, and Orchards about

1 Part.
Natura

Phil. 3.20

Heb. 3.6
Psal. 147.2

it, He layes out a way to it, (*Christ is the way*) He opens a gate into
it, (*Christ is the gate*) And when hee hath done all this, (built his
house, furnished it, planted about it, made it accessible, and opened
the gate) then hee keepes house, as well as builds a house, he feeds
us, and feasts us in his house, as well as he lodges us, and places us
in it. And as Christ professes what his owne Diet was, what he fed
upon, (*My meat is to doe the will of my Father*) so our meat is to
know the will of the Father; Every man, even in nature, hath that
appetite, that desire, to know God. And therefore if God have made
100 any man, and not given him meanes to know him, he is but a good
Builder, he is no good Housekeeper, He gives him lodging, but he
gives him no meat; But *the eyes of all wait upon thee, and thou givest
them their meat in due season. All,* (not onely we) wait upon God;
and he gives them *Their* meat, though not our meat, (The Word and
the Sacraments) yet *Their* meat, such as they are able to digest and
endue. Even in nature, *He is the confidence of all the ends of the
earth, and of them that are a far off, upon the Sea.* That is his daily
bread, which even the naturall man begs at Gods hand, and God
affords it him.
110   The most precious and costly dishes are alwaies reserved for the last
services, but yet there is wholesome meat before too. The cleare light
is in the Gospel, but there is light in Nature too. At the last Supper,
(the Supper of the Lambe in Heaven) there is no bill of fare, there
are no particular dishes named there. It is impossible to tell us what
we shall feed upon, what we shall be feasted with, at the Marriage
Supper of the Lamb; Our way of knowing God there cannot be expressed. At that Supper of the Lambe, which is here, here in our way
homewards, that is, in the Sacramentall Supper of the Lambe, it is
very hard to tell, what we feed upon; How that meat is dressed, how
120 the Body and Blood of Christ is received by us, at that Supper, in
that Sacrament, is hard to be expressed, hard to be conceived, for the
way and manner thereof. So also in the former meale, that which we
have called the Dinner, which is The knowledge which the Jews had
in the Law, it was not easie to distinguish the taste, and the nature of
every dish, and to finde the signification in every Type, and in every
Ceremony. There are some difficulties (if curious men take the matter
in hand, and be too inquisitive) even in the Gospel; more in the

Marginal references:
Ioh. 14.6
Matt. 7.13

Ioh. 10.7

Ioh. 4.34

Psal. 145.15

Revel. 19.9

Law; most of all in Nature. But yet, even in this first refection, this
first meale, that God sets before man, (which is our knowledge of
¹³⁰ God in Nature) because wee are then in Gods House, (all this World,
and the next make God but one House) though God doe not give

Psal. 63.5
81.16

Marrow and fatnesse, (as *David* speaks) though he doe not *feed them
with the fat of the wheat, nor satisfie them wtih honey out of the
Rock,* (for the Gospel is the honey, and Christ is the Rock) yet, even
in Nature, hee gives sufficient meanes to know him, though they
come to neither of the other Meales, neither to the Jews Dinner, The
benefit of the Law, nor to the Christians Supper, either when they
feed upon the Lamb in the Sacrament, or when they feed with the
Lamb in the possession and fruition of Heaven.

¹⁴⁰   Though therefore the Septuagint, in their Translation of the
Psalms, have, in the Title of this Psalme, added this, *A Psalme of
Ieremy and Ezekiel, when they were departing out of the Captivity
of Babylon,* intimating therein, that it is a Psalme made in contemplation of that blessed place which we are to go to, (as, literally, it was
of their happie state in their restitution from Babylon to Jerusalem)
And though the ancient Church, by appropriating this Psalme to the
office of the dead, to the service at Burials, intimate also, that this
Psalme is intended of that fulnesse of knowledge, and Joy, and Glory,
which they have that are departed in the Lord, yet the Holy Ghost
¹⁵⁰ stops, as upon the way, before we come thither, and, since we must
lie in an Inne, that is, Lodge in this World, he enables the World to
entertaine us, as well as to lodge us, and hath provided, that the
World, the very world it selfe, (before wee consider the Law in the
World, or the Church in the World, or Glory in the next World)
This very World, that is, Nature, and no more, should give such an
universall light of the knowledge of God, as that he should bee *The
confidence of all the ends of the Earth, and of them that are a farre
off upon the Sea.*

And therefore as men that come to great places, and preferments,
¹⁶⁰ when they have entred by a faire and wide gate of Honour, but yet
are laid downe upon hard beds of trouble and anxiety in those places,
(for, when the body seemes in the sight of men, to go on in an easie
amble, the minde is every day (if not all day) in a shrewd and dis-
easefull trot) As those men will sometimes say, It was better with me,

when I was in a lower place, and fortune, and will remember, being Bishops, the pleasures they had when they were Schoole-boyes, and yet, for all this, intermit not their thankfulnesse to God, who hath raised them to that height, and those meanes of glorifying him: so, howsoever we abound with joy and thankfulnesse, for these gracious
170 and glorious Illustrations of the Law, and the Gospel, and beames of future Glory, which we have in the Christian Church, Let us reflect often upon our beginning, upon the consideration of Gods first bene-fits, which he hath given to us all in Nature, *That light, by which he* Iohn 1.9 *enlighteneth every man that commeth into the World,* That he hath given us a reasonable soule capable of grace, here, (that, he hath denied no man, and no other creature hath that) That he hath given us an immortal soul capable of glory hereafter, (and that, that im-mortality he hath denied no man, and no other creature hath that.) Consider we alwaies the grace of God, to be the Sun it selfe, but the
180 nature of man, and his naturall faculties to be the Sphear, in which that Sun, that Grace moves. Consider we the Grace of God to be the soule it self, but the naturall faculties of man, to be as a body, which ministers Organs for that soule, that Grace to worke by. That so, as how much soever I feare the hand of a mighty man, that strikes, yet I have a more immediate feare of the sword he strikes with; So, though I impute justly my sins, and my feares of judgements for them, to Gods withdrawing, or to my neglecting his grace, yet I looke also upon that which is next me, Nature, and naturall light, and naturall faculties, and that I consider how I use to use them; whether
190 I be as watchfull upon my tongue, that that minister no tentation to others, and upon mine eye, that that receive no tentation from others, as by the light of Nature, I might, and as some morall Men, without addition of particular Grace, have done. That so, first for my selfe, I be not apt to lay any thing upon God, and to say, that hee starved me, though he should not bid me to the Jews dinner, in giving me the light of the Law, nor bid me to the Christians Supper, in giving me the light of the Gospell, because he hath given me a competent refec-tion even in Nature. And then, that for others, I may first say with the Apostle, *That they are without excuse, who doe not see the* Rom. 1.20
200 *invisible God, in the visible Creature,* and may say also with him, *O* 11.33 *altitudo!* The wayes of the Lord are past my finding out; And there-

fore to those, who doe open their eyes to that light of Nature, in the best exaltation thereof, God does not hide himselfe, though he have not manifested to me, by what way he manifests himselfe to them. For, God disappoints none, and he is *The confidence of all the ends of the Earth, and of them who are a farre off upon the Sea.*

Psal. 37.5
Commit thy way unto the Lord, sayes *David;* And he sayes more, then our Translation seemes to expresse; The margin hath expressed it; for, according to the Originall word, *Galal,* it is in the Margin, not
²¹⁰ *Commit,* but *Roll thy way upon the Lord;* which may very well imply, and intend this precept, Carry thy Rolling trench up to God,
Gen. 18.23
and gather upon him; As *Abraham,* when he beat the price with God for Sodom, from fifty, to ten, rolled his Petition upon God, so roll thy wayes upon him, come up to him in a thankfull acknowledgement, what he hath done for thee, in the Gospel, in the Law, and in Nature; And then, as *Tertullian* sayes of publique Prayers, *Obsidemus Deum,* In the Prayers of the Congregation wee besiege God, So this way wee entrench our selves before God, so, as that nothing can beat us out of our trenches; for, if all the Canons of the Church beat upon me, so
²²⁰ that I be by Excommunication removed from the assistances of the Church, (though I be inexcusable, if I labour not my Reconciliation, and my Absolution) yet, before that be effected, I am still in my first trench, still I am a man, still I have a soule capable of Grace, still I have the light of Nature, and some presence of God in that; though I be attenuated, I am not annihilated, though by my former abuses of Gods graces, and my contumacy, I be cast back to the ends of the earth, and a far off upon the Sea, yet even there, God is the confidence of all them; As long as I consider that I have such a soule, capable of Grace and Glory, I cannot despaire.
²³⁰ Thus Nature makes Pearls, Thus Grace makes Saints. A drop of dew hardens, and then another drop fals, and spreads it selfe, and cloathes that former drop, and then another, and another, and becomes so many shels and films that invest that first seminall drop, and so (they say) there is a pearle in Nature. A good soule takes first Gods first drop into his consideration, what he hath shed upon him in Nature, and then his second coate, what in the Law, and successively his other manifold graces, as so many shels, and films, in the Christian Church, and so we are sure, there is a Saint.

Roll thy wayes upon God; And (as it followes in the same verse)
²⁴⁰ *Spera in eo, & ipse faciet;* we translate it, *Trust in him, and he shall
bring it to passe;* Begin at *Alpha,* and hee shall bring it to *Omega:*
Consider thy selfe but in the state of Hope, (for the state of Nature
is but a state of Hope, a state of Capablenesse; In Nature wee have
the capacity of Grace, but not Grace in possession, in Nature) *Et ipse
faciet,* sayes that Text, God shall doe, God shall work; There is no
more in the Originall but so, *Ipse faciet;* Not God shall doe it, or doe
this, or doe that, but doe all; doe but consider that God hath done
something for thee, and he shall doe all, for, *He is the confidence of
all the ends of the earth, and of them that are a farre off upon the Sea.*
²⁵⁰ Here is a new Mathematiques; without change of Elevation, or
parallax, I that live in this Climate, and stand under this Meridian,
looke up and fixe my self upon God, And they that are under my
feete, looke up to that place, which is above them, And as divers, as
contrary as our places are, we all fixe at once upon one God, and
meet in one Center; but we doe not so upon one Sunne, nor upon one
constellation, or configuration in the Heavens; when we see it, those
Antipodes doe not; but they, and we see God at once. How various
formes of Religion soever passe us through divers wayes, yet by the
very light and power of Nature, we meet in one God; and for so
²⁶⁰ much, as may make God accessible to us, and make us inexcusable
towards him, there is light enough in this dawning of the day, refec-
tion enough in this first meale, The knowledge of God, which we
have in Nature; That alone discharges God, and condemns us; for,
by that, *He is,* that is, He offers himselfe to be, *The confidence of all
the ends of the Earth, and of them who are a far of upon the Sea;*
that is, of all mankinde.

But then, *Lunæ radiis non maturescit botrus,* fruits may be seene
by the Mooneshine, but the Mooneshine will not ripen them. Therefore a Sunne rises unto us, in the law, and in the Prophets, and gives
²⁷⁰ us another manner of light, then we had in nature. *The way of the
wicked is as Darknesse,* sayes *Solomon;* Wherein? It follows, *They
know not at what they stumble.* A man that calls himselfe to no kinde
of account, that takes no candle into his hand, never knowes at what
he stumbles, nor what occasions his sin. But by the light of nature,
if he will looke upon his owne infirmities, his own deformities, his

[2 Part.
Lex]

Prov. 4.19

own inclinations, he may know at what he stumbles, what that is that

Rom. 3.20
Rom. 5.13
Rom. 7.7

leads him into tentation. For, though S. *Paul* say, That *by the law is the knowledge of sin,* And, *Sin is not imputed when there is no law;* And againe, *I had not knowne sin, but by the law;* in some of these

²⁸⁰ places, the law is not intended onely of the law of the Jews, but of the law of nature in our hearts, (for, by that law, every man knows that he sins) And then, sin is not onely intended of sin produced into act, but sin in the heart; as the Apostle instances there, *I had not knowne lust, except the law had said, Thou shalt not covet.* Of some sinnes, there is no cleare evidence given by the light of nature: That the law supplied; and more then that. The law did not onely shew, what was sin, but gave some light of remedy against sin, and restitution after sin, by those sacrifices, which, though they were ineffectuall in themselves, yet involved, and represented Christ, who was their salvation.

²⁹⁰ So then, God was to the Jews, in generall, as he was to his principall

Deut. 34.1

servant amongst them, *Moses;* He saw the land of promise, but he entred not into it; The Jews saw Christ, but embraced him not. *Abraham* saw his day, and rejoyced; They saw it, that is, they might have seen it, but winked at it. *Luther* sayes well, *Iudæi habuere jus mendicandi,* The Jews had a licence to beg, They had a Breve, and might gather, They had a Covenant, and might plead with God; But they did not; and therefore, though they were inexcusable for their neglect of the light of Nature, and more inexcusable for resisting the light of the law, That they and we might be absolutely inexcusable,

³⁰⁰ if we continued in darknesse after that, God set up another light, the light of the Gospel, which is our third and last part, wrapped up in those first words of our Text, *By terrible things, in righteousnesse, wilt thou answer us, O God of our salvation.*

3 Part.
Ecclesia
Christi-
ana

This word, *Salvation, Iashang,* is the roote of the name of *Iesus.* In the beginning of the Primitive Church, when the followers of Christ left or discontinued their being called *the Disciples,* and *the Faithfull,* and *the Brethren,* and *the Professors,* as they had been called before, and would bring the Name of their founder, Christ Jesus, into more evidence and manifestation, yet they were not called

³¹⁰ by the Name of *Iesus,* but from *Christ;* at Antioch first they were

Acts 11.26

called *Christians.* For, it is well distinguished, That the Name of

Bonavent.

Iesus, as it signifies a *Saviour,* first contemplates God, and the Divine nature, (which onely could save us) And then hath relation to Man, and the Humane nature, without assuming of which, the Sonne of God could not have saved us that way, that God had proposed, The satisfaction of his Justice; And then, the Name of *Christ,* (as it signifies *Anointed,* and appointed to a certaine purpose, as to die for us) first contemplates Man, and the Humane nature, which onely could die, And then hath relation to God, and the Divine nature. So that 320 Jesus is God, and Man in Him; And Christ is Man, and God in Him. So the Name *Iesus* seemes to taste of more Mystery, and more Incomprehensiblenesse; And the Name of *Christ,* of more Humility, and Appliablenesse.

And with this lower Name, to be called *Christians* from *Christ,* was the Church of God contented; Whereas a later race of men in the Romane Church, will needs take their Denomination from *Iesus* himselfe; But I know not whether they meane our *Iesus* or no. *Iosephus* remembers two (at least) of that name, *Iesus,* that were infamous malefactors, and men of blood; and they may deduce themselves from 330 such a *Iesus.* And a Jesuit teaches us, that it is the common opinion, that *Barrabas* the murderer, was by his proper Name called *Iesus;* that his name was *Iesus Barrabas;* and that therefore Pilate made that difference upon our Saviour, *Iesus Nazarenus, This is Iesus of Nazareth,* and not *Iesus Barrabas;* and from that *Iesus, Iesus Barrabas* they may deduce themselves. And we know also, that that mischievous sorcerer, was called by that Name, *Bar-jesu,* The Sonne of Jesus. From which *Iesus* amongst these, they will make their extraction, let them chuse. As amongst the Jesuits, the bloodiest of them all, (even to the drawing of the sacred blood of Kings) is, by his name, 340 *Mariana;* So all the rest of them, both in that respect, of sucking blood, and occasioning massacres, and other respects too, are rather Marianits then Jesuits, Idolaters of the blessed Virgin *Mary,* then worshippers of Jesus.

We consist in the Humility of the Ancients; we are *Christians, Iesus* is meerly a *Saviour,* A name of Mystery, *Christ* is *Anointed,* A name of Communication, of Accommodation, of Imitation; And so this name, the name of *Christ,* is *Oleum effusum,* (as the Spouse speaks) An oyntment, a perfume powred out upon us, and we are *Christians.* In the name of *Iesus,* S. *Paul* abounded, but in the Name

Josephus

Lorinus
Act. 13.6

Ibid.

Cant. 1.3

Corn. Lap.
Eph. 1.10

I Cor. 1.12

Psal. 19.5

350 of *Christ* more; for, (as a Jesuit gives us the account) he repeats the name of *Iesus* almost three hundred times, but the name of *Christ* more then foure hundred, in his Epistles. In this Church then, which is gathered in the Name of *Christ,* (though in the power and merit of *Iesus*) This light which we speake of, This knowledge of God, and means of salvation, is in the highest exaltation. In the state of nature, we consider this light, as the Sunne, to be risen at the Moluccæ, in the farthest East; In the state of the law, we consider it, as the Sunne come to Ormus, the first Quadrant; But in the Gospel, to be come to the Canaries, the fortunate Ilands, the first Meridian. 360 Now, whatsoever is beyond this, is Westward, towards a Declination. If we will goe farther then to be Christians, and those doctrines, which the whole Christian Church hath ever beleeved, if we will be of *Cephas,* and of *Apollos,* if we will call our selves, or endanger, and give occasion to others, to call us from the Names of men, Papists, or Lutherans, or Calvinists, we depart from the true glory and serenity, from the lustre and splendor of this Sunne; This is *Tabernaculum Solis,* Here in the Christian Church, God hath set a Tabernacle for the Sunne; And, as in nature, Man hath light enough to discerne the principles of Reason; So in the Christian Church, (considered with-370 out subdivisions of Names, and Sects) a Christian hath light enough of all things necessary to salvation.

So then, still roll thy wayes upon God, Gather upon him nearer and nearer; for, all these are emanations of lights from him, that he might be found, and seen, and knowne by thee. The looking upon God, by the first light of Nature, is, to catechize, and examine thy selfe, whether thou doe governe, and employ thy naturall faculties to his glory; whether thou doe shut thine eyes at a tentation, stop thine eares at a blasphemy upon God, or a defamation upon thy neighbour; and withhold thy hand from blood and bribes, and thy feet from fellow-380 ship in sin. The looking upon God, by the second light, the light of the law, is, to discerne by that, that God hath alwayes had a peculiar people of his own, and gathered them, and contained them in his worship, by certain visible, sensible Ordinances and Institutions, Sacraments, and Sacrifices, and rituall Ceremonies, and to argue and conclude out of Gods former proceedings with them, his greatnesse and his goodnesse towards the present world. And then, to see God by that last and best light, the light of the Christian Church, is, to be content with so much of God, as God hath revealed of himselfe to his Church; And (as it is expressed here) to heare him answer thee, *By terrible things in righteousnesse;* for, that he does *as he is the God of our salvation,* that is, as he works in the Christian Church; which is our last Consideration; *By terrible, &c.*

In this Consideration, (Gods proceeding with us in the Christian Church) this observation meets us first, That Gods conversation with us there, is called an *Answering;* (*He shall answer us*) Now if we looke that God should answer us, we must say something to God; and our way of speaking to God, is by petition, by prayer. If we present no petition, if we pray not, we can looke for no answer, for we aske none. *Esaias is very bold,* (saith S. *Paul*) *when he sayes, That God was found of them that sought him not, and made manifest to them that asked not after him;* Yet though it were boldly said, it was truly said; so early, and so powerfull is Gods preventing grace towards us. So it is a very ordinary phrase amongst the Prophets, *God answered, and said* thus, and thus, when the Prophet had asked nothing of God. But here we are upon Gods proceeding with man in the Christian Church; and so, God answers not, but to our petitions, to our prayers. In a Sermon, God speaks to the Congregation, but he answers onely that soule, that hath been with him at Prayers before. A man may pray in the street, in the fields, in a fayre; but it is a more acceptable and more effectuall prayer, when we shut our doores, and observe our stationary houres for private prayer in our Chamber; and in our Chamber, when we pray upon our knees, then in our beds. But the greatest power of all, is in the publique prayer of the Congregation.

It is a good remembrance that *Damascene* gives, *Non quia gentes quædam faciunt, à nobis linquenda;* We must not forbeare things onely therefore, because the Gentiles, or the Jewes used them. The Gentiles, particularly the Romans, (before they were Christians) had a set Service, a prescribed forme of Common prayer in their Temples; and they had a particular Officer in that State, who was *Conditor precum,* that made their Collects, and Prayers upon emergent occasions; And *Omni lustro,* every five yeares there was a review, and an alteration in their Prayers, and the state of things was presumed to

Respondet, ergo Orandum

Rom. 10.20

Damasc.

have received so much change in that time, as that it was fit to change some of their Prayers and Collects. It must not therefore seeme strange, that at the first, there were certaine Collects appointed in our Church; nor that others, upon just occasion, be added.

Gods blessing here, in the Christian Church, (for, to that we limit this consideration) is, that here *He will answer us;* Therefore, here
430 we must ask; Here, our asking is our communion at Prayer: And therefore they that undervalue, or neglect the prayers of the Church, have not that title to the benefit of the Sermon; for though God doe speake in the Sermon, yet hee answers, that is, applies himselfe, by his Spirit, onely to them, who have prayed to him before. If they have joyned in prayer, they have their interest, and shall feele their Consolation in all the promises of the Gospel, shed upon the Congregation, in the Sermon. Have you asked by prayer, *Is there no Balme in*

Esay. 53.5 *Gilead?* He answers you by me, Yes, there is Balme; *Hee was wounded for your transgressions, and with his stripes you are healed;*
440 His blood is your *Balme,* his Sacrament is your *Gilead.* Have you

1 Sam. 13.19 asked by prayer, *Is there no Smith in Israel?* No meanes to discharge my selfe of my fetters, and chaines, of my temporall, and spirituall Encumbrances? God answers thee, Yes, there is; He bids you but

Act. 12.7 looke about, and you shall finde your selfe in *Peters* case; *The Angel of the Lord present, A light shining, and his chaines falling off:* All your manacles locked upon the hands, All your chaines loaded upon the legges, All your stripes numbred upon the back of Christ Jesus. You have said in your prayers here, (*Lord, from whom all good counsails doe proceed*) And God answers you from hence, *The Angel*
450 *of the great Counsell shall dwell with you, and direct you.* You have said in your prayers, *Lighten our darknesse,* and God answers you by

Esay. 60.19 mee, (as he did his former people by *Esay*) *The Lord shall be unto thee an everlasting light, and thy God thy glory.* Petition God at prayers, and God shall answer all your petitions at the Sermon. There we begin, (if wee will make profit of a Sermon) at Prayers; And thither wee returne againe, (if we have made profit by a Sermon) in

Confes. due time, to prayers. For, that is S. *Augustines* holy Circle, in which

l. 1. c. 1 hee walkes from Prayers to the Sermon, and from the Sermon, next day to Prayers againe. *Invocat te fides mea,* sayes he to God; Here I
460 stand or kneele in thy presence, and in the power of faith, to pray to

thee. But where had I this faith, that makes my prayer acceptable? *Dedisti mihi per ministerium Prædicatoris;* I had it at the Sermon, I had it, saith he, by the ministery of the Preacher; but I had it therefore, because thy Spirit prepared me by prayer before; And I have it therefore, that is, to that end, that I might returne faithfully to prayers againe. As hee is *The God of our salvation,* (that is, As he works in the Christian Church) *he answers us:* If we aske by prayer, he applies the Sermon; And, *He answers by terrible things, in right-eousnesse.*

470   These two words, (*Terribilia per Iustitiam*) *By Terrible things in Righteousnesse,* are ordinarily by our Expositors taken, to intimate a confidence, that God imprints by the Ordinance of his Church, that by this right use of Prayer and Preaching, they shall alwayes be delivered from their enemies, or from what may bee most terrible unto them. In which exposition, *Righteousnesse* signifies faithful-nesse, and *Terrible things* signifie miraculous deliverances from, and terrible Judgements upon his, and our enemies. Therefore is God called, *Deus fidelis, The faithfull God;* for, that faithfulnesse implies a Covenant, made before, (and there entred his Mercy, that hee
480 would make that Covenant) and it implies also the assurance of the performance thereof, for there enters his faithfulnesse. So he is called, *Fidelis Creator, (We commit our soules to God, as to a faithfull Creator)* He had an eternall gracious purpose upon us, to create us, and he hath faithfully accomplished it. So, *Fidelis quia vocavit, Hee is faithfull in having called us;* That he had decreed, and that he hath done. So Christ is called, *Fidelis Pontifex, A mercifull and a faithfull high Priest; Mercifull* in offering himselfe for us, *faithfull* in apply-ing himselfe to us. So Gods whole word is called so often, so very often *Testimonium fidele, A faithfull witnesse,* an evidence that can-
490 not deceive, nor mislead us. Therefore we may be sure, that what-soever God hath promised to his Church, (And whatsoever God hath done upon the enemies of his Church heretofore, those very per-formances to them, are promises to us, of the like succours in the like distresses) he will performe, re-performe, multiply performances thereof upon us. *Thy counsails of old are faithfulnesse and truth;* That is, whatsoever thou didst decree, was done even then, in the infallibility of that Decree; And when that Decree came to be exe-

Terribilia per Iusti-tiam

Deut. 7.9

1 Pet. 4.19

1 Thes. 5.24

Heb. 2.17

Psal. 19.8

Esay. 25.1

cuted, and actually done, in that very execution of that former Decree was enwrapped a new Decree, That the same should be done over
500 and over againe for us, when soever wee needed it. So that then, casting up our account, from the destruction of Babel, by all the plagues of Egypt, through the depopulation of Canaan, and the massacre in *Sennacheribs* Army, to the swallowing of the Invincible Navy upon our Seas, and the bringing to light that Infernall, that subterranean Treason in our Land, we may argue, and assume, *That the God of our salvation will answer us by terrible things,* by multi-plying of miracles, and ministring supplies, to the confusion of his, and our enemies, for, *By terrible things in righteousnesse, will the God of our salvation answer us.*

Per Iusti- 510   So then, his Judgements are these *Terribilia,* Terrible, fearefull
tiam   things; And hee is faithfull in his Covenant, and by terrible Judge-ments he will answer, that is, satisfie our expectation. And that is a convenient sense of these words. But, the word, which we translate *Righteousnesse* here, is *Tzadok,* and *Tzadok* is not faithfulnesse, but holinesse; And these *Terrible things* are Reverend things; and so *Tremellius* translates it, and well; *Per res Reverendas, By Reverend things,* things to which there belongs a Reverence, *thou shalt answer us.* And thus, the sense of this place will be, That the God of our salvation, (that is, God working in the Christian Church) calls us
520 to Holinesse, to Righteousnesse, by Terrible things; not Terrible, in the way and nature of revenge; but Terrible, that is, stupendious, reverend, mysterious: That so we should not make Religion too homely a thing, but come alwayes to all Acts, and Exercises of Religion, with reverence, with feare, and trembling, and make a dif-ference, between Religious, and Civill Actions.

In the frame and constitution of al Religions, these Materials, these Elements have ever entred; Some words of a remote signification, not vulgarly understood, some actions of a kinde of halfe-horror and amazement, some places of reservation and retirednesse, and appro-
530 priation to some sacred persons, and inaccessible to all others. Not to speake of the services, and sacrifices of the Gentiles, and those selfe-manglings and lacerations of the Priests of *Isis,* and of the Priests of *Baal,* (faintly counterfaited in the scourgings and flagellations in the Roman Church) In that very discipline which was delivered from

God, by *Moses,* the service was full of mysterie, and horror, and reservation, *By terrible things,* (Sacrifices of blood in manifold effusions) *God answered them,* then. So, the matter of Doctrine was delivered mysteriously, and with much reservation, and in-intelligible-nesse, as *Tertullian* speaks. The Joy and Glory of Heaven was not
540 easily understood by their temporall abundances of Milke, and Honey, and Oyle, and Wine; and yet, in these (and scarce any other way) was Heaven presented, and notified to that people by *Moses.* Christ, a Messias, a Saviour of the World, by shedding his blood for it, was not easily discerned in their Types and Sacrifices; And yet so, and scarce any other way was Christ revealed unto them. God sayes, *I have multiplied visions, and used similitudes, by the ministery of the Prophets.* They were Visions, they were Similitudes, not plaine and evident things, obvious to every understanding, that God led his people by. And there was an Order of Doctors amongst the Jews that
550 professed that way, To teach the people by Parables and darke sayings; and these were the powerfullest Teachers amongst them, for they had their very name (*Mosselim*) from power and dominion; They had a power, a dominion over the affections of their Disciples, because teaching them by an obscure way, they created an admiration, and a reverence in their hearers, and laid a necessity upon them, of returning againe to them, for the interpretation and signification of those darke Parables. Many thinke that *Moses* cites these obscure Doctors, these *Mosselim,* in that place, in the booke of Numbers, when he sayes, *Wherefore they that speake in Proverbs, say* thus, and
560 thus, And so he proceeds in a way and words, as hard to be understood, as any place in all his Books. *David* professes this of himselfe often; *I will open darke sayings upon my Harpe,* And, *I will open my mouth in a Parable.* And this was the way of *Solomon;* for that very word is the Title of his booke of Proverbs. And in this way of teaching, our Saviour abounded, and excelled; for when it is said, *He taught them as one having authority,* And when it is said, *They were astonished at his Doctrine, for his word was with Power,* they refer that to this manner of teaching, that hee astonished them with these reserved and darke sayings, and by the subsequent interpretation
570 thereof, gained a reverend estimation amongst them, that he onely could lead them to a desire to know, (that darke way encreased their

Hos. 12.10

Sandæi
symbolica
fol. 108

Num. 21.27

Psal. 49.4
78.2

Matt. 7.29
Luke 4.32

desire) and then he onely satisfie them with the knowledge of those things which concerned their salvation. For these Parables, and comparisons of a remote signification, were called by the Jews, *Potestates,* Powers, Powerfull insinuations, as, amongst the Grecians, the same things were called *Axiomata,* Dignities; And of Christ it is said,

Mat. 13.34   *Without a Parable spake he not.*

So that God in the Old, and Christ in the New Testament, hath conditioned his Doctrine, and his Religion (that is, his outward wor-
580 ship) so, as that evermore there should be preserved a Majesty, and a reverentiall feare, and an awfull discrimination of Divine things from Civill, and evermore something reserved to be inquired after, and laid up in the mouth of the Priest, that the People might acknowledge an obligation from him, in the exposition, and application thereof. Nay, this way of *answering us by terrible things,* (that is, by things that imprint a holy horror, and a Religious reverence) is much more in the Christian Church, then it can have beene in any other Religion; Because, if wee consider the Jews, (which is the onely Religion, that can enter into any comparison with the Christian, in this kinde) yet,
590 we looke more directly and more immediately upon God in Christ, then they could, who saw him but by way of Prophecie, a future thing that should be done after; we looke upon God, in History, in matter of fact, upon things done, and set before our eyes; and so that Majesty, and that holy amazement, is more to us then ever it was to any other Religion, because we have a nearer approximation, and vicinity to God in Christ, then any others had, in any representations of their Gods; and it is a more dazeling thing to looke upon the Sun, in a direct, then in an oblique or side line. And therefore, the love of God, which is so often proposed unto us, is as often seasoned with the
600 feare of God; nay, all our Religious affections are reduced to that one,

Mal. 1.6   To a reverentiall feare; If he be a *Master,* he cals for *feare,* and, If he be a *Father,* he calls for *honor;* And honour implies a reverentiall

Psal. 34.11   feare. And that is the Art that *David* professes to teach, *Artem timendi, Come ye children, and hearken unto me, and I will teach you the feare of the Lord.* That you thinke not Divinity an Occupation, nor Church-Service a recreation; but still remember, That *the God of our Salvation* (God working in the Christian Church) *will answer you;* but yet, *by terrible things;* that is, by not being over-

fellowly with God, nor over-homely with places, and acts of Religion;
⁶¹⁰ which, it may be an advancement to your Devotion and edification, to
consider, in some particulars in the Christian Church.

And first, consider we it, in our manners, and conversation. Christ
sayes, *Henceforth I call you not servants, but friends.* But, howsoever
Christ called him *friend,* that was come to the feast without the
wedding garment, he *cast him out,* because he made no difference of
that place from another. First then, remember by what terrible things
God answers thee in the Christian Church, when he comes to that
round and peremptory issue, *Qui non crediderit, damnabitur,* He
that beleeves not every Article of the Christian faith, and with so
⁶²⁰ stedfast a belief, as that he would dye for it, *Damnabitur,* (no modifi-
cation, no mollification, no going lesse) He shal be damned. Consider too the nature of Excommunication, That it teares a man from
the body of Christ Jesus; That that man withers that is torne off, and
Christ himselfe is wounded in it. Consider the insupportable penances
that were laid upon sinners, by those penitentiall Canons, that went
through the Church in those Primitive times; when, for many sins
which we passe through now, without so much as taking knowledge
that they are sins, men were not admitted to the Communion all their
lives, no, nor easily upon their death-beds. Consider how dangerously
⁶³⁰ an abuse of that great doctrine of Predestination may bring thee to
thinke, that God is bound to thee, and thou not bound to him, That
thou maiest renounce him, and he must embrace thee, and so make
thee too familiar with God, and too homely with Religion, upon presumption of a Decree. Consider that when thou preparest any uncleane action, in any sinfull nakednesse, God is not onely present with
thee in that roome then, but then tels thee, That at the day of Judgement thou must stand in his presence, and in the presence of all the
World, not onely naked, but in that foule, and sinfull, and uncleane
action of nakednesse, which thou committedst then; Consider all this
⁶⁴⁰ and confesse, that for matter of manners and conversation, *The God*
of thy Salvation answers thee by terrible things. And so it is also, if
we consider Prayer in the Church.

Gods House is the house of Prayer; It is his Court of Requests;
There he receives petitions, there he gives Order upon them. And you
come to God in his House, as though you came to keepe him com-

In moribus
Iohn 15.15
Mat. 22.12

Marke 16.16

In oratione

pany, to sit downe, and talke with him halfe an houre; or you come as Ambassadors, covered in his presence, as though ye came from as great a Prince as he. You meet below, and there make your bargaines, for biting, for devouring Usury, and then you come up hither to ⁶⁵⁰ prayers, and so make God your Broker. You rob, and spoile, and eat his people as bread, by Extortion, and bribery, and deceitfull waights and measures, and deluding oathes in buying and selling, and then come hither, and so make God your Receiver, and his house a den of Thieves. His house is *Sanctum Sanctorum,* The holiest of holies, and you make it onely *Sanctuarium;* It should be a place sanctified by your devotions, and you make it onely a Sanctuary to priviledge Malefactors, A place that may redeeme you from the ill opinion of men, who must in charity be bound to thinke well of you, because they see you here. *Offer this to one of your Princes,* (as God argues ⁶⁶⁰ in the Prophet) and see, if he will suffer his house to be prophaned by such uncivill abuses; And, *Terribilis Rex, The Lord most high is terrible, and a great King over all the earth;* and, *Terribilis super omnes Deos, More terrible then all other Gods.* Let thy Master be thy god, or thy Mistresse thy god, thy Belly be thy god, or thy Back be thy god, thy fields be thy god, or thy chests be thy god, *Terribilis super omnes Deos,* The Lord is terrible above all gods, *A great God, and a great King above all gods.* You come, and call upon him by his name here, But *Magnum & terribile, Glorious and fearefull is the name of the Lord thy God.* And, as if the Son of God were but the Son of ⁶⁷⁰ some Lord, that had beene your Schoole-fellow in your youth, and so you continued a boldnesse to him ever after, so, because you have beene brought up with Christ from your cradle, and catechized in his name, his name becomes lesse reverend unto you, And *Sanctum & terribile,* Holy, and reverend, Holy and terrible should his name be.

Consider the resolution that God hath taken upon the Hypocrite, and his prayer; *What is the hope of the Hypocrite, when God taketh away his soule? Will God heare his cry? They have not cryed unto me with their hearts, when they have howled upon their beds.* Consider, that error in the matter of our prayer frustrates the prayer and ⁶⁸⁰ makes it ineffectuall. *Zebedees* Sons would have beene placed at the right hand, and at the left hand of Christ, and were not heard. Error in the manner may frustrate our prayer, and make it ineffectuall too.

Psal. 47.3
96.4

95.3

Deut. 28.58

Psal. 111.9

Iob 27.8
Hos. 7.14

Mat. 20.21

Ye ask, and are not heard, because ye ask amisse. It is amisse, if it be
not referred to his will, (*Lord if thou wilt, thou canst make me
clean.*) It is amisse, if it be not asked in faith, (*Let not him that
wavereth, thinke he shall receive any thing of the Lord.*) It is amisse,
if prayer be discontinued, intermitted, done by fits, (*Pray incessantly*)
And it is so too, if it be not vehement; for Christ was *in an Agony* in
his prayer, and *his sweat was as great drops of blood.* Of prayers without these conditions, God sayes, *When you spread forth your hands,
I will hide my eyes, & when you make many prayers, I will not
heare you.* Their prayer shall not only be ineffectuall, but even their
prayer shall be *an abomination;* And not only an abomination to
God, but destruction upon themselves; for *Their prayer shall be
turned to sin.* And, when they shall not be heard for themselves, no
body else shall be heard for them; (*Though these three men, Noah,
Iob, and Daniel, stood for them, they should not deliver them;*)
Though the whole Congregation consisted of Saints, they shall not
be heard for him, nay, they shall be forbidden to pray for him, forbidden to mention, or mean him in their prayers, as *Ieremy* was.
When God leaves you no way of reconciliation but prayer, and then
layes these heavy and terrible conditions upon prayer, Confesse that
though he be *the God of your salvation,* and do *answer you,* yet *By
terrible things doth the God of your salvation answer you.* And consider this againe, as in manners, and in prayer, so in his other Ordinance of Preaching.

Thinke with your selves what God lookes for from you, and what
you give him, in that Exercise. Because God cals *Preaching foolishnesse,* you take God at his word, and you thinke Preaching a thing
under you. Hence is it, that you take so much liberty in censuring and
comparing Preacher and Preacher, nay Sermon and Sermon from the
same Preacher; as though we preached for wagers, and as though
coine were to be valued from the inscription meerely, and the image,
and the person, and not for the metall. You measure all by persons;
and yet, *Non erubescitis faciem Sacerdotis, You respect not the person
of the Priest,* you give not so much reverence to Gods Ordinance, as
he does. In no Church of Christendome but ours, doth the Preacher
preach uncovered. And for all this good, and humble, and reverend
example, (fit to be continued by us) cannot we keepe you uncovered

Iam. 4.3
Luke 5.12
Iam. 1.6

1 Thes. 5.17
Luke 22.44

Esay. 1.15

Prov. 28.9
Psal. 109.7

Ezek. 14.14

*In conci-
onibus*
1 Cor. 1.21

Lam. 4.16

⁷²⁰ till the Text be read. All the Sermon is not Gods word, but all the Sermon is Gods Ordinance, and the Text is certainly his word. There is no salvation but by faith, nor faith but by hearing, nor hearing but by preaching; and they that thinke meanliest of the Keyes of the Church, and speake faintliest of the Absolution of the Church, will yet allow, That those Keyes lock, and unlock in Preaching; That Absolution is conferred, or withheld in Preaching, That the proposing of the promises of the Gospel in preaching, is that binding and loosing on earth, which bindes and looses in heaven. And then, though Christ have bid us, *Preach the Gospel to every creature,* yet, ⁷³⁰ in his own great Sermon in the Mount, he hath forbidden us, *to give holy things to dogs, or to cast pearle before swine, lest they trample them, and turne and rend us.* So that if all those manifold and fearfull judgements, which swell in every Chapter, and blow in every verse, and thunder in every line of every Booke of the Bible, fall upon all them that come hither, as well, if they turne, and rend, that is, Calumniate us, the person of the Preacher, as if they trample upon the pearles, that is, undervalue the Doctrine, and the Ordinance it selfe; If his terrible Judgements fall upon every uncharitable mis-interpretation of that which is said here, and upon every irreverence in this ⁷⁴⁰ place, and in this action; Confesse, that though he be *the God of your salvation,* and doe *answer you,* yet, *by terrible things doth the God of your salvation answer you.* And confesse it also, as in manners, and in prayers, and in preaching, so in the holy and blessed Sacrament.

This Sacrament of the Body and Blood of our Saviour, *Luther* calls safely, *Venerabile & adorabile;* for certainly, whatsoever that is which we see, that which we receive, is to be adored; for, we receive Christ. He is *Res Sacramenti,* The forme, the Essence, the substance, the soule of the Sacrament; And *Sacramentum sine re Sacramenti, mors est,* To take the body, and not the soule, the bread, and not ⁷⁵⁰ Christ, is death. But he that feels Christ, in the receiving of the Sacrament, and will not bend his knee, would scarce bend his knee, if he saw him. The first of that royall Family, which thinks it selfe the greatest in Christendome at this day, The House of Austrich, had the first marks of their Greatnesse, The Empire, brought into that House, for a particular reverence done to the holy and blessed Sacrament. What the bread and wine is, or what becomes of it, *Damascen* thinks

Marginal notes:

Mar. 16.15

Mat. 7.6

In Sacramento

Bernar.

Alvarez de Auxil.
Epist. ad Phil. 3
Damasc.

impertinent to be inquired. He thinks he hath said enough; (and so may we doe) *Migrat in substantiam animæ;* There is the true Transubstantiation, that when I have received it worthily, it becomes my
760 very soule; that is, My soule growes up into a better state, and habitude by it, and I have the more soule for it, the more sanctified, the more deified soule by that Sacrament.

Now this Sacrament, which as it is ministred to us, is but a Sacrament, but as it is offered to God, is a Sacrifice too, is a fearfull, a terrible thing. If the sacrifices of the Law, the blood of Goats and Rammes, were so, how fearfull, how terrible, how reverentiall a thing is the blood of this immaculate Lambe, the Sonne of God? And though God doe so abound in goodnesse towards us, *Vt possint injuriata Sacramenta prodesse reversis,* (as S. *Cyprian* excellently ex-
770 presses it) That that Sacrament which we have injured and abused, received unworthily, or irreverently, at one time, may yet benefit us, and be the savour and seale of life unto us, at another, yet when you heare that terrible Thunder break upon you, *That the unworthy receiver eats and drinks his own damnation,* That he makes Christ Jesus, who is the propitiation of all the world, his damnation; And then, That not to have come to a severe examination of the Conscience before, and to a sincere detestation of the sin, and to a formed, and fixed, and deliberate, and determinate resolution against that sin, at the receiving of the Sacrament, (which, alas, how few doe? Is there one that does
780 it? There is scarce one) That this makes a man an unworthy receiver of the Sacrament, That thus we make a *mock of the Sonne of God,* thus *we tread the blood of the Covenant under foot, and despite the Spirit of grace;* And that for this, at the last day, we shall be ranked with *Iudas,* and not onely with *Iudas,* as a negligent despiser, but with *Iudas,* as an actuall betrayer of the blood of Christ Jesus. Consider well, with what fearfull Conditions even this seale of your reconciliation is accompanied, and though you may not doubt, but that God, *the God of your salvation does answer you,* yet you must confesse too, That it is *by terrible things,* that he does it. And, as it is so
790 in matter of manners, and so in our prayers, and so in our preaching, and so in the Sacrament, so is it also at the houre of our Death, which is as far as we can pursue this Meditation, (for, after Death we can aske nothing at Gods hands, and therefore God makes us no answer)

Cyprian

1 Cor. 11.29

Heb. 10.29

And therefore with that Conclusion of all, we shall conclude all, *That by terrible things, the God of our salvation answers us,* at the houre of our death.

In morte   Though death be but a sleepe, yet it is a sleepe that an Earth-quake cannot wake; And yet there is a Trumpet that will, when that hand of God, that gathered dust to make these bodies, shall crumble these 800 bodies into dust againe, when that soule that evaporated it selfe in unnecessary disputations in this world, shall make such fearfull and distempered conclusions, as to see God onely by absence, (never to see him face to face) And to know God onely by ignorance, (never to know him *sicuti est,* as he is) (for he is All mercy) And to possesse immortality, and impossibility of dying onely in a continuall dying; when, as a Cabinet whose key were lost, must be broken up, and torne in pieces, before the Jewell that was laid up in it, can be taken out; so thy body, (the Cabinet of thy soule) must be shaken and shivered by violent sicknesse, before that soule can goe out, And when 810 it is thus gone out, must answer for all the imperfections of that body, which body polluted it, And yet, though this soule be such a loser by that body, it is not perfectly well, nor fully satisfied, till it be reunited to that body againe; when thou remembrest, (and, oh, never forget

Mat. 26.38   it) that Christ himselfe *was heavy in his soule unto Death,* That
Mat. 26.39   Christ himselfe came to a *Si possibile, If it be possible, let this Cup*
Mat. 27.46   *passe;* That he came to a *Quare dereliquisti,* a bitter sense of Gods dereliction, and forsaking of him, when thou considerest all this, compose thy selfe for death, but thinke it not a light matter to dye. Death made the Lyon of Judah to roare; and doe not thou thinke, 820 that that which we call going away like a Lambe, doth more testifie a conformity with Christ, then a strong sense, and bitter agony, and colluctation with death, doth. Christ gave us the Rule, in the Example; He taught us what we should doe, by his doing it; And he pre-admitted a fearfull apprehension of death. A Lambe is a Hieroglyphique of Patience, but not of stupidity. And death was Christs *Consummatum est,* All ended in death; yet he had sense of death; How much more doth a sad sense of our transmigration belong to us, to whom death is no *Consummatum est,* but an *In principio;* our account, and our everlasting state begins but then.

Psal. 130.4   830   *Apud te propitiatio, ut timearis;* In this knot we tie up all; *With*

thee there is mercy, that thou mightest be feared. There is a holy feare,
that does not onely consist with an assurance of mercy, but induces,
constitutes that assurance. *Pavor operantibus iniquitatem,* sayes Pro. 21.15
Solomon; Pavor, horror, and servile feare, jealousie and suspition of
God, diffidence, and distrust in his mercy, and a bosome-prophecy of
self-destruction; *Destruction* it selfe, (so we translate it) *be upon the
workers of iniquity; Pavor operantibus iniquitatem;* And yet sayes
that wise King, *Beatus qui semper Pavidus; Blessed is that man that* Pro. 28.14
always fears; who, though he always hope, and beleeve the good
⁸⁴⁰ that God will shew him, yet also feares the evills, that God might
justly multiply upon him; Blessed is he that looks upon God with
assurance, but upon himselfe with feare. For, though God have given
us light, by which we may see him, even in Nature, (for, *He is the
confidence of all the ends of the Earth, and of them that are a far of
upon the Sea*) Though God have given us a clearer light in the Law,
and experience of his providence upon his people throughout the Old
Testament, Though God have abundantly, infinitely multiplied these
lights and these helpes to us in the Christian Church, where he is *the
God of salvation,* yet, as *he answers us by terrible things,* (in that first
⁸⁵⁰ acceptation of the words which I proposed to you) that is, Gives us
assurances, by miraculous testimonies in our behalfe, that he will
answer our patient expectation, by terrible Judgements and Revenges
upon our enemies, *In his Righteousnesse,* that is, In his faithfulnesse,
according to his Promises, and according to his performances of those
Promises, to his former people; So in the words, considered the other
way, In his Holinesse, that is, in his wayes of imprinting Holinesse in
us, He answers us *by terrible things,* in all those particulars, which we
have presented unto you; By infusing faith; but with that terrible
addition, *Damnabitur,* He that beleeveth not, shall be damned; He
⁸⁶⁰ answers us, by composing our manners, and rectifying our life and
conversation; but with terrible additions of censures, and Excommunications, and tearings off from his own body, which is a death to
us, and a wound to him; He answers us by enabling us to speake to
him in Prayer; but with terrible additions, for the matter, for the
manner, for the measure of our Prayer, which being neglected, our
very Prayer is turned to sin. He answers us in Preaching; but with
that terrible commination, that even his word may be the savor of

death unto death. He answers us in the Sacrament; but with that terrible perplexity and distraction, that he that seemes to be a *Iohn,* or
870 a *Peter,* a Loving, or a Beloved Disciple, may be a *Iudas,* and he that seems to have received the seale of his reconciliation, may have eat and drunke his own Damnation. And he answers us at the houre of death; but with this terrible obligation, That even then I make sure my salvation with feare and trembling. That so we imagine not a God of wax, whom we can melt, and mold, when, and how we will; That we make not the Church a Market, That an over-homelines and familiarity with God in the acts of Religion, bring us not to an irreverence, nor indifferency of places; But that, as the Militant Church is the porch of the Triumphant, so our reverence here, may
880 have some proportion to that reverence which is exhibited there,

Revel. 4.10

where the Elders cast their Crownes before the Throne, and continue in that holy and reverend acclamation, *Thou art worthy, O Lord, to receive Glory, and Honor, and Power;* for, (as we may adde from this Text) *By terrible things, O God of our salvation, doest thou answer us in righteousnesse.*

The fifth of my Prebend Sermons upon my five Psalmes:
Preached at S. Pauls.

Psal. 66.3. *Say unto God, How terrible art thou in thy works! Through the greatnesse of thy Power shall thine Enemies submit themselves unto thee.*

IT is well said, (so well, as that more then one of the Fathers seeme to have delighted themselves in having said it) *Titulus Clavis,* The Title of the Psalme, is the Key of the Psalme; the Title opens the whole Psalme. The Church of Rome will needs keepe the Key of heaven, and the key to that Key, the Scriptures, wrapped up in that Translation, which in no case must be departed from. There, the key of this Psalm, (the Title thereof) hath one bar wrested, that is, made otherwise, then he that made the Key, (the Holy Ghost) intended it; And another bar inserted, that is, one clause added, which the Holy
10 Ghost added not. Where we reade, in the Title, *Victori, To the chiefe Musician,* they reade, *In finem, A Psalme directed upon the end.* I think, they meane upon the later times, because it is in a great part, a Propheticall Psalme, of the calling of the Gentiles. But after this change, they also adde, *Resurrectionis, A Psalme concerning the Resurrection;* and that is not in the Hebrew, nor any thing in the place thereof. And, after one Author in that Church had charged the Jewes, That they had rased that clause out of the Hebrew, and that it

Leo Castr.

160

was in the Hebrew at first, A learned, and a laborious Jesuit, (for Lorinus
truely, Schooles may confesse the Jesuits to bee learned, for they have
²⁰ assisted there; and States, and Councell-tables may confesse the Jesuits
to be laborious, for they have troubled them there) hee, I say, after he
had chidden his fellow, for saying, That this word had ever been in
the Hebrew, or was razed out from thence by the Jewes, concludes
roundly, *Vndecunque advenerit,* Howsoever those Additions, which
are not in the Hebrew, came into our Translation, *Authoritatem
habent, & retineri debent,* Their very being there, gives them Authen-
tikenesse, and Authority, and there they must be. That this, in the
Title of this Psalme, be there, wee are content, as long as you know,
that this particular, (That this Psalme by the Title thereof concerns
³⁰ the Resurrection) is not in the Originall, but added by some Expositor
of the Psalmes; you may take knowledge too, That that addition hath
beene accepted and followed, by many, and ancient, and reverend
Expositors, almost all of the Easterne, and many of the Westerne
Church too; and therefore, for our use and accommodation, may well
be accepted by us also.

We consider ordinarily three Resurrections: A spirituall Resurrection, a Resurrection from sinne, by Grace in the Church; A temporall
Resurrection, a Resurrection from trouble, and calamity in the world;
And an eternall Resurrection, a Resurrection after which no part of
⁴⁰ man shall die, or suffer againe, the Resurrection into Glory. Of the
first, The Resurrection from sinne, is that intended in *Esay, Arise, and* Esay 60.1
*shine, for thy light is come, and the glory of the Lord is risen upon
thee.* Of the later Resurrection, is that harmonious straine of all the
Apostles in their Creed intended, *I beleeve the Resurrection of the
body.* And of the third Resurrection, from oppressions and calamities
which the servants of God suffer in this life, some of our later men Calvin
understand that place of *Iob, I know that my Redeemer liveth, and* Iob. 19. 26
that in my flesh I shall see God; And that place of *Ezekiel* all under- Ezek. 37
stand of that Resurrection, where God saith to the Prophet, *Sonne of*
⁵⁰ *man, can these bones live?* Can these men thus ruined, thus dispersed,
bee restored againe by a resurrection in this world? And to this
resurrection from the pressures and tribulations of this life, doe those
Interpreters, who interpret this Psalme, of a Resurrection, refer this
our Text, (*Say unto God, How terrible art thou in thy works!*

Through the greatnesse of thy power shall thine enemies submit themselves unto thee.) Consider how powerfully God hath, and you cannot doubt, but that God will give them a Resurrection in this world, who rely upon him, and use his meanes, whensoever any calamity hath dejected them, ruined them, scattered them in the eyes ⁶⁰ of men. Say unto the Lord, That he hath done it, and the Lord will say unto thee, that he will doe it againe, and againe for thee.

Divisio   We call *Noah, Ianus,* because hee had two faces, in this respect, That hee looked into the former, and into the later world, he saw the times before, and after the flood. *David* in this Text, is a *Ianus* too; He looks two wayes, he hath a Prospect, and a Retrospect, he looks backward and forward, what God had done, and what God would doe. For, as we have one great comfort in this, That Prophecies are become Histories, that whatsoever was said by the mouthes of the Prophets, concerning our salvation in Christ, is effected, (so prophecies are made ⁷⁰ histories) so have wee another comfort in this Text, That Histories are made Prophecies; That whatsoever we reade that God had formerly done, in the reliefe of his oppressed servants, wee are thereby assured that he can, that he will doe them againe; and so Histories are made Prophecies: And upon these two pillars, A thankfull acknowledgement of that which God hath done, And a faithfull assurance that God will doe so againe, shall this present Exercise of your devotions be raysed; And these are our two parts. *Dicite Deo, Say unto God, How terrible art thou in thy works!* (that part is Historicall, of things past) *In multitudine virtutis, In the greatnesse of thy power, shall thine enemies submit themselves unto thee,* (that part is Propheticall, of things to come.)

In the History wee are to turne many leafes, and many in the Prophecy too, to passe many steps, to put out many branches in each. In the first, these; *Dicite, say ye;* where we consider first, The Person that enjoyns this publike acknowledgement and thanksgiving, It is *David,* and *David* as a King; for to Him, to the King, the ordering of publike actions, even in the service of God appertans. *David, David* the King speaks this, by way of counsell, and perswasion, and concurrence to all the world, (for so in the beginning, and in some other passages of the Psalme, it is *Omnis terra, All yee lands,* Verse 1. and *All the earth,* Verse 4.) *David* doth what he can, that all the world might concurre in one manner of serving God. By way of Assistance he extends to all, And by way of Injunction and commandement to all his, to all that are under his government, *Dicite, say you,* that is, you shall say, you shall serve God thus. And as he gives counsell to all, and gives lawes to all his subjects, so he submits himselfe to the same law; For, (as wee shall see in some parts of the Psalme, to which the Text refers) he professes in his particular, that he will say and doe, whatsoever hee bids them doe, and say; *My house shall serve the* ¹⁰⁰ *Lord,* sayes *Ioshua;* But it is, *Ego, & domus mea, I and my house;* himselfe would serve God aright too.

Iosh. 24.15

From such a consideration of the persons, in the Historicall part, wee shall passe to the commandement, to the duty it selfe; That is, first *Dicite, say.* It is more then *Cogitate,* to Consider Gods former goodnesse; more then *Admirari,* to Admire Gods former goodnesse; speculations, and extasies are not sufficient services of God; *Dicite, Say unto God,* Declare, manifest, publish your zeale, is more then *Cogitate,* Consider it, thinke of it; but it is lesse then *Facite,* To come to action; wee must declare our thankfull zeale to Gods cause, we ¹¹⁰ must not modifie, not disguise that; But, for the particular wayes of promoving, and advancing that cause, in matter of action, we must refer that to them, to whom God hath referred it. The Duty is a Commemoration of Benefits; *Dicite,* Speake of it, ascribe it, attribute it to the right Author; Who is that? That is the next Consideration, *Dicite Deo, Say unto God; Non vobis,* Not to your owne Wisdome, or Power, *Non Sanctis,* Not to the care and protection of Saints or Angels, *Sed nomini ejus da gloriam,* Onely unto his name be all the glory ascribed. And then, that which fals within this commandement, this Consideration, is *Opera ejus,* The works of God, (*How terrible* ¹²⁰ *art thou in thy works!*) It is not *Decreta ejus, Arcana ejus,* The secrets of his State, the wayes of his government, unrevealed Decrees, but those things, in which he hath manifested himselfe to man, *Opera,* his works. Consider his works, and consider them so as this commandement enjoynes, that is, *How terrible God is in them;* Determine not your Consideration upon the worke it self, for so you may think too lightly of it, That it is but some naturall Accident, or some imposture and false Miracle, or illusion, Or you may thinke of it with an amazement, with a stupidity, with a consternation, when you con-

sider not from whom the worke comes, consider God in the worke;
130 And God so, as that though he be terrible in that worke, yet, he is so
terrible but so, as the word of this Text expresses this terriblenesse,
which word is *Norah,* and *Norah* is but *Reverendus,* it is a terror of
Reverence, not a terror of Confusion, that the Consideration of God
in his works should possesse us withall.

And in those plaine and smooth paths, wee shall walke through the
first part, The historicall part, what God hath formerly done, (*Say
unto God, how terrible art thou in thy works!*) from thence we descend to the other, The Propheticall part, what, upon our performance of this duty, God will surely do in our behalfe; he will subdue
140 those enemies, which, because they are ours, are his; *In multitudine
virtutis, In the greatnesse of thy power, shall thine enemies submit
themselves unto thee.* Where we shall see first, That even God himselfe hath enemies; no man therefore can be free from them; And
then we shall see, whom God cals enemies here, Those who are enemies to his cause, and to his friends; All those, if we will speake
Davids language, the Holy Ghosts language, we must call Gods enemies. And these enemies nothing can mollifie, nothing can reduce,
but Power; faire meanes, and perswasion will not worke upon them;
Preaching, Disputing will not doe it; It must be Power, and great-
150 nesse of power, and greatnesse of Gods Power. The Law is Power,
and it is Gods Power; All just Laws are from God. One Act of this
Power (an occasionall executing of Laws at some few times, against
the enemies of Gods truth) will not serve; there must be a constant
continuation of the execution thereof; nor will that serve, if that be
done onely for worldly respects, to raise money, and not rather to
draw them, who are under those Laws, to the right worship of God,
in the truth of his Religion. And yet all, that even all this, This power,
this great power, his power shall worke upon these, his, and our
enemies, is but this, *They shall submit themselves,* sayes the text, but
160 how? *Mentientur tibi,* (as it is in the Originall, and as you finde it in
the Margin) They shall dissemble, they shall lie, they shall yeeld a
fained obedience, they shall make as though they were good Subjects,
but not be so. And yet, even this, Though their submission be but
dissembled, but counterfaited, *David* puts amongst Gods blessings to
a State, and to a Church; It is some blessing, when Gods enemies dare

not appeare, and justifie themselves, and their Cause, as it is a heavy discouragement, when they dare do that. Though God doe not so far consummate their happinesse, as that their enemies shall be truly reconciled, or throughly rooted out, yet he shall afford them so much
170 happinesse, as that they shall doe them no harme.

And, Beloved, this distribution of the text, which I have given you, is rather a Paraphrase, then a Division, and therefore the rest will rather be a Repetition, then a Dilatation; And I shall onely give some such note, and marke, upon every particular branch, as may returne them, and fix them in your memories, and not enlarge my selfe far in any of them, for I know, the time will not admit it.

First then, we remember you, in the first branch of the first part, that *David,* in that Capacity, as King, institutes those Orders, which the Church is to observe in the publique service of God. For, the King
180 is King of men; not of bodies onely, but of soules too; And of Christian men; of us, not onely as we worship one God, but as we are to expresse that worship in the outward acts of Religion in the Church. God hath called himselfe King; and he hath called Kings Gods. And when we looke upon the actions of Kings, we determine not our selves in that person, but in God working in that person. As *it is not I that doe any good, but the grace of God in me,* So it is not the King that commands, but the power of God in the King. For, as in a Commission from the King, the King himselfe workes in his Commissioners, and their just Act is the Kings Act: So in the Kings lawfull
190 working upon his Subjects, God works, and the Kings acts are Gods acts.

That abstinence therefore, and that forbearance which the Roman Church hath used, from declaring whether the Laws of secular Magistrates do bind the Conscience, or no, that is, whether a man sin in breaking a Temporall Law, or no, (for, though it have beene disputed in their books, and though the Bishop of that Church were supplicated in the Trent Councell, to declare it, yet he would never be brought to it) that abstinence, I say, of theirs, though it give them one great advantage, yet it gives us another. For, by keeping it still
200 undetermined, and undecided, how far the Laws of temporall Princes doe binde us, they keepe up that power, which is so profitable to them, that is, To divide Kings and Subjects, and maintaine jealousies

1 Part
Rex
gubernat
Ecclesiam

1 Cor. 15.10

betweene them, because, if the breach of any Law, constitute a sin, then enters the jurisdiction of Rome; for, that is the ground of their indirect power over Princes, *In ordine ad spiritualia,* that in any action, which may conduce to sin, they may meddle, and direct, and constraine temporall Princes. That is their advantage, in their forbearing to declare this doctrine; And then, our advantage is, That this enervates, and weakens, nay destroyes and annihilates that ordi-
210 nary argument, That there must be alwayes a Visible Church, in which every man may have cleare resolution, and infallible satisfaction, in all scruples that arise in him, and that the Roman Church is that Seat, and Throne of Infallibility. For, how does the Roman Church give any man infallible satisfaction, whether these or these things, grounded upon the temporall Laws of secular Princes, be sins or no, when as that Church hath not, nor will not come to a determination in that point? How shall they come to the Sacrament? how shall they go out of the world with a cleare conscience, when many things lye upon them which they know not, nor can be informed by
220 their Confessors, whether they be sins or no? And thus it is in divers other points besides this; They pretend to give satisfaction and peace in all cases, and pretend to be the onely true Church for that, and yet leave the conscience in ignorance, and in distemper, and distresse, and distraction in many particulars.

The Law of the Prince is rooted in the power of God. The roote of all is Order, and the orderer of all is the King; And what the good Kings of Judah, and the religious Kings of the Primitive Christian Church did, every King may, nay, should do. For, both the Tables are committed to him; (as well the first that concernes our religious
230 duties to God, as the other that concernes our Civill duties to men.) So is the Arke, where those Tables are kept, and so is the Temple, where that Arke is kept; all committed to him; and he oversees the manner of the religious service of God. And therefore it is, that in the Schooles we call Sedition and Rebellion, Sacriledge; for, though the trespasse seeme to be directed but upon a man, yet in that man, whose office (and consequently his person) is sacred, God is opposed, and violated. And it is impiously said of a Jesuit, (I may easily be

Gretzer   beleeved of that Jesuit, if any other might be excepted) *Non est Regum etiam veram doctrinam confirmare,* The King hath nothing

²⁴⁰ to doe with Religion, neither doth it belong to him to establish any forme of Religion in his Kingdome, though it bee the right Religion, and though it be but by way of Confirmation.

This then *David, David* as a King takes to be in his care, in his office, To rectifie and settle Religion, that is, the outward worship of God. And this he intimates, this he conveyes by way of counsaile, and perswasion to all the world; he would faine have all agree in one service of God. Therefore he enters the Psalme so, *Iubilate omnes terræ, Rejoyce all ye lands;* and, *Adoret te omnis terra, All the earth shall worship thee;* and againe, *Venite & audite omnes, Come and heare* ²⁵⁰ *all ye that feare God.* For, as S. *Cyprian* sayes of Bishops, That every Bishop is an universall Bishop, That is, must take into his care and contemplation, not onely his owne particular Dioces, but the whole Catholique Church: So every Christian King is a King of the whole Christian world, that is, must study, and take into his care, not onely his own kingdome, but all others too. For, it is not onely the municipall law of that kingdome, by which he is bound to see his own subjects, in all cases, righted, but in the whole law of Nations every King hath an interest. My soule may be King, that is, reside principally in my heart, or in my braine, but it neglects not the remoter parts of ²⁶⁰ my body. *David* maintains Religion at home; but he assists, as much as he can, the establishing of that Religion abroad too.

David endevours that, perʃwades that every where; but he will be sure of it at home; There he enjoyns it, there he commands it; *Dicite,* sayes he, *Say;* that is, This you shall say, you shall serve God thus. We cannot provide, that there shall be no Wolves in the world, but we have provided that there shall be no Wolves in this kingdome. Idolatry will be, but there needs be none amongst us. Idolaters were round about the children of Israel in the land of promise; They could not make all those Proselytes; but yet they kept their own station. ²⁷⁰ When the Arian heresie had so surrounded the world, as that *Vniversa fere Orientalis Ecclesia,* Almost all the Eastern Church, And *Cuncti pene Latini Episcopi, aut vi, aut fraude decepti,* Almost all the Bishops of the Westerne Church, were deceived, or threatned out of their Religion into Arianisme; Insomuch, that S. *Hilarie* gives a note of an hundred and five Bishops of note, noted with that heresie; When that one Bishop, who will needs be all alone, the Bishop of

Omnibus persuadet

Ver. 1
Ver. 4
Ver. 16

Suis imperat

Nicephor.

Vinc. Lyra

Hilar.

Hieron.
De Roma pont.
1.4. c.9

Rome, *Liberius,* so far subscribed to that heresie, (as S. *Hieroms* expresse words are) that *Bellarmine* himselfe does not onely not deny it, but finds himselfe bound, and finds it hard for him to prove, That ²⁸⁰ though *Liberius* did outwardly professe himselfe to be an Arian, yet in his heart he was none; yet for all this impetuousnesse of this flood of this heresie, *Athanasius,* as Bishop, excommunicated the Arians in his Dioces, And *Constantine,* as Emperor, banished them out of his Dominions. *Athanasius* would have been glad, if no other Church, *Constantine* would have been glad, if no other State would have received them; When they could not prevaile so far, yet they did that which was possible, and most proper to them, they preserved the true worship of the true God in their own Jurisdiction.

Ipse facit,
quod jubet

²⁹⁰ *David* could not have done that, if he had not had a true zeale to Gods truth, in his own heart. And therefore, as we have an intimation of his desire to reduce the whole world, and a testimony of his earnestnesse towards his own Subjects, so we have an assurance, that in his own particular, he was constantly established in this truth. He

Ver. 5
Ver. 8
Ver. 16
Psal. 145.3

cals to all, (*Come and see the works of God*) And more particularly to all his, (*O blesse our God yee people*) but he proposes himselfe to their consideration too, (*I will declare what he hath done for my soule.*) *Great is the Lord, and greatly to be feared,* sayes this religious King, in another Psalme; And that is a Proclamation, a Remonstrance

Ver. 4

to all the world. He addes, *One generation shall declare thy works*
³⁰⁰ *to another;* And that is a propagation to the ends of the world. But

Ver. 5

all this is rooted in that which is personall, and follows after, *I will speake of the glorious honour of thy Majesty;* And that is a protestation for his own particular. And to the same purpose is that which follows in the next verse, *Men shall speake of the might of thy terrible acts;* They shall, that is, They should; and, I would all men would, sayes *David;* But, whether they doe, or no, *I will declare thy greatnesse,* sayes he there; I will not be defective in my particular. And *David* was to be trusted with a pious endevour amongst his Neighbours, and with a pious care over all his own subjects, as long as he
³¹⁰ nourished, and declared so pious a disposition in his own person. And truly, it is an injurious, it is a disloyall suspition, and jealousie, it is an ungodly fascination of our own happinesse, to doubt of good effects abroad, and of a blessed assurance at home, as long as the zeale

of Gods truth remains so constantly in his heart, and flowes out so declaratorily in his actions, in whose person God assures both our temporall safety, and our Religion.

    We passe now from this consideration of the persons; which, though it be fixed here, in the highest, in Kings, extends to all, to whom any power is committed, To Magistrates, to Masters, to Fathers, ³²⁰ All are bound to propagate Gods truth to others, but especially to those who are under their charge; And this they shall best doe, if themselves be the Example. So far we have proceeded, and we come now to the Duty, as it is here more particularly expressed, *Dicite, Say unto God,* Publish, declare, manifest your zeale. Christ is *Verbum, The Word,* and that excludes silence; but Christ is also λόγος, and that excludes rashnesse, and impertinence in our speech. *Inter cæteras Dei appellationes, Sermonem veneramur,* Amongst Gods other Names, we honour that, that he is *the Word;* That implies a Communication, Gods goodnesse in speaking to us, and an obligation ³³⁰ upon us, to speake to him. For, Beloved, That standing of the Sunne and Moone, which gave occasion to the drawing of so much blood of the Amorites, is, in the Originall, not *Siste Sol,* but *Sile Sol;* He does not bid the Sunne and Moone stand still, but he bids them say nothing, make no noise, no motion so. Be the Sunne the Magistrate, and be the Moone, the Church, *Si sileant,* if they be silent, command not, pray not, avow not Gods cause, the case is dangerous. The *Holy Ghost* fell in *fiery tongues,* he inflamed them, and inflamed them to speake. Divers dumb men were presented to Christ; but if they were *dumb,* they were *deafe* too, and some of them *blinde.* Upon men that ³⁴⁰ are dumb, that is, speechlesse in avowing him, God heaps other mischievous impediments too; Deafnesse, They shall not heare him in his word, and Blindnesse, They shall not see him in his works.

    Dicite, Say, sayes *David,* Delight to speake of God, and with God, and for God; *Dicite,* say something. We told you, this was *Magis quàm Cogitare,* That there was more required then to thinke of God. Consideration, Meditation, Speculation, Contemplation upon God, and divine objects, have their place, and their season; But this is more then that; And more then Admiration too; for all these may determine in extasies, and in stupidities, and in uselesse and frivolous ³⁵⁰ imaginations. Gold may be beat so thin, as that it may be blowne

Marginal notes:

Dicite

Nazianz.

Josh. 10.12

Acts 2.3

Mat. 12.22
Mar. 7.32

Magis quàm cogitare

away; And Speculations, even of divine things, may be blowne to that thinnesse, to that subtilty, as that all may evaporate, never fixed, never applied to any use. God had conceived in himselfe, from all eternity, certaine Idea's, certaine patterns of all things, which he would create. But these Idea's, these conceptions produced not a creature, not a worme, not a weed; but then, *Dixit, & facta sunt,* God spoke, and all things were made. Inward speculations, nay, inward zeale, nay, inward prayers, are not full performances of our Duty. God heares willingliest, when men heare too; when we speake alowd
360 in the eares of men, and publish, and declare, and manifest, and avow our zeale to his glory.

Minùs quàm   It is a duty, which in every private man, goes beyond the *Cogitare,*
facere   and the *Admirari;* but yet not so far as to a *Facite,* in the private man. Private men must thinke piously, and seriously, and speake zealously, and seasonably of the cause of God. But this does not authorize, nor justifie such a forwardnesse in any private man, as to come to actions, though he, in a rectified conscience, apprehend, that Gods cause might be advantaged by those actions of his. For, matter of action requires publique warrant, and is not safely grounded upon private zeale.
Origen   370 When *Peter,* out of his own zeale, drew his sword for Christ, *Nondum manifestè conceperat Euangelium patientiæ,* He was not yet well instructed in the patience of the Gospel; Nay, he was submitted to the
Mat. 26.52   sentence of the law, out of the mouth of the supreme Judge, *All they that take the sword* (that take it before it be given them by Authority) *shall perish by the sword.* The first law, that was given to the new
Gen. 9.4   world, after the Flood, was against *the eating of blood.* God would not have man so familiar with blood. And the second commandement,
Gen. 9.6   was against *the shedding of blood,* (*Who so sheddeth mans blood, by man shall his blood be shed.*) Nay, not onely where *Peter* was
380 over-forward of himself, to defend Christ by armes, but where *Iohn* and *Iames* were too vehement, and importunate upon Christ, to give them leave to revenge the wrong done to him upon the Samaritans,
Luke 9.55   (*Wilt thou that we command fire to come down from heaven, and consume them?*) Christ rebukes them, and tells them, *They knew not of what spirit they were;* that is, of what spirit they ought to be. They knew, sayes S. *Hierome,* they had no power of their own; They goe to him who had; And they doe not say, *Domine jube,* Lord doe

thou doe it; but, Thou shalt never appeare in it, never be seene in it, onely let us alone, and we will revenge thee, and consume them. Though they went no farther then this, yet this rash, and precipitate importunity in *Iames* and *Iohn,* as well as that hasty comming to action in *Peter,* was displeasing to Christ; *Dicite,* speake; so far goes the duty of this Text; Speake by way of Counsell, you that are Counsellors to Princes, And, by way of Exhortation, you that are Preachers to the people; but leave the *Facite,* matter of action, to them in whose hearts, and by whose hands, and thorough whose commandments God works.

We are yet in our first, in our Historicall part, Commemoration; and there we made it, (in our distribution and paraphrase) our next step, what we are to commemorate, to employ this *Dicite,* this speaking upon; and it is upon Gods works; (*Say unto God, how terrible art thou in thy works!*) So that the subject of our speech, (let it bee in holy Conferences, and Discourses, let it be in Gods Ordinance, Preaching) is not to speake of the unrevealed Decrees of God, of his internall, and eternall purposes in himselfe, but of his works, of those things in which he hath declared, and manifested himselfe to us. God gave not always to his Church, the Manifestation of the pillar of Fire, but a pillar of Cloud too; And, though it were a Cloud, yet it was a Pillar; In a holy, and devout, and modest ignorance of those things which God hath not revealed to us, we are better settled, and supported by a better Pillar, then in an over-curious, and impertinent inquisition of things reserved to God himselfe, or shut up in their breasts, of whom God hath said, *Ye are gods.* God would not shew *all himselfe* to *Moses,* as well as he loved him, and as freely as he conversed with him, He shewed him but *his hinder parts.* Let that be his Decrees then, when in his due time they came to execution; for then, and not till then, they are works. And God would not suffer *Moses* his body to be seene, when it was dead, because then it could not speake to them, it could not instruct them, it could not direct them in any duty, if they transgressed from any. God himselfe would not be spoken to by us, but as hee speaks of himselfe; and he speaks in his works. And as among men, some may Build, and some may Write, and wee call both by one name, (wee call his Buildings, and wee call his Books, his Works) so if wee will speake of God, this

Opera

Exod. 33.23

Deut. 34.6

World which he hath built, and these Scriptures which he hath written, are his Works, and we speak of God in his Works, (which is
the commandement of this Text) when we speak of him so, as he
hath manifested himselfe in his miracles, and as hee hath declared
himselfe in his Scriptures; for both these are his Works. There are
430 Decrees in God, but we can take out no Copies of them, till God himselfe exemplifie them, in the execution of them; The accomplishing
of the Decree is the best publishing, the best notifying of the Decree.
But, of his Works we can take Copies; for, his Scriptures are his
Works, and we have them by Translations and Illustrations, made
appliable to every understanding; All the promises of his Scriptures
belong to all. And, for his Miracles, (his Miracles are also his Works)
we have an assurance, That whatsoever God hath done for any, he
will doe againe for us.

Deus ipse, in
operibus illis,
considerandus

Psal. 66.5
Verse 16

Heb. 13.8

It is then his Works upon which we fix this Commemoration, and
440 this glorifying of God; but so, as that wee determine not upon the
Work it selfe, but God in the Work, (*Say unto God,* (to Him) *how*
terrible art thou, (that God) *in thy Works!*) It may bee of use to you,
to receive this note, Then when it is said in this Psalme, *Come, and*
see the Works of God, and after, *Come, and heare all yee that feare*
God, in both places it is not, *Venite,* but *Ite,* It is *Lechu,* not *Come,*
but *Goe,* Goe out, Goe forth, abroad, to consider God in his Works;
Goe as farre as you can, stop not in your selves, nor stop not in any
other, till you come to God himselfe. If you consider the Scriptures to
be his Works, make not Scriptures of your owne; which you doe,
450 if you make them subject to your private interpretation. My soule
speaks in my tongue, else I could make no sound; My tongue speaks
in English, else I should not be understood by the Congregation. So
God speaks by his Sonne, in the Gospel; but then, the Gospel speaks
in the Church, that every man may heare. *Ite,* goe forth, stay not in
your selves, if you will heare him. And so, for matter of Action, and
Protection, come not home to your selves, stay not in your selves, not
in a confidence in your owne power, and wisedome, but *Ite,* goe forth,
goe forth into Ægypt, goe forth into Babylon, and look who delivered
your Predecessors, (predecessors in Affliction, predecessors in Mercy)
460 and that God, who is *Yesterday, and to day, and the same for ever,*
shall doe the same things, which he did yesterday, to day, and for

ever. Turne alwayes to the Commemoration of Works, but not your owne; *Ite,* goe forth, goe farther then that, Then your selves, farther then the Angels, and Saints in heaven; That when you commemorate your deliverance from an Invasion, and your deliverance from the Vault, you doe not ascribe these deliverances to those Saints, upon whose dayes they were wrought; In all your Commemorations, (and commemorations are prayers, and God receives that which wee offer for a Thanksgiving for former Benefits, as a prayer for future) *Ite,* 470 goe forth, by the river to the spring, by the branch to the root, by the worke to God himselfe, and *Dicite,* say unto him, say of him, *Quam terribilis Tu in Tuis,* which sets us upon another step in this part, To consider what this Terriblenesse is, that God expresses in his works.

Though there be a difference between *timor,* and *terror,* (feare and terror) yet the difference is not so great, but that both may fall upon a good man; Not onely a feare of God must, but a terror of God may fall upon the Best. When God talked with *Abraham, a horror of great darknesse fell upon him,* sayes that Text. The Father of lights, and the God of all comfort present, and present in an action of Mercy, 480 and yet, a horror of great darknesse fell upon *Abraham.* When God talked personally, and presentially with *Moses, Moses hid his face, for* (sayes that Text) *he was afraid to looke upon God.* When I look upon God, as I am bid to doe in this Text, in those terrible Judgements, which he hath executed upon some men, and see that there is nothing between mee and the same Judgement, (for I have sinned the same sinnes, and God is the same God) I am not able of my selfe to dye that glasse, that spectacle, thorow which I looke upon this God, in what colour I will; whether this glasse shall be black, through my despaire, and so I shall see God in the cloud of my sinnes, or red in 490 the blood of Christ Jesus, and I shall see God in a Bath of the blood of his Sonne, whether I shall see God as a Dove with an Olive branch, (peace to my soule) or as an Eagle, a vulture to prey, and to prey everlastingly upon mee, whether in the deepe floods of Tribulation, spirituall or temporall, I shall see God as an Arke to take mee in, or as a Whale to swallow mee; and if his Whale doe swallow mee, (the Tribulation devour me) whether his purpose bee to restore mee, or to consume me, I, I of my selfe cannot tell. I cannot look upon God, in what line I will, nor take hold of God, by what handle I will; Hee

Terribilis

Gen. 15.12

Exod. 3.6

is a terrible God, I take him so; And then I cannot discontinue, I can-
⁵⁰⁰ not breake off this terriblenesse, and say, Hee hath beene terrible to
that man, and there is an end of his terror; it reaches not to me. Why
not to me? In me there is no merit, nor shadow of merit; In God there
is no change, nor shadow of change. I am the same sinner, he is the
same God; still the same desperate sinner, still the same terrible
God.

Reverendus

But *terrible in his works*, sayes our Text; Terrible so, as hee hath
declared himselfe to be in his works. His Works are, as we said before, his Actions, and his Scriptures. In his Actions we see him Terrible upon disobedient Resisters of his Graces, and Despisers of the
⁵¹⁰ meanes thereof, not upon others, wee have no examples of that. In
his word, we accept this word in which he hath beene pleased to
expresse himselfe, *Norah,* which is rather *Reverendus,* then *Terribilis,*
as that word is used, *I gave him life and peace, for the feare wherewith*

Mal. 2.5

he feared me, and was afraid before my Name. So that this Terriblenesse, which we are called upon to professe of God, is a Reverentiall,
a Majesticall, not a Tyrannicall terriblenesse. And therefore hee that
conceives a God, that hath made man of flesh and blood, and yet
exacts that purity of an Angel in that flesh, A God that would provide himselfe no better glory, then to damne man, A God who lest
⁵²⁰ hee should love man, and be reconciled to man, hath enwrapped him
in an inevitable necessity of sinning, A God who hath received
enough, and enough for the satisfaction of all men, and yet, (not in
consideration of their future sinnes, but meerely because he hated
them before they were sinners, or before they were any thing) hath
made it impossible, for the greatest part of men, to have any benefit
of that large satisfaction; This is not such a Terriblenesse as arises
out of his Works, (his Actions, or his Scriptures) for God hath never
said, never done any such thing, as should make us lodge such conceptions of God in our selves, or lay such imputations upon him.

Psal. 2.11 ⁵³⁰ The true feare of God is true wisedome. It is true Joy; *Rejoice in*
trembling, saith *David;* There is no rejoycing without this feare;
there is no Riches without it; *Reverentia Iehovæ,* The feare of the
Lord is his treasure, and that is the best treasure. Thus farre we are

---

† Some words seem to have been omitted here, as there is no principal
verb to agree with "And therefore hee..." at the beginning of the sentence.

to goe; *Let us serve God with reverence, and godly feare,* (godly Heb. 12.28
feare is but a Reverence, it is not a Jealousie, a suspition of God.) And
let us doe it upon the reason that followes in the same place, *For our
God is a consuming fire,* There is all his terriblenesse; he is *a consuming fire* to his enemies, but he is *our God;* and God is love: And therefore to conceive a cruell God, a God that hated us, even to damnation,
540 before we were, (as some, who have departed from the sense and
modesty of the Ancients, have adventured to say) or to conceive a
God so cruell, as that at our death, or in our way, he will afford us
no assurance, that hee is ours, and we his, but let us live and die in
anxiety and torture of conscience, in jealousie and suspition of his
good purpose towards us in the salvation of our soules, (as those of
the Romane Heresie teach) to conceive such a God as from all eternity meant to damne me, or such a God as would never make me
know, and be sure that I should bee saved, this is not to professe God
to be terrible in his works; For, his Actions are his works, and his
550 Scriptures are his works, and God hath never done, or said any thing
to induce so terrible an opinion of him.

And so we have done with all those pieces, which in our para-
phrasticall distribution of the text, at beginning, did constitute our
first, our Historicall part, *Davids* retrospect, his commemoration of
former blessings; In which he proposes a duty, a declaration of Gods
goodnesse, *Dicite,* publish it, speake of it; He proposes Religious
duties, in that capacity, as he is King; (Religion is the Kings care)
He proposes, by way of Counsaile to all; by way of Commandment
to his owne Subjects; And by a more powerfull way, then either
560 counsaile or Commandment, that is, by Example, by doing that himselfe, which he counsailes, and commands others to doe. *Dicite, Say,*
speake; It is a duty more then thinking, and lesse then doing; Every
man is bound to speake for the advancement of Gods cause, but when
it comes to action, that is not the private mans office, but belongs to
the publique, or him, who is the Publique, *David* himselfe, the King.
The duty is Commemoration, *Dicite, Say,* speake, but *Dicite Deo,* Do
this *to God;* ascribe not your deliverances to your Armies, and Navies,
by Sea, or Land; no, nor to Saints in Heaven, but to God onely. Nor
are ye called upon to contemplate God in his Essence, or in his De-
570 crees, but in his *works;* In his Actions, in his Scriptures; In both those

you shall find him *terrible,* that is, Reverend, majesticall, though never tyrannicall, nor cruell. Passe we now, according to our order laid downe at first, to our second part, the Propheticall part, *Davids* prospect for the future; and gather wee something from the particular branches of that, *Through the greatnesse of thy power, thine enemies shall submit themselves unto thee.*

In this, our first consideration is, that God himselfe hath enemies; and then, how should we hope to be, nay, why would wee wish to be without them? God had good, that is, Glory from his enemies; 580 And we may have good, that is, advantage in the way to glory, by the exercise of our patience, from enemies too. Those for whom God had done most, the Angels, turned enemies first; vex not thou thy selfe, if those whom thou hast loved best, hate thee deadliest. There is a love, in which it aggravates thy condemnation, that thou art so much loved; Does not God recompence that, if there be such a hate, as that thou art the better, and that thy salvation is exalted, for having beene hated? And that profit, the righteous have from enemies. *God loved us then, when we were his enemies,* and we frustrate his exemplar love to us, if we love not enemies too. The word *Hostis,* (which 590 is a word of heavy signification, and implies devastation, and all the mischiefes of war) is not read in all the New Testament: *Inimicus,* that is, *non amicus,* unfriendly, is read there often, very very often. There is an enmity which may consist with Euangelicall charity; but a hostility, that carries in it a denotation of revenge, of extirpation, of annihilation, that cannot. This gives us some light, how far we may, and may not hate enemies. God had enemies to whom he never returned, The Angels that opposed him; and that is, because they oppose him still, and are, by their owne perversenesse, incapable of reconciliation. We were enemies to God too; but being *enemies,* we 600 were *reconciled to God by the death of his Son.*

As then actual reconciliation makes us actually friends, so in differences which may be reconciled, we should not be too severe enemies, but maintaine in our selves a disposition of friendship; but, in those things, which are in their nature irreconciliable, we must be irreconciliable too. There is an enmity which God himselfe hath made, and made perpetuall: *Ponam inimicitias,* sayes God; God puts an enmity betweene the seed of the Serpent, and the seed of the woman; And,

2 Part
Habet Deus hostes

Rom. 5.8

Rom. 5.10

Gen. 3.15

those whom God joynes, let no man sever, those whom God severs, let no man joyne. The Schoole presents it well; wee are to consider
610 an enemy formally, or materially; that is, that which makes him an enemy, or that which makes him a man. In that which makes him a man, hee hath the Image of God in him, and by that is capable of grace and glory; and therefore, that wee may not hate, which excludes all personall, and all nationall hatred. In that which makes him an enemy he hath the Image of the Devill, infidelity towards God, perfidiousnesse towards man, Heresie towards God, infectious manners towards man; and, that we must alwaies hate; for, that is *Odium perfectum,* A hate that may consist with a perfect man, nay, a hate that constitutes love it selfe; I do not love a man, except I hate
620 his vices, because those vices are the enemies, and the destruction of that friend whom I love.

God himselfe hath enemies, *Thine enemies shall submit,* sayes the text, to God; There thou hast one comfort, though thou have enemies too; but the greater comfort is, That God cals thine enemies his. *Nolite tangere Christos meos,* sayes God of all holy people; you were as good touch me, as touch any of them, for, *they are the apple of mine eye.* Our Saviour Christ never expostulated for himselfe; never said, why scourged you me? why spit you upon me? why crucifie you me? as long as their rage determined in his person, he opened
630 not his mouth; when *Saul* extended the violence to the Church, to his servants, then Christ came to that, *Saul, Saul, why persecutest thou me? Cains* trespasse against God himselfe was, that he would binde God to an acceptation of his Sacrifice; And for that God comes no farther, but to *Why doest thou thus?* but in his trespasse upon his brother, God proceeds so much farther, as to say, *Now art thou cursed from the earth. Ieroboam* suffered Idolatry, and God let him alone; that concerned but God himselfe. But when *Ieroboam* stretched forth his hand to lay hold on the Prophet, his hand withered. Here is a holy league, Defensive, and Offensive; God shall not onely protect
640 us from others, but he shall fight for us against them; our enemies are his enemies.

And beloved, it is well that it is so; for, if we were left to our selves, we were remedilesse. *It is his mercy that we are not consumed,* by his indignation, by himselfe; But it must be the exercise of his power, if

*Inimici tui,
Dei sunt
inimici*
Psal. 105.15
17.8

Acts 9

Gen. 4.6

Ver. 11

1 King 13.4

*Magnitudo
potentiæ*

we be not consumed by his, and our enemies; for, there is but that
one way in the text, that can bring these enemies to any thing, that is,
In multitudine virtutis tuæ, In the greatnesse of thy power. It must
be *power;* Intreaty, Appliablenesse, Conformity, Facility, Patience
does not serve. It must be Power, and *His power;* To assist our selves
⁶⁵⁰ by his enemies, by Witches, or by Idolaters, is not his power. It is
Power that does all; for, the name that God is manifested in, in all
the making of the World, in the first of Genesis, is *Elohim,* and that
is *Deus fortis,* The powerfull God. It is *Power,* and it is *His power;*
for, his name is *Dominus tzebaoth,* The Lord of Hosts. Hosts and
Armies of which he is not the Generall, are but great insurrections,
great rebellions. And then, as it is *Power,* and *His power,* so it is
the greatnesse of his Power; His Power extended, exalted. It is in the
Originall, *Berob, In multitudine fortitudinis,* in thy manifold power,
in thy multiplied power. *Moses* considers the assurance that they

Deut. 20.4   ⁶⁶⁰ might have in God, in this, That God fought their battails (*The Lord
your God goeth with you, to fight for you against your enemies, and
save you.*) There was his power declared, and exercised one way;
and then in this, That he had afforded them particular Laws, for their
direction in all their actions, Religious, and Civill; (*To what Nation
is God come so neare? what people have Lawes and Ordinances, such
as we have?*) So that, where God defends us by Armies, and directs
us by just Lawes, that is *Multitudo fortitudinis, The greatnesse of his
power,* his power magnified, his power multiplied upon us.

Mentientur   Now, through this *power,* and not without this power, this double
⁶⁷⁰ power, Law and Armes, *Thine enemies shall submit themselves unto
thee,* sayes our text. And then, is all the danger at an end? shall we
be safe then? Not then. The word is *Cacash,* and *Cacash* is but *Mendacem fieri,* to be brought to lie, to dissemble, to equivocate, to modifie, to temporize, to counterfait, to make as though they were our
friends, in an outward conformity. And there are enemies of God,
whom no power of Armies or Lawes can bring any farther then that,
To hold their tongues, and to hold their hands, but to withhold their

Iosh. 9   hearts from us still. So the Gibeonites deceived *Ioshua,* in the like-
nesse of Ambassadors; *Ioshuahs* power made them lie unto him. So
⁶⁸⁰ *Pharaoh* deceived and deluded *Moses* and *Aaron;* Every Act of power
brought *Pharaoh* to lie unto them. I direct not your thoughts upon

publique Considerations; It is not my end; It is not my way: My
way and end is to bring you home to your selves, and to consider
there, That we are full of weakenesses in our selves, full of enemies,
sinfull tentations about us; That onely the power of God, his power
multiplied, that is, The receiving of his word, (that is, the power of
Law) The receiving of his corrections (that is, the power of his Hosts)
can make our enemies, our sinfull tentations submit, and when they
do so, it is but a lie, They returne to us, and we turne to them againe,
690 *In the greatnesse of thy power shall thine enemies submit unto thee.*

But then, (which is our last step and Conclusion) even this, That
these enemies shall be forced to such a submission, to any submission,
though disguised and counterfait, is, in this Text, presented for a
Consolation; There is a comfort even in this, That those enemies shall
be faine to lie, that they shall not dare to avow their malice, nor to
blaspheme God in open professions. There is a conditionall blessing
proposed to Gods people; (*O that my people had hearkned unto me!
O that Israel had walked in my wayes!*) What had been their recompence? This. *The haters of the Lord should have submitted them-*
700 *selves unto them.* Should they in earnest? No truly; there is the same
word, They should have lyed unto them, they should have made as
though they had submitted themselves; and that, God presents for a
great degree of his mercy to them. And therefore, as in thy particular
Conscience, though God doe not take away that *Stimulum carnis,*
and that *Angelum Satanæ,* though he doe not extinguish all lusts and
concupiscencies in thee, yet if those lusts prevaile not over thee, if they
command not, if they divert thee not from the sense, and service of
God, thou hast good reason to blesse God for this, to rest in this, and
to call it peace of conscience: So hast thou reason too to call it Peace
710 in the Church, and peace in the State, when Gods enemies, though
they be not rooted out, though they be not disposed to a hearty Allegeance, and just Obedience, yet they must be subject, they must submit themselves whether they wil or no, and though they wil wish no
good, yet they shall be able to doe no harme. For, the Holy Ghost
declares this to be an exercise of power, of Gods power, of the greatnesse of Gods power, that his enemies submit themselves, though with
a fained obedience.

Consolatio

Psal. 81.15

Commentary and Listings of Sources

Notes to the Five Prebend Sermons

Commentary and Listings of Sources

The following set of notes is intended to elucidate difficult or abstruse aspects of the Prebend sermons and to indicate a context for them in the age and within the whole of Donne's life and work; to document Donne's sources and practices in quoting Scripture so as to highlight the most essential factor in his preaching; and to identify and substantiate, where possible, Donne's drawing of material from the Fathers, the Schoolmen, and other writers and commentators. In sum, I have tried to trace for a series of five sermons the intricate process by which Donne developed a chosen text into a finished formal discourse, and on account of which, in Walton's words, "The latter part of his life may be said to be a continual study. . . ." To pursue my intention meant to evoke in some measure the resources of Donne's sensibility, and I have had, therefore, to assume a working knowledge of Latin on the reader's part. I have tried not to presume upon this but, instead, to extract from sources, to expand contractions in and regularize texts, to summarize or quote—directly or indirectly—in English at points where material indebtedness is not at issue.

In my explanatory notes some works are cited under the abbreviations given below:

BCP

Liturgiae Britannicae, or The Several Editions of the Book of Common Prayer of the Church of England, From Its Compilation to the Last Revision . . . Arranged to Shew Their Respective Variations, ed. William Keeling. London, 1842.

Black's Law Dict.

Black's Law Dictionary: Definitions of the Terms and Phrases of American and English Jurisprudence, Ancient and Modern, 4th ed. St. Paul, Minn.: West Publishing Co., 1951.

Devotions

Devotions upon Emergent Occasions by John Donne, ed. John Sparrow. Cambridge: Cambridge University Press, 1923.

EP	*Of the Laws of Ecclesiastical Polity,* in *The Works of . . . Richard Hooker,* ed. John Keble and rev. R. W. Church and F. Paget. 7th ed. 3 vols. Oxford, 1888. (The sequence of numbers in references indicates book, chapter, and section.)
Essays	*Essays in Divinity by John Donne,* ed. Evelyn M. Simpson. Oxford: Clarendon Press, 1952.
OED	*The Oxford English Dictionary, Being A Corrected Re-Issue . . . of A New English Dictionary on Historical Principles . . . ,* ed. James A. H. Murray, Henry Bradley, W. A. Craigie, and C. T. Onions. 13 vols. Oxford: Clarendon Press, 1933.
Preb I, II, etc.	First, Second . . . Prebend Sermon.
Sermons or P-S	*The Sermons of John Donne,* ed. George R. Potter and Evelyn M. Simpson. 10 vols. Berkeley and Los Angeles: University of California Press, 1954–1963.
LXXX S	*LXXX Sermons Preached by That Learned and Reverend Divine, Iohn Donne, Dr in Divinitie, Late Deane of the Cathedral Church of S. PAULS, London.* London, 1640.

The following learned journals are cited by initials:

ELH	*A Journal of English Literary History.*
JEGP	*Journal of English and Germanic Philology.*
PMLA	*Publications of the Modern Language Association.*
RES	*Review of English Studies.*
SEL	*Studies in English Literature.*

In undertaking to verify Donne's Biblical references, I have followed Don Cameron Allen's invaluable lead in "Dean Donne Sets His Text," *ELH,* X (1943), 208–229, where methods of quotation and versions utilized in *LXXX Sermons* are discussed. To save space, I have usually not commented on Donne's exact citation of a version except where there is some unusual circumstance. Thus, the lack of a note will signal that Donne's wording corresponds with that of some version of the Bible. What version it is can be ascertained from Appendix B, which comprises a gathering of all quotations and allusions that I have been able to identify, and versions used, organized under several headings in line-by-line listings. In my notes the scope has necessarily been somewhat narrower than Allen's article and covers only the Latin and English versions used by Donne in the Prebend sermons. The Greek Bible plays virtually no role; there is a single, indirect reference to the Septuagint (Preb IV, 140–144) and one reference to *"Axiomata"* (Preb IV, 576). By contrast Hebrew words occur with relative frequency. They are always transliterated according to a standard seventeenth-century system, whose salient features are described by Mrs. Simpson (Appendix, *Sermons,* X, 329). Because Donne himself transliterates and because inability to read Hebrew is widespread, I have cited the most accessible and complete modern transliterations, those of James Strong, which are organized as in seventeenth-century lexicons and present along with a basic form (e.g., a primary root) its various renderings in different contexts. I have used this short reference:

Strong's *Concise Dict.*   *A Concise Dictionary of the Words in the Hebrew Bible; With Their Renderings in the Authorized English Version,* by James Strong, bound with his *Exhaustive Concordance of the Bible.* New York and Nashville, 1894.

Although Donne was steeped in the Vulgate as updated with the revisions prescribed by the Council of Trent, Allen's article demonstrated that he also had a lively if unscholarly interest in the variety of Latin versions by both Roman and Reformed translators that were available in his day. Some of this variety is more apparent than real. The revised Vulgate and Sebastian Munster very often coincide, and the Preface to the edition bearing Vatablus's name states that the text in the column labeled "NOVA" is a reworking of Santis Pagnini's, which is praised here and elsewhere for its fidelity to Hebraisms. Nevertheless, I have checked Donne's Latin citations and allusions against each of the versions listed below.

Moreover, in listing the Latin versions here, and the English versions subsequently, I have included mention of holdings given in W. Sparrow Simpson's *S. Paul's Cathedral Library. A Catalogue of Bibles, Rituals, and Rare Books* . . . (London, 1893). These may afford some indication of the availability of these editions to Donne. Unfortunately there can be no certainty, for in most cases the date of addition to the Cathedral library is unknown, and Geoffrey Keynes' Appendix on Books from Donne's Library in his *Bibliography of Dr. John Donne,* 3rd ed. (Cambridge: Cambridge University Press, 1958) lists no Bibles.

These Latin editions have been consulted in annotating the Prebend sermons:

Beza	Theodorus Beza's translation of the Greek New Testament, printed in parallel columns with Immanuel Tremellius's translation of the Syriac New Testament. For the title, see under "Trem" below.
Eras	*Novum Instrumentum omne, diligenter ab ER-ASMO ROTERDAMO recognitum & emendatum, non solum ad graecam veritatem, verum etiam ad multorem utriusque linguae* [i.e., both Greek and Latin] *codicum, eorumque veterum simul & emendatorum fidem.* . . . Basle, 1516.
Muns	*Hebraica Biblia, latina planeque nova Sebast.* [*iani*] *Munsteri translatione.* . . . Basle, 1546. Cited uniquely at Preb II, 537–538, 579–580; Preb III, 349; Preb V, 247–248. Shared readings with Pagn at Preb IV, 470; Preb V, 471–472.
Pagn	*HEBRAICORUM BIBLIORUM, Veteris Testamenti Latina interpretatio, opera olim X[S]antis Pagnini Lucensis: nunc verò Benedicti Ariae Montani Hispalensis, Francisci Raphelengii Alnetani, Guidonis, & Nicolai Fabriciorum Boderianorum fratrum collato studio, ad Hebraicam dictionem diligentissimè expensa.* . . . Antwerp, [1569–1572]. Cited uniquely at Preb I, 533–535; Preb II, 437 mg. Shared readings with Muns given above. (Simpson, p. 4, records possession of an edition of 1571–1572.)
T-J	*Testamenti Veteris Biblia Sacra, sive, Libri Canonici . . . Latini recèns ex Hebraeo facti, brevibusque*

Trem

Scholiis illustrati ab Immanuele Tremellio & Francisco Junio . . . : quibus etiam adjunximus Novi Testamenti libros ex sermone Syro ab eodem Tremellio, & ex Graeco à Theodoro Beza in Latinum versos, notisque itidem illustratos. Secunda cura Francisci Junii. London, 1593.

T-J cited uniquely at Preb II, 704; Preb IV, 516; Preb V, 512, 532. Shared readings with Vatab at Preb III, 44, 91, 103, 555, 558–559. (Simpson, p. 6, records possession of an edition of 1597.)

Vatab

Biblia Sacra cum duplici translatione [the Vulgate and a revision of Santis Pagnini's version], *& Scholiis Francisci Vatabli, nunc denuò à plurimus, quibus scatabant, erroribus repurgatis.* 2 vols. Salamañca, 1584. Shared readings with T-J given above. (Simpson, p. 3, records possession of a polyglot edition of 1599 which incorporates Vatablus's work.)

Vulg

Biblia Sacra Vulgatae Editionis, Sixti V. et Clementis VIII. jussu recognita atque edita. Editio nova, Versiculis distincta. London, 1849. (Simpson, p. 6, records the possession of two Vulgates of 1618 containing the Tridentine text.)

In citing English versions of Scripture, Donne tended to rely upon the popular Geneva Bible, with its spirited Protestant glosses, in the earlier years of his ministry. Only in the later years, roughly after his appointment to the Deanery of St. Paul's, did the Authorized Version gain precedence. Donne's preference for the Geneva version in the face of the literarily superior and officially commissioned translation of 1611 is a curious and seemingly significant fact, but it is impossible to infer any strain of unorthodoxy. The unexceptionable Lancelot Andrewes customarily set his text and quoted from the Geneva version as well as the Vulgate—also Donne's favorite Latin version. Happily for my purposes, Donne makes a unique display of his recourse to all of the vernacular Bibles authorized for use in the Church of England, and also to the Wyclif "Later Version," in the third Prebend sermon (ll. 414–422; cf. ll. 589–590, 619). It is also notable that Donne nowhere reveals acquaintance with the Douai-Rheims Bible, the translation made by exiled English Catholics.

The English versions used in annotating the Prebend sermons are as follows:

AV
The Holy Bible, A Facsimile in a reduced size of the Authorized Version published in the year 1611, with an introduction by A. W. Pollard, and illustrative documents. London: Oxford University Press, 1911. (Simpson, p. 13, records possession only of copies dated 1637 and later.)

Bish
The Holy Bible, conteyning the Olde Testament and the Newe. Authorised and appoynted to be read in Churches. [The Bishops', or Parker's, Bible.] London, 1595.
(Simpson, p. 12, records possession of three copies, including a "very imperfect" first edition of 1568.)

Genv
The Bible translated according to the Ebrew and Greeke, and conferred with the best translations in divers languages. With most profitable annotations upon all the hard places and other things of great importance. [The Geneva, or Breeches, Bible.] London, 1600. (Simpson, pp. 13–14, records possession only of a "Third Part" in an edition of 1583.)

Gr B
The Byble in Englyshe, that is to say, the content of al the holy Scripture, both of the olde, and newe testament. . . . This is the Byble apoynted to the use of the churches. [The Great, or Cranmer's, Bible.] London, 1541. (Simpson, pp. 8–9, 12, records possession of two editions of 1540 and three of 1541 as well as a number of later editions.)

Wyc LV
The Wyclif "Later Version" (c. 1384) reprinted in *The Holy Bible, containing the Old and New Testaments, with the apocryphal books, in the earliest English versions made from the Latin Vulgate by John Wycliffe and his followers,* ed. Josiah Forshall and Sir Frederic Madden. Oxford, 1850.

From my documentation of Donne's non-Biblical sources it will be seen that he is prolific and usually entirely accurate in his citations of the Latin Fathers. He cites the Scholastics as accurately but much less often. Because of its accessibility, inclusiveness, and reprintings of many seventeenth-century texts, I have used (despite its unevenness):

PL   *Patrologiae cursus completus, bibliotheca omnium*
                            SS. patrum, doctorum, scriptorumque ecclesiasti-
                            corum. Series latina, ed. J. P. Migne *et al.* 221 vols.
                            Paris, 1844–1903.

The less direct influence of Aquinas on Donne often makes it possible to quote in English, for which I have employed:

ST   St. Thomas Aquinas, *Summa Theologica. Literally*
                            Translated by Fathers of the English Dominican
                            Province. 3 vols. New York: Benziger Bros., 1947.

The following list indicates where in the Prebend sermons Donne's citations of the Latin Fathers and the Scholastics occur. I enclose in parentheses line numbers of passages for which I have not found a source. (Indirect indebtedness is not included here.)

St. Ambrose: Preb III, 354–355.
St. Augustine: Preb I, 31–36 (Possidius); II, 76, 339–348, 349–351, 401–408,
    427; III, 471–482, 483–490, 496–499, 552–554; IV, 457–466.
St. Bernard: Preb III, 460, 490–494; IV, 345–349, 748–750.
St. Cyprian: (Preb IV, 768–772); V, 250–253.
St. Gregory the Great: (Preb III, 545–548).
St. Hilary: Preb III, 354–355; V, 274–275.
St. Isidore of Seville: Preb I, 231–233.
St. Jerome: Preb II, 29–30, 530; III, 468–471; V, 277–278, 386–387.
Tertullian: Preb II, 265–271; IV, 216–217, (538–539).
St. Vincentius Lerinensis (Vincent of Lérins): Preb V, 271–274.
St. Thomas Aquinas (or "the Schoole"): Preb III, 443–448; IV, 1–2, 10–16;
    V, 233–236.
St. Bonaventure: Preb IV, 311–319.

The paucity of Donne's use of the Bible in Greek makes it unsurprising that his acquaintance with the Greek Fathers and other Greek writers is at one remove—that is, in Latin translation. Trying to discover what translations Donne in fact used has been my most difficult undertaking, but I have met with moderate success. Where I have been unable to identify Donne's Latin translation but have located a presumptive source in the Greek original, I have translated from:

PG   *Patrologiae cursus completus, bibliotheca omnium*
                           SS. patrum, doctorum, scriptorumque ecclesiasti-
                           corum. Series graeca, ed. J. P. Migne *et al.* 161
                           vols. Paris, 1857–1904.

Otherwise, the following list indicates the occurrences of Donne's citations of the Greek Fathers and Greek writers, and translations used, in the Prebend sermons. Again, parentheses signal an unknown or uncertain source.

St. Athanasius: Preb I, 59–73: tr. Angelus Politianus, 74–85: tr. Petrus
    Nannius Alcmarianus, perhaps with later revision.
St. Basil the Great: Preb I, 6–9: tr. Godefridus Tilmannus.
St. (John) Chrysostom: (Preb I, 292–295); II, 15–17.
(St. John) Damascene: (Preb IV, 415–417), 756–762: tr. Frontus Ducaeus.
St. Gregory Nazianzenus: (Preb V, 326–328: tr. Petrus Mosellanus.)
Nicephorus Callistus Xanthopulus: Preb V, 270–271: tr. Johannes Langus.
Origen: Preb V, 370–372: tr. unknown, of medieval provenience, printed
    in Jacob Merlin's ed. (1512).
Aristotle: Preb III, 441–442: *"vetusta translatio latina".*
Epictetus: (Preb II, 336–339.)
(Flavius) Josephus: Preb IV, 327–329.
Philo Judaeus: Preb III, 529–533.

A final miscellaneous category of sources used in the Prebend sermons defies general description. I wish, however, to call attention to the fact that Donne's (unacknowledged) use of Erasmus's *Adagia* for proverbial lore has the interesting result of displacing the standard source, Pliny's *Historia Naturalis,* from first position.

Adagia: Preb I, 209–212; III, 533–536; IV, 267–268.
Historia Naturalis: Preb II, 155–168 and mg.; (IV, 230–238).

Reformed writers and commentators, other than translators of the Bible:

Calvin: (Preb I, 335); V, 45–46.
Luther: (Preb IV, 294–295); 744–745: tr. Justus Jonas.
Melanchthon: (Preb I, 335–336).

Roman Catholic writers and commentators, other than translators of the Bible:

Didacus Alvarez: Preb IV, 752–755 and mg.
(St.) Robert Bellarmine: Preb v, 278–282 and mg.
Jacob Gretzer: (Preb V, 237–242.)
Cornelius à Lapide: Preb II, 159–168; IV, 350–352 and mg.
Johannes Lorinus; Preb IV, 330–336 and mg.; V, 16–27 and mg.
Juan de Mariana: Preb IV, 338–340.
(Luis de Molina: Preb I, 328–329.)
Maximilianus Sandaeus: Preb IV, 552 mg.
(Nicholas Serarius: Preb I, 608–609.)

Notes to the First Prebend Sermon

I.3–6: See Introduction, note 10. Cf. Hooker, *EP,* V.xxxvii.2: "What is there necessary for man to know which the Psalms are not able to teach?"

I.6–9: "Psalmis est profligandis daemonibus ac depellendis quoddam amuletum" (*Homilia in Psalmum primum ... Godefrido Tilmanno ... interpretè, Divi Basilii Magni ... omnia quae in hunc diem latino sermone donata sunt opera* [Antwerp, 1568], p. 62 A).

I.12–13: Luke 24.44 (Genv): "All must be fulfilled which are written of mee in the Lawe of Moses, and in the Prophets, and in the Psalmes"; (Bish): "all must (needes) bee fulfilled which were written of mee in the Law of Moses, and in the Prophetes and in the Psalmes." The AV is much less close to Donne's italics than both of these.

I.13–15: The Sadducees and the Pharisees (here called "the Scribes"), the main Jewish religious factions at the time of Christ, disputed the regard in which Scripture was to be held. Although both accorded highest authority to the Torah or Pentateuch, the Pharisees put later Scripture (the Prophets and other sacred writings) on an equal plane. Donne's assertion is misleading, for the Sadducees did admit later Scripture as a lower order of tradition, not divinely transmitted like the Torah but spiritually useful nevertheless. (See the references in James Hastings, *et al., Encyclopedia of Religion and Ethics* [New York: Charles Scribner's Sons, 1921], XI, 44.) Cf. Donne's historical and allegorical excursus on the Pharisees and Sadducees in *Sermons,* IX.6.372–433.

I.22–31: The Gradual Psalms, a group comprising nos. 120–134 in the AV, are each prefixed with a Hebrew title which the AV renders as "A Song of Degrees"

and St. Jerome as *"Canticum graduum."* The meaning of this title remains somewhat uncertain, the
present general opinion being that it alludes to the
recitation of these Psalms at the going up of pil-
grims to Jerusalem for annual festivals.

I.31–36:   In the AV numbering, the Penitential Psalms are 6,
32, 38, 51, 102, 130, and 143. Donne's regard for
them is evinced in three surviving series of sermons
on Penitential Psalms (*Sermons,* II, nos. 1–6; V, nos.
15–19 and VI, no. 1; IX, nos. 11–18). For confirmation of the story about St. Augustine, see ch. 31 of
the *Vita* written by a disciple and younger contemporary, Possidius (*PL,* XXXII, 63–64). Izaak Walton tells in his *Life of Donne* about the analogous
(and yet revealingly different) deathbed meditations by Donne on the portrait of himself in his
shroud.

I.36–41:   Cf. for example *Synopsis Criticorum Aliorumque S.
Scripturae Interpretum,* in *Opera Matthaei Poli . . .*
(London, 1674), IV, 636: "Censent viri eruditi
cantatos a Christo hymnos qui Paschate cani solerent,
quales sunt Psal. 114, & sequentes (Grotius): vel a
Psal. 113. ad Psal. 118 inclusivè (Buxtorsius). Hunc
hymnum vocabant, *hymnum* magnum vel, *Halleluja
magnum* (Drusius)."

I.43:   Donne refers to the Cathedral Church of St. Paul,
not to the Church of England.

I.44–57:   See Introduction, pp. 5–6 on Donne's Prebendal
duties and the idea underlying the Prebend sermons.

I.59:   curious: studious, attentive.

I.59–73:   See *In Psalmos Opusculum Angelo Politiano Interpretè,* in *Divi Athanasii Alexandrini . . . Opera
omnia, quae quidem hactenus latinitate donata sunt*
(London, 1532), p. 239^r: "Potest igitur unusquisque

in psalmi motum statumque animae suae deprehendere." The *Opusculum* (pp. 239^r–241^v) prescribes several Psalms *"adversus insidiantes"* but the sixty-second (in AV numbering; the sixty-first in the Septuagint and Vulgate) is not among them. However, the *Opusculum* appears to be a shortened version of St. Athanasius's *Letter to Marcellinus on Interpretation of Psalms,* which includes the following advice: "Against those who rush savagely upon you and want to take your life, put on the meekness you have from your God and be of good courage: for as long as those men remain thus, so much the longer stand your ground in the Lord and say then the sixty-first." I have translated from *PG,* XXVII, 33.

I.60:

exquisite: minute, careful.

I.74–75:

Donne is referring to the work headed *"Contra omnes haereses sermo"* and contained, for example, in *Sancti Patris Nostri Athanasii . . . Opera quae reperiuntur omnia. Editio · Nova juxta Parisinam ANNI MDCXXVI adornata* (Cologne, 1686), I, 1077–1087. The Preface claims that this edition is an emended version of Petrus Nannius Alcmarianus's 1555 translation, which was first published at Basle in 1556, and at Paris in 1572 and after. That Donne used this translation is confirmed by the correspondence of his quotation at *Sermons,* I.6.200 with I, 1078: "Duo quoque cum eo latrones erant in suspendio, altero execrantè, altero dicentè, *Quid execramur justum, nos secundum scelera nostra affigimur."*

I.80–83:

The Socinians, an anti-Trinitarian sect of the sixteenth century, arose out of the teachings of Lelius (1525–1562) and Faustus (1539–1604) Socinus that Christ was a man who earned divine status by his marvelous acts. Socinian hostility to St. Athanasius (here focused in a scurrilous pun which Donne cannot resist repeating) would have stemmed from his vigorous opposition to Arianism, a fourth-century anti-Trinitarian heresy. It derived its name from Arius (c. 250–c. 336) who taught that Christ was neither divine nor eternal but rather a perfectly good, and therefore glorified, creature of God. John Cosin, a conservative Anglican contemporary of Donne's, explicitly compares the Arians and Socinians (*Works* [Oxford, 1853], I, 280). Regarding the particular growth of rationalism in English theological method which was branded "Socinianism" from about 1650 onward (and is nowhere at issue in Donne), see H. J. McLachlan, *Socinianism in Seventeenth-Century England* (London: Oxford University Press, 1951).

I.92:   On the use of Latin headings for the parts of the sermon and the influence of classical oratory on homiletic form, see W. Fraser Mitchell, *English Pulpit Oratory from Andrewes to Tillotson* (London: Society for Promoting Christian Knowledge, 1932), pp. 41–130.

I.99–105:   On Donne's practice of choosing texts which can function as summaries of larger portions of Scripture, see Joan Webber, *Contrary Music: The Prose Style of John Donne* (Madison, Wis.: University of Wisconsin Press, 1963), p. 16, and Introduction, p. 42 above.

I.101–102:   Psalm 62.8 (AV): "Trust in him at all times . . . God is a refuge for us."

I.119:   mediocrity: the quality or condition of being intermediate between two extremes; a mean state or condition. (The word also has a quasi-technical reference to the Aristotelian notion of the mean.)

I.127–129:   The fascination of the black arts is theologically castigated (and implicitly attested) in King James's little treatise, *Daemonologie* (1597). See the Bodley

Head Quarto reprint, ed. G. B. Harrison (New York: G. B. Putnam and Co., 1924), pp. 6–8, 24–26, on the sins entailed by witchcraft. Donne's other reference to "Saints, or Angels" is, of course, an anti-Roman aside; cf. his *Second Anniversary,* ll. 511–518.

I.147–154:   Donne follows St. Augustine in understanding the divine image in man as the expression of the Persons of the Trinity in the three faculties of the soul. The concept has important implications for Donne's preaching (see Introduction, pp. 30–34). St. Augustine's Trinitarian line of thought, moreover, has its source in Biblical grammar: specifically, the plural verb in Gen. 1.26. In Donne's time, conversely, a proof of the Triune nature of God was regularly derived from this verse together with Gen. 1.1, which contains a plural subject. See Arnold Williams, *The Common Expositor: An Account of the Commentaries on Genesis, 1527–1633* (Chapel Hill, N.C.: University of North Carolina Press, 1948), pp. 243–245. Donne refers with approval to this Trinitarian construction (*Sermons,* III.5.336–354; VIII.1.654–671; IX.3.17–21) but considers it to fall short of the kind of proof necessary in doctrinal matters.

I.150:   Heb. 1.5 (Bish, AV): "For unto which of the Angels said he at any time, Thou art my sonne, this day have I begotten thee? . . ."

I.155–156:   undervalue: insufficiency in worth. Cf. *Sermons,* I.1.54. The substantive is rare, according to the *OED,* which cites Bacon, *The Advancement of Learning,* I, To the King—3.

I.161:   aliened: the earlier form of "alienated."

I.165–172:   Cf. Aquinas's argument (*ST,* pars I^a, q. x, art. 2): "The idea of eternity follows immutability. . . . Hence, as God is supremely immutable, it supremely belongs to Him to be eternal. Nor is He eternal only, but He is His own eternity; whereas, no other being is its own duration, as no other is its own being. Now God is His own uniform being; and hence, as He is His own essence, so He is His own eternity." On the distinction between natural incorruptibility and immortality, on the one hand, and incorruptibility and immortality conferred by God, on the other, see *ST,* pars Iª, q. xcvii, art. 2.

I.171–172:   Allusion is to 1 Cor. 15.53,54.

I.172–180:   Donne's interest in angelology remained as intense in his sermons (see, e.g., *Sermons,* IV.2.582–630; IV.3.1408–1428; VIII.3.365–492; VIII.16 *passim;* X.1.117–212) as in his poem "Air and Angels." Mary Paton Ramsay discusses this interest as one of the major, and specifically Thomistic, survivals of medieval thought in Donne (*Les Doctrines médiévales chez Donne* [London: Oxford University Press, 1917], pp. 190–217); cf. in particular Aquinas's conception of angels as intellectual essences, that is, absolutely incorporeal beings (*ST,* pars Iª, q. l, art. 1), which Donne adopts and defends in his sermons. But angelology was an equally intense seventeenth-century interest because of the political inferences to be drawn from the ranks and nature of the heavenly beings. The chief Anglican work is John Salkeld's *A Treatise of Angels* (London, 1613); Puritan literature on the subject is dealt with by Michael Walzer, *The Revolution of the Saints* (Cambridge, Mass.: Harvard University Press, 1965), pp. 160–166. The definitive treatment is Robert West's *Milton and the Angels* (Athens, Ga.: University of Georgia Press, 1955).

I.181:   Donne's phrasing does not correspond with any Latin version at Luke 6.35. Tremellius reads "filii Excelsi"; the Vulgate, Beza, and Vatablus read "filii Altissimi." The closest approximation is Vatablus's marginal note, *"Filii Dei,"* beside this verse.

I.181–182:

Latin versions (Vulg, Trem, Beza, Vatab) read "semen ipsius" in I John 3.9 and "filium Dei" in verse 10.

I.182–183:

2 Peter 1.4 (Vulg, Beza, Eras, Vatab): "divinae consortes naturae."

I.184–190:

"Deos ipsos" would appear to be Donne's own emphatic phrase based on the text alluded to in the next line, and to which P-S bracket a reference, Ps. 82.6. It reads "Ego dixi: Dii estis" (Vulg, Muns); "I have said, Yee are Gods" (AV). Although Donne glances at a political application of this text at l. 189, he omits the assertion, frequent elsewhere (*Sermons,* II.15.78; IV.7.288; IV.13.346; V.3.284–287; VI.12.104–111; VIII.15.236), that the verse is God's confirmation of the divine right of kings. A widespread use of this text and this interpretation is a mark of Elizabethan and Stuart preaching; Charles H. and Katherine George report, in fact, more extravagant assertions of divine right among Puritan than among conservative Anglican preachers (*The Protestant Mind of the English Reformation: 1570–1640* (Princeton, N.J.: Princeton University Press, 1961), pp. 211–223, esp. 216, 222, where Perkins and Andrewes on Psalm 82.6 are cited). Yet the *locus classicus* remains James I's speech to Parliament shortly after the Gunpowder Plot: "Kings are in the word of GOD it selfe called Gods, as being his Lieutenants and Vice-gerents on earth, and so adorned and furnished with some sparkles of the Divinitie" (*The Political Works,* ed. C. H. McIlwain [Cambridge, Mass.: Harvard University Press, 1918], p. 281). However, this interpretation of Psalm 82.6 is of much earlier date and is found, for example, in Lyra's Gloss on the verse. See R. W. and A. J. Carlyle, *A History of Medieval Political Theory in the West* (Edinburgh and London: W. Blackwood and Sons, 1903); J. N. Figgis, *The Divine Right of Kings,* 2nd ed. (Cambridge: Cambridge University Press, 1914).

I.191–192 and mg: P-S bracket a reference to Psalm 8.4, which in all English versions reads "What is man, that thou art mindfull of him?"

I.197–199:   These lines are a tissue of Scriptural allusions— "Love of the Father" (1 John 3.1); "Price of the Sonne" (1 Cor. 6.20, 7.23, connected typologically with Zech. 11.12); "Temple of the Holy Ghost" (1 Cor. 6.19); "Signet upon Gods hand" (Jer. 22.24; Hag. 2.23); "Apple of Gods eye" (Deut. 32.10; Psalm 17.8; Lam. 2.18; Zech. 2.8).

I.200:   evacuate: empty, deplete by purging or vomiting (in Donne's time, also by bleeding or sudorifics); evaporate: convert or turn into vapor; extenuate: make thin or lean, render emaciated or shrunken. "Metaphysical" wit emerges in Donne's verbal racking of human nature.

I.202:   contributary: parallel form of "contributory."

I.209–212:   Cf. *Essays in Divinity,* p. 65: "But of the treasures of his mercy, he hath made us the Stewards, by dispensing to one another. For first, he hath redeemed man by man, and then he hath made *Hominem homini Deum.*" As Mrs. Simpson remarks in her note on this passage in the *Essays,* the proverb is found in Erasmus's *Adagiorum Chiliades quatuor cum sesquicenturia* (ed. Stephanus, 1558), Chil. I, cent. i.69, where, along with Suidas's original Greek formulation, there is a commentary on the various human offices which were considered in antiquity (by Hesiod, Cicero, Horace, Virgil, Pliny, and St. Gregory Nazianzenus among others) to have a godlike function.

I.214:   In his *Commentary on the Minor Prophets* (1625), Cornelius à Lapide says that according to the mystical sense of Obad. 1.21, as given by St. Augustine, Clarius, Vatablus, and others, "saviours" signifies

"Christ and the Apostles" and "Sion" "the Christian Church" (*Commentarii in Scripturam Sacram* [London and Paris, 1868], VII, 370). In *Sermons,* V.18.481–487; X.5.90–94, Donne utilizes, however, St. Jerome's interpretation of this verse (also reproduced in Lyra's Gloss) where it becomes an allegory of the Pentacostal descent of the Holy Ghost upon the founders of the Church.

I.218–220:   On the Godlike prerogative of temporal authority, see the note to ll. 184–190 above.

I.222–225:   The definition of the separate but equal functions of priest and prince originated with Pope Gelasius (d. 496), who derived them from the earthly offices of Christ (McIlwain, Introduction, *Political Works of James I,* p. xxi).

I.229:   Exod. 4.16 (Bish, AV): "Thou shalt be to him in stead of God."

I.231–233:   St. Isidore of Seville, *Liber sententiarum,* III.li.6: "Cognoscant principes saeculi Deo debere se rationem reddere propter Ecclesiam, quam a Christo suscipiunt" (*PL,* LXXXIII, 723).

I.236–238:   Heb. 4.15 (Bish, AV): "For wee have not an high Priest which cannot bee touched with the feeling of our infirmities; but was in all points tempted like as wee are." The identification of Christ as "a great high Priest" prompted typological readings of much of the Old Testament.

I.239–240:   Deut. 16.18 (AV): "Judges and officers shalt thou make thee in all thy gates."

I.244 mg.:   I follow P-S in emending *LXXX S's* inaccurate "Judg. 6."

I.251:   increpation: chiding, rebuke. The noun derives from Tertullian.

I.252:   2 Chron. 16.12 (AV): "In his disease hee sought not to the LORD, but to the Physicians." The "case" (as Donne calls it) of King Asa troubled him sorely in his own illness; see the fourth Expostulation and Prayer of his *Devotions*.

I.254–255:   The first allusion is perhaps to the two recorded dealings of King Solomon with merchants (1 Kings 10.15, 28; 2 Chron. 1.16, 9.14); the second is surely to the same King's summoning of skilled workmen for the building of the Temple (1 Kings 5.6, 7.14). Donne refers to the latter incident as an example of a human contract showing trust (*Sermons*, VII.18. 105–110).

I.259:   detort: an obsolete form of "distort."

I.263–266:   The necessity of having a useful occupation and the inexcusability of remissness or delay in pursuing it are often dealt with in Donne's preaching (e.g., *Sermons*, II.3.360–376; VII.3.363–390; VIII.7.130– 147). Potter points out an especially striking resemblance between a letter to Sir Henry Goodyer written, perhaps, in 1608 and a sermon dated 24 March 1617 (Introduction, *Sermons*, I, 128); it may be that the sermon passages reflect obliquely Donne's uneasiness at having waited until the age of forty-two to take holy orders. But autobiographical inferences are not required; the theme of a "calling" for each and every individual redounds in English preaching of the age. See the discussion in C. H. and K. George, *The Protestant Mind*, pp. 126–143.

I.266:   sustentation: the keeping up or preservation of a condition or state, especially human life.

I.270 mg.:   I follow P-S in emending *LXXX S's* inaccurate "Esay 40.15."

I.274–276:   Allusion is to 2 Cor. 2.16 where preachers of the Gospel are characterized as "the savour of life unto life" to those who are saved and to 1 Cor. 3.6, where the AV reads: "I have planted, Apollos watered: but God gave the encrease."

I.278:   uncontroulably: incontrovertibly, indisputably.

I.282–283:   On the distinction between the "sense" and the "use" of a text and Donne's handling of the two, see Introduction, pp. 42–44. "Our translation" is, of course, the Authorized Version of the Bible.

I.287–331:   The degrees of authorization which Donne assigns to several Roman tenets do not entirely fit the facts. It is true that the Council of Trent (1545–1563) expressly affirmed Transubstantiation in the Mass (Session 13, ch. 4 and Canon 2) as well as the efficacy of prayer for the dead (Session 25, Decree Concerning Purgatory). However, far from offering "the worship of Images and Reliques" to the faithful, the Council prescribed a method of instruction in the proper honoring of religious objects which included stern warnings against idolatry (Session 25, On the Invocation, Veneration, and Relics of Saints, and on Sacred Images). For texts in English, see *The Canons and Decrees of the Council of Trent,* tr. J. Waterworth (London, 1848), pp. 78, 82, 232–235. Although Spanish piety particularly desired enunciation of the doctrine of the Immaculate Conception of Mary, this was withheld both in the Council's Decree on Original Sin (Session 1) and in the Constitutions of Sixtus IV. The doctrine ultimately became dogma with a Bull of Pius IX in 1854, having long been a matter of popular though unofficial assent. It is interesting to compare Donne's comment in *Biathanatos* (c. 1607) that "our Lady is said to be preserv'd from originall sinne" (facs. 1st ed. by J. William Hebel [New York: Facsimile Text Society, 1930], p. 175) with the scathing irony he directs against Melchior Canus, who attempted to establish the doctrine (*Sermons,* VII.4.183–97).

I.292–295: The Latin phrase would seem to be a "Resultance" (the term used by Walton for Donne's synoptic notes on his reading) rather than an exact quotation. It occurs twice elsewhere (*Sermons,* IV.9.279; IV.14. 445) without attribution to anyone. The closest approximations in sense which I have found are Homily 11 on John 1.14 (PG, *LIX,* 79–80), English version in *The Homilies of S. John Chrysostom* (Oxford and London, 1848), IV, 91; and Tertullian, *Adversus Praxean,* ch. x (PL, II, 189). Cf. John Whitgift, *Works,* Parker Soc. XLVII (1851), 179: "That God could do it, and therefore hath done it, is no good reason."

I.297: the Schoole: In a strict etymological sense, the educational program of the medieval universities, i.e., the monastic *scholae;* in a broader sense, Scholastic theology and philosophy, which aimed at greater understanding of the truths of divine revelation through the rational operations of analogy, analysis, correlation, definition, and systematization. Among the Schoolmen or Scholastics, St. Thomas Aquinas is by far the most frequently cited in the sermons, and at times Donne uses "the Schoole" as an informal synonym for the *Summae.*

I.303–305: Donne names Tertullian, St. Epiphanius, St. Chrysostom, St. Augustine, and St. Ambrose as early Fathers who permitted or advocated prayers for the dead (*Sermons,* VII.6.199–325).

I.311–319: Criticism of the Council of Trent for having flouted the originally Thomistic distinction between "necessary" and "indifferent" matters of faith is a widespread and constant theme in English preaching from the time of Jewel onward. See the negative comments of Perkins, Sibbes, Cosin, and others in C. H. and K. George, *The Protestant Mind,* p. 386.

I.317–318: unmaintenable: unmaintainable. This is the earliest use of the word cited in the *OED.*

I.319–331:

This passage adverts pointedly to a major fault asserted by Anglican critics of the science of casuistry (cases of conscience) as practiced in the Roman Church. The literature of Roman casuistry reached enormous proportions in the period from 1560 to 1660 due, primarily, to the efforts of Jesuits like Bellarmine, Cajetan, and Suarez; Reformed (and specifically Anglican) casuistry was a competing development of the later decades. The fault which Donne attacks is the referral of a doubting conscience to openly conflicting authorities, on the basis of which a so-called probable determination was to be reached. The problem with such help, in Donne's view, was that it was no help at all: see his more detailed criticism in *Sermons,* IV.8.442–457. Cf. Taylor's remark in the Preface to *Ductor Dubitantium* (1660) that further doubts of conscience are the only likely issue when authorities conflict; *"alii aiunt, alii negant, utrumque probabile"* makes for "sceptic theology," not moral resolution. Donne himself in *Pseudo-Martyr* (1610) exposed the at best only probable reasoning whereby English Catholics who refused to take the Oath of Allegiance to their King could be regarded as martyrs for their faith, and then proceeded to erode much (if not all) of the probable ground by citing evidence of earlier Popes' acknowledgments of superior temporal authority. Relevant further discussion can be found in A. E. Malloch, "John Donne and the Casuists," *SEL,* II (1962), 57–76; and H. R. McAdoo, *The Structure of Caroline Moral Theology* (London: Longmans, Green, and Co., 1949).

I.322–327:

"From 1617 to 1656, Philip III and Philip IV made the Immaculate Conception [of Mary] a matter of state policy, by long and earnest efforts with the papacy to decide it affirmatively" (H. C. Lea, *A History of the Inquisition of Spain* [New York and London: Macmillan, 1907], IV, 359, and documents cited there).

I.323:   P-S unaccountably read "them" between "raysed" and "so"; I restore the reading of *LXXX S.*

I.327–328:   During Charles I's reign, the Papal Court repeatedly received reports that "the English Catholics, disrupted by the dissensions of the clergy [over the nature and order of ecclesiastical jurisdiction in England], were becoming further demoralized through lack of clear guidance on such questions as the Oath of Allegiance" (Gordon Albion, *Charles I and the Court of Rome* [London: Burns, Oates and Washburne, 1935], p. 117).

I.328–329:   The theological dispute in the Roman Church over "the Concurrence of Grace, and Free-will" arose in connection with the doctrines of Luis de Molina (1535–1600), a Spanish Jesuit. In his *Concordia liberi arbitrii cum gratiae donis* Molina maintained, despite minor inconsistencies, that the efficacy of grace ultimately stems not from its nature as a free divine gift (*ab intrinseco*) but from man's voluntary cooperation, foreknown by God, with this gift. The conflict between the Jesuits, the chief defenders of Molina's doctrines, and the Dominicans, his chief opponents, was the cause of a special Congregation at Rome (1598–1607), which left undecided the points at issue. Between 1607 and 1610, if not earlier, Donne was steeping himself in the literature of religious controversy and apparently retained a strong recollection of the virulence of this particular one. See his other comments in *Sermons,* VII.4.274–286; X.7.523–531.

I.332–36:   I have not found a source for these comparisons of philosophers and Reformers.

I.340:   Amen: a Hebrew word meaning true, faithful, certain, was appended to sentences as a form of affirmation: hence, its use at the end of a prayer to signify earnest desire or assurance of being heard.

I.341:

Since the whole clause "These things saith the Amen" is Scriptural, it should presumably be in italics but is not in *LXXX S.*

I.342–351:

A Biblical concordance quickly confirms this observation on style, from which Donne draws customary spiritual implications. Two examples of the redoubling referred to occur in John 16.16–23, the Gospel appointed in the *BCP* for the third Sunday after Easter. This was the occasion of the first Prebend sermon.

I.352–354:

"Go to" is found in the Prophets at Isa. 5.5 and Jer. 18.11. But, as P-S note in a bracketed marginal reference, Donne is citing James 4.13, which in the AV reads, "Goe to now ye that say, To day or to morrow wee will goe into such a city and continue there a yere, and buy, and sell, and get gaine." Thus "Prophet" is a slip for "Apostle."

I.356–359:

Donne is apparently conflating the opening words of the Athanasian Creed (which, under the rubric *"Quicunque vult,"* is printed in sixteenth- and seventeenth-century editions of the *BCP* between Evening Prayer and The Litany) with the formula of excommunication in the Tridentine Canons. The latter actually begin *"Si quis dicet,"* state a noxious proposition, and conclude with pronouncing *Anathema,* the Hebrew word for "accursed," which is found in 1 Cor. 16.22: "If any man love not the Lord Jesus Christ, let him be *Anathema. . . ."* The verse, which served as the Tridentine model, was used by Donne as the text of one sermon (*Sermons,* II, no. 15). On the history of the formulas and ceremonies used in excommunication and their use in "The Curse," "The Bracelet," and "The Expostulation," see Robert A. Bryan, "John Donne's Use of the Anathema," *JEGP,* LXI (1962), 305–312.

I.359–361:

LXXX S reads "Goe to you" and "So also, goe to you" and "Goe to you" in accordance with AV

	punctuation (see note to ll. 352–354 above), but I have followed P-S in inserting commas for clarity.

I.361–369: This reproof is directed mainly at Puritans who emphasized the doctrine of reprobation (predestination to damnation). Charles and Katherine George contend that Donne's humane reluctance throughout his preaching to affirm reprobation is unique among English divines of his time. See *The Protestant Mind,* pp. 68–70.

I.372 mg.: The comparison which follows may have been prompted by the gloss on Psalm 62.9, the sermon text, in the AV; it gives "alike" as a variant reading for "altogether."

I.374–378: Hooker also treats this "Probleme": "For by reason of man's imbecility and proneness to elation of mind, too high a flow of prosperity is dangerous; too low an ebb again as dangerous, for that the virtue of patience is rare, and the hand of necessity stronger than ordinary virtue is able to withstand" (*EP,* V.1xxvi.5).

I.374–375 and mg.: Derived from Cicero and Quintilian, the art of formal disputation on a set topic was a staple of grammar-school and university education in the Renaissance. The more familiar form in which the influence of classical disputation is felt in Donne's work is Scholastic method, as instanced in his youthful *Paradoxes and Problems* (c. 1592?). But about 1598, when Donne was seeking court employment, he participated in a literary debate originating in the Earl of Essex's circle on the question "Which kind of life is best, that at Court, that in the City, or that in the Country?" A fine verse letter to Sir Henry Wotton ("Sir, more then kisses . . .") was the result; for other particulars see W. Milgate, ed., *John Donne: The Satires, Epigrams and Verse Letters* (Oxford: Clarendon Press, 1967), pp. 225–226.

Donne remarks on the persistent effects of training in classical oratory at ll. 554–556 in this sermon and on the shared ancestry of "Homilies, Sermons, Lectures, Orations, . . . and your owne or your fellowes Themes, or Problemes, or Commonplaces . . . when you went to Schoole, or to the University" in *Sermons*, VIII.10.22–40.

I.381–382:   The italicized phrase is no quotation but a summary of the Lord's words in Matt. 25.34–36.

I.385–386:   Exod. 23.3 (AV): "Neither shalt thou countenance a poore man in his cause."

I.386–387:   More of Lev. 19.15 (AV), which Donne quotes freely, clarifies its meaning: "Ye shall doe no unrighteousnes in judgement; thou shalt not respect the person of the poore, nor honour the person of the mightie. . . ." Cf. the moral exposition drawn from this text in *Sermons*, VII.6.346–356, 386–392.

I.393:   The sixth of the Thirty-nine Articles authorizes the use of the Apocrypha "for example of life and instruction of manners." Like the Lessons from the Apocrypha in the *BCP*, this citation conforms to the principle.

I.394–396:   Isa. 51.21 (Vulg): "Audi hoc, paupercula, et ebria non a vino"; the italicized English words appear to be Donne's translation of this Latin version, for the English versions read "thou miserable & drunken, (howbeit not with wine)" (Bish); "thou miserable and drunken, but not with wine" (Genv); "thou afflicted, and drunken, but not with wine" (AV). Allen ("Dean Donne Sets His Text," p. 226) remarks on this practice. For other occurrences, see Appendix B, pp. 353–354.

I.408:   Prov. 10.15 (Vulg, Muns): "pavor pauperum"; (AV) "the destruction of the poore is their povertie."

I.415–418:   Cf. Bacon's "Of Adversity": "But to speak in a mean. The virtue of Prosperity is temperance, the virtue of Adversity is fortitude; which in morals is the more heroical virtue. Prosperity is the blessing of the Old Testament; Adversity is the blessing of the New; which carrieth the greater benediction, and the clearer revelation of God's favour."

I.416:   doubt: anticipate with apprehension, apprehend something feared or undesired (*OED,* sense 6a).

I.425–431:   Cf. Hooker, *EP,* I.ii.4: "The general end of God's external working is the exercise of his most glorious and most abundant virtue. Which abundance doth shew itself in variety, and for that cause this variety is oftentimes in Scripture exprest by the name of *riches* (Eph. 1.7; Phil. 4.19; Col. 2.3)."

I.426–429:   The four Biblical references would seem to have been taken from a concordance entry "Riches."

I.426–427:   Rom. 2.4 (Gr B, Bish, AV): "despisest thou the riches of his goodnesse."

I.427–428:   Rom. 11.33 (AV): "O the depth of the riches both of the wisdome and knowledge of God."

I.433:   comminations: threatenings of punishment or vengeance, especially divine punishment or vengeance.

I.435–436:   P-S read "with all their labors and industry, to sustaine . . ."; I restore the punctuation of *LXXX S,* which conveys a more natural oral rhythm.

I.437:   shrewd: grievous, serious, sore; in an intensive use qualifying a word denoting something bad or undesirable in itself.

I.441:   Incorrigible: "Incapable of being corrected, amended, or improved; . . . in English law, a species of habitual offender" (*Black's Law Dict.,* p. 907). For texts of laws passed in James I's reign against "incorrigible and dangerous Rogues," see C. J. Ribton-Turner, *A History of Vagrants and Vagrancy* (London, 1887), pp. 133, 141. Inveighing against able-bodied beggars was frequent from the English pulpit of the day: see *Sermons,* III.5.200–208; VIII.12.277–288; C. H. and K. George, *The Protestant Mind,* pp. 158–159, give other references.

I.442:

accommodation: adaptation (of a word, expression, *etc.*) to something different from its original purpose. A technical homiletic term in the seventeenth century.

I.451–453:

Donne's familiarity with the traditional religious dimensions given to this question is revealed in a letter of uncertain date: "For divers mindes out of the same thing often draw contrary conclusions. . . . And as often out of contrary things men draw one conclusion: as to the *Roman* Church, magnificence and splendor hath ever been an argument of Gods favour, and poverty & affliction, to the *Greek*" (*Letters to Severall Persons of Honour,* ed. C. E. Merrill, Jr. [New York: Sturgis and Walton Co., 1910], p. 62).

I.471–478:

Cf. Hooker, *EP,* V.xlvii.2: "In reference to other creatures of this inferior world man's worth and excellency is admired. Compared with God, the truest inscription wherewith we can circle so base a coin is that of David, '*Universa vanitas est omnis homo:* whosoever hath the name of a mortal man, there is in him whatsoever the name of vanity doth comprehend' (Psalm 39.5)."

I.481:

Any of several sources could have supplied Donne with these remarks. St. Jerome's *Liber de nominibus Hebraicis* reads: "Abel, luctus, sive vanitas, vel vapor, aut miserabilis"; "Cain possessio, vel acquisitio, vel lamentatio" (*PL,* XXIII, 817, 820). Cf. Lyra's Gloss on Gen. 4.1,2 (*PL,* CXIII, 98) and Lapide's note on the same verses (*Commentarii in Scripturam Sacram,* I, 97).

I.482–509:

This depiction of the emptiness of acclamation and popular favor is one among many in a subclass of medieval and Renaissance set pieces on the variability of fortune. Here the vividness of visualization and the reference to Christ's humiliation on the way to Golgotha only shortly after the Triumphal Entry are particularly reminiscent of Shakespeare's and Daniel's depictions of Bolingbroke's London reception and the disgrace of the deposed King Richard (*Richard II,* V.ii; *The First Fowre Bookes of the civile warres* . . . , bk. II, sts. 62–64, 76–77, 83–85).

I.492:

hoysed: hoisted.

I.495–502:

This is evidently an allusion to the English Separatist—that is, extreme Puritan—refugee ministers whose conventicles were allowed to flourish first in Calvinist Holland, later in America (where a few dozen persons had settled at Plymouth six years before the delivery of this sermon). Of the group to which Donne apparently refers, the best-known names included Hugh Peters, later Cromwell's chaplain; John Paget, a Presbyterian who relocated in Amsterdam after being expelled from his Cheshire ministry; William Ames, the learned author of works attacking ceremonies and of a system of casuistry which defended the liberty of the individual conscience; John Forbes, a Scotsman, who set up in Delft after James I banished him and became famous as the Presbyterian minister to the English Merchant Adventurers; and John Davenport, a London vicar with Independent sympathies, who in 1633 eluded prosecution in the Court of High Commission by fleeing in disguise to Holland and thence, eventually, to the New World to escape Laud's drive toward religious uniformity. See the discussion in H. R. Trevor-Roper, *Archbishop Laud,* 2nd ed. (London: Macmillan, 1963), pp. 244–257. It should be understood that Donne's negative reflections arise from his longing for the unity of the Church and apply to separatism, not to colonization itself. He was responsive to the promise of America, as attested by his attempt to get himself appointed Secretary for Virginia (1609) and in his sermon of 1622 before the Honorable Company of the Virginian Plantation (*Sermons,* IV, no. 10). Ironically, Donne's words here were to have much more point in the years immediately following as a result of the coercive measures of the High Church party with which he was principally aligned. G. M. Trevelyan (*England under the Stuarts,* 12th ed. rev. [London: Methuen and Co. Ltd., 1925], pp. 173–174) states that Laud's policies were accountable for the emigration of 20,000 Englishmen to New England between 1628 and 1640. A more recent and detailed discussion of the matter is Allen French's *Charles I and the Puritan Upheaval: A Study of the Causes of the Great Migration* (London: Allen and Unwin, 1955).

I.505: Allusion is to the mocking address to Christ recorded in all English versions at Matt. 27.29 (except Genv); Mark 15.18; and John 19.3.

I.507: *"Crucifige eum"* occurs in Latin versions at Mark 15.13,14; Luke 23.21; and John 19.6.

I.508: "Beelzebub" is the title given in the Gospels to "the prince of the devils," whose agent Christ's enemies claimed he was (Matt. 12.24; Mark 3.22; Luke 11.15). On the obscure derivation of the name, see *The Oxford Dictionary of the Christian Church,* ed. F. L. Cross (London: Oxford University Press, 1957), p. 149.

I.520–522:   Cf. with Donne's precise observations and extraction of moral significance from the phrasing of his text the blunting found in Joseph Hall's "A Paraphrase upon the Hard Texts of the Whole Divine Scripture," *Works* (Oxford, 1837), III, 198–199: "Certainly, man, of what degree or estate soever, is mere vanity, and utterly deceitful in the trust that is put in them. . . ."

I.529–531:   See the questions directed to the ordinand by the presiding bishop in The Form of Ordering Priests in the *BCP, viz.:* "Are you determined . . . to instruct the people committed to your charge . . . ?" "Will you then give your faithful diligence always so to minister the Doctrine and Sacraments and the Discipline of Christ, as the Lord hath commanded, and as this Realm hath received the same . . . so that you may teach the people committed to your Cure and Charge, with all diligence to keep and observe the same?"

I.531–533:   *Chasab,* or *kāzāb* in modern transliteration, is a noun from the Hebrew root *kāzab;* as Donne says, it has the literal meaning of "to lie or deceive" and the figurative meaning of "to fail." (See no. 3576 in Strong's *Concise Dict.,* p. 55.)

I.533–535:   Donne's italicized Latin answers uniquely to Pagnini's interlinear translation of Isa. 58.11, which reads "non cuius aquae mentientur." The other Latin versions differ markedly from this and from each other. Donne's italicized English does not even resemble any English version and thus is, presumably, his literal rendering of Pagnini's Latin and the original Hebrew. The literalism is sound; the form of *Chasab* occurring in Isa. 58.11 is a third person plural imperfect, signifying ongoing action.

I.536–540:   Despite the continued use of personal pronouns, there is no discernible personal animus in Donne's remarks on the failure of courtiers to act on their promises to suitors. Another tone entirely emanates from the letters written near the close of his long and futile efforts to gain civil employment (1602–1614), a tone of moody desperation alternating with obsequiousness. See R. C. Bald, *John Donne: A Life* (New York and Oxford: Oxford University Press, 1970), pp. 290–297.

I.544–545:　In his youthful "Satire IV," ll. 237–238, Donne had deferred to "Preachers which are/ Seas of Wit and Arts" as the most competent scourgers of courtiers' vices. Topicality, however, remains subordinate to more basic and broad moral emphases in his preaching; the implication here is of conscious policy. Contrast the practice of Joseph Hall, another satirist turned Anglican (though more Puritanical) divine, especially in *The Great Imposter* and *The Fashions of the World,* two sermons which denounce the times (*Works,* V, 136–149, 246–257).

I.556–559:　Donne's italicized English phrases appear to be literal translations of unique Vulgate readings at Prov. 27.7 and Jer. 10.14, for they correspond to no English version.

I.559:　over-weening: thinking too highly of, over-esteeming.

I.560–562:　Allusion is to Gen. 3.6, 7, 10.

I.565:　Donne's use of disparate sources in pairing one of his infrequent classical allusions with a Biblical one emphasizes his point that disparately motivated violations of the sacred incur the same extreme punishment. Uzza's intentions were innocent in laying a steadying hand on the Ark of the Covenant while it was in transport; Acteon's voyeurism was not (see Ovid, *Metamorphoses,* bk. III, fab. 3).

I.574–575:   Low, leather-soled shoes with embroidered uppers are worn at solemn pontifical masses by bishops of the Roman Church generally, but at Rome they are worn only by the Pope. Not wearing shoes is a means of practicing poverty and humility used by some monastics.

I.576:   The Society of Jesus was organized by St. Ignatius Loyola and received papal approval in 1540. For other indications of Donne's hostility to the order, see Preb IV, 325–43.

I.578:   "Minorites" is an older name for the Order of Friars Minor (Franciscans) founded by St. Francis of Assisi in 1209; its rule is distinguished by the imposition of complete poverty on the order as a whole, not simply on individual friars. The "Minims" (*Ordo Fratrum Minimorum*) were organized by St. Francis of Paola in 1435; their name bespeaks their intention of exercising humility as a chief virtue by considering themselves the least (*minimi*) of all religious persons and orders.

I.579:   Repeated objects of Donne's ridicule (*Sermons,* I.3.970; II.14.398; III.4.38; IV.3.1131), the Nullans or Brothers of the Common Life were organized by Gerard Groote (1340–1384) and found mostly in the Low Countries until their disappearance in the period of the Reformation. Luther mentions having received part of his education from the "Nullbrüder" (Otto Scheel, *Martin Luther* [Tübingen: J. C. B. Mohr, 1916], I, 70). I am indebted for this information on the Nullans to Professors Paul Droulers and Garcia Villoslada of the Pontifical Gregorian University, Rome.

I.585:   competency: sufficiency, without superfluity, of the means of life; a livable estate or income.

I.593–603:

This theme of the danger of self-reliance is awesomely orchestrated in the second Prebend sermon, ll. 193–219.

I.608–609:

Cf. "The Storm," l. 14: "th'ayres middle marble roome"; *Second Anniversary,* ll. 191–192: "no desire to know, nor sense,/Whether th'ayres middle region be intense. . . ." Burton remarks ("Air rectified," *Anatomy of Melancholy,* pt. II, sec. ii, mem. 3) on Teneriffe and other places that "are highly elevated, near the middle region, and therefore cold, *ob paucam solarium radiorum refractionem,* as Serrarius answers, *com. in 3. cap Josua quaest. 5. Abulensis, quaest. 37."* It is reasonable to infer that Serarius's commentary on Joshua was also Donne's source, for he cites it explicitly in *Sermons,* III.15.222 mg. (There is no direct evidence of Donne's knowledge of the relevant passage in Tostatus Abulensis, only of a general familiarity with this author.) For a list of Donne's references to post-patristic commentators, see Appendix, *Sermons,* X, 387–401. W. Milgate (*Satires, Epigrams and Verse Letters,* p. 204) cites a parallel passage in *Blundeville his Exercises* (1594). H. J. C. Grierson, in *The Poems of John Donne* (Oxford: Clarendon Press, 1912), II, 134, traces the old cosmological belief in the intense coldness of the middle region of the air to Pliny. His account, however (*Natural History,* bk. II, chs. 38, 45–47), emphasizes the turbulent currents and the enormous variations in temperature resulting from the location of the middle region between "an unlimited quantity from the upper element of air and an unlimited quantity of terrestrial vapour" (Loeb ed., 1944, tr. H. Rackham, I, 247).

I.609–611:

The opposite (a favorable) view of mediocrity is taken by the Puritan John Downame: "The meane estate is much to bee preferred before the greatest prosperity . . . because it is most safe. . . . The meane estate . . . preserveth us from forgetfulnesse of God, irreligion and prophanesse, which accompanieth prosperity, from the use of unlawfull meanes to maintaine our state, and from unpatiency, murmuring and repining against God to which we are tempted in poverty and adversitie" (*The Plea of the Poore* [London, 1616], pp. 372–375, quoted in C. H. and K. George, *The Protestant Mind,* p. 162). Donne himself advocates "mediocrity" in religious concerns (*Sermons,* III.7.448).

I.612, 615, 627:   It may be the influence of traditional typology and not simple error that leads Donne to call David "the Prophet" instead of "the Psalmist," the usual title.

I.619:   bladder: float made from a prepared and inflated animal bladder.

I.630–631:   Psalm 39.5 (AV): "verily every man at his best state is altogether vanitie"; (Genv): "surely every man in his best state is altogether vanitie."

I.635–637:   The image of a scale or balance is magnificently enlarged upon in the second Prebend sermon, ll. 73–219.

I.644–645:   Jer. 17.5 (Genv, AV): "Cursed be the man that trusteth in man, and maketh flesh his arme."

I.647–648:   Matt. 16.17 (Genv, AV): "Flesh and blood hath not revealed it unto thee."

I.660:   Psalm 62.11 (AV): "God hath spoken once; twice have I heard this."

I.662–663:   Psalm 62.6 (AV): "He onely is my rocke and my salvation; he is my defence."

I.664:   Psalm 62.7 (AV): "In God is . . . my glorie: . . . my refuge is in God."

I.684–686:   Mic. 7.5 (AV): "Trust yee not in a friend, put ye not confidence in a guide: keepe the doores of thy mouth from her that lyeth in thy bosome."

I.688–689:   Mic. 7.7 (AV): "Therefore I will looke unto the LORD: I will waite for the God of my salvation: my God will heare me."

Notes to the Second Prebend Sermon

Sermon heading: The date is given in Old Style; the year in New Style is 1626.

II.7 and mg.: I emend *LXXX S*'s inexact reference to "Cant. 1.3" to correlate with the cited Latin (Vulgate) text. Cf. Donne's *"Oleum effusum"* passage with St. Bernard's celebrated *Sermo* XV *in Cantica*, 1–4, where the phrase becomes an exultant refrain (*PL*, CLXXXIII, 844–846); see also the note to Preb IV, 345–349.

II.9: Searcloth (cerecloth): a cloth smeared or impregnated with wax or some glutinous matter, used as a bandage. The *OED* cites, besides this place, Charles Butler's *The feminine monarchie; or a treatise concerning bees*, x (1623), Z iij: "A Cere-cloth to refresh the wearied Sinewes and tired Muscles. . . ." souples: softens or mollifies by applying an unguent, *etc.; OED*, 4, obsolete.

II.13–15: The late fourth-century compilation of ecclesiastical regulations known as the *Apostolical Constitutions* enjoins (bk. II, ch. 59): "When thou instructest the people, ô bishop, command and exhort them to come constantly to church morning and evening every day . . . singing psalms and praying in the Lord's house: in the morning saying the sixty-second Psalm [63 in AV], and in the evening the hundred and fortieth" (tr. James Donaldson, *Ante-Nicene Christian Library* [Edinburgh, 1870], XVII, 87–88. Cf. *PG*, I, 744).

II.15–17: St. (John) Chrysostom, *Exposition of Ps.* 140, commands on the authority of the Antiochene Fathers the daily recitation of certain Psalms at certain times; the sixty-second (63 in AV) is assigned to the early morning hours. He goes on to praise this Psalm for its intense, eloquent expression of the soul's desire for God in what the Migne editors conjecture is a fragment of a now-lost exposition of the whole Psalm (*PG*, LV, 427–428). Cf. "Testè S. Chrysostomo, olim in Ecclesiâ appellabatur: Psalmus matutinus" (In Psal. 62 Commentarium, *Scripturae Sacrae Cursus Completus* [Paris, 1839], XV, 658).

II.21–24:   On Donne's Prebendal duties, see Introduction, pp. 5–6.

II.25:   Gomer: *"omer"* in modern transliteration; a Hebrew measure of volume, roughly equal to two-thirds of a gallon, prescribed for the gathering of manna (Exod. 16.16, 18, 22). Cf. *Sermons,* I.2.530.

II.27–29:   Donne characteristically saw his texts as epitomes of larger sections of Scripture. Cf. ll. 59–62 of the fourth Prebend sermon and Introduction, p. 42.

II.29–30:   St. Jerome, *Breviarium in Psalmos:* "Quid est titulus, nisi clavis? Ut ita dixerim, in domum non ingreditur nisi per clavum, hoc est, per titulum intelligitur in cujus persona cantatur" (*PL*, XXVI, 872). Cf. St. Hilary, *Prologus in Librum Psalmorum* (*PL,* IX, 236). Donne makes the remark also in *Sermons,* II.2.1–4.

II.31:   The AV reads the title of Psalm 63 as "A Psalme of David, when hee was in the wildernesse of Judah." This is the title in St. Jerome's third and final translation of the Psalms, the so-called *Hebrew Psalter:* "Psalmus David cum esset in deserto Juda" (*PL,* XXVIII, 1235). But St. Jerome's earlier *Gallican Psalter,* which the Vulgate incorporates, had read "Psalmus David cum esset in deserto Idumaeae" (*PL,* XXVI, 1060).

II.32–49:   Joan Webber analyzes Donne's division of his text and the Christian view of time which it betokens (*Contrary Music,* pp. 151–152).

II.44–45:   The circle is very frequently used by Donne as an emblem of the divine nature. See, e.g., Preb III, 384–387; Preb IV, 254–255; *Essays in Divinity*, pp. 38–39; *Devotions*, p. 4; *Sermons*, III.11.346–347; VI.8.189–198; cf. II.9.107–112. W. Milgate, citing F. L. Huntley, *Sir Thomas Browne* (Ann Arbor, Mich.: University of Michigan Press, 1962), pp. 108–109, 139, asserts that the God-circle commonplace is of unknown origin but is ascribed to Hermes Trismegistus in twelfth-century sources (*Satires, Epigrams, and Verse Letters of Donne*, p. 270). Whatever the intermediate history of the image, it is noteworthy that, since the beginnings of philosophy, nonanthropomorphic representations of God have employed the image of a sphere. Distinct stages in the development of the image can be traced. Xenophanes argued that God does not resemble the human form in any way; Parmenides asserted that Being is a sphere (without calling it God); Empedocles effected a synthesis in maintaining that God is a sphere. (See fragments Xen. B23, Par. B8, and Emp. B29 in H. Diels and W. Kranz, *Die Fragmente der Vorsokratiker*, 5th ed. [Berlin: Weidmann, 1934]; and discussions in Werner Jaeger's *The Theology of the Early Greek Philosophers*, tr. Edward S. Robinson [Oxford: Clarendon Press, 1947], Chapter 8, and G. S. Kirk's and J. E. Raven's *The Pre-Socratic Philosophers* [Cambridge: Cambridge University Press, 1964], p. 326.) In Plato and Aristotle, moreover, the sphere and circular movement constantly carry divine associations. In the *Timaeus*, 33B, Plato says that God fittingly made the world a sphere since its perfect and uniform shape embraces all life; in the *Laws*, bk. X, 898A-B, he says that perfect circular revolution has the closest possible affinity and likeness to the movement of Intelligence or Mind. Aristotle (*De Caelo*, 269a20) remarks that the circle is primary, perfect, simple, and prior to all other forms, and that any bodily substance possessing the form of a circle is more divine than any other. It is evident that, for Aristotle and for Donne, astronomy is a major link in the association of circularity and divinity. Jungian overtones in Donne's circle imagery are analyzed by Mary Ellen Williams, *John Donne's "Orbe of Man . . . Inexplicable Mistery": A Study of Donne's Use of Archetypal Images in the Round,* unpub. diss. University of Michigan, 1964.

II.48:   fixation: fact or condition of being fixed. The earliest citation in the OED for this sense of the word (1b) is to one of Donne's sermons.

II.49:   Heb. 13.8 (Bish): "Jesus Christ yesterday, and to day, and the same for ever"; (AV): "Jesus Christ the same yesterday, and to day, and for ever."

II.57:   Psalm 63.1 (AV): "My flesh longeth for thee in a drie and thirstie lande, where no water is."

II.67:   Donne's frequent references to the "branches" of his text and discourse (e.g., *Sermons,* II.5.2–3; IV.3.139–140; IV.11.299; VII.10.97; IX.13.89–91) carry felicitous suggestions of the organic unity of his best sermons. (Cf. Joan Webber, *Contrary Music,* p. 158.) The botanical associations are sometimes pursued, presumably as an expansion on the Augustinian metaphor which depicts Scripture as a post-Edenic, and now lawful and necessary, Tree of Life (see *Sermons,* I.8.44–50, 269–296; VIII.5.64–71).

II.76:   2 Cor. 4.17 (Vulg, Eras): "gloriae pondus." Donne variously interpreted the "pondus animae" as "love of pureness," the weight and ballast of the soul (*Sermons,* I.3.794–834), as peace of conscience (V.10.37; IX.4.231 f.), and as the love of God (IX.11.299). The last is the closest to St. Augustine's *Epistola LV* (*Ad Inquis. Januarii*), bk. II, ch. 10, sec. 18, which Mrs. Simpson cites as Donne's source (Appendix, *Sermons,* X, 376).

II.82:   Donne's italicized Latin does not approximate any Latin version at Exod. 8.24. The closest is the Vulgate's "Et venit musca gravissima." Since Donne cites the exact reading of the Vulgate at Exod. 9.3 in the preceding line, this is undoubtedly an informal reference, made from memory and in passing, to the same version.

II.84:   Job 7.20 (Bish, AV): "That I am a burden to my selfe."

II.86:   Lam. 3.7 (Vulg): "aggravit compedem meum"; (Muns) "aggravavit vincula mea."

II.88–89:   Matt. 20.12 (Genv, AV): "us, which have borne the burden, and heate of the day."

II.89, 92, 97–98:   Prov. 27.3 (Genv, AV): "A stone is heavie, and the sand weightie"; (AV): "but a fooles wrath is heavier then them both."

II.94:   comminatory: denunciatory, threatening; commonitory: serving to admonish.

II.99:   morosity: moroseness. The first occurrence of this now rare word cited by the *OED* is from a sermon of Donne's.

II.101–102:   For David on vanity, see Psalm 39.5,11; for Solomon, see Eccles. 1.2, 3.19, 12.8. "Levity" is not found in the AV.

II.105:   Despite lack of textual support in the Gospels (which give other particulars of her life), Mary Magdalene, one of Christ's followers, was traditionally identified with the "woman who was a sinner" and anointed Christ's feet in Simon's house (Luke 7.37). This is the source of her reputation for profligacy (the "lightnesse" on which Donne puns). Cf. his earlier pursuit of the moral and metaphorical richness of the burden of sin (*Sermons,* II, no. 4).

II.106:

In the apocryphal Book of Susanna, which narrates her solicitation and false accusation by two elders, her beauty and chastity are dwelt on in verses 2, 22–23, 27, and 31.

II.107–108:

Allusion is, broadly, to the overtures and treachery of Potiphar's wife toward Joseph, described in Gen. 39, and in particular to verse 6: "Joseph was a goodly person, and well favoured."

II.109:

Dives: Latin for "rich," commonly taken (by way of the Vulgate) as the proper name of the rich man in the parable in Luke 16.19–31.

II.110–111:

Eccles. 5.13 (AV): "There is a sore evill which I have seene under the Sun, namely riches kept for the owners therof to their hurt." Donne preached a somber sermon on this verse at Whitehall in 1620 (*Sermons,* III, no. 1).

II.116:

delinquents: persons failing in duty or obligation; more generally, offenders (especially in a legal sense).

II.120 and mg:

P-S bracket a reference to Job 1.1. But the more appropriate text is 1.8 (AV): "an upright man, one that feareth God, and escheweth evill." The incidents subsequently referred to by Donne are narrated in Job 1.12–2.13.

II.124–126 and mg.:

P-S bracket a reference to 1 Sam. 13.14, which in all versions reads "the Lord hath sought him a man after his owne heart." The words, spoken to Saul, refer to David; the subsequent incidents are narrated in 2 Sam. 13, 15–18.

II.128–129:

Matt. 4.1 (Genv, AV): "led up of the Spirit into the wildernesse, to be tempted of the devill."

II.133:

Herodians: A Jewish party, mainly political, who were partisans of the Herodian or Idumaean dynasty (chiefly under Herod Antipas, 4 B.C.–39 A.D.), and lax in their adherence to Judaism.

II.138:   Allusion is to Psalm 22.6, which in the English versions (except Geneva) reads "But I am a worme, and no man; a reproach of men, and despised of the people," a verse construed typologically as an anticipation of Christ's words in his humiliation and suffering (see *Sermons,* VIII.5.449–450). Donne was fond of the text and cited it very frequently, oftenest, however, in its historical sense as David's recognition of the debasement of human nature in sin. See, e.g., *Sermons,* II.11.289–290; III.15.427; IV.14.85; IX.5.208; IX.8.676.

II.142–143:   2 Cor. 4.17 (Gr B, Bish, AV): "an exceeding and eternall waight."

II.147–149:   Matt. 21.44 (AV): "And whosoever shall fall on this stone, shalbe broken: but on whom soever it shall fall, it will grinde him to powder." One of the most compelling among Donne's earlier attempts at figurative exposition was a sermon preached on this text before the Countess of Montgomery in 1619 (*Sermons,* II, no. 8). Cf. Winfried Schleiner's brief analysis in *The Imagery of John Donne's Sermons* (Providence, R.I.: Brown University Press, 1970), pp. 188–189. In the present instance Donne's mention of "accommodation" signals a different figurative, but also strongly moral, construction.

II.155–158:   Pliny, *Natural History,* bk. XXVII, chs. 98–99, Loeb ed., 1956, tr. W. H. S. Jones, VII, 448–449: "Among all plants nothing is more wonderful than lithospermum. . . . The plant is about five inches high, with ligneous little branches of the thickness of a rush. Near the leaves it grows . . . little stones, white and round as pearls, as big as a chick-pea but hard as a stone. . . . "

II.159–168:   It is probable that Donne is drawing on Lapide, *Commentaria in Ezechielem Prophetam* (1621), cap. xxxvi: *"Cor lapideum* est voluntas in impietate et peccatis obstinata et indurata ut lapis, qualis fuit Judaeorum: sic cor hirsutum et pilosum reipsa habuisse Hermogenem, Leonidam, Aristomenem, Messenum, Lysandrum, esseque hominum durorum, asperorum et crudelium, tradunt Plinius libr. xi. 37, Plutarch. in Parall. et Rhodig. lib. iv. cap. 16" (*Commentarii in Scripturam Sacram,* VI, 1251). Cf. Pliny's *Natural History,* bk. XI, ch. 70, on the incidents leading to the discovery of the "shaggy heart" of Aristomenes, the Messenian.

II.161–162:   Ezek. 36.26 (Genv): "I will take away the stonie heart out of your body, and I will give you an heart of flesh"; (AV) "I will take away the stonie heart out of your flesh, and I will give you an heart of flesh." Ezek. 11.19 differs only in reading "their flesh" and "give them." Cf. St. Augustine's extended remarks on this text in *De .gratia et libero arbitrio,* cap. xiv, secs. 29,30 (*PL,* XLIV, 898), which may have influenced Donne's treatment here since concepts of grace developed in that work are mentioned at ll.444–450 of the present sermon.

II.170–172:   Rev. 16.9 (AV): "And men were scorched with great heat, and blasphemed the Name of God, which hath power over these plagues: and they repented not, to give him glory."

II.174:   Rev. 16.11 (AV): "And blasphemed the God of heaven . . . and repented not of their deeds."

II.175–176:   Donne's inaccuracy, that is, the inaccurate knowledge of his time is exceptional; in general the seventeenth century had reliable understanding of Biblical weights and measures. But the talent, the standard large weight in Mesopotamia, Canaan, and Israel, was the equivalent in Biblical times of about 75 pounds.

(*The Interpreter's Dictionary of the Bible,* ed. G. A. Buttrick *et al.* (New York and Nashville: Abingdon Press, 1962), IV, 510–511.

II.176–179 and mg.: I adopt P-S's emendation of "ver. 29," the erroneous marginal reference in *LXXX S.* Rev. 16.21 (Genv, Bish, AV): "Men blasphemed God, because of the plague . . . ; for the plague therof was exceedingly great."

II.185: spittle (now spital): a house or place for receiving the indigent or diseased.

II.189: Donne's play on "passion" and "Action" exemplifies the wit which is a recurring manifestation of the strain exerted by divine mystery upon human thought and language. Cf. Erich Auerbach's discussion of *"passio"* as used in patristic writings (*Literary Language and Its Public in Late Latin Antiquity and in the Middle Ages,* tr. Ralph Manheim [New York: Pantheon Books, 1965], pp. 67–81) and Walter J. Ong's study of Aquinas and the Victorines in "Wit and Mystery: A Revaluation in Medieval Latin Hymnody," *Speculum,* XXII (1947), 310–341.

II.206–207: There is an echo of Psalm 38.2 (Gr B, Bish, AV), "For thine arrowes sticke fast in me; and thy hand presseth me sore," the text of one of a series of sermons on this Psalm which Donne preached at Lincoln's Inn. In the sermon on Psalm 38.2 he used the traditional figurative interpretation (derived from Origen, whom Donne cites) of God's "arrows" as "tentations" and "tribulations" (*Sermons,* II.1.219–746). This sermon has been analyzed by Dennis Quinn, "Donne's Christian Eloquence," *ELH,* XXVII (1960), 287–289; by Miss Webber, *Contrary Music,* pp. 167–170; and by Schleiner, *The Imagery of Donne's Sermons,* pp. 167–169.

II.228: On the particulars of angelic movement as conceived by Donne, see *Essays,* p. 37, and Preb II, 730–733 (text and note).

II.232–234: Psalm 78.60,61 (AV): "He forsooke the tabernacle of Shiloh . . . And delivered his strength into captivitie, and his glory into the enemies hand."

II.237: Psalm 27.4 (AV): "that will I seeke after"; (Genv, Bish): "which I will require." (Vulgate: "hanc requiram.")

II.242–245: Psalm 84.3 (AV): "Yea the sparrowe hath found an house, and the swallow a nest for her selfe, where she may lay her young."

II.246–247: Luke 12.7; Matt. 10.31 (AV): "yee are of more value then many sparrowes." Donne's interrogative may be the effect of the respective preceding verses, Luke 12.6 and Matt. 10.29, or of the question regarding the "foules of the aire" in Matt. 6.26 (AV): "Are yee not much better then they?"

II.248–279: This passage shows notable affinities with Hooker, *EP,* V.xxiv.2: "The good which we do by public prayer is more than in private can be done, for that besides the benefit which here is no less procured to ourselves, the whole Church is much bettered by our good example; . . . In which considerations the Prophet David so often voweth unto God the sacrifice of praise and thanksgiving in the congregation (Ps. 26.12, 34.1), so earnestly exhorteth others to sing praises unto the Lord in his courts, in his sanctuary, before the memorial of his holiness (Ps. 30.4, 96.9); and so much complaineth of his own uncomfortable exile, wherein although he sustained many most grievous indignities and endured the want of sundry both pleasures and honours before enjoyed, yet as if this one were his only grief and the rest not felt, his speeches are all of the heavenly benefit of public assemblies and the happiness of such as had free access thereunto (Ps. 27.4, 42.4, 84.1)." Cf. the slightly earlier passage from Hooker, cited in the note to ll. 265–271, which Donne parallels not only in content but also in Biblical citations.

II.250–251:   The religious "vehemence" is inferred from an ellipsis in the Hebrew.

II.257–258:   Dan. 6.10 (Bish): "the windowes of his chamber toward Hierusalem stoode open"; (Genv, AV): "his windowes (window: Genv) being open in his chamber toward Hierusalem."

II.264–265:   Donne's reference to 1 Kings 8.44,45 is so free that it cannot be correlated with any specific English translation. The condition of captivity is actually dealt with in verses 47–49.

II.265–271:   See Tertullian, *Liber de Oratione,* cap. i (*PL,* I, 1254–1255), or "On Prayer," tr. S. Thelwall, in *The Ante-Nicene Fathers,* ed. Roberts and Donaldson, III, 681: "And what is the Lord Christ's—as this method of praying is—that is not heavenly? And so . . . let us consider His heavenly wisdom: first, touching the precept of praying secretly, whereby He exacted man's faith, that he should be confident that the sight and hearing of Almighty God are present beneath roofs, and extend even unto the secret place; and required modesty in faith [*modestia fidei*], that it should offer its religious homage to Him alone, whom it believed to see and to hear everywhere." The subsequent lines correspond closely in sense (but not in wording) to Tertullian's *Apologeticus adversus Gentes pro Christianis,* cap. xxxix: "Coimus in coetum et congregationem, ut ad Deum, quasi manu facta, precationibus ambiamus" (*PL,* I, 532). (Sister Emily Joseph Daly's translation of this sentence in *Tertullian: Apologetical Works,* The Fathers of the Church X [New York: Cima Publishing Co., 1950] 98, reads as follows: "We come together for a meeting and a congregation, in order to besiege God with prayers, like an army in battle formation.") Since the Index Latinitatis to Tertullian in Migne records no instance of *obsidere,* the likeliest supposition is that Donne was here quoting, imprecisely, from memory. The supposition is strengthened by the fact that Tertullian's exact wording is cited by Donne in *Sermons,* V.11.270–271; on the contrary, the phrasing of the second Prebend sermon recurs at V.14.148–149. (Cf. V.18.12–15.) Like Donne, Hooker was struck by this sentence of Tertullian's and cites it in *EP,* V.xxiv.1: "I speak no otherwise concerning the force of public prayer in the Church of God, than before me Tertullian hath done."

II.272–273 and mg.:   P-S bracket a reference to Psalm 84.4, which reads (AV): "Blessed are they that dwell in thy house: they wilbe still praysing thee."

II.284–304:   Christian caution in excommunicating is emphasized by Tertullian, *Apologeticus,* ch. 39 (PL, I, 532); and Hooker cites his authority on the subject (*EP,* VI.iv.15): "Evil persons are not rashly, and as we list, to be thrust from communion with the Church; insomuch that, if we cannot proceed against them by any orderly course of judgment, they are rather to be suffered for the time than molested." The history of Anglican attitudes toward excommunication shows interesting change. The earlier attitude (which continues through Hooker and Donne) is well expressed by John Whitgift, who cites Calvin's and Bullinger's reproofs to the Anabaptists for their claim that there is no true church approved by God where excommunication is not wielded (see *Works,* Parker Soc. XLVII [1851], 186). Laud's later attitude, however, was that the potent instrument of excommunication ought to be used in enforcing church discipline, which he did (H. R. Trevor-Roper, *Archbishop Laud,* pp. 103, 155). But the more temperate minds of Hooker and Donne remained aware of attendant human limitations: "As for the act of excommunication, it neither shutteth out from the mystical [body of Christ], nor clean from the visible [Church of Christ], but only from fellowship with the visible in holy duties" (*EP,* III.i.13). Donne's "damne-damme" pun in ll. 300–301 exactly captures the violence and ambiguity of the proceeding. Cf. Joan Webber's examples of his "wordplay in which the word is apparently made a metaphor of itself" (*Contrary Music,* p. 138).

II.304–305:   Recusant: any person, especially a Roman Catholic, who refused to comply with the law requiring attendance at the services of the Church of England. Libertin(e): one who holds free, unorthodox opinions about religion; a free-thinker. Separatist: one who advocates ecclesiastical separation, particularly a member of any of the sects separated from the Church of England. In the seventeenth century the term was applied chiefly to the Independents and those who agreed with them in rejecting all ecclesiastical authority outside the individual congregation. Its purview included, of course, the immigrants to Holland and New England.

II.336–339:   See The *Discourses of Epictetus,* bk. I, ch. 2, tr. P. E. Matheson (Oxford: Clarendon Press, 1916), p. 51: "Of one thing beware, O man; . . . do not sell your will cheap. The great, heroic style, it may be, belongs to others, to Socrates and men like him. . . . 'What am I to do then? Since I have no natural gifts, am I to make no effort for that reason?' Heaven forbid: Epictetus is not better than Socrates: if only he is as good as Socrates I am content." Donne repeats the exemplum in *Sermons,* IV.3.375–379; VIII.7.216–219, and, significantly, VI.5.217–224, where (as in the source) only Socrates is named as a model. The unlikelihood that Epictetus would take as a model Plato, a philosophical adversary, and the secondhand nature of all knowledge of Epictetus (he wrote nothing, but his disciple Flavius Arrianus compiled his teachings) complicate the question of Donne's source and his fidelity to it. He does, however, invoke Arrian by name on Epictetus (*Sermons,* VII.16.488–494) and might have known such a representative work as, e.g., Flavius Arrianus's *Commentarius disputationum . . . Epicteti, Graece & Latine, interpretè Iacobo Schegkio . . .*, published with *Epicteti Stoici Philosophi Enchiridion* (Geneva, 1594). The relevant passage, in lib. III, cap. 26 (p. 433), reads "Proinde ne existimes dumtaxat exemplum me habere hominis non occupati & vacui domesticis negociis, quique nec uxorem, nec liberos, nec patriam, nec amicos aut propinquos habeat a quibus detorqueri aut distrahi potuerit: proferre Socratem libet. . . . "

II.339–348: For the characterization of the divine ideas "in the Schoole," see Aquinas, *ST,* pars Iᵃ, q. xv, art. 3, where St. Augustine's *De diversis quaestionibus,* lib. I, q. 46 is cited. This Donne makes use of here (as noted in Simpson, Appendix, *Sermons,* X, 382), quoting somewhat freely from "De ideis" where it reads: "tanta in eis vis constituitur, ut nisi his intellectis sapiens esse nemo possit" (*PL,* XL, 29). Donne reverted to consideration of the Platonic and neo-Platonic notion of the divine ideas in the fifth Prebend sermon, ll. 353–357; cf. *Essays,* pp. 60–61; *Sermons,* IV.3.348–355, 470–493; IX.2.206–217; IX.12.55–59. According to Miss Ramsay, Donne's observations accord with the theological mainstream from St. Anselm through St. Albertus Magnus (*Les Doctrines médiévales chez Donne,* pp. 155–159). Cf. Hooker, *EP,* I.ii.1,5; Milton, *Paradise Lost,* VII. 557; on God's "great Idea" to which the Creation answers.

II.348–352: St. Augustine, *In Joannis Evangelium,* tract. I.16: "*Omnia,* ergo, fratres, *omnia* omnino *per ipsum facta sunt, et sine ipso factum est nihil.* Sed quomodo per ipsum facta sunt omnia? *Quod factum est, in illo vita est*" (*PL,* XXXV, 1387). (The Vulgate ends verse 3 with "quod factum est" and begins verse 4 with "in ipso vita erat.") Aquinas's *Catena Aurea,* moreover, cites Augustine, *Enarratio in Psalmum* civ, Bede's commentary on John 1.4, and Origen's second homily on John as authority for this interpretation and punctuation (*Commentary on the Four Gospels Collected Out of the Works of the Fathers* [Oxford and London, 1874], IV, 15–17). But Lapide cites Tertullian, St. Ambrose, and St. Cyril among others giving a different division and sense (*Commentarii in Scripturam Sacram,* VIII, 877).

II.352–359:

Donne may be indebted to Lapide's *Comm. in Epist. ad Hebraeos* (1614), cap. xi, which notes of this verse: "Id est, ut ex non entibus et non existentibus fierent entia et existentia. Est metalepsis: quae enim non sunt, nec existunt, sunt invisibilia. . . . In Graeco est verborum metathesis, μὴ ἐκ φαινομένων, pro ἐκ μὴ φαινομένων. Secundo, Ludov. Molina et Ribera hic *ex invisibilibus,* id est, inquiunt, ex rationibus aeternis ideisque rerum, quae fuerunt ab aeterno, invisibiles et reconditae in mente et Verbo Dei, tanquam in arte et exemplari suo, creata sunt omnia, ut existerent fierentque visibilia, utque suae ideae et similitudini, quam habent in mente divina, apte responderent. Ita D. Thomas, qui ad hoc citat illud Boetii lib. 3 de Consolatione" (*Commentarii in Scripturam Sacram,* IX, 977). For Greek Fathers on this passage, see St. Chrysostom's Homily 22 on the Epistle to the Hebrews (*PG,* LXIII, 153–154) and Theodoret's *Compendium haereticarum fabularum* (*PG,* LXXXIII, 464).

II.353–354:

Heb. 11.3 (AV): "things which are seene were not made of things which doe appeare."

II.364–365:

Gen. 1.26 (Vulg): "Faciamus hominem ad imaginem, et similitudinem nostram." Consistently construed as an intimation of the Trinity, this (in Latin or in English) is perhaps the most frequently cited text in Donne. See, e.g., *Sermons,* I.8.154; II.2.15; II.11.521; II.17.69; V.7.212; V.14.393; VI.7.159; VI.13.132; VI.14.1; VIII.1.666. See also Introduction,

p. 30 on the implications of this verse in Donne's Augustinian conception of human psychology.

II.394–401:   In Hebrew and other Semitic tongues, verbs do not indicate past, present, and future time (as in Indo-European languages) but only completed (perfect) or uncompleted (imperfect) actions. (See Simpson, Appendix, *Sermons,* X, 344.) While ordinary discourse in the narrative books of Scripture uses the imperfect in speaking of events that have not yet happened, oracular utterances in many passages in the prophetic books employ the perfect, exhibiting the assurance of the speaker regarding God's purposes.

II.401–408:   St. Augustine, *Enarratio in Psalmum* lxii.1: "Quis inde non gaudeat? Quis non et ea quae nondum venerunt ventura speret, propter illa quae jam tanta impleta sunt? . . . Modicum quod restat venturum esse credamus, quando jam videmus tanta quae tunc futura erant, modo compleri" (*PL,* XXXVI, 748).

II.427:   St. Augustine, *Sermo* XXVI: "Eligit tamen, et habet electos, quos creaturus est eligendos: habet autem apud se ipsum, non in natura sua, sed in praescientia sua" (*PL,* XXXVIII, 173).

II.437 mg.:   Donne's heading seems to derive from Pagnini's unique reading at Psalm 63.7, "Quia fuisti auxilium mihi." (The Vulgate reads "quia fuisti adjutor meus"; other versions have "auxilium" but lack "quia" constructions.)

II.444–457:   St. Augustine distinguishes operating grace (the sole working of God upon the human will) from co-operating grace (the grace which works with man's love of God, to strengthen and perfect it) in *De gratia et libero arbitrio,* cap. xvii.33 (*PL,* XLIV, 901). Another Augustinian distinction, best made in *Sermo* CCCLXVI.7 (*PL,* XXXIX, 1650), concerns "first" or prevenient or antecedent grace (the un-merited gift of God by which man in a natural state is disposed to respond to divine redemption) and subsequent grace (the help which God gives man after conversion to resist sin and temptation, and the mercy which God extends when man fails in resist-ing but repents). As here in Donne, the two distinc-tions tend to converge in St. Augustine's work—e.g., in *Contra Julianum*, bk. I, ch. xcv (*PL*, XLV, 1112) —probably because of their similar underlying pur-pose: to preserve and balance the efficacy of divine grace and of human free will. Donne goes out of his way to insist on these Augustinian notions in the face of such current and rival doctrines of grace as Molina's, which as expounded in *Concordia liberi arbitrii cum gratiae donis* (1588) placed crucial em-phasis on the free cooperation of the human will with divine grace and thence became the basis of Jesuit teaching, or the theological system of Jacobus Arminius (formally set forth in the *Remonstrance* of 1610), whose moderate doctrine of election, be-lief that man could resist divine grace, and broad-ened view of redemption became important in later seventeenth-century Anglican thought. But Donne had received the gold medal of the Synod of Dort (1618–19), which made an official condemnation of Arminian teachings on justification; he also expli-citly condemned Molina and his disciples as early as the *Essays in Divinity* (p. 50), which predate his ordination.

II.453–454:   Mark 9.24 (Genv): "Lord, I beleeve: helpe my un-beliefe"; (AV): "Lord, I beleeve; help thou mine unbeliefe."

II.469:   *Gnazar*, or *'āzar* in modern transliteration, derives from a root meaning "to surround," i.e., "to protect" or "to aid" (See no. 5826 in Strong's *Concise Dict.,* p. 87). A noun from this root, *'ēzer*—help, succor—is used to describe the purpose of Eve's creation in

Gen. 2.18; the AV renders it "an help meet." (Cf. Donne's observation on *Gnazar* at *Sermons,* IV.15. 432–433.)

II.479:

inchoations: beginnings, commencements. Donne's usage closely resembles Hooker's, as cited in the *OED:* "the inchoation of those graces, the consummation whereof dependeth on mysteries ensuing."

II.499:

Donne employs a phrase from the Vulgate rendering of his text.

II.508–516:

Cf. Andrewes, *Ninety-six Sermons* (Oxford, 1843), V, 504: "Now, as for the Scripture . . . when there is any ill spoken of which we are to resist, then it is commended to us as an armoury, whence we may fetch any kind of weapon which we shall need, either offensive as 'a sword,' or defensive as 'a shield'."

II.512–513:

Sword: Eph. 6.17; Heb. 4.12; Deut. 33.29; Psalm 17.13, *etc.; Target* (buckler): 2 Sam. 22.31; Psalm 18.2,30, 91.4; Prov. 2.7, *etc.;* Wall: Isa. 26.1, 60.18 (interpreted typologically); *Tower:* Psalm 61.3; Prov. 18.10 (Genv, AV); *Rocke:* Psalm 18.2 (AV)— St. Paul also observes (1 Cor. 10.4) that the rock from which the Israelites were supplied with water was a type of Christ; *Hill:* Psalms 3.4, 15.1, 24.3, 99.9 (Gr B, Bish, AV); Ezek. 34.26, *etc.*

II.515:

The title which the AV translates "Lord of Hosts" is either *"Dominus exercituum"* or *"Dominus virtutum"* in the Vulgate. It occurs, among many other places, at 1 Sam. 1.11; 2 Sam. 7.27; Psalms 24.10, 59.5, 84.1; Isa. 47.4; Jer. 10.16; Mal. 1.14.

II.516–519:

Notable classical examples are the armor forged by Hephaestus for Achilles, which is described in bk. XVIII of the *Iliad,* and the armor presented to Aeneas by Venus at the end of bk. VIII of the *Aeneid.*

II.520:   Allusion is to 1 Sam. 17.4–7, where Goliath's armor
                            is described.

II.525–527:   Isa. 59.17 (AV): "For he put on righteousnesse as a
                            brestplate, and an helmet of salvation upon his head."
                            Donne's assertion in l. 527 refers to verse 20: "And
                            the redeemer shall come to Sion."

II.530:   St. Jerome's *Prologus galeatus* or *Helmeted Prologue*
                            (i.e., one which makes a capital defense) was orig-
                            inally prefixed to 1 Kings, the book which he recom-
                            mended as an introduction to Bible study. Later it
                            was placed before Genesis, its position in the Vulgate.
                            The *Prologus* cites peculiarities of written Hebrew,
                            lists the canonical books of the Old and New Testa-
                            ments (subdivided as to kinds) and the books of
                            the Apocrypha, and discourses briefly on the variety
                            of the Scriptures. Then, following a protestation of
                            humility and regard for "Hebrew truth" as well as
                            openness to acknowledge error and receive correc-
                            tion, St. Jerome inveighs against frivolous or cap-
                            tious criticism and asks true Christians for their
                            prayers to combat would-be detractors of his work.

II.537–538, 579–580:   Donne is here following Munster's unique reading
                            of the latter half of his text: "ideo sub umbra alarum
                            tuarum exultans cantabo."

II.541–568:   The *locus classicus* on the much treated subject of the
                            names of God is, of course, Aquinas, *ST*, pars Iᵃ,
                            q. 13, arts. 1–12, which contains a profusion of
                            patristic citations. Donne reveals a general indebted-
                            ness to this source as well as possible particular
                            echoes; cf. lines 554–556 with q. 13, art. 7, obj. 1,
                            "Ambrose says (*De Fide*, I) that this name *Lord*
                            is the name of power"; lines 563–568 with q. 13, art.
                            11, "It is written that when Moses asked, *If they
                            should say to me, What is His name? what shall
                            I say to them?* the Lord answered him, *Thus shalt
                            thou say to them, HE WHO IS hath sent me to you*

(Exod. 3.13, 14). Therefore this name *HE WHO IS,* most properly belongs to God. . . . For it does not signify form, but simply existence itself. Hence, since the existence of God is His essence itself . . . , it is clear that among other names this one specially denominates God." See also Donne's disquisition on the names of God in the *Essays,* pp. 23–26, where there is a marginal reference to this place in Aquinas. Here, moreover, Donne is making some conventional remarks about Hebrew etymology and grammar. *Elohim,* in modern transliteration *'elôhîm,* means strictly "gods"; the discomfort caused by this vestige of polytheism, in Donne's time and later, was eased by such explanations as that of a "plural of majesty" or a plural with intensive force (Donne's option). While these are rejected by modern scholars of Hebrew, the form *Elohim,* especially in its linking with a singular verb in its first occurrence (Gen. 1.1), was an important piece of evidence among sixteenth- and seventeenth-century commentators for proving the doctrine of the Trinity. (See note to ll. 147–154 of the first Prebend sermon.) *Adonai,* the second name of God, is accurately defined. *Jehovah* (more properly, *Yahweh*), is the form of the Tetragrammaton which prevailed in Donne's day due to the popularizing of a medieval error about the unpronounced name of God. (See *The Oxford Dictionary of the Christian Church,* p. 717, and references given there.) Regarding *Jehovah,* Donne draws upon the thought forms of Greek and Latin Christianity (considerations "of Essence, of Being, of Subsistence") rather than those of Old Testament Jewish theology, which considered and knew God in his acts. The manuscript form YHWH is a third person singular imperfect of the verb "to become," "to happen," with the meaning "I will be (cause to be) what I will be (cause to be)." The Tetragrammaton does not involve predication but, rather, stands for the inexhaustible source of divine potential. When Hellenized Jews abandoned their native historicism and became philosophers, then the scruples against voicing the Tetragrammaton arose, along with the kind of hypostatizing that Donne performs.

II.546–550:   This passage is a reprise of two prominent considerations (ll. 208–256, 657–682) in the first Prebend sermon.

II.557:   *dominium:* in the civil and old English law, ownership; property in the largest sense, including both the right of property and the right of possession or use. An exhaustive discussion is found in bk. II (*De acquirendo rerum dominio*) of the thirteenth-century treatise *De Legibus et Consuetudinibus* by Henry de Bracton (ed. and tr. Sir Travers Twiss, London, 1878). Cf. Aquinas, *ST,* pars II^{a}II^{ae}, q. 66, art. 1: "Sic habet homo naturale dominium exteriorum rerum quia per rationem et voluntatem potest uti rebus exterioribus ad suam utilitatem."

II.565–566:   Allusion is to Exod. 3.13,14.

II.597–600 and mg.:   I follow P-S's correction of *LXXX S*'s erroneous marginal reference, "Ex. 19.14." Exod. 19.4 (AV): "Ye have seene what I did unto the Egyptians, and how I bare you on Eagles wings, and brought you unto my selfe."

II.600–602:   Ezek. 1.24 (Genv, AV): "I heard the noise of their wings, like the noise of great waters, as the voice of the Almightie . . . as the noise of an hoste." Verses 5–9,23 give rise to the notion that these "living creatures" are cherubim. (Donne's "Cherubims" is ungrammatical, a double—Hebrew and English—plural. On the shortcomings of his knowledge of Hebrew, see D. C. Allen, "Dean Donne Sets His Text," pp. 212–219.)

II.602–604:   Jer. 49.22 (AV): "He shall . . . spread his wings over Bozrah: and at that day shall the heart of the mightie men of Edom, be as the heart of a woman in her pangs."

II.607–610: Dan. 3.17,18 (Genv, AV): "Our God . . . is able to deliver us. . . . But if not, bee it knowen unto thee, O king, that we will not serve thy gods."

II.620–621: Matt. 23.37 (Genv, Bish, AV): "O Hierusalem, Hierusalem . . . how often would I have gathered thy children together . . . as a hen gathereth her chickens under her wings."

II.625–626: E.g., Psalms 17.8, 36.7, 57.1, 61.4, 91.4. Donne demonstrates the spiritual utility of a Biblical concordance.

II.635–640: At *Sermons,* VIII.5.206–207, Donne says that Melancholy is made "the seat of Religion . . . by the Papist." But Puritan diffidence (shading into despair) regarding emphatic doctrines of election and reprobation evoked, notably, Richard Sibbes's spate of consolatory writings between 1637 and 1639 (*Bowels Opened, The Bruised Reede and Smoaking Flax, The Riches of Mercie, The Saints Cordials, etc.*). Robert Burton claims that his treatment of "Religious Melancholy" in pt. III, sect. 4 of the *Anatomy* (1620) is the first sifting of the evidence in a "controverted" matter. Lawrence Babb surveys the pronouncements of other medical writers of the age in *The Elizabethan Malady* (East Lansing, Mich.: Michigan State University Press, 1951), pp. 47–54.

II.640–643: Donne apparently adverts to the nonenforcement of the Penal Code against recusants, which had begun in 1623 under King James during negotiations for the Spanish match and had continued under Charles. George Abbot, Archbishop of Canterbury, whom Charles caused to be sequestered in 1627, traces the history of developments in complaining against nonenforcement (*Stuart Tracts, 1603–93,* ed. C. H. Firth

[Westminster: Camden Society, 1903], pp. 343–344).
On the eventual turning of the tide at the time of
the Long Parliament in 1640, see Gordon Albion,
Charles I and the Court of Rome, pp. 338–357.

II.647–650:

In the course of his own "bodily disease" during
the winter of 1623–24, Donne brooded as follows
in the *Devotions* (p. 69): "But what have I done,
either to *breed,* or to *breath* these *vapors?* They
tell me it is my *Melancholy;* Did I infuse, did I
drinke in *Melancholly* into my selfe? It is my
thoughtfulnesse; was I not made to thinke? It is my
study; doth not my *Calling* call for that? I have don
nothing, wilfully, perversely toward it, yet must
suffer in it, die by it." Cf. "To Mr. T. W." ("At
once, from hence"), ll. 7–10; and Jonson's altogether different tone in "To Heaven": "Good, and
great God, can I not thinke of thee,/But it must,
straight, my melancholy bee?"

II.654–658:

Cf. *Sermons,* VI.14.298–300; IX.18.1–2; X.6.455–457.

II.660:

Cf. Donne's sermon on the New World's potential
(IV, no. 10), preached in 1622 before the Honorable
Company of the Virginian Plantation.

II.667:

Donne was fond of the intensive redoubling in the
Vulgate's *"morte morieris"* and cited it repeatedly
in his preaching. See l. 171 of the third Prebend
sermon and *Sermons,* I.2.187; II.2.295; III.3.442;
VII.14.202; VIII.7.527; VIII.8.663; IX.5.655.

II.668:

Chaiim, or chayim, in Gen. 2.17, is a masculine plural
form of the adjective *chay* ("alive"), which can function as a noun in its feminine singular and masculine plural forms. (See no. 2416 in Strong's *Concise
Dict.,* p. 38.) Donne's *"vitarum"* is apparently a
somewhat misleading attempt at a literal Latin
equivalent, not a citation from any existing Latin
translation.

II.676, 677:	Matt. 25.23 (Genv): "Enter in into thy masters joye"; (AV): "enter thou into the joy of thy lord."
II.679 mg.:	I follow P-S's emendation of "verse 24," the erroneous reference in *LXXX S.*
II.684–687:	This passage briefly anticipates a more developed consideration in the fifth Prebend sermon (ll. 577–641).
II.693–696:	The theme of conformity to Christ, often expressed in strongly physical terms, is prominent in Donne's preaching; see, notably, *Sermons,* II.9.488–555; II.14.469–491; X.11.579–673.
II.700:	St. Augustine, *Enarratio in Psalmum* lxii.16: "Semper enim ille major est, quantumcumque creverimus" (*PL,* XXXVI, 758).
II.704 and mg.:	P-S bracket a reference to Gen. 1.2, which Donne cites in the unique Tremellius-Junius reading: "incubabat superficiei aquarum." (Cf. the Vulgate's "Spiritus Dei ferebatur super aquas.")
II.708–710:	wardship: a species of legal custody in England, whereby the guardian was entrusted with and held accountable for the person and lands of an heir under fourteen years of age (*Black's Law Dict.,* p. 1755).
II.723–730:	The sequence of celestial phenomena is the same as that in the celebrated passage on the soul's flight in the *Second Anniversary,* ll. 195–206. Donne's view that the soul was not required to await the Last Judgment but might enjoy beatitude immediately after death was a late development in the teaching of the Western Church, first appearing in the seventh century and not enunciated as dogma until Pope Benedict XII's *De statu animarum ante generale judicium* (1336). Helen Gardner suggests that imaginative appeal rather than vestigial Roman convic-

tions determined Donne's position, anomalous in a Protestant (Appendix A, *The Divine Poems of John Donne* [Oxford: Clarendon Press, 1952], p. 116). Cf. *Sermons,* VII.15.486–489.

II.730–732: These brief allusions to angelic movement are more in keeping with the early explicit views of Aquinas, as set out in his uncompleted commentary on Boethius's *De Trinitate,* than with the later, general treatment given in *ST,* pars Iᵃ, q. lxii, art. 1, e.g., "The angel does not acquire such beatitude by any discursive motion, as man does, but . . . is straightway in possession of it, owing to his natural dignity." (See also q. lviii, art. 3, and Donne's "Obsequies to the Lord Harrington," ll. 81–100, which expatiates on the passage just cited.) However, in q. v, art. 4, ad obj. 3 of the early commentary St. Thomas says that motion cannot be predicated of the angels in the proper and natural sense of the term as applied to physical bodies. For angels, being pure intelligences like God himself, cannot be localized in time or space. But, in a manner of speaking, they can be said to move in exercising their intellects and wills (motion understood as operation) or in functioning as second principles (in accordance with the First Cause, the will of God—which Donne apparently has in mind here) when they enter into relations with, or influence, things in time and space. See *St. Thomas Aquinas, The Division and Methods of the Sciences: Questions V and VI of his Commentary on the De Trinitate of Boethius,* tr. Armand Maurer (Toronto: Pontifical Institute of Mediaeval Studies, 1953), p. 43.

II.738: John 16.24 (all versions): "Your joy may be full."

II.739–740: John 16.22 (Genv): "Your ioye shall no man take from you"; (AV): "Your joy no man taketh from you."

II.743–744: Cf. "Obsequies to the Lord Harington," ll. 31–36.

Notes to the Third Prebend Sermon

III.1–14:   See Introduction, pp. 5–6.

III.9–10:   "Sacrifice of Praise" echoes Jer. 33.11, Heb. 13.15, and the opening of the second paragraph of the Invocation following the Oblation in the Order for Holy Communion, *BCP.*

III.11,12:   Quire (choir): There is a play on two meanings— one, "the part of a church or cathedral eastward of the nave, where the services are performed," the other (*OED,* 1a), now obsolete, "the clergy of a cathedral or collegiate church engaged in performing divine service."

III.18–26:   Cf. Donne's other map images used in dividing his texts (*Sermons,* IV.7.63; VI.14.298–300; VII.17.29– 30).

III.32:   ambition (of): ardent desire of anything considered advantageous or creditable; *OED,* 3.

III.34:   Cf. "Obsequies to the Lord Harington," ll. 37–39, where Donne calls the "deeds of good men" the perspective glass by which heavenly "Vertues, indeed remote, seem to be neare."

III.35:   tincture: a slight infusion or trace (of some element or quality). Cf. *OED,* 6, the now obsolete alchemical meaning, which may have a metaphorical bearing: "A supposed spiritual principle or immaterial substance whose character or quality may be infused into material things; the quintessence, spirit, or soul of a thing." On Donne's use of alchemical images and their context, see Edgar H. Duncan, "Donne's Alchemical Figures," *ELH,* IX (1942), 257–285; W. A. Murray, "Donne and Paracelsus," *RES,* XXV (1949), 115–123.

III.43:   On *rectus corde*, cf. *Sermons*, IX.18.565–592.

III.44:   retribution: repayment, recompense for some service
                   or merit; *OED*, 1, now rare.

III.44–45:   Donne's text reads "laudabuntur omnes recti corde"
                   (Vulg) and "gloriabuntur omnes" in Tremellius-
                   Junius and Vatablus.

III.49–53:   See note to Preb I, 361–369; cf. *Sermons*, II.6.276–
                   287.

III.51–56:   On the centrality of the idea that the glory of God
                   was the first and final purpose of the creation of
                   man, see E. Randolph Daniel, "Reconciliation, Cove-
                   nant and Election: A Study in the Theology of John
                   Donne," *Anglican Theological Review*, XLVIII
                   (1966), 16. Cf. Aquinas, *ST*, pars Iᵃ, q. 47, art. 2,
                   where it is argued that the imparting of God's good-
                   ness, not the punishment of sin, was the purpose of
                   the creation of the physical universe.

III.66:   sinister: There seems to be punning on more than
                   one sense of the word, e.g., "dishonest, unfair; not
                   straightforward, underhand" (*OED*, 3); "erring,
                   erroneous, astray from the right path" (4c, rare in
                   17th c., now obsolete).

III.69–73:   Cf. the reference to "squint lefthandedness" in "To
                   the Countess of Bedford" ("Reason is our Soules
                   left hand"), l. 5. Here, however, the development of
                   the images out of the Vulgate "recti" (where the
                   AV reading is "upright in heart") demonstrates
                   notably both Donne's Latinate sensibility and his
                   emphasis on moral significance through "dilation"
                   of Biblical figures of speech.

III.72:   withall: therewith (*OED*, 2).

III.91:   Bulloyn: bullion; precious metal in the mass.

III.108: Matt. 25.21 (Vulg, Trem): "Euge serve bone".

III.111–115: Donne here affirms the substance of the tenth of the Thirty-nine Articles, "Of Free-Will," regarding preventing (antecedent, anticipant) grace and subsequent (concomitant, auxiliant) grace: "Wherefore we have no power to do good works pleasant and acceptable to God, without the grace of God by Christ preventing us, that we may have a good will, and working with us, when we have that good will." Upon the denial by Pelagius, a fifth-century Welsh monk, that any assistance of divine grace was necessary for salvation, St. Augustine sought in *De gratia et libero arbitrio* to differentiate and clarify the operations of grace with respect to free will which were subsequently codified by Aquinas, *ST,* pars I^{a}II^{ae}, q. 111, arts. 2,3. (See also note to Preb II, 444–457.) In Donne's day the term "semi-Pelagianism" expressed the opprobrium in which critics of the Spanish Jesuit Molina held his *Concordia liberi arbitrii cum gratiae donis* (see note to Preb I, 328–329). See also the brief definitions in *Sermons,* IX.1.733–735.

III.115: obsequious: compliant with the will or wishes of another, especially, a superior (a now rare sense).

III.122: Prov. 8.31 (AV): "My delights were with the sonnes of men."

III.123–126: Eph. 3.6,7,8,10 (Genv, AV): "the Gospel: Whereof I was (am: Genv) made a Minister, according to (by: Genv) the gift of the grace of God . . . that I should preach among the Gentiles . . . To the intent that now unto (unto the: AV) principalities (i.e., 'the Angels': Genv gloss) and powers in heavenly places, might be knowen by the church, the manifold wisedome of God."

III.127–128: Allusion is to Eph. 3.9; all English versions substantially concur with the AV reading: "the fellowship of the mysterie, which from the beginning of the world, hath bene hid in God." Cf. Col. 1.26.

III.128–131: Aquinas (*ST*, pars I^a, q. 57, art. 5) affirms that the angels know the mysteries of grace only if and when God wills.

III.133: entendment: way of understanding (something); conception or interpretation of a matter (*OED*, 2; obsolete).

III.134–135: *Secundum allegata & Probata:* "According to the things alleged and proved," the legal phrase for the evidence on which judgment is based (*Black's Law Dict.*, p. 1521). Cf. *Sermons*, III.7.273; IX.4.457.

III.138–176: On Donne's frequent and passionate decrying of the doctrine of predestination to damnation, see note to 11. 361–369 of the first Prebend sermon and *Sermons*, II.7.220–226; III.12.244–246.

III.140 mg.: I follow P-S's emendation of "Gen. 18.17," the inaccurate reference in *LXXX S.*

III.147: P-S bracket a marginal reference to Gen. 1.27, where this Latin phrase occurs (in the Vulg and T-J). This text is important in St. Augustine's (and hence Donne's) view of man, for it requires the inference that human nature was at first perfectly good (see, e.g., *PL*, XXXV, 2319–2320; XL, 786, 806, 1023; XLII, 1207).

III.147–149: *"Ad Imaginem Diabolicam"* is Donne's own coinage paralleling the Biblical phrase cited in the preceding note. Allen mentions similar inventiveness ("Dean Donne Sets His Text," p. 225).

III.153: 1 Peter 5.8 (all versions): "the devill, as a roaring Lion, walketh about, seeking whom he may devoure."

III.161–162:   Cf. Philo Judaeus, *Questions and Answers on Genesis,* bk. I, ch. 20, tr. Ralph Marcus (Loeb ed., 1953), p. 12: "Why does [God] bring all the animals to the man that he may give names to them? Scripture has cleared up the great perplexity of those who are lovers of wisdom by showing that names exist by being given and not by nature, since each is an apt and naturally suitable name through the skillful calculation of a wise man who is pre-eminent in knowledge. And very proper to the mind of the wise man alone, or rather to the first of earth-born creatures, is the giving of names. . . . For as he was the first to see living creatures, so he was the first to be worthy of being lord over all and the first introducer and author of the giving of names. . . . We must, however, also suppose that the giving of names was so exact that so soon as he gave the name and the animal heard it, it was affected as if by the phenomenon of a familiar and related name being spoken." Origen's belief, influenced by Philo and in its turn influential on the Church Fathers, was that the name accords with the nature. See *Contra Celsum,* tr. Henry Chadwick (Cambridge: Cambridge University Press, 1953), pp. 23, 299–301.

III.167,168:   P-S bracket references for Donne's allusions to 1 John 3.12 (AV: "Cain, who . . . slewe his brother") and to Matt. 10.4 (AV: "Judas Iscariot, who also betrayed him").

III.169–171:   As in ll. 147–149 above, Donne has apparently coined *"morte moriendum"* on the basis of the Vulgate *"morte morieris"* in Gen. 2.17. See also the note to l. 667 of the second Prebend sermon.

III.191:   Gen. 1.1 (Gr B, Bish): "In the beginning God created heaven and earth"; (Genv, AV): "the Heaven, and the Earth."

III.197–203:   For the Roman Church, following Aquinas, *In 4 libros sententiarum magistri Petri Lombardi,* III.22,

q. ii, art. 1, "limbo" designates, first, the interim—
and now nonexistent—place or state where the souls
of the just who lived before the time of Christ
awaited their redemption upon his Harrowing of
Hell (*limbus* or *infernus sanctorum patrum*), and
second, the permanent place or state of unbaptized
children and others who die without personal guilt
but are excluded from the Beatific Vision because of
original sin (*limbus puerorum* or *infantium*). The
first, the limbo of the patriarchs, was uniformly regarded as a happy condition, but the limbo of the
children was held to be some kind of damnation,
despite wide divergence about its exact nature in the
troubled history of the doctrine. The extremes are
represented by the Augustinian view that unbaptized
children shared the general pains of hell (*De pec-
catorum meritis et remissione*, I.16 (*PL*, XLIV, 120);
Contra Julianum, V.44 (*PL*, XLIV, 809) and the
gradually developed Thomistic position that theirs is
a state of perpetual happiness on the natural level
(*In sententias Petri Lombardi;* III.22, q. ii, art. 1;
Quaestiones disputatae de malo, V, art. 3). However,
in Donne's day a compromise opinion was advanced
in Bellarmine's *De amissione gratiae et statu peccati*,
iv–vii, the second of his *Controversiae* which appeared between 1586 and 1593. Bellarmine contended
that the souls in the limbo of children incur no
physical torment (*poena sensus*) but do suffer the
pain of deprivation of the sight of God (*poena
damni*). This is essentially a return to the doctrines
of Abelard (*Expositio in Ep Pauli ad Rom.*, ii.5:
PL, CLXXVIII, 870), Peter Lombard (*Sententiarum
Libri quatuor*, II, dist. xxxiii.5: *PL*, CXCII, 730), and
the majority of the Scholastics.

III.209–215:   A Biblical concordance readily confirms these remarks, another manifestation of Donne's persistent
interest—shared with Origen, the Latin Church
Fathers, and St. Bernard—in the spiritual overtones
(moral sense) of a text.

III.216–217:	*Vox dolentis:* voice of one in pain; *Increpantis:* of one chiding, rebuking, reproving.
III.225–226 and mg.:	I restore the correct reference of *LXXX S*, which P-S unaccountably alter to "Esay. 16.29." Isa. 16.9 (AV): "I wil bewaile with the weeping of Jazer, the Vine of Sibmah: I wil water thee with my teares."
III.226:	Isa. 1.24 (Genv, AV): "Ah, I will . . . avenge me of mine enemies."
III.228 mg.:	I follow P-S in emending "Ezek. 16.11," the erroneous reference in *LXXX S*.
III.231:	Irregularity: in ecclesiastical usage, an infraction of the rules governing those in holy orders; an impediment or disqualification by which a person is debarred from ordination, discharge of clerical functions, or ecclesiastical advancement; *OED*, 1c; the earliest sense in English. Besides wittily hypothesizing the necessity of God's conformity with canon law, Donne may be glancing at the "irregularity" investigation made by a royal commission after Archbishop Abbot's accidental homicide of a gamekeeper in 1621. The proceedings are described by S. R. Gardiner, *History of England, 1603–1642* (London, 1887–1891), IV, 139–140.
III.242–244:	Cf. St. Ambrose's vivid imaging of the serpent as a type of carnal indulgence in *Liber de Paradiso*, ch. xv (*PL*, XIV, 329).
III.243:	Allusion is to God's curse on the serpent in Gen. 3.14.
III.250–251:	See the note to Donne's observations on melancholy in ll. 635–640 of the second Prebend sermon.
III.259–260:	*Iashar, yāshār* in modern transliteration, means "righteous, straight, upright" (see no. 3477 in

Strong's *Concise Dict.*, p. 53). Valentinus Schindlerus (*Lexicon Pentaglotton* [Hanover, 1612], col. 820) gives the basic meanings of *rectus, aequus, planus esse, probatus esse.* Donne's reference is to the masculine singular; the form in his text is masculine plural.

III.261–262:   Allusion is to Jacob's vision, described in Gen. 28.12.

III.263–267:   Cf. Preb II, 367–384.

III.271–295:   A lesser but still notable parallel to this passage is found in *Sermons,* IX.18.565–575.

III.284–285:   Recognition that a compass needle does not point at the true north but makes an angle with the absolute meridian was first certain in the fifteenth century, despite claims (based on vague passages) that variation—or declination—was known to the eleventh-century Chinese and to Roger Bacon at the time he wrote his *Opus minus* (1266). Some of the compasses used by Columbus on his second (1493) voyage had their needles mounted askew to correct for variation. In *De magnete* (1600), however, William Gilbert first hypothesized that the directive power of the compass is due to the earth's being a great magnet itself. Donne alludes to *De magnete* regarding the "Magnetique force" which unifies the world in the *First Anniversary,* ll. 219–222, and in the *Essays in Divinity.* See Charles M. Coffin, *John Donne and the New Philosophy* (New York: Columbia University Press, 1937), pp. 84–87.

III.285–287:   To the naked eye, the pole star (Polaris) is the star nearest the north celestial pole and the brightest star in the constellation Ursa Minor. Its proximity to the pole gives it an apparently constant position all night and all year. This together with its moderate brightness makes it a convenient object for use in determining latitude and north-south direction in the northern hemisphere. The *OED* cites Richard Eden's

The decades of the newe worlde or west India (tr. 1555): "The starre which we caule the pole starre or northe starre . . . is not the very poynte of the pole Artyke."

III.292–295:   Cf. "Goodfriday, 1613," ll. 23–24: "that endless height which is/ Zenith to us, and to'our Antipodes"; *Sermons*, IV.1.509–519.

III.297–298:   Prov. 23.26 (Muns): "Praebe mihi fili mi cor tuum"; (Vulg): "Praebe fili mi cor tuum mihi"; (AV): "My sonne, give me thine heart."

III.311–321:   On the arguments of the more traditionalist Anglican clergy against Puritanically minded attempts to make the visible church (the parish) congruent with the invisible church (God's elect), see C. H. and K. George, *The Protestant Mind*, pp. 314–318.

III.324:   On "Recusancy," see note to ll. 304–305 of the second Prebend sermon.

III.327:   collaterall: lying aside from the main subject, purpose, or line of action.

III.328:   occasion: pretext, excuse; *OED*, 2b, now obsolete.

III.333–334:   2 Sam. 1.21 (all versions): "according to thine own heart hast thou done all these great things."

III.342–343 and mg.:   I follow P-S's correction of "Psal. 35.11," the erroneous reference in *LXXX S*. Donne's two allusions give the gist of the places cited but are too free to correspond to any particular English version.

III.345:   adprecation (appreciation): the action of praying for or invoking a blessing on another; a devout wish.

III.345–346:   Although the allusion is somewhat unclear, Donne is presumably recalling Psalm 42.2, which reads (Gr B, Bish, Genv): "When shall I come to (and: Genv) appeare before the presence of God?" The

AV omits "the presence of." The closest Latin versions of the verse are (T-J): "quando accedam, ut appaream in conspectu Dei?" and (Muns, Vatab): "quando veniam ut appaream conspectui dei?"

III.346–347: Again, Donne's italics are very free, but the words appear to be a conflation of parts of Psalm 51.11,12 (Genv, AV): "Cast me not away from thy presence; . . . Restore unto (to: Genv) me the joy of thy salvation."

III.349–350: Donne cites Munster's exact Latin reading; Psalm 119.11 (AV): "Thy word have I hidde in mine heart." Perhaps the amplification which follows was prompted in part by a verse from the lesson for Evening Prayer on the twenty-second Sunday after Trinity (November 5 in 1626), Prov. 3.32 (AV): "For the froward is abomination to the Lord: but his secret is with the righteous."

III.351–353: Psalm 40.10 (Genv, AV): "I have not hid thy righteousness within my heart; . . . I have not concealed . . . thy truth, from the great congregation."

III.354–355: St. Hilary, *Tractatus in cxviii Psalmum:* "Ita enim dixit: *In corde meo abscondi eloquia tua, ut non peccarem tibi:* quia cum caetera peccata secundum differentias rerum aut in nos ipsos aut in alios exsererentur; tamen tum fierent in Deum propria, cum quae occultorum cordium essent condenda secreto, haec in profanae cogitationis scientiam proderentur" (*PL*, IX.513–514). St. Ambrose, *In Psalmum cxviii Expositio:* "*In corde meo,* inquit, *abscondi eloquia tua, ut non peccem tibi. . . .* Peccat enim Deo, qui commissa sibi secreta mysteria putaverit indignis esse vulganda. . . . Cave ergo ne divitias tuas perfidis prodas: . . . quanto magis sermonem Dei cordis nostri gremio debemus operire, debemus abscondere!" (*PL*, XV, 1284–1285).

III.355–356: "Pearles before swine" alludes to Matt. 7.6.

III.356:   inferre: bring on, induce, occasion (*OED*, 1; obsolete).

III.366:   Psalm 119.19 (Vulg): "Incola . . . sum . . .: non abscondas a me mandata tua"; (T-J): "Peregrinante me in hac terra, ne abscondas a me praecepta tua."

III.369–375:   Sir Thomas Browne thought otherwise, as he confessed in *Religio Medici,* pt. I, sect. 3: "We have reformed from them, not against them; . . . and therefore I am not scrupulous to converse and live with them, to enter their Churches in defect of ours, and either pray with them, or for them. I could never perceive any rational Consequence from those many Texts which prohibit the Children of Israel to pollute themselves with the Temples of the Heathens; we being all Christians, and not divided by such detested impieties as might prophane our Prayers, or the place wherein we make them; or that a resolved Conscience may not adore her Creator any where, especially in places devoted to his Service" (*Works,* ed. Geoffrey Keynes [London: Faber & Gwyer Ltd., 1928], I, 6–7).

III.384–387:   Cf. Preb II, 44–45 and note; "To the Countess of Bedford" ("Honour is so sublime perfection"), ll. 46–48.

III.395–397:   The observation about God's mercy is very Augustinian; see, e.g., *Enarrationes in Psalmum lviii* where it is remarked of the Psalmist's phrasing: *"Deus meus misericordia mea.* Non invenit impletus bonis Dei, quid appellaret Deum suum, nisi misericordiam suam. O nomen, sub quo nemini desperandum est! *Deus meus,* inquit, *misericordia mea"* (*PL,* XXXVI, 712–713).

III.397–398:   Curses upon anyone who tampers with Scripture are standard in rabbinical literature, but I have not found a curse pertaining specifically to the Psalter. Clear examples of the standard sort occur in *The*

Babylonian Talmud, ed. I. Epstein (London: Soncino Press, 1959): *Seder Neziḳin Sanhedrin,* ch. xi, 99ᵃ, and *Aboth,* ch. iii. See also the article "Bible Canon" in *The Jewish Encyclopedia,* ed. Isidore Singer (New York and London: Funk and Wagnalls Co., n.d.), III, 143, 149, which cites the famous passage in the Midrash concerning additions, " 'And further . . . my son, be admonished,' saith God; 'Twenty-four books have I written for you. . . . He who reads one verse not written in the twenty-four books . . . will find no salvation. . . .' " and reproduces these warnings with regard to the Torah: "Any prophet who attempts to annul one of its laws will be punished by death"; "Before him who denies its divine origin the doors of hell shall never close, and he shall be condemned to stay therein eternally."

III.413:

Halal, or *hālal* in modern transliteration, is the third person singular masculine perfect form of a root with the original meaning of "to be clear, to shine" having sound and color associations. Its derivative meanings include "to exult, to celebrate, to commend, to glory, to give light, to be worthy of praise"—all of which Donne draws upon in this sermon. (See Strong's *Concise Dict.,* no. 1984, p. 33.)

III.414–422:

This comparison of English translations of the Bible, unique in Donne's preaching, is made a means of drawing out the various meanings of a key word in order to develop the spiritual and moral significance of the text in the second half of the sermon. Donne successively cites Psalm 64.10 in the Great Bible of 1539 (whose Psalter the *BCP* incorporates), the so-called Bishop's Bible of 1568, the Authorized Version of 1611, and the Later Version (c. 1395–1397) of the "Wyclif" Bible. The versions read as follows:

(Gr B): "The righteous shal rejoyce in the lorde and put his trust in hym: and all they that are true of hert shalbe glad."

(Bish): "The righteous wyll rejoyce in God, and put his trust in hym: and all they that be upright hearted wylbe glad."
(AV): text cited at head of sermon.
(Wyc LV): "The iust man schal be glad in the Lord, and schal hope in him; and alle men of riȝtful herte schulen be preisid."

III.423–428: Donne's transliteration, *Iithhalelu,* and gloss upon it are substantially accurate. The point of departure is the third person masculine plural imperfect indicative—*yihalelû* in modern transliteration. To produce the reflexive form *yithhalelû* the letter *taw* ("th"), the sign of the reflexive conjugation, is inserted between the prefix and the consonants of the root.

III.430–431 and mg.: P-S bracket a reference to John 5.35, which reads (AV): "He was a burning and a shining light"; (Genv): "He was a burning and a shining candle." Donne preached two sermons mainly devoted to the life and witness of St. John the Baptist (*Sermons,* IV, nos. 5,8).

III.433–435: A form of *hâlal* does occur in Psalm 78.63, which the AV renders "given in marriage."

III.441–448: Like Aquinas, Donne calls Aristotle "the Philosopher." The first citation is an exact Latin rendering of *Rhetoric,* I.ix.1367^{b}26–27. See *Aristoteles Ars Rhetorica, accedit vetusta translatio latina,* ann. L. Spengel (Leipzig, 1868), I, 213: "Est autem laus sermo elucidans magnitudinem virtutis." (Cf. Plato, *Protagoras,* 337^b.) Donne proceeds to quotation and close paraphrase of Aquinas, *ST,* pars II^{a}II^{ae}, q. 103, art. 1, ad obj. 3: "Praise is distinguished from honour . . . because by paying honour to a person we bear witness to a person's excelling goodness absolutely, whereas by praising him we bear witness to his goodness in reference to an end (*in ordine ad finem*): thus we praise one that works well for an end. On the other hand, honour is given even to the best, which is not referred to an end, but has already arrived at the end (*sed iam sunt in fine*), according to the Philosopher, *Ethic.* i.5."

III.451:

interlocutory: pronounced during the course of a court action, not finally decisive. (The legal sense.)

III.458–460:

Prov. 22.1 (AV): "A Good name is rather to be chosen then great riches, and loving favour rather then silver & golde."

III.460:

St. Bernard, *Sermo LXXI in Cantica:* "Habent et mores colores suos, habent et odores" (*PL,* CLXXXIII, 1121).

III.468–471:

St. Jerome, *Epistola* CXXIII.15: "Fuge personas, in quibus potest malae conversationis esse suspicio, nec paratum habeas illud è trivio: Sufficit mihi conscientia mea: non curo quid de me loquantur homines" (*PL,* XXII, 1056).

III.471–482:

St. Augustine, *De bono viduitatis,* cap. xxii: "Nec audiendi sunt, sive viri sancti, sive feminae, quando reprehensa in aliqua negligentia sua, per quam fit ut in malam veniant suspicionem, unde suam vitam longe abesse sciunt, dicunt sibi coram Deo sufficere conscientiam, existimationem hominum non imprudenter solum, verum etiam crudeliter contemnentes; cum occidunt animas aliorum, sive blasphemantium viam Dei, quibus secundum suam suspicionem quasi turpis quae casta est displicet vita sanctorum, sive etiam cum excusatione imitantium, non quod vident, sed quod putant. Proinde quisquis a criminibus flagitiorum atque facinorum vitam suam custodit, sibi bene facit: quisquis autem etiam famam, et in alios misericors est" (*PL,* XL, 448).

III.483–490:

St. Augustine, *Epistolarum Classis I.*22: "Sed tamen ab eis qui se honorant nec totum nec nihil accipiendo, et id quod accipitur laudis aut honoris, non propter

se qui totus coram Deo esse debet et humana con-
temnare, sed propter illos accipiatur quibus consulere
non potest, si nimia dejectione vilescat" (*PL,*
XXXIII, 93).

III.490–494: St. Bernard, *Sermo LXXXIII de Diversis: "Mel in-
venisti? noli multum comedere, ne forte satiatus
evomas illud* (Prov. 25.16). Potest non incongrue
hoc loco mellis nomine favor humanae laudis intelligi: meritoque non ab omni, sed immoderato mellis
hujus edulio prohibemur" (*PL,* CLXXXIII, 700–
701).

III.494–495: Donne implies in alluding to the commandment regarding the Tree of Knowledge in Gen. 2.17 that
such absolute prohibitions are exceptional; God is
usually moderately permissive toward man.

III.496–499: St. Augustine, *Sermo CCCXXXIX—In die Ordina-
tionis suae:* "Laudari autem a bene viventibus, si
dicam nolo, mentior: si dicam volo, timeo ne sim
inanitatis appetentior quam soliditatis" (*PL,*
XXXVIII, 1480). The subsequent remark on the
apostles' "holy complacency" when their preaching
pleased their auditors occurs also at *Sermons,* II.17.
379–380; I have not found the Augustinian source.

III.509–511: *The Babylonian Talmud: Seder Zera'im Berakoth,*
tr. Maurice Simon (London: Soncino Press, 1959),
p. 14: "R.(abbi) Eleazar b.[en] Abina says: Who-
ever recites [the psalm] *Praise of David* (note: Ps.
CXLV) three times daily, is sure to inherit the world
to come." Cf. J. M. Neale and R. F. Littledale, *A
Commentary on the Psalms: from Primitive and
Mediaeval Writers* . . . , 2nd ed. (London, 1874),
IV, 383: "It is said in the Talmud: 'Everyone who
repeats the Tehillah of David [145. Psalm] thrice a
day may be sure that he is a child of the world to
come. And why? Not merely because the Psalm is
alphabetical (for that the 119th is, and in an eight-
fold degree), nor only because it praises GOD's

providence over all creation (for that the Great Hallel does, 136.25), but because it unites both these properties in itself.' "

III.516:   *Iithhalelu*: see note to ll. 423–428 above.

III.521–523:   Zeph. 3.19,20 (AV): "I will get them praise and fame in every land . . . for I will make you a name and a praise among all people of the earth."

III.529–533:   "On Joseph," *Philo,* tr. F. H. Colson (Loeb ed., 1935), VI, 173: "As for the difference between cooks and physicians, it is a matter of common knowledge. The physician devotes all his energies solely to preparing what is wholesome, even if it is unpalatable, while the cook deals with the pleasant only and has no thought of what is beneficial." The distinction originates in Plato's *Gorgias,* 463–464, 500B–501A; where Socrates compares on the one hand rhetoric and cookery (both are concerned with pleasure), and on the other political justice and medicine (their end is the good).

III.533–536:   According to Erasmus, *Adagiorum Chiliades quatuor cum sesquicenturia* (1558), Chil. II, cent. i.96, pp. 384–385, the original form of this proverb is Aristophanes' βαλλ' ἐς κόρακας: Id est, Abi ad corvos, perinde valet quasi dicas, Abi in malam crucem, in malam rem, atque in exitium." Erasmus then cites the saying of Diogenes the Cynic, which Donne adapts: "Satius est ad corvos devenire, quam ad adulatores. Quod hi & vivos & bonos etiam viros devorarent."

III.537:   Although *LXXX S* prints no italics, Donne is quoting exactly from Psalm 10.3 (AV), "the covetous, whom the Lord abhorreth."

III.542:   Subsidy man: one who pays toward a subsidy, which, in English law, is an aid, tax, or tribute granted by

Parliament to the King for the urgent occasions of the realm, and levied on every subject of ability, according to the value of his lands or goods (*Black's Law Dict.*, p. 1597). Cf. John Cowell's definition of "Subsidie" in *The Interpreter: . . . Wherein is set foorth the true meaning of all, or the most part of such Words and Termes, as are mentioned in the Lawe Writers, or Statutes of this victorious and renowned Kingdome* (Cambridge, 1607), Rrr 1. A spiritual construction on "Subsidy man" occurs earlier, and appropriately, in a sermon of Donne's at Lincoln's Inn (*Sermons*, II.10.57).

III.543: condigne: merited, fitting, adequate (*OED*, 3). Since the end of the seventeenth century the word has been obsolete (or archaic) except when used of appropriate punishment, as in the Tudor Acts of Parliament.

III.543–544: Allusion is to the so-called "Golden Rule" given in Matt. 7.12.

III.545–548: References to the human desire for praise and warnings against succumbing to it are exceedingly frequent in the works of Gregory the Great. The nearest approximation to Donne's citation which I have found is "Et plerumque contingit ut hi qui ad bona opera recte intentione non veniunt, cum placere se hominibus vident, ad exercenda haec eadem opera vehementius accendantur" (*Moralia in Job*, lib.XIII: *PL*, LXXV, 1015).

III.552–554: St. Augustine, *Epistolarum Classis III*, 231: "Ecce quid quaerebat in laude hominem, ubi etiam [Apostolus] dicebat, *De caetero, fratres, quaecumque sunt vera, quaecumque pudica, quaecumque casta, quaecumque sancta, quaecumque charissima, quaecumque bonae famae, si qua virtus, si qua laus, haec cogitate: quae didicistis et accepistis, et audistis et vidistis in me, haec agite; et Deus pacis erit vobiscum*

(Philipp. 4.8,9). Caetera igitur, quae supra commemoravi, virtutis nomine amplexus est, dicens, *si qua virtus:* illud autem quod subjecit, *quaecumque bonae famae,* alio uno verbo congruo prosecutus est dicendo, *si qua laus.* Quod itaque ait, *Si hominibus placerem, Christi servus non essem* (Galat. 1.10), sic utique accipiendum tanquam dixerit: Si bona quae facio, fine laudis humanae facerem, laudis amore tumescerem. Volebat ergo Apostolus placere omnibus, et eis placere gaudebat, non quorum laudibus tumescebat in seipso, sed quos laudatus aedificabat in Christo" (*PL,* XXXIII, 1024).

III.562–563,568–569:   Allen, "Dean Donne Sets His Text," p. 213, criticizes Donne's misleading assertion that "the Hebrew hath no Superlatives," since grammars of the day gave instruction in the equivalent special construction. But Donne's concern here is less with accurate linguistic description than with the spiritual intimations of a solecism in "the language which the Holy Ghost spake."

III.589–590:   "Our three Translations" refers to the three successive sixteenth-century versions prepared for official use in the Church of England. Donne's italics reproduce the reading of the Great Bible, with an added "thereof"; see the note to ll. 413–422 above.

III.596–600 and mg.:   The cited texts all contain forms of *hālal,* which the AV renders in the following italicized words. Psalm 75.4: "I said unto the *fooles,* Deale not *foolishly";* Isa. 44.25: "(The Lord) maketh diviners *mad;* . . . turneth wisemen backward, and maketh their knowledge *foolish";* Job 12.17: "He . . . maketh the Judges *fooles."*

III.607,617:   I follow P-S in italicizing the *"in"* of *"in futuro aeterno,"* which is set in roman type in *LXXX S.* Both *"in futuro aeterno"* and *"in aeterno"* appear to be Donne's coinages. Neither is found in the Vulgate, which has *"in aeternum"* very frequently. See F. P. Dutripon, *Concordantiae Bibliorum Sacrorum Vulgatae Editionis* (Paris, 1838).

III.612:   towards: An uncertain predicate-adjectival usage, now also obsolete. The *OED* (B II 4b) questioningly submits the following definition: "Towards some end or purpose; (as a contribution) toward something."

III.619–625:   Aquinas, *ST,* pars III Supp., q. 85, art. 1, affirms the approximation, insofar as possible, of the beatified body to the qualities of the soul. Cf. Donne's earlier adaptation of the idea in "A Funeral Elegy," ll. 59–62.

III.625–626:   2 Peter 1.4 (Genv, AV): "That . . . you might bee partakers of the divine nature"; I Cor. 6.17 (Gr B, Bish, AV, Genv): "He that is joyned (coupled: Bish) unto the Lord, is one spirit."

III.630–641:   In *ST,* pars III Supp., q. 92, arts. 1–3, Aquinas discusses the Beatific Vision (vision of the divine essence which the blessed enjoy). Cf. his theory of how God can be known by his creatures, pars I^a, q. 12, esp. arts. 6–10.

III.638:   riches: a variant of Middle English "richesse," often treated mistakenly as a plural. Donne's singular verb is correct. Cf. "riches is" in the *Second Anniversary,* l. 233.

III.648–653:   A godly death is depicted traditionally, as conformity with Christ; note the echo of the last words from the cross as given in Luke 23.46 (AV), "Father, into thy hands I commend my spirit." Cf. the death speech in *Everyman.*

III.659–671:   Donne's preaching is characterized by dramatic and varied use of the first person, well discussed by Joan

Webber (*Contrary Music,* pp. 115–120). Note the autobiographical reflections in his emphasis on the moral impact of his sermons (ll. 663–65; cf. *Sermons,* IX.6.8–12) and the reference to his late ordination (ll. 692–693). On the other hand, a generalizing effect is created by the constant echoes in Donne's phraseology of the parable of the Kingdom of Heaven in Matt. 25.34–46. Cf. Preb I, 381–382.

III.668–671:   One of Donne's favorite rhetorical figures is antimetabole, which George Puttenham aptly termed "Counterchange" and described as follows: "Ye have a figure which takes a couple of words to play with . . . , and by making them to chaunge and shift one into others place they do very pretily exchange and shift the sense" (*Arte of English Poesy,* bk. III).

III.679:   Hosanna(es): "Save now!" or "Save, pray!", an exclamation occurring, e.g., in Psalm 118.25 and used by the Jews as an appeal for deliverance as well as the praising of God. The latter use was taken over by the Christian Church. See Matt. 21.9,15; Mark 11.9,10; John 13.13.

III.680–682:   Donne is correct but unspecific. *Hallelujah,* meaning "Praise (ye) the Lord," is a compound composed of the plural verb *hallelū* and *"jah"* (or *"Yah"*), the first syllable of "Jehovah" ("Yahweh").

III.685:   Allusion is to Psalm 22.14, which reads (AV): "my heart . . . is melted in the midst of my bowels."

III.686–688:   Matt. 25.21 (Vulg, Trem): 'Euge serve bone"; (Genv): "It is well done good servant and faithfull . . . , enter into thy masters joy"; (AV): "Well done, good and faithfull servant: . . . enter thou into the joy of thy lord." This text is cited earlier at ll. 108–109 above and at ll. 676–677 of the second Prebend sermon.

III.689:   1 Cor. 9.16 (Vulg, Eras): "Vae enim mihi est, si non evangelizavero"; (Beza, Vatab): "vae autem mihi est, nisi evangelizem"; (Trem): "vae autem mihi nisi evangelizavero."

III.709:   "Numbered with thy Saints in glory everlasting" occurs in the canticle *Te Deum laudamus* in the Order for Morning Prayer in the *BCP*.

Notes to the Fourth Prebend Sermon

Sermon heading: The date is given in Old Style; in New Style the year is 1627.

IV.1–2,10–16:   *Ex nihilo nihil fit* ("From nothing, nothing is made") was originally an Eleatic and especially Parmenidean principle: see fragment 28 B 8 in Diels-Kranz. It was adopted much later by the medieval Schoolmen as an accurate statement about material causation. The great exception to the principle was God's creation of the world (*creatio ex nihilo*), when something was made out of nothing. St. Augustine very often affirms (or meditates on) *creatio ex nihilo,* notably in bk. XI, ch. 5 of the *Confessions,* whence Donne's stylistic redoubling here may derive: "Quomodo fecisti, Deus, caelum et terram? Non utique in caelo neque in terra fecisti caelum et terram . . . : neque in universo mundo fecisti universum mundum, quia non erat, ubi fieret, antequam fieret, ut esset" (*PL, XXXII,* 812. Cf. bk. XII, chs. 7–8: XXXII, 828–829; *Contra Julianum,* V.42: XLV, 1479). Other important discussions are found in St. Anselm, St. Bonaventure, and especially St. Thomas Aquinas, whose definition of a miracle as something done outside the order of created nature is echoed here by Donne. "Miraculum proprie dicitur, quod fit praeter ordinem totius naturae creatae, sub quo ordine continetur omnis virtus creaturae" (*ST,* pars Iᵃ, q. cxiv, art. 4); "haec autem, quae praeter ordinem communiter in rebus statutum quandoque divinitus fiunt, miracula dici solent" (*Summa contra Gentiles,* lib. III, cap. 101). The witty linkage of *creatio ex nihilo* with the divine ordinance of preaching (as manifestations, respectively, of the generative and regenerative power of the Word) appears to be Donne's own, although St. Chrysostom, St. Gregory the Great, and St. Bernard may have provided a lead in the violent images (e.g., the transformation of beasts into men) which they use to describe the conversion of sinners by the working of the Holy Ghost. See Schleiner's remarks on the rhetoric in such cases, *The Imagery of Donne's Sermons,* pp. 34–36. Cf. with Donne's entire *exordium* the reflections in the *Essays,* p. 28 on creation *ex nihilo,* and p. 81 on miracles.

IV.5:   infatuate: turn into folly, confound, frustrate.

IV.7–8:   Cf. ll. 173–176 of the fifth Prebend sermon, where after an extraordinarily prolonged division of the text Donne promises not to exceed his time limit. One hour was the customary length of a sermon in the earlier seventeenth century. Donne frequently alludes to the standard (*Sermons,* I.8.318–321; III.10. 39–42; IV.15.519–520; VI.7.36–37; VII.14.716; IX.14. 4–5; X.5.540); his adherence to it is specially remarked on in the funeral elegies by Mr. R. B. and Sidney Godolphin (*Poems of Donne,* ed. Grierson, I, 356, 363). Accepting all this testimony requires the conclusion that Donne expanded his sermons considerably when he wrote them out for publication, since the versions of many which we possess take longer than an hour to read aloud. See Robert L. Hickey, "Donne's Delivery," *Tennessee Studies in Literature,* IX (1964), 40–41.

IV.15:   reluctation: struggle, resistance, opposition of things or persons.

IV.40–42:   Allusion is to the parable told by Jesus in Luke 14.16–24 and Matt. 22.2–14.

IV.47:   Rev. 3.20 (all versions): "Behold, I stand at the doore, and knocke: If any man heare my voyce and open the doore, I will come in to him, and will sup with him, and he with me."

IV.52–53:   Rev. 19.9 (AV): "Blessed are they which are called unto the marriage supper of the Lambe."

IV.59–62:   On this kind of characteristic textual comment, see Introduction, p. 42.

IV.67–69:   Cf. *Sermons*, V.18.476–477. The word "salvation" in the AV rendering of Psalm 65.5 translates the Hebrew noun *yēsha'*, which derives from the root *yāsha'* (Donne's *"Iashang"*) meaning properly "to be open, wide, or free" and by implication "to be safe" or, causatively, "to free, succor, defend, deliver, save, or bring salvation." See nos. 3467, 3468 in Strong's *Concise Dict.*, p. 53. Valentinus Schindlerus's list of meanings (*Lexicon Pentaglotton*, col. 818) includes *"salus, liberatio, redemtio"* [*sic*]. The other allusion to "the very Name of *Iesus*" refers to *Yᵉhôwshûwa'* (a proper noun meaning "Yahweh-saved") or to *Yêshûwa'* ("He will save"), the Hebrew source-words for the Greek Iησοῦς. See nos. 3091, 3442 in Strong's *Concise Dict.*, pp. 48, 53; also no. 2424 in Strong's *Dictionary of the Words in the Greek Testament*, likewise publ. and bound with his *Exhaustive Concordance* (New York and Nashville, 1890), p. 37. Cf. St. Jerome's *Liber de nominibus Hebraicis* (*PL, XXIII*, 899 *et passim*): "Jesus, salvator."

IV.88:   Heb. 3.6 (Genv): "Christ is as the Sonne, over his own house, whose house we are"; (Bish, AV): "Christ as a sonne over his owne house; whose house are wee."

IV.89:   Psalm 147.2 (all versions): "The Lord doth build up Jerusalem."

IV.91:   John 14.6 (Gr B, Bish, AV): "Jesus saith unto him, I am the Way." Cf. with Donne's figurative progression a passage in St. Hilary's *Tractatus in lxvii Psalmum*: "Religiosae autem viae doctrina Christus est, quam se esse in Evangeliis ostendit, dicens: *Ego sum veritas, via et vita* (John 14.6); et rursum:

Nemo ad Patrem vadit, nisi per me (ibid). Et hunc esse viam, ipse ille connexus sibi psalmi sermo testatur. Quae *in terra,* id est, vel ex terra ortis, vel terram inhabitantibus cognoscibilis, et nota praestanda est. *Ut cognoscamus in terra viam tuam, in omnibus gentibus salutare tuum.* Jesum salutare ac salutarem dici, ipse ille proprietatis sermo loquitur. Nam quod nobiscum *salutare* est, id apud Hebraeum Jesus est" (*PL,* IX, 439).

IV.92:   Matt. 7.13,14 (AV): "Enter ye in at the strait gate . . . strait is the gate and narrow is the way which leadeth unto life." Cf. St. Gregory, *Moralia in Job,* lib. VI, cap. 3: "Quis alius portae nomine, nisi mediator Dei et hominem debet intelligi, qui ait: *Ego sum ostium, per me si quis introierit, salvabitur"* (*PL,* LXXV, 751), and *Homiliae in Ezechielem,* lib. II: "Portam autem Dominum dicimus, quia per ipsum intramus ad ipsum" (*PL,* LXXVI, 1035).

IV.97:   John 4.34 (AV): "My meat is, to doe the will of him that sent mee."

IV.106:   endue: pass into the stomach, digest (*OED,* II 2; obsolete).

IV.117–122:   Donne's circumspection is typically Anglican; cf. the twenty-eighth of the Thirty-nine Articles, "Of the Lord's Supper," which (in the context of acrimonious and assertive sixteenth-century controversy about this Sacrament) precludes holding of the doctrine of Transubstantiation or taking a Zwinglian memorialist position but makes no definite positive pronouncement on the means or manner of receiving the Real Presence of Christ. A similar reticence is found in the conclusion of the first part of "An Homily of the Worthy receiving and reverent esteeming of the Sacrament of the Body and Blood of Christ" in the *Second Tome of Homilies.*

IV.132 mg.:   *LXXX S* reads "Ps. 63.6" in correspondence with
                    Vulgate numbering, but since the allusion is in
                    English, I emend with P-S.

IV.132–134:   Psalm 81.16 (Genv): "And God would have fed
                    them with the fat of wheat, and with honie out of
                    the rocke would I have sufficed thee"; (AV): "He
                    should have fedde them also with the finest of the
                    wheat: and with honie out of the rocke, should I
                    have satisfied thee."

IV.134:   Cf. Rabanus Maurus, *Allegoriae in Sacram Scrip-
                    turam:* "*Mel,* doctrina Christi, ut in cantico Deuter-
                    onomii [32.13]: 'Sugerunt mel de petra,' id est, dul-
                    cem susceperunt doctrinam a Christo"; "*Petra* est
                    Christus, ut in Psalmis [77.20]: 'Percussit petram et
                    fluxerunt aquae,' quod Judaicus populus Christum
                    crucifixum percusserunt, et fluxerunt ab eo dona
                    gratiae" (*PL*, CXII, 997, 1028).

IV.136–139:   In medieval exegesis the Scriptures are commonly
                    compared to a meal. See, e.g., Peter Lombard's *Com-
                    mentarium in Psalmos,* where, citing Cassiodorus, it
                    is asserted: "Aliud totum, mensa, sacra Scriptura est,
                    quia sicut in mensa diversa fercula ad refectionem
                    corporis ponuntur, ita in sacra Scriptura diversae
                    sententiae ad saginam animarum. . . . Hanc mensam
                    habuerunt Judaei, dum mandata Dei coluerunt"
                    (*PL*, CXCI, 637), and Alanus de Insulis's *Sermo
                    IV,* which represents the Scriptures as a meal of milk
                    (the historical sense), bread (the allegorical sense),
                    and honey (the tropological sense) (*PL*, CCX, 209).
                    But Rabanus Maurus's collection of connotations is
                    closest to Donne's associative development: "*Mensa*
                    est Vetus Testamentum, ut in Evangelio [Matt.
                    15.27]: 'Catelli edunt de micis quae cadunt de mensa
                    dominorum,' id est, humilis gentium subtilitatem
                    Veteris Testamenti per intellectum comedit. *Mensa,*
                    sacrum altare, unde accipimus corpus Domini Christi
                    et sanguinem, ut in libro Ecclesiastici [31.12]: 'Ad

magnam mensam sedisti, diligenter attende quae apposita sunt tibi,' id est, sacramenta corporis et sanguinis Domini, quae in altari sumus fidei oculo contingit" (*Allegoriae in Sacram Scripturam, PL,* CXII, 998).

IV.140–145:

Donne supplies a good literal translation of the title which is given this Psalm in later texts of the Septuagint. Although this lengthy title is lacking in the Hebrew, Syriac, and Chaldee versions of the Psalter, and in earlier manuscripts of the Septuagint, it is found in Origen's *Hexapla* whence it was taken by St. Jerome (and used by St. Augustine) in the belief that it was authoritative. St. Jerome rendered it as follows in his Gallican Psalter, which also is the Vulgate version: *"In finem, Psalmus David, Canticum Ieremiae, et Ezechielis populo transmigrationis, cum inciperent exire"* (*PL,* XXIX, 241–242). Even if (as is likely) Donne's scanty Greek sufficed for the purposes here, some Latin source like Jerome or Augustine (*PL,* XXXVI, 772) may well have alerted his attention to the variety of titles for the Psalm.

IV.146–149:

Because Psalm 65.2, "O thou that hearest prayer, unto thee shall all flesh come," was anciently regarded as a prophecy of the resurrection of the body, the whole Psalm was incorporated into the Office of the Dead in the Western Church (Neale and Littledale, *A Commentary on the Psalms,* 3rd ed., I, 50–52; II, 344). The liturgical section of the late fourth-century *Apostolical Constitutions* indicates that another of Donne's Prebend Psalms, the 63rd, was also used in this Office in conjunction with the 67th. See James Donaldson's translation in the *Ante-Nicene Christian Library,* XVII, 233.

IV.151:

In direct contrast to the metaphorical usage here, "Inne" is a recurrent metaphor for the body (the house of the soul) in Donne's poems; see his "Metempsychosis", l. 181; *Second Anniversary,* l. 175; and the devotional application in *La Corona,* iii.1–5.

IV.159–166:   This passage exemplifies the increased essayistic ten-
               dency in Donne's mature preaching, as associative
               development dominates. Cf. Bacon's "Of Great
               Place": "Certainly great persons had need to borrow
               other men's opinions, to think themselves happy;
               for if they judge by their own feeling, they cannot
               find it: but if they think with themselves what other
               men think of them, and that other men would fain
               be as they are, then they are happy as it were by re-
               port; when perhaps they find the contrary within."

IV.163:   shrewd: vexatious, irksome (*OED,* 4; obsolete).

IV.173–174:   John 1.9 (Genv, AV): "That was the true Light,
               which lighteth every man that commeth into the
               world."

IV.174–178:   Aquinas identifies the qualities of rationality and
               immortality possessed by the human soul (*ST,* II^a
               II^{ae}, q. 164, art. 1, ad obj. 1): "Forma autem homi-
               nis est anima rationalis, quae est de se immortalis."

IV.179–181:   Donne here, as frequently in his work, is making
               figurative use of the Ptolemaic conception of the
               universe, in which the solid, stationary sphere of the
               earth was envisaged as being surrounded by ten
               hollow, concentric, revolving spheres with variously
               attached celestial bodies. The sphere to which the sun
               was attached was the fourth, counting outward from
               the earth. Cf. "Goodfriday, 1613," l. 1: "Let mans
               Soule be a Spheare"; "Obsequies to the Lord Haring-
               ton," l. 4: "Gods great organ, this whole Spheare."

IV.193:   St. Augustine contrasts particular grace (*gratia spe-
               cialiter*) and general grace (*gratia generaliter*) in
               bk. I, ch. 25 of his *Retractations.* He denotes by par-
               ticular grace the special Jewish dispensation in the
               Law and the Prophets, and by general grace the
               sum of the ways and means by which God effects
               man's reconciliation (*PL,* XXXII, 624).

IV.199–201: Donne's italics are too free to be correlated with any specific English version. *"O altitudo"* occurs uniquely in the Vulgate. Cf. Browne's celebrated acknowledgment in *Religio Medici,* pt. I, sect. 9: "I love to lose myself in a mystery, to pursue my Reason to an *O altitudo!"*

IV.208–210: "The Margin" is that of the AV; Donne's italics reproduce its gloss exactly. The word rendered in the text as "Commit" derives from the Hebrew primary root *gālal* which, as Donne says, has the literal meaning of "to roll" and figurative meanings including "to commit" and "to trust" (See no. 1556 in Strong's *Concise Dict.,* p. 27).

IV.216–217: Tertullian, *Apologetica,* ch. 39 (*PL,* I, 532). See note to Preb II, 265–271. Donne proceeds characteristically, by way of a pun on "Canon," to dilate the military figure implicit in the (apparently misremembered) verb from Tertullian.

IV.230–238: The analogy between pearls and saints stems from traditional allegorical interpretations of Scripture on which the *Pearl* Poet drew earlier in depicting the young beatified Margaret. These are catalogued, e.g., by Rabanus Maurus: "Per *margaritas* hominis justi, ut in Apocalypsi [21.21]: 'Duodecim margaritae, duodecim portae,' quod homines sancti per fidem apostolorum aditum habent ad regnum celeste"; *"Margarita* est caeleste desiderium, ut in Evangelio [Matt. 13.46], 'Inventa una pretiosa margarita,' id est, concepto in mente desiderio caelesti" (*PL,* CXII, 996). Also, a sermon on Matt. 13.45 among the suppositious works of St. Bernard interprets the "pretiosa margarita" as "religio sancta, pura et immaculata, in qua homo vivit purius" (*PL,* CLXXXIV, 1131). Donne's treatment, however, differs from the tradition in its focus on process, the (pseudo-) organic stages of which come out of Pliny's *Natural History,* bk. IX, ch. 54: "The source and breeding-ground of pearls are shells not much differing from oyster-shells. These, we are told, when stimulated by the generative season of the year gape open as it were and are filled with dewy pregnancy, and subsequently when heavy are delivered, and the offspring of the shells are pearls. . . . If they are well fed in due season, the offspring also grows in size. . . . Indeed a healthy offspring is formed with a skin of many thicknesses" (Loeb ed., III, 235–237). Donne also uses this account at *Sermons*, II.15.3–9.

IV.241:   *Alpha* and *Omega*, the first and last letters of the Greek alphabet, are used not only proverbially to designate the beginning and end of something but also especially by the Christian Church to denote God's infinitude and eternity. (See Rev. 1.8, 21.6, and 22.13, which refer to Christ.) The Greek letters probably derived their function from the corresponding one of the Hebrew for "truth," *'emeth,* which begins with the first and ends with the last letter of the Hebrew alphabet.

IV.250–256:   Here Donne outdoes even the dazzling cosmic figures of the often quoted passage in a letter to Sir Henry Goodyer: "You know I never fettered nor imprisoned the word Religion; not . . . immuring it in a *Rome,* or a *Wittemberg,* or a *Geneva;* they are all virtuall beams of one Sun, and wheresoever they finde clay hearts, they harden them, and moulder them into dust; and they entender and mollifie waxen. They are not so contrary as the North and South Poles; and [as?] that they are connatural pieces of one circle. Religion is Christianity" (*Letters,* ed. Merrill, p. 25).

IV.254–255:   On circle imagery relating to God, see the note to ll. 44–45 of the second Prebend sermon.

IV.257–259:   Cf. *Essays,* ed. Simpson, p. 51: "Synagogue and Church is the same thing, and of the Church, *Roman* and *Reformed,* and all other distinctions of place, Discipline, or Person, but one Church, journying to one *Hierusalem.*"

IV.267:

The deficient heading for the second part of the sermon (see Introduction, pp. 60–61; cf. margins at ll. 78, 304) surely belongs here, in something like the form I have supplied. If Donne did not omit the heading himself, it might have been dropped by the typesetter for *LXXX Sermons.* There it should appear in a position which might easily be overlooked in page composition: just under the running heading at the top, at a point in the margin even with the first line of type.

IV.267–268:

Erasmus, *Adagiorum Chiliades quatuor cum sesquicenturia,* Chil. IV, cent. viii.73, includes this proverb and comments on it: "Plutarchus hunc Iovis senarium ceu proverbialem adfert, differens quod luna quoniam radios habet imbecilliores quam sol, excitare possit humores, concoquere non possit. Μέλας γὰρ αὐταῖς οὐ πεπαίνεται βότρυς. Id est, Neque enim his niger maturus efficitur botrus. Convenit in eos qui conantur quod ob defectum virium non queunt perficere. . . . In αὐταῖς subaudiendum est ἀκτῖσιν, id est radiis."

IV.293:

Allusion is to John 8.56.

IV.294–295:

I have not located this particular phrase in any of Luther's Latin works or in any sixteenth-century Latin translation of his German works. However, Donne's citation has every evidence of being genuine. The Jews' inexcusability for their disbelief in the Christian dispensation after having been uniquely favored with the Law is an almost endlessly repeated theme in Luther's writing, perhaps because it leads naturally into his central doctrine—justification not by works under the Law but by faith in Christ alone (*sola fides*). In particular, the Jews' special prerogative as God's Chosen People and their abuse of it are the subjects of Luther's vituperative *Von den Juden und ihren Lügen* (1543), which in Justus Jonas's translation (1544) under the title *De Iudaeis et eorum mendaciis,* circulated both singly and in the (abortive) sixteenth-century editions of Luther's *Opera omnia.*

IV.295:   According to John Cowell's *The Interpreter* (1607), L 1, *"Brief (breve)* . . . in our common lawe, signifieth a writ, whereby a man is summoned to answer to any action: or (more largely) any precept of the king in writing, issuing out of any court, whereby he commaundeth any thing to be done, for the furtherance of justice or good order."

IV.304:   See note to ll. 67–69 above.

IV.305–311:   The followers of Jesus are referred to as "disciples" in Acts 11.26 (the standard name in the Gospels for the twelve who had been personally chosen) and as "saints and faithful brethren in Christ" by St. Paul at Col. 1.2 (cf. 1 Cor. 1.9; Eph. 1.1). Those who hold the faith are said to have "professed" Christ (1 Tim. 6.12; Heb. 3.1, 4.14, 10.23). Cf. *Sermons,* VI.6.198–208; IX.1.282–300.

IV.311–319:   St. Bonaventure, *In lib. III Sententiarum M. Petri Lombardi,* dist. xviii, dub. 2: "Clarificatio autem nominis ipsius Christi in hoc consistit, ut communiter homines noverint, illum qui in humana natura apparebat, esse Filium Dei et redemptorem mundi. . . . Et sic clarificatio nominis Christi est manifestatio cognitionis habitae de Christo, qua cognoscitur esse *Dei Filius* et *Christus* et *Iesus;* . . . Nam *Filius Dei* nominat personam in *una* natura; *Christus* autem et *Iesus* nominant personam in *duabus* naturis; sed *Christus* nominat personam in *humana* natura relata ad divinam, quia dicitur *unctus. Iesus* autem nominat personam in *divina* natura relata ad humanam, quia *Iesus* dicitur Salvator esse" (*Opera Omnia*

[Quaracchi, 1887], III, 394). The notes to the passage indicate correlations with St. Augustine and the *Glossa Ordinaria*.

IV.325–343:   This anti-Roman foray takes as its target the Jesuits, or Society of Jesus, founded by St. Ignatius Loyola and sanctioned formally by the Pope in 1540. In England, where the Jesuits first arrived in 1580 (R. C. Bald, *John Donne: A Life,* p. 39), they were objects of fear and abhorrence for the line of reasoning implied here: their teaching that the end (upholding of papal supremacy) justified the means, from which they deduced the Pope's right to excommunicate and depose sovereigns and also condoned the assassination of recalcitrant excommunicated sovereigns. The near-success of the Gunpowder Plot in 1605 confirmed the English popular mind in its worst suspicions of the Jesuits. Donne's *Ignatuis His Conclave* (1611), ed. Timothy Healy (Oxford: Clarendon Press, 1969), and other anti-Jesuit passages in the sermons manifest the grim wit and make the "king-killers" charge found here. In the overall context of such attacks, this digression is a model of brevity and finesse—despite Mrs. Simpson's censures (*Sermons,* VII, 28).

IV.327–329:   Flavius Josephus (37–?95 A.D.) mentions a total of six men named Jesus, excluding Jesus of Nazareth, in *The Jewish Wars* and *The Jewish Antiquities*. Most were worthy priests and civil servants. The only negative reflections are upon one Jesus, son of Shaphat, leader of a band of robbers, and another Jesus, a plebian, son of Ananus, who became a public nuisance through his mad, prophetic cries and suffered a cruel accidental death in the siege of Jerusalem (*Jewish Wars,* III.ix.7; VI.v.3). In "A Second Sermon Preached at White-hall. April 19. 1618" Donne is much more accurate about the number and identity of Jesuses in Josephus (*Sermons,* I.9.376–380; cf. III.14.352–355).

IV.330–336 and mg.:   Ioannis Lorini Societatis Iesu, *In Actus Apostolorum Commentaria: . . . Recognita, correcta, restituta, locupletata* (London, 1609), p. 524 B, comments as follows on Acts 13.6: "Sed meminisse Bedam oportuit, nomen IESVS, vulgare tunc multorum fuisse, tametsi postea soli Domino nostro jure attributum. Ita ut opinio sit (certum Auctorem non legi) Barrabam latronem proprio nomine Iesum vocatum, atque idcirco Pilatum differentiae causa addidisse, *qui dicitur CHRISTVS* (Mat. 27.17)." Donne gets the gist of Lorinus but mistakes the Biblical reference, substituting Pilate's stipulation "This is Jesus of Nazareth" at John 19.19 for the one in Matthew that Lorinus quotes. P-S signal their recognition of the substitution by bracketing a marginal reference "John 19.19" at l. 333 and moving *LXXX S*'s reference to "Act. 13.6" down to replace its "Ibid." These alterations, however, ignore the source passage in Lorinus, with which the margin of *LXXX S* makes good sense. I restore its readings. (Cf. Donne's explicit citation of Lorinus's *Commentary on Acts* at *Sermons*, VI.6.219–220.)

IV.338–340:   Juan de Mariana (1536–1624), a Spanish Jesuit, historian, and political theorist, gained widespread notoriety because of his view of tyrannicide in *De rege et regis institutione* (1599), which amounted to a qualified condoning of the act. Mariana decried purely political assassination but admitted a desperate remedy as a last resort, when a state flagrantly violated the public welfare. The qualifications were lost in the universal odium attached to his name and to the Jesuit order, especially after the assassination of Henry IV of France (1610).

IV.345–349:   There are apparent reminiscences here of St. Bernard's sublime *Sermo XV in Cantica,* e.g., "O nomen benedictum! O oleum usquequaque effusum! . . . Particeps nominis sum, sum et haereditatis, Christianus sum; frater Christi sum. . . . Effuso est plenitudo divinitatis, habitans super terram corporaliter, ut de ille plenitudine omnes . . . diceremus: Oleum effusum nomen tuum" (*PL,* CLXXXIII, 845–846). But, equally, reflections on the virtues of the names Jesus and Christ are frequent in patristic literature. See St. Ambrose (*PL,* XVI, 757) and St. Jerome (*PL,* XXVI, 263).

IV.349:   Allusion is to Phil. 4.12,13.

IV.350–352:   Cornelius à Lapide, *Commentarium in Epist. ad Ephesios* (1614), cap. i: "Nimirum ita satiari nomine Christi non poterat Paulus, ut eum, ut ita dicam, superflue, et singulis saepe versibus nominaret. Hinc nomen *Jesu* in parvis et paucis hisce quatuordecim epistolis suis repetit ducenties decies novies, *Christi* nomen quadringenties et semel" (*Comm. in Scripturam Sacram,* IX, 499).

IV.355–360:   Donne apparently has in mind a world map on the order of Gerardus Mercator's celebrated projection, *Nova et aucta orbis terrae descriptio* (1569). At the easternmost edge of Mercator's map, at 180° longitude as charted in this projection, lie the Moluccas, an island group of the Malay archipelago. Ormus (modern Hormuz)—the strait between the Persian Gulf and the Gulf of Oman, and the island in the strait—is located in this projection at almost precisely 90° longitude, hence, at "the first Quadrant" whether the phrase is taken to refer to one-quarter of the sun's journey around the earth or to the notation of position used in the map. Again, in Mercator's projection zero degrees longitude (in Donne's words, "the first Meridian," and in modern terminology "the prime meridian") intersects the westernmost of the Canary Islands. This is the halfway point of the "natural" (24-hour) day, as opposed to the "artificial" day (sunrise to sunset), when the natural day is correlated with the distribution of land masses on the Mercator map. But Donne also brings in the conception of the artificial day in the suggestion that the sun *ante meridiem* rises over the Eastern hemisphere and sets *post meridiem* over the Western hemisphere. Although this suggestion makes no sense in terms of actual empirical observation, it can be seen as a natural outgrowth of the intuitive notion of a cycle as having a rise-and-fall or upswing-downswing movement. This suggestion is made in Donne's use of "Declination" here in the now-obsolete sense (*OED*, 4) of "a sinking into a lower position, a descent toward setting" rather than in its more usual geomagnetic or astronomical senses, neither of which fit. Cf. the essentially similar passage at the beginning of a sermon probably delivered two weeks after the fourth Prebend sermon (*Sermons*, VII.14.8–14); the memorable metaphorical reflection on post-meridial light in "A Lecture upon the Shadow," ll. 25–26; and the play on the concepts of natural and artificial day in "To the Countess of Bedford" ("You have refin'd mee"), ll. 19–24, which Helen Gardner elucidates in "Notes on Donne's Verse Letters," *Modern Language Review*, XLI (1946), 319. See also Schleiner, *The Imagery of Donne's Sermons*, pp. 90–93, on the rhetorical effect of Donne's use of geographical names.

IV.366–367 and mg.:   Psalm 19.5 (Vulg): In sole posuit tabernaculum suum"; (Muns, Pagn): "soli posuit tabernaculum in eis" (i.e., the heavens). I restore *LXXX S*'s marginal reference, which P-S (strangely, because Latin is being cited) adjust to "Psal. 19.4," the notation of the AV. William Whitaker's *A Disputation on Holy Scripture, against the Papists, especially Bellarmine and Stapleton*, Parker Soc. XLVI (1849), 469, provides a contemporary Anglican sidelight on this text. He attacks the inaccurate Vulgate reading—which St. Jerome himself emended in his third and final translation of the Psalms, the so-called *Hebrew Psalter*—and Bellarmine's use of the Vulgate reading in *De Ecclesia*, lib. III, cap. 12, to prove the visibility of the Church. Another fault of Bellarmine's is the use of a figure of speech to establish doctrine. Cf. Donne's legitimate spiritual extension of the figure to the Christian Church.

IV.383:

sensible: perceptible by the senses (*OED*, I 1; now rare).

IV.399–401:

Rom. 10.20 (AV): "But Esaias is very bold, and saith, I was found of them that sought me not: I was made manifest unto them, that asked not after me."

IV.402:

On preventing grace, see note to ll. 111–115 of the third Prebend sermon.

IV.403–405:

This stylistic peculiarity occurs especially in the book of Job (e.g., 38.1, 40.1,6). Cf. Jer. 23.35,37.

IV.409–414:

P-S's emendation of *LXXX S*'s "houses" in l. 411 to "houres" clarifies Donne's reference to the ancient Christian custom of observing set times of the day for prayer. In the Roman Church these came to be called "canonical hours" because the recitation of the seven separate daily services contained in the Breviary was required of all clerics on whom the Divine Office was imposed. No particular provision was made for the lay Christian's use of the fixed devotional routine in the Breviary. When the *BCP* came into being, it combined and condensed the seven services for the canonical hours into the Orders for Morning and Evening Prayer, also leaving private prayer unregulated. Although there is naturally great insistence on the necessity of public prayer in the Church among Anglo-Catholics (see, e.g., "An Homily of the Place and Time of Prayer" in the *Second Tome of Homilies,* and Preb II, 220–279), there is additional strong stress by High Churchmen on setting aside several stipulated times each day for personal devotion. See *Sermons,* VII.10.435, where Donne exhorts that "stationary times of the day, and night too" be maintained for prayer, and IX.14.412–417, where he rejects the Roman system of canonical hours but defends set devotions. The strongest recommendation is John Cosin's (quoted in *Anglicanism,* ed. P. E. More and F. L. Cross [Milwaukee, Wis.: Morehouse Publishing Co., 1935], p. 629): "As we are common Christians we should go to our prayers three times a day: *At evening, and morning, and at noon-day will I praise Thee* (Ps. 55.17). But as we are specially separated from other Christians to be priests and prophets, we should go to them seven times a day, *Seven times a day do I praise thee* (Ps. 119.164)." To implement this (Scripturally prescribed) program Cosin compiled and published *A Collection of Private Devotions* (1627), which P. G. Stanwood solidly places in its religious, political, and general historical context; see the Introduction to his edition (Oxford: Clarendon Press, 1967).

IV.415–417:

The closest approximation to the italicized Latin which I have found is a passage in St. John of Damascus's (Damascene's) first *Apologetical Oration against Those Who Throw Down Sacred Images;* I translate from *PG,* XCIV, 1256–1257: "At any rate, until you pervert their uses, people detest not the reverencing of our icons but the uses of the idolatrous Greeks. Therefore it is not necessary on account of the absurd use of the Greeks to abolish ours, which has developed in a holy way." However, neither of the two sixteenth-century Latin translations (Godefridus Tilmannus's and Petrus Franciscus Zinus's) which I have checked corresponds to Donne's wording. His knowledge of the work is revealed in his reference to "Damascen" and "that great Sermon of his, *De Imaginibus*" in *Sermons,* VIII.5.711–12.

IV.417–425:

I have not located a general Roman or specifically patristic source for this narration.

IV.421: emergent: unexpectedly arising, not specially provided for; *OED*, 5, rare. Cf. Donne's title, *Devotions
upon Emergent Occasions.*

IV.425,426: A "Collect" or gathering together of the various concerns of worshipers in a single prayer is, strictly
speaking, the prayer preceding the Epistle in the Eu-
charistic Office and, more generally, a short prayer
containing an invocation, petition, and ascription of
glory, which can occur at any point in a liturgical
sequence. The Collects in the *BCP* are mostly translated from earlier service books like the Sarum Use,
but several admirable ones were composed by Cranmer. A few more were added in the seventeenth century, including the Collect on the Gunpowder Plot,
one "emergent occasion" which Donne mentions at
ll. 504–505, as part of The Form of Prayer for the
Fifth of November which was drawn up by James
I's bishops and issued on his authority in 1606. On
the history of this and the other so-called "state-
services," see *The Annotated Book of Common
Prayer,* ed. J. H. Blunt (London, 1884), pp. 703–
705.

IV.437–453: Here application is made of the Augustinian principle of the harmony of the two Testaments as Donne
in a characteristic manner projects an imagined dia-
logue, with Scripture as script. The device is discussed by Joan Webber in *Contrary Music,* pp. 99–
100.

IV.437–438 and mg.: As P-S note in a bracketed reference, Donne's italics
exactly reproduce the AV wording in Jer. 8.22.

IV.438–439: Isa. 53.5 (Genv, AV): "But he was wounded for
our transgressions, . . . and with his stripes we are
healed."

IV.441 mg.: I adopt P-S's emendation of *LXXX S*'s imprecise
citation, "1 Sam. 13.18."

IV.448–451:

The second Collect at Evening Prayer in the *BCP* begins "O God, from whom all holy desires, all good counsels, and all just works do proceed"; this Collect is followed by the third, For Aid against All Perils, which opens: "Lighten our darkness, we beseech thee, O Lord." As Donne explains elsewhere, "Christ himselfe is called *The Angel of the great Councell,* according to the *Septuagint* [mg.: Esay 9.6]" (*Sermons,* III.5.249–250; cf. IV.1.56; IV.6.473; IX.3.578). But the phrase occurs in patristic literature also as a name of Jesus. See, e.g., St. Hilary's *De Trinitate,* lib. IV, cap. 26 (*PL,* X, 116); Tertullian's *Liber de Carne Christi,* cap. xiv (*PL,* II, 823); St. Phoebadius's *De Filii Divinitate et Consubstantialitate Tractatus,* cap. viii (*PL,* XX, 46). These Fathers, moreover, identify Christ with the visitant angels of Gen. 21.17,18, and 28.13. Cf. *Sermons,* VIII.8.967.

IV.459–466:

Note Donne's exceptionally exact marginal citation of St. Augustine, *Liber Confessionum,* I.1: "Invocat te, Domine, fides mea, quam dedisti mihi, quam inspirasti mihi per humanitatem filii tui, per ministerium praedicatoris tui" (*PL,* XXXII, 661).

IV.470–475:

Donne's Latin is closest to Munster's and Pagnini's shared reading *"Terribilia in iustitia";* the Vulgate, by contrast, reads *"Mirabile in aequitate."* St. Augustine's influential *Enarrationes in Psalmos* provides a purely individual interpretation of this difficult phrase, referring it to the marvels of the soul's growth in goodness (*PL,* XXXVI, 779–780); Hall's "A Paraphrase upon the Hard Texts of the Whole Divine Scripture" (*Works,* III, 199) does, however, give a construction similar to Donne's: "O God, thou, in thine infinite justice, wilt answer the prayers and supplications of thy Church, in marvellous deliverances, and in fearful plagues upon thine enemies."

IV.482–483:

1 Peter 4.19 (Vulg, Vatab): "qui fideli Creatori commendent animas suas"; (Trem): "tamquam cre-

atori fidele"; (Genv, AV): "Wherefore let them that suffer according to the will of God, commit their soules (AV: the keeping of their soules) to him . . . , as unto a faithfull Creator."

IV.484–485:   Donne deviates fundamentally from both Latin and English versions. I Thess. 5.24 (Vulg, Beza, Trem, Vatab): "Fidelis est, qui vocavit vos"; (AV): "Faithful is hee that calleth you."

IV.486–487:   Heb. 2.17 (AV): "a mercifull and faithfull high Priest."

IV.489 and mg.:   Because the italicized English words are not from an English version but rather Donne's literal translation of the Vulgate phrase preceding, I restore *LXXX S*'s marginal reference (which P-S unaccountably emend to accord with the AV).

IV.501–505:   Allusion is, successively, to Gen. 11.9 (the destruction of Babel); Exod. 7–11 (the plagues of Egypt); Judges 1.1–17 (the depopulation of Canaan); 2 Kings 19.35 and 2 Chron. 32.21 (the massacre in Sennacherib's army); the defeat of the Spanish Armada by the English navy in 1588; and the discovery of the Gunpowder Plot in 1605. Linking of the Armada and Gunpowder Plot deliverances is a standard piece of evidence in Donne for the providential view of history. Cf. Preb V, 464–469 and *Sermons,* II.11.100; III.4.368; IV.3.213. See also Andrewes' long series of Gunpowder Plot sermons, especially the one for 1607 in which the deliverance is compared with the ending of the Babylonian Captivity (*Ninety-six Sermons* [1853], IV, 237–242).

IV.513:   convenient: suitable, appropriate to the purpose; *OED,* 4, now obsolete.

IV.513–515:   *Tsadok,* or *tsĕdĕq* in modern transliteration, is a noun from a Hebrew root with the basic meaning of "to be right in itself, to be right as is, to cause to be right." (See no. 6663 in Strong's *Concise Dict.,* p. 99.) As Mrs. Simpson points out (Appendix, *Sermons,* X, 338), Donne is somewhat misleading, since the masculine adjectival form actually occurring in his text is *tsâdeq,* which he would perhaps have written *Tsadik.* (See Strong's no. 6664.) Donne's comment focuses on the (admittedly correct) primary root. An interesting discussion of the developments in Jewish ethical concepts which relate to the word *tsâdeq* is found in Norman Snaith's *The Distinctive Ideas of the Old Testament* (London: Epworth Press, 1944), pp. 68–74.

IV.515–518: Psalm 65.6 (Tr-J): "Res reverendas in justitia proloqueris nobis, ô Deus salutis nostrae; fiducia omnium extremitatum terrae & maris longinquorum." "Res reverendas" has the note: "Id est, augustissimas promissiones in futurum, comprehensas verbo tuo."

IV.522–525: Religious ceremonial (by which "'a difference, between Religious, and Civill Actions" is overtly made) was a vexed issue in Anglicanism because of the violent anti-Romanism of the Puritan faction. The conservative position, which was Donne's, is well exemplified by Andrewes' admonitions: "Look to the text then, and let no man persuade you but that God requireth a reverent carriage, even of the body itself. . . . For believe this, as it may be superstitiously used, so it may irreligiously be neglected also" (*Ninety-six Sermons,* II, 337). Cf. the collected opinions on "Ceremonies" in *Anglicanism,* ed. More and Cross, pp. 541–546. Other insistence on reverence is made by Donne at ll. 608–609 and in Preb V, 474–551.

IV.524: Allusion is to Phil. 2.12 (Gr B, Bish, AV): "Worke out your owne salvation with feare, and trembling."

IV.529: reservation: in ecclesiastical usage, the action or practice of preserving a thing for some particular purpose. Appropriation, which also has a specialized ecclesiastical sense, is reservation for disposal by a particular person or persons.

IV.532–533:　　　The explicit patristic source (and hence a likely one for Donne) on the cultic excesses of the priests of Isis is Lactantius, *De falsa religione,* bk. I, ch. xxi: "Isidis Ægyptia sacra sunt, quatenus filium parvulum vel perdiderit, vel invenerit. Nam primo sacerdotes ejus, deglabrato corpore, pectora sua tundunt; lamentantur, sicut ipsa, cum perdidit, fecerat" (*PL,* VI, 235). (Lactantius seems to mistake the object of Isis's grief as memorialized in the ritual: it was her brother-husband, Osiris, and not her son, Horus. See E. A. Wallis Budge, *Osiris and the Egyptian Resurrection* [New York: G. P. Putnam's Sons, 1911], II, 293–296.) The desperate self-wounding of the priests of Baal is referred to in 1 Kings 18.28.

IV.534–537:　　　Prescriptions for various blood sacrifices occur in Lev. 1–9, 16, 22–23.

IV.538–539:　　　No form of "in-intelliblenesse" is found in Tertullian, whose "adventurous Latin" (as Donne characterized it elsewhere) does embrace *"ininventibilia," "ininvestigabiles,"* and *"ininterpretabili"* (*PL,* I, 238, 286, 564). However, *"inintelligibile"* or *"inintelligibilia"* occurs three times in St. Hilary (*PL,* X, 76, 79–80, 81) and once in St. Ambrose (*PL,* XVI, 44).

IV.540–541:　　　Allusion is, successively, to Exod. 3.8 and Psalm 23.5.

IV.549–577 and mg.: Donne's exceptionally exact marginal reference is to the Dutch Jesuit Maximilianus Sandaeus's *Symbolica ex omni antiquitate sacra, ac profana, in artis formam redacta, oratoribus, poetis et universe philologis ad omnem commoditatem amoenae eruditionis concinnata,* of which I have located a quarto edition of 1626 in the Bibliothèque Nationale, Paris. It is not wholly clear who are being designated as the *Mosse-*

lim, for the implication here is of an order dating
from Biblical times. Yet definite identification of a
group of rabbis with frequent pedagogical use of the
mâshâl (maxim of a metaphorical nature, hence,
parable or proverb) traces only to post-Biblical times,
specifically, to the Palestinian (as distinct from the
Babylonian) teachers whose precepts are contained
in the Talmud and Midrash. See *The Universal Jewish Encyclopedia* (New York: Universal Jewish Encyclopedia, Inc., 1942), VII, 394–395. Donne does,
however, correctly note (when *LXXX S*'s erroneous
marginal references are adjusted, as below) that
Num. 21.27, Psalm 49.4, and Psalm 78.2 all contain
occurrences of *mâshâl,* the root meanings of which
are (1) "to have authority, to rule," and (2) "to
compare." (One form is *Mish^ele,* the Hebrew title
for the Book of Proverbs.) There is a philological
dispute regarding the relation (and priority) of these
disparate meanings; the dominant line of thought
now is that the association of authoritativeness arose
out of the impressive effect of a similitude. But in
Biblical occurrences of the masculine plural *Mosselim,* or *moshâlîm* in modern transliteration, the
meaning is either "rulers" or "coiners of parables."
(See nos. 4910, 4912 in Strong's *Concise Dict.,* p.
74.) Although Donne's *"Potestates"* (l. 574) is an
acceptable rendering of the force of the Hebrew
mâshâl, and *"Axiomata"* (l. 576) can betoken
"things of dignity" as well as "maxims, principles"
in Greek, the imputation regarding Matt. 13.34 is
misleading. The Greek word used there is παραβολαῖ,
from which English "parables" comes. The interesting association in Hebrew of intellectual authority
with a powerful use of figurative language seems to
recur as an historical phenomenon in the seventeenth-
century technique of "strong-lined" preaching, which
is analyzed by George Williamson in "Strong Lines"
(1936), reprinted in *Seventeenth-Century Contexts*
(Chicago: University of Chicago Press, 1961), pp.
120–131.

IV.559,562,565 mg.:   I adopt P-S's emendations of, respectively, "Num. 21.7," "Psal. 77.2," and "Matt. 7.19," the erroneous references in *LXXX S*.

IV.562–563:   Psalm 49.4 (AV): "I will open my darke saying upon the harpe."

IV.597–598:   Cf. "Satire III," ll. 87–88: "mysteries/ Are like the Sunne, dazling, yet plaine to all eyes."

IV.600–601:   Allusion is to Psalm 5.7; cf. Heb. 12.28.

IV.603–605 and mg.:   I follow P-S's emendation of *LXXX S*'s reference to "Psal. 34.12," because *"Artem timendi"* does not occur in any Latin version at this place. Typical readings include (Vulg, Muns, Pagn): "timorem Domini"; (T-J): "reverentiam Jehovae." The Latin phrase must be Donne's coinage. Psalm 34.11 (Gr B, Bish, AV): "Come, yee children, hearken unto (and hearken unto: Gr B, Bish) me: I will teach you the feare of the Lord."

IV.608–609:   over-fellowly, over-homely: obsolete synonyms for "overfamiliarly." Cf. *Sermons,* VIII.5.311–313.

IV.613 mg.:   I follow P-S's emendation of *LXXX S*'s reference to "Iohn 15.14."

IV.618:   Mark 16.16 (Vulg, Beza, Eras, Vatab): "qui . . . non crediderit, condemnabitur." Donne repeatedly cited this text with his own substitution of *"damnabitur"* (*Sermons,* IV.7.550; V.13.358; VII.16.175; VIII.1.-200; VIII.15.651).

IV.621–624:   The source of this traditional conception is St. Paul's habitual reference to the Church as the body of Christ (Rom. 12.5; 1 Cor.10.16–17, 12.12; Eph. 1.22–23, 4.12; Col. 1.18, 2.19). On excommunication, see note to ll. 284–304 of the second Prebend sermon.

IV.624–628:   Cf. *Sermons,* III.14.673–678. Donne reveals accurate historical knowledge. Under the ancient Christian system of public penance (a term deriving from *poena,* punishment), a sinner would voluntarily or under threat of excommunication petition his bishop for admission to the special order of penitents. The order was assigned a distinctive garb and place at worship, was not allowed to receive Communion, and was subjected to an arduous course of prayer, almsgiving, and fasting. (Cf. Andrewes' commendation of these traditional means in *Ninety-six Sermons* I, 356–374.) How long one remained in the order of penitents depended on the gravity of the sin, and, although the penitent was eventually granted full restoration, severe rules remained in force— including, in the earliest known system, lifelong bodily continence. Because permission to undergo penance was granted only once in a lifetime, petitions for it in the early Church were frequently postponed until the approach of death. See also Donne's tracing of the link between penance and indulgences (*Sermons,* VII.6.818–825). For a full collection of texts and analytical commentary, see O. D. Watkins' *A History of Penance: Being a Study of the Authorities (A) For the whole Church to A.D. 450, (B) For the Western Church from A.D. 450 to A.D. 1215,* 2 vols. (London and New York: Longmans, Green, and Co., 1920).

IV.630:   "that great doctrine of Predestination": This basic and perennially vexed theological point has to do with the existence of a divine decree by which certain persons will infallibly receive salvation. The decree is suggested but not explicitly affirmed in OT references to the "Book of Life" (e.g., Psalm 69.29; Exod. 32.32; Dan. 12.1). In both the NT Gospels and Epistles, however, predestination is affirmed (e.g., Matt. 20.23; John 10.29; Rom. 8.28–30; Eph. 1.3–14; cf. 2 Tim. 1.9; 1 Cor. 4.7). In the Western Church St. Augustine was the first great proponent of predestination. He taught, mainly in the anti-Pelagian tracts, that predestination is a perfect expression of God's justice and foreknowledge, which appears incomprehensible only because of limited human understanding. In the Eastern Church St. John Damascene sought to reconcile predestination with Origen's stress on the universal saving will of God by predicating an "antecedent" divine intent that all men be saved, which is modified in consequence of the sins of some, who are then consigned to eternal punishment. Medieval Scholastics—Peter Lombard, St. Bonaventure, St. Thomas Aquinas—undertook to synthesize the Western and Eastern views into a single doctrine of God's absolute goodness and omnipotence. Predestination became a fundamental concern of the Reformers, especially Calvin, who rejected the universal saving intent of God and maintained equally strongly the gratuitous predestination of the elect and the gratuitous (and certain) reprobation of the damned, who are denied salvation by an initial divine determination and not any personal fault. Opposition to the Calvinistic position was officially countermanded by the Synod of Dort (1618–19) and by the Confession of the Westminster Assembly (1646), the latter of which declared that the Fall of man caused a limitation to the elect of (previously intended) salvation for all. Donne's own views on predestination have been the occasion of misunderstanding by Itrat Husain (*The Dogmatic and Mystical Theology of John Donne* [London: Society for Promoting Christian Knowledge, 1938], pp. 104–111) and William R. Mueller (*John Donne, Preacher* [Princeton, N.J.: Princeton University Press, 1962], pp. 186–189), who confused predestination with reprobation and asserted that Donne rejected both. As E. Randolph Daniel, "Reconciliation, Covenant and Election: A Study in the Theology of John Donne," *Anglican Theological Review,* XLVIII (1966), 17, points out, Donne's actual position was defense of the positive aspects (election) and rejection of the negative aspects (reprobation), which is precisely that of the seventeenth of the Thirty-nine Articles, "Of Predestination and Election."

IV.643:

Allusion is to Isa. 56.7. Jesus is recorded as citing this text in Matt. 21.13; Mark 11.17; Luke 19.46.

IV.644–674:

A different sidelight is found in the "Report of Attorney General Noy and Dr. Rives as to the Profanation of S. Paul's Cathedral. 1631," in *Documents Illustrating the History of S. Paul's Cathedral,* ed. W. Sparrow Simpson, Camden Soc. n.s. XXVI (1880), 131–132, where "the neglect and suffrance of the Deane and Chapter in tymes past" is blamed for the "inordinate noyse" of playing children, and the "walkinge" and "talkinge" of persons of quality during divine service in the church. But the complaints were not limited to conduct at St. Paul's. Cf. *Constitutions and Canons Ecclesiasticall, Treated upon by the Bishop of London, . . . and the rest of the Bishops and clergie . . . And agreed upon with the Kings Maiesties Licence. . . . Anno Dom. 1603* (London, 1612), D 1ᵛ, which prescribes that "Reverence and attention" are "to be used within the Church in time of Divine Service" and specifically that no men are to cover their heads except in cases of infirmity, that there is to be no disturbance by walking and talking, and that there is to be reverence done at the name of Jesus, kneeling at the prayers, and standing at the Creed, according to the Prayer Book rubrics. See also Andrewes' sermon at Whitehall on Easter 1621: "I know not how, our carriage, a many of us, is so loose; covered we sit, sitting we pray; standing, or walking, or as it takes us in the head, we receive; as if Christ were so gentle a person, we might touch Him, do to Him what we list, He would take all well" (*Ninety-six Sermons,* III, 33). R. C. Bald gives other references in his discussion of public behavior in the Cathedral while Donne was Dean (*John Donne: A Life,* pp. 402–405).

IV.649–650,653: Usury: in older English law, interest on money; increase for the loan of money; the taking of any compensation whatever for the use of money (*Black's Law Dict.*, p. 1714). John Cowell, *The Interpreter* (1607), L 1ᵛ, remarks that *"Broker (brocarius)* seemeth to come from the French (*broieur. i. tritor*) that is a gryneder or breaker into small peeces. Because he that is of that trade, to deall in maters of mony and marchandise betwene Englishe men and strangers, doth draw the bargaine to particulars, and the parties to conclusion, not forgetting to grinde out something to his owne profit" and, at Hhh 4ᵛ, that *"Receyver (Receptor, or Receptator)* generally and indefinitely used, is as with the Civilians, so also with us, used commonly in the evill part, for such as receive stollen goods from theeves, and conceale them."

IV.654–655: As all Latin versions read, the *Sanctum Sanctorum* (Holy of Holies, or, in the AV rendering, "the most holy place") was the innermost recess of the Jewish Tabernacle and later of the Temple, where the Ark of God (Ark of the Covenant) was kept. This place was entered only once yearly by the high priest, on the Feast of Atonement. See Exod. 26–30; Lev. 16; 2 Chron. 3,4,35; Heb. 9.1–10. *Sanctuarium* (holy place) was the medieval term for the consecrated building and grounds of a church where, by canon law, a fugitive from justice or a debtor was immune from arrest and punishment; hence, by extension, the right of such immunity also became known as "sanctuary."

IV.659 and mg.: P-S bracket a reference to Mal. 1.8, which reads (Gr B): "Offre it unto thy prince"; (Bish, Genv): "offer it now unto (to: Bish) thy prince"; (AV): "offer it now unto thy governour."

IV.661–662 and mg.: Because the Latin phrase is in first position, I restore the citation of *LXXX S*, which P-S emend to correspond to the AV. Psalm 47.2 (AV): "the LORD most high is terrible; he is a great King over all the earth."

IV.662–663:   The italicized English words appear to be Donne's literal translation of the Vulgate, for they do not correspond with any version at Psalm 96.4. The AV reads, for example, "the LORD is great . . . hee is to be feared above all Gods."

IV.668–669:   Here the italicized Latin words correspond to no version at Deut. 28.58. They read (Vulg, Muns): "nomen . . . gloriosum et terribile"; (Pagn): "gloriosum & terribilem"; (Vatab): "gloriosum & tremendum"; (Tr-J): "gloriosissimum & summe reverendum." All English versions read: "this glorious and fearefull Name, (of: Gr B) THE LORD THY GOD."

IV.673 mg.:   I adopt P-S's emendation of *LXXX S*'s erroneous "Psal. 111.4."

IV.677–678:   Hos. 7.14 (Genv): "they have not cryed unto me with their hearts, when they howled upon their beds."

IV.683:   James 4.3 (all versions): "Ye aske, and receive not, because ye aske amisse."

IV.685–686:   James 1.7 (AV): "For let not that man ("he that wavereth"—verse 6) thinke that he shall receive any thing of the LORD."

IV.687:   1 Thess. 5.17 (Gr B, Bish, Genv): "Pray continually"; (AV): "Pray without ceasing."

IV.690–692:   Isa. 1.15 (AV): "When ye spread foorth your handes, I will hide mine eyes . . . : yea, when yee make many prayers I will not heare."

IV.692–693:   Prov. 28.9 (AV): "his prayer shalbe abomination."

IV.694–695:   Psalm 109.6 (Gr B, Bish, Genv): "Let his praier be turned into sinne." Psalm 109.7 (AV): "let his prayer become sinne."

IV.696–697:   Donne's italics are too free to correlate with any English version at Ezek. 14.14.

IV.699–700:   Allusion is to Jer. 7.16, 11.14, 14.11.

IV.712:   wagers: The *OED* gives one meaning of the noun as "a contest for a prize" (1615).

IV.715–716:   Donne misquotes the unique Vulgate reading at Lam. 4.16: "facies sacerdotum non erubuerunt"; (AV): "they respected not the persons of the priests."

IV.724–726:   Absolution is the formal act by a bishop or priest of pronouncing Christ's forgiveness of sins to those who have confessed their offense and declared themselves penitent. At the Reformation the traditional doctrine that the forgiveness of Christ is administered on earth through an ordained priesthood was first contested. Hooker clarifies Anglican objections to Roman claims about the sacramental nature of absolution and the pre-eminence of priestly power over the sinner's penitence, affirming that the minister's power is only declaratory and that the efficacy of absolution depends on a genuine change of heart in the sinner (*EP*, VI.vi.1–9). In the services of the Church of England, declaratory absolution, the statement by the priest that God does forgive the penitent, follows after general confession by the congregation in the Orders for Morning and Evening Prayer. Donne argues here that even those who attribute least to priestly absolution (the more Puritanically minded) will allow that its declaratory function is subsumed in the declaratory function of preaching, which he then proceeds to praise in a characteristic fashion.

IV.727–728:   Allusion is, successively, to Matt. 18.18 and 16.19.

IV.730–732:   Matt. 7.6 (AV): "Give not that which is holy unto
                     the dogs, neither cast ye your pearles before swine:
                     lest they trample them under their feete, and turne
                     againe and rent you."

IV.744–745:   The closest approximation which I have found
                     occurs in the section entitled *"De Adoratione Sacra-
                     menti"* in the *Libellus Doc. Martini Lutheri, de
                     Sacramento Eucharistiae, ad Valdenses fratres, è ger-
                     manico translatus per I. Ionam* (Wittenberg, 1526),
                     C^r–C ii^v. (The original tract, *Vom Anbeten des Sac-
                     raments des heiligen Leichnams Jesu Christi* [1523],
                     is noteworthy for Luther's use throughout of the
                     term "the Sacrament of the Body and Blood"—
                     which Donne also uses here—instead of Luther's
                     much more usual later term, "the Sacrament of the
                     Altar.") In the section cited, Luther makes a pre-
                     liminary distinction between *"orare"* or *"opus oris"*
                     and *"adorare"* or *"opus . . . totius corporis,"* but he
                     proceeds to argue that the more crucial difference be-
                     tween perfunctory and heartfelt adoration (or wor-
                     ship) cannot be gauged by outward appearances. It
                     is certain that the worshiper who truly believes the
                     Body and Blood of Christ to be present will draw
                     near to communicate *"reverenter & religiosè."* Yet
                     he must be left free to perform or withhold outward
                     acts of adoration, as he wills, in order to assure the
                     genuineness of the *"reverentia & honor divinus"*
                     which Luther terms the only due response to Christ's
                     Presence in the Sacrament. Donne's unequivocal en-
                     dorsement of adoration gives the misleading impres-
                     sion that Luther prescribes it, ignoring his qualifica-
                     tions.

IV.747–748:   Allusion (perhaps intentionally cryptic) is to a suc-
                     cession of several passages in the Third Part of the
                     Summa Theologica: Aquinas's definition of *forma
                     sacramenti* as the words of consecration which ac-

company the exterior sign or material elements of a sacrament and give them their meaning (q. 72, art. 4); his determination of the meaning of the words of consecration to be *substantia formae sacramentalis,* the essence of the sacramental form (q. 60, art. 7); and, most germanely, the Thomistic account of Transubstantiation as conversion of the pre-existing substance of the bread and wine into the substance of Christ's body through the form of the sacrament, that is, the words "This is my body and blood" (q. 76, arts. 1,2; q. 78, art. 1).

IV.748–750: St. Bernard, *Epistola ad Fratres de Monte Dei,* I.x: "Sacramentum enim sine re Sacramenti sumenti mors est" (*PL,* CLXXXIV, 327).

IV.752–755: The incident to which Donne refers is narrated in Didacus Alvarez's *De auxiliis divinae gratiae et humani arbitrii viribus et libertate* . . . (London, 1621), fol. A 2ᵛ, near the end of the dedicatory letter to King Philip III of Spain: "Si quis enim originem, causamque tantae felicitatis quaerat, non aliunde Gentis Austriacae Imperium gloriosum, quam a Sanctissimo Eucharistiae Sacramento, hoc est, ab omnium gratiarum fonte profectum esse fatebitur. Notissimum est eximium illud, & numquam satis laudatum pietatis, & religionis exemplum, quod Rudolphus Comes Aspurg. Regibus, & Principibus praebuit Christianis. Cum enim die quadam intenderet venationi, & obvium haberet in itinere Sacerdotum pauperem, Viaticum infirmo in villa existenti deportantem, ut audivit sacratissimum Domini nostri IESU CHRISTI corpus adesse, relicta venatione, quam insequebatur, accessit ex equo celeriter descendit, ac genibus super nudam, & coelesti pluvia madidam terram flexis, Sacrosanctum devotissime pluvia defendebatur, exuit, & super humeros Sacerdotis sanctum Christi Domini corpus deportantis, reverenter imposuit, ne a pluvia aliquid detrimenti sacra EUCHARISTIA in itinere pateretur. Mira res: Non post longum tempus idem

RUDOLPHUS, qui, ut debita reverentia sanctam adoraret Hostiam praetereuntem, descenderat." Presumably the vividly visualizable details impressed themselves in Donne's memory. I am indebted to my colleague Alan H. Nelson for transcribing this passage for me from the British Museum copy.

IV.756–762:

A close approximation of Donne's italicized phrase is found in a passage in the first of St. John Damascene's two (suppositious) *Epistolae ad Zachariam, de corpore & sanguine Christi,* tr. Frontus Ducaeus (1603) and printed in *Opera omnia quae exstant . . . ,* ed. M. Lequien (Paris, 1712), I, 656: "Post summationem autem iam incorruptibile est, ad consistentiam & in substantiam animae nostrae transiens: incorruptibile, inquam . . . ut nos ab omni corruptela vindicet. Ita sentimus, ita quoque credimus." This passage concludes a running parallel between the mysteries of the Incarnation and the Eucharist developed in the letter. Damascene elaborates correspondences between events in the life of Christ—Nativity, Transfiguration, Crucifixion, Resurrection, and Ascension—and the ritual of the Mass, declaring that questions *de modo* are in both cases impertinent. What the reverent receiver at the altar must do is the same as what the reverent hearer of the Gospel must do—believe and acknowledge that Christ is among, and indeed in, man. Exactly the same line of thought is found in bk. IV, ch. 14 of Damascene's much better known and undoubtedly genuine *De Fide Orthodoxa* (*PG*, XCIV, 1144–1145), but I have found no Latin translation which approaches the wording given by Donne.

IV.767:

Allusion is to St. John the Baptist's reference, in John 1.29, 36, to Christ as the Lamb of God (a reference itself derived from Isa. 53.7). The *Agnus Dei,* a formula invocation beginning "O Lamb of God," is recited thrice by the celebrant priest just prior to the Communion in the Roman Mass. Perhaps

Donne's associations here reflect the religious experience of his childhood.

IV.768–772: In view of Donne's usual accuracy elsewhere in citing Latin Fathers and in view of the unremitting severity toward the "lapsed" (those who, under the threat of Roman imperial prosecution, performed the idolatrous acts required by the state religion) and other profaners of the sacraments of the Church for which St. Cyprian is well known, this is an incomprehensible reference. The nearest idea is contained in the anonymous *Liber de Rebaptismate,* which in two manuscript copies is attributed to St. Cyprian and was printed with his works from the seventeenth century onward. The treatise is now believed to have been written by an adversary at the height of the rebaptism controversy (254–255 A.D.) in which St. Cyprian actively participated (W. Hartel, ed., *S. . . . Cypriani Opera Omnia* [Vienna, 1871], III.iii.52; E. W. Benson, *Cyprian: His Life, His Times, His Work* [London and New York, 1897], pp. 390–392). The author of *De Rebaptismate* asks on what grounds the Church purports to distinguish valid baptism by ill-living, ignorant, or misguided bishops within its ranks from so-called illicit baptism by heretics, which yet is performed with water in the name of the Trinity. He argues, addressing St. Cyprian, that the Church cannot presume to set limits on the workings of divine grace: "Sed enim, virorum optime, reddamus et permittamus virtutibus caelestibus vires suas, et dignitationi divinae majestatis concedamus operationes proprias" (*PL,* III, 1243). To the contrary, St. Cyprian in his undoubted works declared baptism by heretics to be of no effect, maintaining that there are no sacraments outside the Church (*Epistolae* lxx, lxxi, lxxiii: *PL,* III, 1073–1082; 1155–1174; IV, 421–425). He wrote the judgment of the seventh Council of Carthage on the necessity of rebaptizing heretics (*PL,* III, 1089–1116). Also he inveighed against other bishops' more lenient policies of readmitting the lapsed to full communion (see *Epistolae* ix–xi, xiii and cap. 16, *Liber de Lapsis: PL,* IV, 256–264, 267–268, 493–494; cf. pseudo-Cyprian, *Sermo de coena Domini,* printed in Erasmus's edition of Cyprian's works [Basle, 1525], pp. 445–451, e.g., "Si cum calice Christi de calice daemoniorum communicas, contumelia est, non religio: injuria, non devotio.") In ch. 25 of *De Lapsis,* the strongest counterevidence to the opinion which Donne ascribes to St. Cyprian, there is a description of a little girl's forced reception of the Eucharist (in accordance with the practice of infant communion in the early Church). She instinctively resisted because her nurse had fed her food offered to idols, but the unsuspecting deacon persisted in making the child communicate. "Tunc sequitur," wrote St. Cyprian, an eyewitness, "singultus et vomitus. In corpore atque ore violato Eucharistia permanere non potuit. Sanctificatus in Domini sanguine potus de pollutis visceribus erupit. Tanta est potestas Domini, tanta majestas!" (*PL,* IV, 500). Is it outrageously literal-minded to wonder if this vivid anecdote was the dim source of a supposedly Cyprianic belief that the injured sacraments might show themselves in reversals?

IV.773–774 and mg.: I adopt P-S's emendation of "1 Cor. 11.27," the inaccurate reference in *LXXX S.* 1 Cor. 11.29 (Gr B, Genv): "He that eateth and drinketh unworthely, eateth and drinketh his own damnation"; (AV): "Hee that eateth and drinketh unworthily, eateth and drinketh damnation to himselfe."

IV.774–775: Allusion is to 1 John 2.1,2 (AV), "If any man sinne, we have an Advocate with the Father, Jesus Christ the righteous: and he is the propitiation for our sinnes," the last of the texts in the words of assurance pronounced by the priest just prior to the *Sursum corda* ("Lift up your hearts") in the Order for Holy Communion in the *BCP.*

IV.778:

determinate: definite, distinct.

IV.781:

Allusion is to the behavior of the soldiers who had custody of Christ during his trial (see Luke 22.63; Matt. 27.29; Mark 15.20).

IV.782–783:

Heb. 10.29 (Gr B, Bish, AV): "Of how much sorer punishment . . . shall hee be thought worthy, who hath troden under foote the Sonne of God, and hath counted the blood of the covenant . . . an unholy thing, and hath done despite unto the spirit of grace?"

IV.791:

Cf. the invocation in the Rosary: "Holy Mary, Mother of God, pray for us sinners, now and at the hour of our death."

IV.797–804:

Several features of the evocation of the Last Things recall 1 Corinthians: death as a sleep and the sounding trumpet (15.51, 52); seeing God face to face and knowing as one is known (13.12). Cf. Holy Sonnet X, l. 7. In addition there are verbal reminiscences of Gen. 3.19 (AV): "dust thou art, and unto dust shalt thou returne," and 1 John 3.2 (all Latin versions): "quoniam videbimus eum sicuti est."

IV.799–800:

Allusion is to Gen. 3.19.

IV.814 and mg.:

I adopt P-S's emendation of "Mat. 26.36," the inaccurate reference in *LXXX S.* Matt. 26.38 (Genv): "My soule is very heavie, even unto the death"; (Gr B): "My soule is heavye, even unto the deeth"; (AV): "My soule is exceeding sorrowfull, even unto death."

IV.816:

Donne's *"Quare"* is found in no Latin edition. The Vulgate and Erasmus read "Ut quid dereliquisti me"; Tremellius reads "Ad quid dereliquisti me?"

IV.817:

dereliction: the action of leaving (with intent not to resume); abandonment. The *OED* cites *Biathanatos* for the first English use of the word.

IV.819–822:   "Lion of Judah" is an epithet applied to Christ in Rev. 5.5. On "Lamb," see l. 767 and note.

IV.822:   colluctation: a wrestling or struggling together; strife; conflict.

IV.824:   preadmitted: admitted beforehand. This is the first usage recorded in the *OED*.

IV.825–826:   Cf. the Venerable Godefridus of Admont, in a sermon on John 21.15, "Feed my lambs": "Hic per agnos simplicitas, mansuetudo vel patientia accipitur" (*PL*, CLXXIV, 903).

IV.826,828–830:   *"Consummatum est"* are Jesus' last words on the Cross (John 19.30) and *"In principio"* are the opening words of Genesis and the Gospel of John as given in all Latin editions.

IV.830–831:   Psalm 130.4 (Vulg): "Apud te propitiatio est: et propter legem tuam sustinui te, Domine." The *"ut timearis"* seems to be a Latinizing of the purpose clause in English versions, i.e., "that thou maiest be feared" (Genv, AV). On this practice, see Allen, "Dean Donne Sets His Text," p. 226.

IV.834:   Pavor: quaking fear. A once rare, now obsolete, Latin loan word.

IV.836–837:   Prov. 21.15 (Genv, AV): "destruction shalbe to the workers of iniquitie."

IV.838–839:   Donne's italics reproduce no English version; they are probably a literal rendering of the Vulgate reading immediately preceding.

IV.850:   acceptation: the sense in which a word or sentence is understood or construed; the received meaning.

IV.852–854:   The theme of God's judgment on enemies is more fully treated in Preb V, 577–690. Cf. the Geneva gloss on Psalm 65.5: "Thou wilt declare thy selfe to be the preserver of thy Church in destroying thy enemies, as thou didest in the Red Sea."

IV.859:   On *"Damnabitur,"* see l. 618 and note.

IV.867 mg.:   As P-S indicate in their bracketed reference to 2 Cor. 2.16, Donne's "savor of death unto death" is an allusion to this verse.

IV.867:   commination: See note to Preb I, 433.

IV.873–874:   See note to l. 524 above.

IV.878–885:   The concluding lines of this sermon recapitulate elements from the end of the first Prebend sermon (ascription of power to God) and from the third Prebend sermon (reverence in the Church Militant reflects that of the Church Triumphant; glorifying God shall be the glory of the blessed).

IV.882–885:   The final observation relies on the Augustinian principle of the harmony of the two Testaments. See Introduction, p. 43.

Notes to the Fifth Prebend Sermon

V.1–4:   See note to ll. 29–30 of the second Prebend sermon.

V.4–6:   Allusion is, specifically, to proceedings at the Council of Trent: first, the claim to spiritual primacy (reiterated in a number of decrees in the reference to "the Roman Church, which is the mother and mistress of all churches"); second, the Decree Concerning the Edition, and the Use of the Sacred Books, which declares that "if any one receive not, as sacred and canonical, the said books [OT with Apocrypha, NT] entire with all their parts, as they have used to be read in the Catholic Church, and as they are contained in the old Latin vulgate edition . . . let him be anathema." The Vulgate was to be adhered to "in public lectures, disputations, sermons and expositions" and no one was "to dare, or presume to reject it under any pretext whatever" (*Canons and Decrees of the Council of Trent,* tr. and ed. J. Waterworth, pp. 19, 56, 107, 157, 278–279). For other criticism, see Preb I, 287–331 and note; *Essays in Divinity,* p. 10.

V.10–16:   *"Victori"* is puzzling. The AV title reads only "To the chiefe Musician, A Song or Psalme"; the Vulgate title reads *"In finem, Canticum Psalmi resurrectionis."* St. Jerome derived this title from the Septuagint. St. Augustine, construing the reference to the Resurrection as a signal of the prophetic nature of the whole Psalm, declares its meaning to be as follows: "Psalmus iste est adversus praesumptionem et superbiam Judaeorum, pro fide Gentium ad eamdem spem resurrectionis vocatarum" (*PL,* XXXVI, 787). This determination of meaning is retained by Cassiodorus (*PL,* LXX, 450–451), Arnobius Junior (*PL,* LIII, 415), and pseudo-Bede (*PL,* XCIII, 820) in their expositions of the Psalm, and by Strabo in the *Glossa Ordinaria* (*PL,* CXIII, 938).

V.16–27:

Joannis Lorinus, *Commentarii in Librum Psalm-orum* (Venice, 1717; orig. pub. 1612–1616), II, 464–465, remarks initially of Psalm 66: "De titulo difficultatem facit postremum nomen *resurrectionis.*" Then he debates the genuineness of the title by surveying the textual evidence in Chaldee, *"in textu Nebiensis,"* in Hebrew, in the Septuagint, and in the Greek and Latin Fathers. In the course of this survey he notes that "Leo castro (*lib.* 3. *Apol.* pag. 347) conqueritur ab Hebraeis abrasum hic resurrectionis *nomen,*" finally concluding: "Quod Castro Hebraeis objicit, facit suo more paulo severiùs. Debuissent multo clariora de resurrectione Christi testimonia ex Psalmis auferre, nec deesset illis modus nomen resurrectionis aliter interpretandi. . . . Undecunque titulus hic aut alii, ut nunc sunt in editione nostra, provenerint, auctoritatem habent ac retineri debent."

V.27–35:

Note the consonance between Donne and Bellarmine regarding the title and traditional interpretation of Psalm 66: "Non habetur in hebraeo nomen *resurrectionis,* neque legitur apud Hilarium; et Theodoretus testatur non esse in editione Septuaginta Interpretum, sed postea additum. Legitur tamen a Sanctis Patribus Hieronymo et Augustino in *Commentario* huius Psalmi, et videtur haec unica vox, a quocumque addita sit, prudentur addita, ut indicaret argumentum Psalmi. Argumentum enim Psalmi est gratiarum actio pro beneficiis Dei, sed potissimum pro perfecta felicitate post omnes finitas calamitates; quod sine dubio in resurrectione erit" (*Explanatio in Psalmos* [Rome: Pontifical Gregorian University Press, 1931; orig. pub. 1611], I, 348).

V.36–40:

Originally a figurative interpretation of St. Augustine's, the notion of a plurality of resurrections had impressed itself on Donne personally during his near-fatal illness in the winter of 1623–1624. See the use of this notion in the twenty-first Expostulation and

Prayer of the *Devotions,* and in his Easter sermon of 1624 (*Sermons,* VI, no. 2).

V.41–43: Isa. 60.1 (AV): "Arise, shine, for thy light is come, and the glory of the LORD is risen upon thee."

V.44–45: "I believe in . . . The Resurrection of the Body" is the penultimate clause in the Apostles' Creed, which is recited after the Canticle or Psalm following the New Testament Lesson in the Orders for Morning and Evening Prayer in the *BCP.*

V.45–46: See Calvin, *Sermons sur le livre de Job,* lxxii: "Maintenant nous voyons l'intention de Job. Il est vrai qu'il ne parle point ici expressement et simplement de la resurrection: mais tant y a que ces mots ne peuvent estre exposez, sinon qu'on cognoisse que Iob a voulu attribuer à Dieu une puissance qui ne se voit point auiourd'hui en l'ordre commun de nature. C'est donc comme s'il disoit, que Dieu ne veut point estre cognu de nous seulement cependant qu'il nous fait de bien . . . mais qu'encores . . . que nous ne vissions que la mort devant nous, il faut que nous soyons resolus que nostre Seigneur ne laissera point d'estre nostre garant. . . . Et c'est une consolation inestimable pour tous fideles, quand ils se voyent opprimez de calomnies en ce monde" (*Corpus Reformatorum,* ed. W. Baum, E. Cunitz, E. Reuss [Brunswick, 1887], LXII, 128–130). Donne repeatedly adverts to this interpretation of Calvin's in his preaching (*Sermons,* III.3.392; IV.1.435; VII.13.739).

V.47–48 and mg.: P-S add a reference to verse 25, which *LXXX S* lacks but does not require. Job 19.25,26 (AV): "I know that my Redeemer liveth, and that . . . in my flesh shall I see God."

V.48–51 and mg.: P-S add a reference to verse 3, the exact text cited in Ezek. 37, but I revert to the adequate citation in *LXXX S.* Expositors who take this verse as a reference to the restitution of the Jews include St. Jerome (*PL,* XXV, 349–350) and Rabanus Maurus, who invokes the authority of Jerome (*PL,* CX, 862). St. Gregory the Great interprets the text more broadly, as alluding to a resurgence of the Church (*PL,* LXXVI, 1031). Cf. *Sermons,* IV.1.573–576 where Donne asserts more accurately that "the Fathers (truly I think more generally more unanimely then in any other place of Scripture)" interpret Ezek. 37.3 as "primarily intended of the last resurrection, and but secundarily of the Jews restitution."

V.51–54:   Unless Donne's recollection is imprecise, it is not clear whom he has in mind. St. Augustine's influential interpretation is that the terrible works (Vulgate *"opera timenda"*) mentioned in this text are the Incarnation and Resurrection of Christ, to which the true Church has held in faith through successive ages of persecution (*PL,* XXXVI, 789–794). This line is followed by Arnobius Junior (*PL,* LIII, 414–415) and pseudo-Bede (*PL,* XCIII, 820–821).

V.62–64:   Cf. Donne's *Metempsychosis,* l. 21, where Noah is addressed as "holy *Janus."*

V.67–74:   The view that prophecy becoming history is the dynamic of the Biblical narrative belongs to St. Augustine; see, e.g., his exclamation on the credibility of the divinely inspired Scriptures in *De civitate Dei,* XVIII.40: "Cui enim melius narranti praeterita credimus, quam qui etiam futura praedixit, quae praesentia iam videmus?" (*PL,* XLI, 600). That prophecy becomes history is also, however, a major theme in Donne's preaching and the main ground of his adjurations to take God at his Word (*Sermons,* I.8.491–499; II.12.369–372; VII.5.498–505; VII.14. 260–262; IX.10.49–56; X.1.230–236).

V.90:   Psalm 66.1 (Vulg, Vatab): "omnis terra."

V.98:

particular (here a substantive): individual person (*OED*, 4b; obsolete).

V.99–100:

Donne gives the exact reading of the Geneva version; the AV reads "as for mee and my house, we will serve the LORD." Donne's Latin is closest to (Vulg, Vatab): "ego autem (quidem: Vatab) et domus mea serviemus Domino."

V.104, 105:

Note in this sermon the introduction, for emphasis, of Latin words and phrases in a manner analogous to Donne's custom in citing Scripture. But of these words and phrases only one is Biblical, the somewhat free allusion to Psalm 115.1; see note to ll. 115–117 below. Cf. St. Jerome's linking of Psalm 115.1 with an exposition of the Psalm from which the text of Donne's fifth Prebend sermon is taken (*PL*, XXVI, 1066).

V.110:

promoving: the obsolete form of "promoting."

V.115–117:

Allusion is to Psalm 115.1 (Vulg, Muns, Pagn): "Non nobis, Domine, non nobis, sed nomine tuo da gloriam."

V.116:

Cf. the *Second Anniversary*, ll. 511–512, where "Prayers to Saints" are termed "mis-devotion."

V.128:

consternation: terror such as to prostrate one's faculties; great dismay. An occurrence in Donne's sermons is the second given in the *OED*.

V.132–133:

Donne's remark is correct. The masculine singular passive reflexive adjective in his text, which he transliterates *Norah*, means "terrible, fearful, awesome" and derives from the Hebrew root *yārē'*, which has the transitive meanings of "to be dreadful, to put in fear, to be had in reverence" (see no. 3372 in Strong's *Concise Dict.*, p. 52). *"Norah"* belongs to the so-called "niphal" adjectival conjugation, which accounts for its *n*-prefix in English. The word is also rendered by the AV as "terrible" when it occurs in other Psalms (e.g., 47.2, 65.5, 68.35). Cf. Victorinus Bythner, *Lyra Prophetica Davidis Regis, sive Analysis Critico-Practica Psalmorum* (London, 1664), p. 251, who translates the locution as *"Quam terribile opera tua."*

V.151–157:   On the nonenforcement of recusancy laws (and for more evidence of Donne's opinion in the matter), see Preb II, 640–643 and note, and Appendix A, p. 332.

V.160–162:   "Submit themselves" in the AV renders a form of the Hebrew primary root *kāhash,* which has the literal meaning "to be untrue in word (lie, feign, disown) or in deed (disappoint, fail, cringe)" and figurative meanings including "to deceive, deny, dissemble, deal falsely, be found liars, and submit selves." (See no. 3584 in Strong's *Concise Dict.,* p. 55.) *"Mentientur tibi"* is the Vulgate rendering. The AV marginal gloss reads: *"Or, yeild* fained *obedience. Heb. lie."* The Geneva gloss reads: "As the faithful shal obey God willingly: so the infideles for feare shal dissemble themselves to be subject."

V.169:   throughly: archaic form of "thoroughly."

V.173:   Dilatation: amplification, enlargement, diffuse treatment (*OED,* 3).

V.177–183,225–230:   Hooker exhaustively sifts Old Testament precedents and authority for the claim that the King is the religious as well as the civil head of the state (*EP,* VIII.i,ii). This is a very widely held view of monarchy in England between 1570 and 1640 (see C. H. and K. George, *The Protestant Mind of the English Reformation,* pp. 211–223). Cf. Preb I, 184–190 and note. Here (l. 183), as there, Donne alludes to Psalm 82.6 (AV): "I have said, Yee are gods"; here also, it seems, Donne alludes to Isa. 43.15 ("I am the

LORD, your Holy one . . . your King") and Mal.
1.14 ("I am a great King, saith the LORD of
hostes"), for these are the only first-person statements
among the many declarations in the Bible that God
is King. Cf. Andrewes' terse reflections on the divine
prerogative of kings as conferred in Psalm 82.6
(*Ninety-six Sermons,* IV, 14, 132).

V.185–186:   Allusion is to 1 Cor. 15.10, which reads (AV): "I
laboured more abundantly then they all, yet not I,
but the grace of God which was with me."

V.192–224:   See the note to Preb I, 319–331. This tissue of anti-
Roman remarks amounts to a summary of basic and
long-standing Anglican charges since the Council of
Trent and the papal bull (1573) which excommunicated Queen Elizabeth and absolved her subjects
from allegiance. As might be expected of the author
of *Pseudo-Martyr,* this passage deals knowledgeably
with current vexed questions in canon law, casuistry,
and diplomacy. Donne adverts first to the strongly
worded but unspecific Trentine decree On Reformation (Session xxv), ch. 20: "The Holy Synod . . .
besides those things which It has ordained touching
ecclesiastical [discipline and] persons, has thought
fit, that Secular princes also be admonished of their
duty . . . And for this cause It admonishes the emperor, kings, republics, and princes, and all and each
of whatsoever state and dignity they be, that . . .
they respect whatsoever is of ecclesiastical right, as
belonging especially to God, and as being under the
cover of his protection" (J. Waterworth, *Canons and
Decrees,* pp. 275–276). The following phrase, "*In
ordine ad spiritualia,*" is alluded to by Donne in
Pseudo-Martyr (London, 1610), p. 357, as the customary term for the extent and nature of papal authority among Roman canonists and apologists. The
term itself hinges on the distinction between *spiritualia* (the jurisdiction, powers, rights, and appur-
tenances of episcopal, and especially papal, authority)

and *temporalia* (the jurisdiction, powers, etc., of civil authority, especially emperors and kings) which was standard although variously drawn in canon law after the time of Leo the Great. This distinction was abrogated (and made, with countless other items, matter of controversy) by Henry VIII's first Act of Supremacy (1534), which declared the King to be the Supreme Head on earth of the Church of England and the contrary assertion to be treasonable. Elizabeth's Act of Supremacy (1559), the second, omitted the ascription of the title but exacted of persons holding office or taking a university degree an oath acknowledging the Queen to be supreme governor of the realm in spiritual and ecclesiastical matters. After the discovery of the Gunpowder Plot, James I imposed in addition a severe Penal Code (1606) upon English Catholics and an Oath of Allegiance to himself which required swearing that the doctrine of the Pope's power to depose princes was "impious, heretical, and damnable." On the lack of direction given English Catholics as to the permissibility of taking the oath, see the note to ll. 327–328 of the first Prebend sermon. See also Gordon Albion's account of the negotiations with Rome concerning the Oath of Allegiance during the reign of Charles I (*Charles I and the Court of Rome,* pp. 249–287).

V.209:   enervates: disparages the power or value of (something). The *OED* quotes from *Biathanatos:* "To enervate and maime . . . that repentance which is admitted for sufficient in the Romane Church."

V.223:   distemper: disordered condition; especially according to medieval physiology, a disturbance in the bodily "humours."

V.228–233:   Allusion is to the traditional observation that the first five of the Ten Commandments (Exod. 20.1–17) propound man's duty to God, and the second five man's duty to man. Donne's assertion that the tables of the

Law are committed to the King is misleading, for they were first entrusted to Moses (Exod. 32.15,16) and their replacements to the priestly tribe of the Levites (see, e.g., 2 Sam. 15.24) before the establishment of the monarchy in Israel. However, in the period of the kings, David is recorded as having "prepared a place for the ark of God" (1 Chron. 15.1) which held the tables (Deut. 10.4,5) and Solomon as having placed the Ark in the Temple which he built (1 Kings 8; 2 Chron. 5).

V.233–236:   See Aquinas, *ST,* pars II^a II^{ae}, q. 99, art. 1, ad obj. 1, where he comments on Gratian's charge of sacrilege against those who take issue with their sovereign: "According to the Philosopher (*Ethic.* i.2) the common good of the nation is a divine thing, wherefore in olden times the rulers of a commonwealth were called divines, as being the ministers of divine providence, according to Wisd. of Sol. vi.5, *Being ministers of His kingdom, you have not judged rightly.* Hence by an extension of the term, whatever savours of irreverence for the sovereign, such as disputing his judgment, and questioning whether one ought to follow it, is called a sacrilege by a kind of likeness." Donne's use of Aquinas here is notably restrained in comparison with Roger Manwaring's assertion in *Religion and Allegiance* (1627) that the penalty of disobeying the King was eternal damnation. But even Laud recognized the extremism of Manwaring's position (C. H. and K. George, *The Protestant Mind,* p. 215).

V.237–242:   Perhaps Donne is giving a "Resultance" of Gretzer's views. Although I have not located the precise italicized words, their gist is contained in the defense of papal prerogatives against Stuart claims which is made in ch. viii, secs. 57–62 of Jacob Gretzer's ΒΑΣΙΛΙΚΟΝ ΔΩΡΟΝ, *sive Commentarius Exegeticus in Serenissimi Magnae Britanniae Regis Jacobi Praefationem Monitoriam; et in Apologiam pro Jura-*

mento Fidelitatis (1610), reprinted in vol. VII of his *Opera omnia* (Ratisbon, 1736). Donne's *Pseudo-Martyr* appeared in the same year and took an opposite stance on the very issues that Gretzer examined.

V.247–248: Psalm 66.1 (Muns): "Jubilate . . . omnes terrae"; (AV): "Make a joyfull noise . . . , all yee lands"; (Genv): "Rejoice . . . all yee inhabitants of the earth." Donne's italicized English phrase is either a conflation of the AV and Geneva or his literal translation of Munster's rendering.

V.249–250: Psalm 66.16 (Vulg): "Venite, audite, et narrabo, omnes." But Allen ("Dean Donne Sets His Text," p. 226) takes Donne's Latin phrase as a translation of the AV's "Come and heare all yee. . . ." rather than an inexact citation of the Vulgate. Cf. Preb IV, 830–831.

V.250–253: Cf. *Sermons*, III.5.172–175. St. Cyprian's celebrated conception of the Christian Church as one indivisible diocese is developed in *Liber de Unitate Ecclesiae*, ch. 5 (*PL*, IV, 516). Donne represents St. Cyprian accurately, but the analogy with a king's function is, of course, Donne's—or, more precisely, that of conservative Anglicans of his age. See C. H. and K. George, *The Protestant Mind*, p. 189.

V.270–271: Donne is evidently paraphrasing a marginal heading from bk. XII, ch. 2 of Nicephorus Callistus Xanthopulus's *Ecclesiasticae Historiae Libri Decem et Octo . . . vero ac studio doctiss. viri Joannis Langi, . . . e Graeco in Latinum sermonem translati . . .* (Frankfurt, 1588), col. 706 D: *"Ecclesias fere in Oriente omnes Ariani tenuere."* The text at this place reads: "Atque Hierosolymis exceptis, per Oriente ecclesiae prope omnes in Arianorum potestate erant."

V.271–274: St. Vincent of Lérins describes Arianism in the Western Church in bk. I, ch. 4 of his *Commonito-*

rium: "Item quando Arianorum venenum non jam portiunculam quamdam, sed pene orbem totum contaminaverat, adeo ut prope cunctis Latini sermonis Episcopis partim vi, partim fraude deceptis, caligo quaedam mentibus offunderetur" (*PL,* L, 642).

V.274–275:   Sixty-five is the actual number of Arian bishops whose names are listed by St. Hilary (*Ex Opere Historico Fragmentum,* II: *PL,* X, 642–643).

V.277–278:   St. Jerome, *Liber de Viris Illustribus,* cap. xcvii: "Fortunatianus, natione Afer, Aquileiensis episcopus, imperante Constantio, in Evangelia, titulis ordinatis, brevi et rustico sermone scripsit commentarios: et in hoc habetur detestabilis, quod Liberium, Romanae urbis episcopum, pro fide ad exsilium pergentem, primus sollicitavit ac fregit, et ad subscriptionem haereseos compulit" (*PL,* XXIII, 735, 738).

V.278–282 and mg.:   Donne's rare exactitude in citing Bellarmine bespeaks his fascination with—and later amusement at—the mental acrobatics required in writing religious controversy. Desperate contortions are indeed evident in Bellarmine's *De Romani Pontificis; Ecclesiastica Hierarchia, in Disputationum . . . de Controversiis Christianae Fidei Adversus Hujus Tempores Haereticos* (orig. pub. 1610), *Opera Omnia* (Venice, 1721), I, 402–403: "Undecimus Pontifex, qui erroris arguitur, est Liberius . . . Tilmannus Heshusius lib. i. de Eccles. cap. 9. audacter affirmat, eum Ariana haeresi infectum fuisse. Et sanè testes habet suae sententiae gravissimos auctores; Athanasium in epist. ad solit. vit. agent. Hieronymum in Chron. & in Catal. script. in Fortunatiano, & Damascum in vita Liberii. Respondeo: de Libero duo esse certa; unum verò dubium. Primò, certum est, eum ab initio Pontificatus usque ad exilium, quod pro Fide Catholica pertulit, acerrimum defensorem fuisse Catholicae religionis. . . . Secundò, certum est, Liberium post reditum ab exilio fuisse etiam vere Orthodoxum et pium."

V.290: reduce: lead or bring back from error in action, conduct, or belief, especially in matters of morality or religion; restore to the truth or right faith (*OED*, 8; obsolete, but very common c. 1600–1700).

V.293: *LXXX S* reads "truth,"; I adopt P-S's emendation.

V.297: Psalm 145.3 (AV): "Great is the LORD, and greatly to be praised."

V.299–300: Psalm 145.4 (AV): "One generation shall praise thy works to another: and declare thy power."

V.301 mg.: *LXXX S*'s reference, "Ver. 6," is inaccurate; I emend with P-S.

V.311–316: Cf. the very similar admonition by Donne during the reign of King James (*Sermons*, III.6.396–401).

V.312: fascination: state of being under a spell or enchantment (*OED*, 1b; obsolete).

V.317–322: Here is a compact example of the way exposition characteristically shades into application in Donne's preaching. Cf. Joan Webber's remarks in *Contrary Music*, pp. 144, 146–147.

V.326–328: See *Divi Gregorii . . . episcopi Nazianzeni, de Theologia liber quartus, Petro Mosellano Protegense interprete*, in *Orationes Trigintaocto, . . . Tractatus, sermones, & libri aliquot. . . .* (Paris, 1532), p. 168 E, opposite the marginal heading *"Sermo.":* "Sed ad filii appellationes, de quibus sermo erat institutus, revertamur. . . . Sermo vero, quoniam ita se habet ad patrem, ut ad mentem sermo. . . . nam & hoc significat λόγος. . . . Tum si qui & propterea, quod rebus omnibus insit, hoc nomen tributum dicat, hic a ratione non omnino aberrabit. Nam quid tandem, quod non τῷ λόγῳ (id est, certa ratione) constet?" Neither this nor any other translation in whatever language can do justice to St. Gregory's original *tour de force,* which devolves through the various meanings of the Greek *logos* as speech, reason, principle (see *PG,* XXXVI, 129). There is no question that this remarkable passage would have been strongly to Donne's tastes if he could have read the Greek text. But since he does not seem to have had a reading knowledge of Greek, it is possible that his source here was a work formerly attributed to St. Gregory Nazianzen under the title *Oration 49* or *First Tractate on the Orthodox Faith, Against the Arians* (*PG,* XXXVI, 674–675), which the Migne editors reassign to St. Phoebadius: "Ratio quaedam est, quae apud Graecos Λόγος nuncupatur. . . . Quae tamen Ratio multis nominibus appellatur: modo Verbus, modo Virtus, modo Sapientia. . . . Et ita cum sit Deus omnia in omnibus, ut per haec vocabula divinarum dispositionum mysteria cognoscantur" (*PL,* XX, 42).

V.330–334:   Donne's Latin phrases do not reproduce the reading of any Latin version at Josh. 10.12, but are used to give emphatic expression to his accurate linguistic observation. The Hebrew primary root *dâmah* has the literal meaning "to be dumb or silent." (See no. 1820 in Strong's *Concise Dict.,* p. 31.) Its form in Josh. 10.12,13 is rendered in various equivalent ways: "stetit" (Vulg); "quievit" (Muns); "substetit" (T-J); and "stand still" (AV).

V.349:   extasies: states of being out of one's senses, thrown into a frenzy or stupor (*OED,* 1); also applied vaguely or inconsistently by early writers to all morbid states characterized by unconsciousness, e.g., swoon, trance, epilepsy (2a); also used by mystical writers as the technical designation for the state of rapture in which the body was supposed to become incapable of sensation while the soul was engaged in the contemplation of divine things (3a). Donne is ironically playing off the various meanings against each other. Very different but still characteristic complexity attends the treatment of the state described in his poem "The Extasie" and the infernal vision attendant on the "extasie" of the narrator of *Ignatius His Conclave.*

V.350–353: Joan Webber (*Contrary Music,* p. 219) quotes Ruth Wallerstein (*Studies in Seventeenth-Century Poetic* [Madison, Wis.: University of Wisconsin Press, 1950], p. 34) to the effect that Donne's image of beaten gold derives from Tertullian. But the tone and details differ markedly. The relevant passage is at the end of cap. xxxvii of *Liber de Anima* (*PL,* II, 759) where the process of beating a mass of gold or silver into leaf, which causes the metal to cover a much larger space and to reveal its luster, is used as an analogy for the way in which the soul fills the growing human body and brings into play its powers.

V.353–357: This is a reprise of the magnificent passage in Preb II, 331–359.

V.356: Allusion is to the repeated phrasing of Latin versions (Vulg, Muns, Vatab) in Gen. 1.3–31.

V.370–372: Origen, *Matthäuserklärung II: Die lateinische Übersetzung der Commentariorum Series,* ed. E. Klostermann, in *Werke* (Leipzig: J. C. Hinrichs, 1933), II, 221: "*Unus* autem eorum, *qui erant cum Iesu,* nondum manifestè concipiens apud se evangelicam patientiam illam traditam sibi à Christo nec pacem, quam dedit discipulis suis . . . *extendens manum* accepit *gladium* et percussit *servum principis sacerdotum et amputavit auriculam eius.*" This Latin text, that of Jacob Merlin's first printed edition of Origen's works (Paris, 1512), was produced principally through collation of three manuscripts: *Codex Gemmeticensis* (10th c.), *Codex Brugensis* (12th c.), and *Codex Londinensis* (12th c.).

V.373–375 and mg.:   I adopt P-S's emendation of "Mat. 26.54," the reference in *LXXX S.* Matt. 26.52 (Gr B, Bish, AV): "all they that take the sword, shall perish with the sword."

V.383–385 and mg.:   P-S bracket an additional reference to verse 54; I return to the adequate notation of *LXXX S.* Luke 9.55 (Genv): "Yee knowe not of what spirit yee are."

V.386–387:   *"Domine jube"* appears to be Donne's extrapolation from St. Jerome's *Epistola cxxi:* "Apostoli . . . dicuntque ad Dominum: *Vis, dicimus, ut ignis descendat de caelo, et consumat eos* (Lu. 9.51)? Pulchre, *Vis,* inquiunt, *dicimus* . . . Ergo ut Apostolorum sermo efficientiam habeat, voluntatis est Domini. Nisi enim ille jusserit, frustra dicunt Apostoli" (*PL,* XXII, 1017).

V.406–409:   Allusion is, principally, to Exod. 13.21,22; Num. 14.14; Neh. 9.12,19.

V.413 and mg.:   P-S bracket a reference to Psalm 82.6, to which the italics allude. On the frequent citation and interpretation of this verse, see notes to ll. 177–183, 225–230 above and to ll. 184–190 of the first Prebend sermon.

V.415:   The English versions concur in reading "my backe parts" in Exod. 33.23; *"his hinder parts"* may be Donne's adaptation from the Vulgate's *"posteriora mea."*

V.423–424:   This is a brief demonstration of Donne's characteristic discovery of spiritual utility in an observation about language (in this case, as rarely, native English).

V.443–447:   Donne's distinction cannot be upheld. *"Lechu,"* or *lᵉ ḳû* in modern transliteration, is an irregular plural imperative form deriving from the Hebrew root *hālaḳ* which means indifferently "come (away)" and "go (away)." (See no. 3212 in Strong's *Concise Dict.*, p. 49.) However, Allen commends this gloss ("Dean Donne Sets His Text," p. 216). Donne's report on the occurrences in Psalm 66.5,16 and the AV renderings is nevertheless correct.

V.457–458:   Cf. the spiritual interpretation of deliverance from Egypt which is the climax of the *Essays in Divinity,* ed. Simpson, pp. 74–76.

V.460:   See note to Preb II, 49.

V.464–466:   See note to Preb IV, 501–505. "Vault" here alludes to the cellar beneath the Palace of Westminster, where the group of disaffected English Catholics who conspired in the Gunpowder Plot concealed the explosives that were to blow up King James and Parliament.

V.469:   I follow P-S in placing a comma after *"Ite,"* which is unpunctuated in *LXXX S.*

V.471–472:   Donne's italics seem to be a free rendering of Psalm 66.3 in Pagnini's reading ("quam terribilis in tuis operibus") or in Munster's ("quam terribilis es in operibus tuis"). Cf. the Vulgate's "quam terribilia sunt opera tua."

V.477–478:   Gen. 15.12 (Bish, AV): "an horrour of great darknesse fell upon him." The verse actually associates the horror with Abraham's falling into a deep sleep at sundown, but the speech of God also appears to be continuous through the entire chapter.

V.478–479:   "The Father of Lights" alludes to James 1.17; "the God of all comfort" to 2 Cor. 1.3. The English versions concur in these readings.

V.481:   presentially: in the way of actual presence; as being present. (Cf. Scholastic Latin *praesentialiter.*)

V.482 mg.:   I follow P-S's emendation of *LXXX S's* misprinted reference, "Exod. 13.6."

V.482–497:   The concurrent associative development of these Biblical allusions along literal and allegorical lines seems to be Donne's own. The point of departure is Christ's comparisons of his Second Coming and the Last Judgment to events in the days of Noah and to the gathering of eagles over a carcass (Matt. 24.27–29; Luke 17.26–37), to which are added references to Noah's dispatching of a dove from the ark after the Flood and her return with an olive branch in her beak, signifying receding waters (Gen. 8.8–11) and to the narrative of Jonah's preservation in the belly of the great fish (Jon. 2), which is later called a whale, (Matt. 12.40). In patristic literature the ark is universally interpreted as a sign of salvation, most commonly of the Church but also sometimes of the sacraments. For specific references, see the Migne *Indices de Allegoriis* (*PL,* CCXIX, 130, 151, 159). Likewise, the eagle is widely taken as a figure of the Devil or of evil people or spirits who torment the just (see *ibid.,* 147, 181, 213). Although the dove is best known as a type for the Holy Ghost or persons acting as his instruments (*ibid.,* 126, 138), Garnerus of St. Victor, elaborating in his *Librii Gregorianum* on the *Moralia in Job,* provides precedent for Donne's view of the dove here: "Columbae nomine, mansuetudo Domini intelligitur" (*PL,* CXCIII, 71). The whale is rarely given allegorical construction by the Fathers, probably because Christ himself used it as a figure for his three-day subjection to death (Luke 11.29, 30); however, St. Gregory the Great uses the whale as a figure for the evil forces, both within and without, which threaten man with destruction (*Moralia in Job,* viii.7: *PL,* LXXV, 824).

V.503 mg.:   As P-S indicate in a bracketed reference, allusion is to James 1.17.

V.512:   On *Norah*, see note to ll. 132–133.

V.513–514:   Mal. 2.5 (Bish, AV): "My covenant was with him of life and peace, and I gave them him (to him: AV), for the feare, wherewith he feared mee, and was afraid before my name."

V.516–529:   Where *LXXX S* ends after "that large satisfaction" (l. 526) with a period, Mrs. Simpson inserts three ellipsis points and registers in a footnote the opinion that some words have been omitted because the sentence is a fragment (*Sermons*, VIII, 124). But an omission need not be supposed, for these lines do express a complete idea. Cf. *Sermons*, V.13.781–823, the famous grand paragraph on damnation, which is composed of absolute "That . . . What" clauses having no grammatical dependence; as Joan Webber (*Contrary Music*, p. 58) says, this "is no sentence at all." In the present case two possible editorial courses suggest themselves: (1) To judge from the parallel clause structure in ll. 526–529 and 548–551, Donne seems to have intended an infinitive construction in ll. 516–526 to correspond to that in ll. 538–551. However, it is difficult to attribute the reading "And therefore hee that conceives" in place of "And therefore to conceive" to a printer's error. Since the irregularity probably stood in Donne's copy, emendation is less to be preferred than the second possibility. (2) It is possible to infer from ordinary license in spoken English a reference in Donne's "This is not such a Terriblenesse" (l. 526) reaching back to "hee that conceives" (ll. 516–517) with the force of "hee conceives not such a Terriblenesse." I have therefore taken the milder remedy and altered *LXXX S*'s period in l. 526 to a semicolon. In Donne's day the semicolon could function grammatically, "when in relative clauses it often shows that the relative pronoun refers, not to the immediately preceding word, but to one some distance away" (Vivian Salmon,

"Early Seventeenth-Century Punctuation as a Guide to Sentence Structure," *RES*, n.s. XIII [1962], 354).

V.530:   Allusion is to Psalm 111.10 and Prov. 9.10, which read (AV): "The feare of the LORD is the beginning of wisedome"; and to Prov. 15.33, which reads (AV): "The feare of the LORD is the instruction of wisedome."

V.530–531:   Psalm 2.11 (AV): "rejoice with trembling."

V.532–533 and mg.:   P-S bracket a reference to Isa. 33.6, which reads (uniquely) in Tremellius-Junius: "reverentia Iehovae est thesaurus ejus" and "The feare of the LORD is his treasure" in the AV.

V.538 and mg.:   P-S bracket a reference to 1 John 4.8, in which the phrase "God is love" occurs, and also take the liberty of italicizing the phrase. I have restored the roman type of *LXXX S*, since there is no necessity of taking such a commonplace as a specific quotation.

V.538–541:   Allusion is to John Calvin's *Institutio Christianae Religionis*, bk. III, ch. 21, where a double predestination (to salvation and to damnation) through an eternal and immutable decree of God, exclusive of any individual human merit or fault, is affirmed. On Donne's views on predestination, see notes to Preb IV, 630, and Preb I, 361–369.

V.541:   modesty: humility toward God (*OED*, 2b; obsolete, once rare). Perhaps Donne's vocabulary is influenced by Tertullian's *"modestia fidei"*; cf. note to Preb II, 265–271.

V.541–546:   Allusion is, apparently, to the Trentine decree On Justification (Session 6), ch. 9: "Each one, when he regards himself, and his own weakness and indisposition, may have fear and apprehension touching his own grace; seeing that no one can know with a certainty of faith, which cannot be subject to error [*cui non potest subesse falsum*], that he has obtained the grace of God" (Waterworth, *Canons and Decrees,* p. 37). But this decree expatiates on Aquinas, *ST,* pars Iᵃ IIᵃᵉ, q. 112, art. 5: "Et sic nullus potest scire se habere gratiam."

V.577–579:   Cf. St. Augustine's remarks on God's enemies in *De civitate Dei,* bk. XII, ch. 3.

V.581–582:   Cf. "To Sir Henry Wotton" ("Sir, more then kisses"), ll. 39–40; *First Anniversary,* ll. 193–195. Aquinas treats the angels' sin of malice in *ST,* pars Iᵃ, q. 63.

V.587–588 and mg.:   *LXXX S* gives the reference as "Rom. 5.10." Actually Donne's italics are a free allusion to verse 8 combined with the reference to men as enemies of God in verse 10. Since the latter is cited below (l. 600), I follow P-S in emending the reference here.

V.589–592:   A Latin dictionary confirms Donne's observation regarding *"hostis"* (which derives from a Sanskrit root meaning "to eat, consume, destroy"); a Vulgate concordance also bears out his remark on NT vocabulary.

V.597–599:   On the obstinacy of the evil angels in their sin and their irreconcilability with God, see Aquinas, *ST,* pars Iᵃ, q. 64, art. 2. But this assumption regarding the evil angels was generally held; cf. the reflections of Milton's Satan on his possible alternatives (*Paradise Lost,* IV, 90: "For never can true reconcilement grow....")

V.606:   Gen. 3.15 (Vulg, Muns): "Inimicitias ponam"; (Vatab): "Ponamque inimicitias."

V.608–609:   Allusion is, broadly, to Matt. 19.6 and Mark 10.9 (AV): "What therefore, God hath joined together,

let not man put asunder" or to the priest's pronouncement after the exchange of vows in The Form of
Solemnization of Matrimony in the *BCP:* "Those
whom God hath joined together, let no man put
asunder." Earlier English versions of the Bible (Gr
B, Bish, Genv) read uniformly: "Let not man therefore put asunder that, which God hath coupled together" in Matt. 19.6, and "Therefore, what God
hath coupled together, let no man separate" at Mark
10.9. Strangely, Donne's phrasing bears the closest
resemblance to the English translation (probably
Coverdale's work) of the rite formulated by Archbishop Hermann of Cologne in his *Consultation*
(1548): "That, that God hath joyned, lette no man
dissever." See *The Annotated Book of Common
Prayer, Being An Historical, Ritual, and Theological
Commentary on the Devotional System of the
Church of England,* ed. John Henry Blunt (London,
1884), pp. 15–16, 454.

V.609–611: Cf. Aquinas, *ST,* pars III^a, q. 49, art. 4, where it is
observed that men become God's enemies through
sin, and yet (reply to obj. 1): "God loves all men as
to their nature, which He Himself made; yet He
hates them with respect to the crimes they commit
against Him, according to Ecclus. 12.3: *The Highest
hateth sinners."*

V.618–621: Allusion is, seemingly, to Psalm 138.22, which in the
closest versions reads (Vulg): "Perfecto odio oderam
illos"; (T-J): "Perfecto odio odi illos?" and also to
St. Augustine, *Enarrationes in Psalmum* cxxxviii:
"Quomodo implebit hoc, nisi illo perfecto odio; ut
hoc in eis oderit quod iniqui sunt, hoc diligat quod
homines sunt?" (*PL,* XXXVII, 1802). Cf. Sermons,
III.18. 197–207; "Satire II", ll.1–2.

V.626–627 and mg.: Although *LXXX S* gives a reference to Psalm 17.8,
which reads (Genv, AV): "Keepe me as the apple

of the eye," a more germane text is Zech. 2.8 (AV): "For thus sayth the LORD . . . , he that toucheth you, toucheth the apple of his eye."

V.629:	determined: terminated, ended.

V.629–630:   Allusion is to Isa. 53.7, which reads (AV): "As a sheep before her shearers is dumbe, so he openeth not his mouth." This text, with the whole of the fifty-third chapter, has traditionally been regarded as one of the major prophecies of Christ's Passion.

V.631 mg.:   P-S add a reference to verse 4, the particular text cited in Acts 9.

V.633–634 and mg.:   Donne's italics are closer to God's question in Gen. 4.10 after the murder of Abel, which reads (all versions): "What hast thou done?" than to the cited question in verse 6 after Cain's offering was rejected: "Why art thou wroth? And why is thy countenance fallen?" But I retain the reference of *LXXX S.* However, I follow P-S in italicizing "thus?" which is set in roman type in *LXXX S.*

V.643 and mg.:   P-S bracket a reference to Lam. 3.22, to which (in the Geneva rendering) Donne's italics allude: "It is the Lords mercies that we are not consumed."

V.651–654:   On Donne's commentary on the names of God, see Preb II, 541–568 and note.

V.658:   Donne cites a Hebrew prepositional phrase whose components are *be,* meaning "in," and *rob,* rendered "greatnesse" in the AV, deriving from the primary root *râbab,* "to multiply or to be multiplied, to be great (in number)." (See nos. 7230, 7231 in Strong's *Concise Dict.,* p. 106.) His Latin phrases here and in l. 667 appear to have been coined in the attempt to specify the exact sense of the Hebrew phrase.

V.660–662:   Deut. 20.4 (all versions): "The Lord your God . . . goeth with you, to fight for you against your enemies, and to (to: AV) save you." I follow P-S in supplying a period at the end of the quotation, which is lacking in *LXXX S.*

V.664–666 and mg.:   P-S bracket a reference to Deut. 4.7,8, to which Donne's italics allude. The verse reads (AV): "For what nation . . . hath God so nigh unto them . . . ? And what nation is there so great, that hath Statutes and Judgements so righteous, as all this Law . . . ?"

V.672–674:   Donne does not cite the third person masculine plural passive verb form in his text but, rather, the Hebrew primary root *Cacash,* or *ḳāhash* in modern transliteration (see note to ll. 160–162 above). *"Mendacem fieri"* appears to be Donne's (or his lexicon's) rendering of the sense of this primary root; the Latin versions read the form in the text as (Vulg, Pagn): "mentientur"; (Muns): "mendaces erunt"; (T-J): "mendaciter se dedunt." Cf. the close parallel in *Sermons,* IX.13.179–86.

V.680–681:   Allusion is to Exod. 8–11.

V.686:   Here, in contrast to l. 526, there may be a textual corruption. *LXXX S* has an opening parenthesis before the first "that is" in this line which I, with P-S, delete because it is not functional as the words stand. Did the typesetter perhaps transpose phrases which originally read "That onely the power of God, (that is, his power multiplied) The receiving of his word, (that is, the power of Law)" *etc.?* Or were some words dropped? The present sense is rather precarious.

V.698–700 and mg.:   P-S add a bracketed reference to verse 13, which is quoted in the italicized clauses in parentheses. I retain *LXXX S*'s reference as adequate, but I follow P-S in emending its Vulgate numbering, "Psal. 80," since the AV is being cited. It reads: "The haters of the LORD should have submitted themselves unto him."

V.704–705 and mg.:   P-S bracket a reference to 2 Cor. 12.7, which reads, e.g., (Vulg): "datus est mihi stimulus carnis meae, angelus satanae"; (Trem): "stimulus carni meae, angelus Satanae"; (Vatab): "stimulus in carne, angelus Satan."

Appendices and Index

Appendix A. The Date of the Fifth Prebend Sermon

Omission of a date from the heading of the fifth Prebend sermon is a disconcerting loose end in the *LXXX Sermons* of 1640, the first and the most carefully prepared of the three folio volumes in which John Donne the younger collected all but a handful of his father's sermons. Although suspicion might fall on the son initially because of the two known cases in *Fifty Sermons* (1649) where he expunged the names of Royalists from his father's headings,[1] no political or other motive for leaving out the date of the fifth Prebend sermon is suggested by the circumstances of publication. In the absence of other kinds of evidence the younger Donne must be considered innocent, and, on the basis of the first-person wording of the Prebend sermon headings, the charge—inadvertence more probably than a sin of omission[2]—laid to the Dean himself.

1. Those of Sir Francis Nethersole, King James' agent to the German princes of the Protestant Union and longtime secretary of the Electress Palatine; and Margaret Washington, a relation by marriage of the Duke of Buckingham. Their names are retained in manuscript copies of Donne's sermons at their respective weddings in February and June of 1621. Mrs. Simpson calls attention to the younger Donne's politic excisions (Introduction, *Sermons*, III, 20–21), and she and Potter also suggest that the imprecise headings on Donne's sermons at christenings may be due to the same tactics (Introduction, *Sermons*, V, 7–8). To complete the picture, there is, moreover, evidence that the younger Donne tinkered with details in publishing his father's letters in 1651; the intention was to make the elder Donne, through his acquaintance and correspondence, seem an intimate of Cromwell's relations and supporters. See R. E. Bennett, "Donne's *Letters to Severall Persons of Honour*," *PMLA*, LVI (1941), 138–140.

2. One cannot entirely discount the possibility that the senior Donne himself thought it discreet to leave unrecorded the date of a sermon which glances repeatedly at current conditions and events. The times were rife with offenses taken and given even where none were intended. Note Donne's panic over the difficulties regarding a sermon he preached before King Charles at Whitehall on April 1, 1627, caused probably by his own melodramatic way of casting a compliment as a state secret; for particulars, see Introduction, *Sermons*, VII, 38–42, the sermon itself, and R. C. Bald, *John Donne: A Life*, pp. 491–494. It was also at this period that the sturdy George Abbot, Archbishop of Canterbury, was sent into confinement (July 1627) and sequestered from his jurisdiction (October 1627) for refusing to comply with King Charles' command to license for

The *terminus ad quem* of the fifth Prebend sermon is January 28, 1627 (N.S.), the date on which the fourth was delivered. There is no discernible correlation between the dates of the first four Prebend sermons and the Sundays for which Psalms 62, 63, 64, and 65 are appointed as readings at Morning or Evening Prayer or Holy Communion. The irregular intervals separating the dated Prebend sermons also give no clue as to when the fifth was preached, but it is reasonable to exclude from consideration the period from July to mid-September (the customary summer recess from London) since we have no indication that Donne ever preached at St. Paul's then,[3] and the Prebend sermons were preached at St. Paul's. However, the topicality of parts of the fifth Prebend sermon raises some possibility of setting a *terminus a quo,* or at least suggesting a plausible period for its delivery. This presumably was the procedure in Potter and Mrs. Simpson's assignment of the fifth Prebend sermon to November or December of 1627,[4] but not a word of explanation is given. My proposal that the date be moved up to the late spring of 1627 is based primarily upon topical allusions (as oblique reflections of certain current events).

The preponderance of topical allusions in the fifth Prebend sermon is general in nature, reflecting the gap between royal policies and popular opinion—especially as voiced in Parliament—in the opening years of Charles I's reign. On the popular side, pleading religious instead of political motives, Donne expresses the mounting discontent over the nonenforcement of the Penal Code since the contraction of the King's French marriage,[5] insisting

---

publication the extravagant assertion of the royal prerogative made in Dr. Robert Sibthorpe's sermon "Apostolical Obedience." See S. R. Gardiner, *A History of England under the Duke of Buckingham and Charles I* (London, 1875), II. 173–175, and what is thought to be Abbot's own narrative of the July proceedings, in C. H. Firth's *Stuart Tracts, 1603–1693* (Westminster: Camden Society, 1903), pp. 309–350.

3. On Donne's summer visits at the country houses of noble friends and at his livings of Sevenoaks and Blunham, see Introductions, *Sermons,* I, 129–130; V, 19. In a letter to Sir Henry Goodyer dating from the summer of 1625 Donne lists among places he usually visited Knole, Hanworth, and Keyston (*Letters to Severall Persons of Honour,* ed. Merrill, p. 202).

4. Introduction, *Sermons,* VIII, 11. Or was their motive simply a more even distribution of the sermons for 1627 before and after the July-September break?

5. Enforcement had been suspended under King James as early as December 1624, but action on the application of English Catholics for remission of fines was deferred until the close of the Parliament session of 1625 to prevent recrimination in the House of Commons. See Gordon Albion, *Charles I and the Court of Rome,* pp. 64, 76, and references given there.

on the necessity of unremitting enforcement of the Oath of Allegiance and of fines on recusants (ll. 151–157, 693–696, 710–714). However, he also makes a strong defense of the royal prerogative which goes beyond citing the usual Scriptural proof text for divine right (ll. 411–413)[6] to advert to the rightfulness of Charles' efforts not only to establish uniformity of religion in England but also to recover the Palatinate for his Protestant brother-in-law, the Elector Frederick (ll. 260–261, 312–313). Already the efforts at recovery, under Buckingham's influence, had led King James into war with Spain in late 1624 and King Charles into war with France as well in early 1627.[7] Donne registers a measure of the crisis of confidence between sovereign and subjects as to domestic and foreign priorities and the means of pursuit: "injurious" and "disloyal suspition" and "doubt" have been cast upon the King, and "Remonstrance" has become a byword (ll. 310, 298).[8] This set of allusions applies to most of the period from 1625 to 1627.

On the other hand, Donne's assertion that "the King himselfe workes in his Commissioners, and their just Act is the Kings Act" (ll. 188–189) may be linked with the collection, from September 1626 through November 1627, of King Charles' forced loan by exactly these means.[9] The purpose of the forced loan (really a levy without Parliamentary grant) was to finance

6. On the particular construction placed upon Psalm 82.6, see the note to Preb I, 184–190.

7. Gardiner, *England under Buckingham and Charles I*, II, 111.

8. The *OED* dates to 1626 the political sense of "remonstrance"—a formal statement of grievances or similar matters of public importance. Charles and his Parliaments exchanged a series prior to the House of Commons' Grand Remonstrance (1641), by which the term is best known.

9. See Gardiner, *England under Buckingham and Charles I*, II, 98–99, 104–106, 112–114, 139, 189. Donne's brief statement here is a minimal response to the call in the King's circular letter of September 21, 1626, that the Church come to relief of the necessities of the State. Moreover, Donne's insistence that recusancy penalties be enforced surely reflects another aspect of feeling attached to the forced loan. The free giving of the English Catholics excited much suspicion of a secret understanding between them and the King and led to renewed demands for their prosecution. Rushworth records that, while members of "Society and Inns of Court, the Benchers of *Lincolns-Inn*" withheld payment, "The Papists at this time were forward and liberal on this occasion, insomuch that it was said in those times [the first half of 1627], That in the Point of Allegiance then in hand, the Papists were exceeding Orthodox" (*Historical Collections of Private Passages of State, Weighty Matters in Law, Remarkable Proceedings in Five Parliaments, Beginning . . . Anno 1618. And Ending . . . Anno 1629. . . .* [London, 1721], I, 422, 423).

Buckingham's expedition to the Isle of Rhé in the face of widespread recalcitrance. The expedition was in preparation all through the spring of 1627 and took place between June 27 and October 30 of that year, ending in disastrous defeat.[10] Reports of the utter miscarrying of the blockade and siege and of the great loss of life sustained by the English were common knowledge at home by mid-November, producing the universal consternation evinced in contemporary comments.[11] Donne in particular must have heard the earliest news. Not only was he well acquainted in court circles, but he also had a son—George, who occupied a special place in his affections—serving as an army officer in the expedition to Rhé. In view of these circumstances and the fact that the fifth Prebend sermon holds out the prospect of "good effects abroad" (ll. 312–313) and of "deliverances" by "your Armies, and Navies, by Sea, or Land" (ll. 567–568),[12] I do not see how a date of November or December of 1627 can be upheld.

Judging from the most specific topical allusion of all, to a "holy league, Defensive, and Offensive" (l. 639), I think that the fifth Prebend sermon was preached in May or June of 1627. The very specificity of the reference bespeaks a fresh issue. Ambassadors of Spain and France had contracted a League Defensive and Offensive against England in March of 1627 at Madrid, and both Louis XIII and Philip IV allude to it in confidential correspondence in April.[13] I have not been able to discover exactly when

10. See, e.g., Mr. Beaulieu's letter to Sir Thomas Puckering from London on November 14, 1627: "the common rumour of the sad and doleful tidings . . . of the utter overthrow of our enterprise of Rhé" and the letter to the Rev. Joseph Mead from London on November 16: "Our army's lingering so long at the Isle of Rhé . . . hath been the occasion of the greatest and shamefullest overthrow the English have received since we lost Normandy" (Sir Thomas Birch, *The Court and Times of Charles the First, Illustrated by Authentic and Confidential Letters, From Various Public and Private Collections* [London, 1848], I, 283, 284).

11. See Gardiner, *England under Buckingham and Charles I*, II, 168; Rushworth, I, 465–466; cf. Clarendon's mention in his *History of the Great Rebellion* of "that notable descent upon the Isle of Rhé, . . . attended with many unprosperous attempts, and then with a miserable retreat, in which the flower of the army was lost."

12. Note also ll. 642–643, "if we were left to our selves we were remedilesse," which is a contrary-to-fact conditional clause. After the news of Rhé the phrase could not have served as spiritual consolation, as here, but only as a reminder of actual fact.

13. Gardiner (II, 123) gives the date of the signing of the League Defensive and Offensive as March 16, Albion (p. 100) as March 20. Albion also points out

news of the League broke at Whitehall, but again Donne's court connections would have placed him among the first and best informed.

If the fifth Prebend sermon is to be dated in the late spring or early summer of 1627, the season appears from the extant sermons (at all times only part of the total) to have been inordinately busy for Donne. Apart from the fifth Prebend sermon there are seven preached between Candlemas (February 2) and Trinity Sunday, which, however, fell late (June 16) in 1627.[14] Very probably Donne then delayed his summer departure from London, for on July 1, 1627 he delivered a sermon at Chelsea in commemoration of his good friend, Magdalen (Herbert) Danvers. He explains that this one compensates for the one he could not preach at her funeral in June, being "under other *Pre-obligations* and *Pre-contracts,* in the services of mine own Profession, which could not be excused, nor avoided."[15] It is therefore entirely possible that the fifth Prebend sermon was preached as late as the latter part of June.

In all events it seems better to postulate a date before rather than after Donne's summer recess because of the number and nature of the textual parallels with the fifth Prebend sermon found in the sermons from the spring of 1627 as opposed to the sermons from the winter and spring of 1627–1628. Admittedly there are reasons for wariness in using textual parallels as evidence at all,[16] but I think the parallels from the sermons both before and after the summer recess can be given some probative weight. Their consistently fortuitous character suggests the oddly assorted content of the conscious mind where for some time some notion or turn of phrase occurs repeatedly and then falls into oblivion. Hence I have allowed these

---

that although the signing had been carried out secretly and both parties refused to given written evidence to the Pope's Nuncio, the solemn word of Richelieu and other French ministers as to its existence had been given for some time prior to Louis's ratification on April 20. The fact of Charles' French queen and some remaining French attendants must have eased the spreading of the secret.

14. *Sermons,* VII, nos. 13–18; VIII, no. 1. With the first two only is there any question as to date (Introduction, *Sermons,* VII, 28–32).

15. *Sermons,* VIII.2.5–7.

16. Negative considerations include the uncertain date of two sermons grouped with those preached in the spring of 1627, the fact that textual parallels do occur at widely spaced intervals in Donne's sermons, and the possibility that the parallels may result not from contiguity in the time at which they were preached but from their being copied out together by Donne when he prepared, with a view toward publication, fuller versions of a number of sermons in a short period of time.

textual parallels a secondary place here. While the fortuitous character of the parallels is really perceived only in a comparison of contexts, the occurrences may be noted briefly in the order in which they appear in the fifth Prebend sermon. The following ten parallels are to be found in the seven sermons from the spring of 1627:

1. A mentioning of Calvin's singular interpretation of Job 19.25,26: Preb V, 44–48; VII.13.739–745.

2. The (Augustinian) observation that in Scripture God's histories are made prophecies and his prophecies histories: Preb V, 67–74; VII.14.257–263.

3. The verbal echo in Preb V, 106–110, *"Dicite, Say unto God,* Declare, manifest, publish your zeale . . . ; wee must declare our thankfull zeale to God's cause, we must not modifie, not disguise that;" and VIII.1.69–70, 70–75: *"Dicentes, Saying,* Publishing, Declaring, without disguises or modifications. . . . No occasional emergencies, no losse, no trouble interrupted their zeale to Gods service."

4. The imputing of base motives to the Roman Church's withholding of pronouncements on certain matters: Preb V, 198–202; VII.15.248–252.

5. A reference to the wide spread of the Arian heresy: Preb V, 270–275; VIII.1.37–38.

6. The combination of the idea that all, especially those in authority, ought to propagate God's truth with the notion of the Divine Word (*Verbum*) and *"Dixit, & facta sunt"*—a free citation of the repeated Vulgate phrase in the first chapter of Genesis: Preb V, 320–331, 356–361; VIII.1. 530–561.

7. The citation of the Vulgate reading *"Siste sol"* in Josh. 10.12: Preb V, 332; VII.14.21.

8. The verbal resemblance in Preb V, 350–351, "Gold may be beat so thin, as that it may be blowne away;" and VII.16.358–359: "as gold is gold still, the heaviest metall of all, yet if it be beat into leaf gold, I can blow it away".

9. The assertion that God does not damn a man "from all eternity" (Preb V, 546–547) or "before he meant to make him" (VII.18.65–66).

10. The construing of the Vulgate reading *"Odium perfectum"* in Psalm 138.22 as a prescription of the ideal attitude toward enemies in religion: Preb V, 616–621; VII.17.348–353.

By contrast, there are only five parallels with the fifth Prebend sermon to be found among Donne's seven extant sermons from the winter and spring of 1627–1628:

1. The similar textual note in Preb V, 112–113, "The Duty is a Commemoration of Benefits; *Dicite,* Speak of it," and VIII.7.173: "The duty in this Text is expressed and limited in speaking."

2. The innuendo against the Roman Church for leaving certain matters unresolved: Preb V, 198–202; VIII.7.324–325.

3. The reference to St. Cyprian's claim that every bishop has a responsibility for the whole Church: Preb V, 250–253; VIII.6.179–181.

4. The combination of the notion of God as Word with allusions to the *"Dixit"* and *"Fiat"* of Genesis: Preb V, 324–328, 356–367; VIII.7.192–198.

5. The combined allusion to James 1.17 and 2 Cor 1.3 in Preb V, 478–479, "The Father of lights, and the God of all comfort present," and in VIII.9.165–169, "But even there God is . . . who is the God of all consolation . . . who is the Father of all lights."[17]

Here, on a combination of topical allusions and textual parallels, I am content to rest my case for a date in May or June of 1627 for the fifth Prebend sermon.

17. In addition, it ought to be noted of the group of sermons from the winter and spring of 1627–28 that two references are used in different senses from those in the fifth Prebend sermon. Cf. the reference to *"Arcana"* in Preb V, 120 and VIII.11.90; and the reference to gold in Preb V, 350–351 and VIII.10.109–111.

Appendix B. Table of English and Latin Citations of Scripture in the Prebend Sermons

Under the first six, principal headings this table lists all of the Scriptural citations and allusions in Latin and English which I have been able to identify in the Prebend sermons. The table is limited to Latin and English because Donne's other citations and allusions (Hebrew here, Greek also in the sermons at large) are isolated, and transliterated, words which do not offer clues as to what version of the Bible Donne was using. This table is intended to illustrate Donne's energetic and eclectic use of most of the English and Latin versions available and, above all, to document very graphically the material role of God's Word among the words of Donne the preacher. Out of a total of 3750 lines in the five Prebend sermons I have culled 615 citations and allusions in Latin and English, making an average of one occurrence in every six lines.

The procedure in compiling this table has been to regularize variations in verse and chapter notation in accordance with the Authorized Version. A citation has been classified as exact if the words—including their sequence, tense, case, and number—conform to some version or versions of the Bible. Variations in spelling, punctuation, and typeface, and omitted words which cause no alteration in phrasing have been disregarded for purposes of classification. An inexact citation has been classified as an allusion when it lacks sufficient identifying features to link it with some specific version (or versions).

In the interests of consistency and objectivity, this table is essentially descriptive, not interpretive. Thus, when one of Donne's citations is listed as corresponding with more than one version, the implication is that these versions share a reading of a text and that Donne consulted one of them. I have preferred not to second-guess him as to which version he did in fact use at any given point. His general practice in his mature preaching—which this table confirms—was to consult the Authorized Version first and Geneva second among English versions, and among Latin versions to revert to the Vulgate. (That is, if he consulted any version at all, for he very often quoted from memory.)

Warning ought to be made as to possible minor distortions in my descriptive approach. The unique correspondence of Donne's citation at Preb V, 90 with the Bishops' Bible is more likely to have been, in reality, a loose reference to the Authorized Version, of which the Bishops' Bible was a progenitor. Donne does not appear ever to have chosen a unique reading from the Great or Bishops' Bibles without saying that he did (as at Preb III, 417–418, 589–590). On the other hand, unique correspondences with any one Latin version have no inherent implausibility. Another possible kind of distortion is that an inexact citation falling between the wording of two versions may have been linked with the one to which it has an entirely accidental but, indeed, closer resemblance. The risk of such distortions is, however, very minor and preferable to a method involving subjective decisions at a number of points.

Unfortunately, description and the categories of citation and allusion do not quite cover everything. There remain English and Latin phrases with obvious Scriptural overtones whose nature does require guesswork in the form of some interpretation. These loose ends have been dealt with individually in the notes to the Prebend sermons, and, on the precedent of Don Cameron Allen's article, to which I have often referred, I have ventured to collect them here under three miscellaneous headings added to the six principal (descriptive) ones. The whole table develops as follows:

    I.   Exact Scriptural Citations in English (Authorized Version unless otherwise specified);

   II.   Inexact Scriptural Citations in English (Authorized Version unless otherwise specified);

  III.   Scriptural Allusions in English;

  IV.   Exact Scriptural Citations in Latin;

   V.   Inexact Scriptural Citations in Latin;

  VI.   Scriptural Allusions in Latin;

 VII.   Literal English Translations of the Vulgate (or of Hebrew);

VIII.   Literal Latin Translations of the Authorized Version;

  IX.   Literal Latin Translations (or Amplifications) of Hebrew.

The following abbreviations are used throughout; see the headnote to the commentary on the Prebend sermons for full bibliographical information (pp. 186–188):

AV:	Authorized (or King James) Version
Bish:	Bishops' (or Parker's) Version
Genv:	Geneva (or Breeches) Bible
Gr B:	Great (or Cranmer's) Bible

Wyc LV: Wyclif's so-called "Later Version" (c. 1384)
Beza: Theodorus Beza's Latin New Testament (a translation of
           the Syriac, not the Greek text)
Eras: Desiderius Erasmus's Latin New Testament
Muns: Sebastian Munster's Latin translation of the Bible
Pagn: Santis Pagnini's Latin translation of the Bible
T-J: Immanuel Tremellius's and Franciscus Junius's Latin Old
           Testament
Trem: Immanuel Tremellius's (incomplete) Latin New Testa-
           ment
Vatab: Franciscus Vatablus's Latin edition of the Bible (an
           emended version of Santis Pagnini's translation)
Vulg: Vulgate edition in a post-Tridentine recension

I. Exact Scriptural Citations in English (AV unless otherwise specified):

Preb I (text in headnote)	Psalm 62.9
I.146–147	Col. 1.15
I.214	Obad. 1.21
I.227–228	Exod. 7.1
I.247–248	Exod. 32.36
I.249–250	Jer. 8.22
I.340	2 Cor. 1.20
I.341	Rev. 3.14
I.389	Matt. 5.3
I.393	Ecclus. 25.2
I.406–407	Prov. 10.15
I.410	Prov. 30.8
I.411–412	Ruth 3.10
I.428	Eph. 3.8
I.429	Eph. 3.16
I.442–443	Matt. 15.26
I.641	Psalm 62.8
Preb II.59–60	Psalm 63.2
II.61–62	Psalm 63.5
II.76–77	2 Cor. 4.17
II.92	Prov. 27.3
II.127–128	Matt. 3.17

	II.130–131	Matt. 17.5
	II.240–241	Psalm 42.2
	II.255–256	Psalm 5.7
	II.475	Psalm 51.15
	II.476	Psalm 81.10
	II.594–595	Isa. 18.1
	II.676, 677	Matt. 25.23 (Genv)
	II.680	Matt. 25.34
	II.692–693, 697–698	Psalm 42.5
Preb	III.109	Matt. 25.21
	III.220–222	Jer. 9.1
	III.230	Ezek. 6.11
	III.336–337	2 Sam. 7.27
	III.366–367	Psalm 119.19
	III.417–418	Psalm 64.10 (Gr B, Bish, Wyclif LV)
	III.433–434	Psalm 78.63
	III.537	Psalm 10.3
	III.549–551	Phil. 4.8
	III.603–604	Psalm 112.6
	III.636–637	Rom. 11.33
	III.653–654	1 Cor. 6.19
	III.687–688	Matt. 25.21, 23 (Genv)
Preb	IV.54–55, 57–58, 63–65, 75–76, 156–158, 205–206, 264–265, 302–303	Psalm 65.5
	IV.102–103	Psalm 145.15
	IV.132	Psalm 63.5
	IV.207	Psalm 37.5
	IV.241–242	Psalm 37.5
	IV.270–272	Prov. 4.19
	IV.277–278	Rom. 3.20
	IV.278	Rom. 5.13
	IV.279	Rom. 7.7
	IV.283–284	Rom. 7.7
	IV.437–438	Jer. 8.22
	IV.452–453	Isa. 60.19
	IV.478	Deut. 7.9

	IV.495	Isa. 25.1
	IV.546–547	Hos. 12.10
	IV.559	Num. 21.27
	IV.562–563	Psalm 78.2
	IV.565–566	Matt. 7.29
	IV.566–567	Luke 4.32
	IV.577	Matt. 13.34
	IV.612	John 15.15
	IV.666–667	Psalm 95.3
	IV.676–677	Job 27.8, 9
	IV.684–685	Luke 5.12
	IV.688–689	Luke 22.44
	IV.708–709	1 Cor. 1.21
	IV.729	Mark 16.15
	IV.815–816	Matt. 26.39
	IV.882–883	Rev. 4.11
Preb	V.10–11	Psalm 66 title
	V.49–50	Ezek. 37.3
	V.54–56, 77–78, 114, 119–120, 136–137, 323–324, 343, 401–402, 441–442, 657, 667–668	Psalm 66.3
	V.90	Psalm 66.1
	V.91	Psalm 66.4
	V.99–100	Josh. 24.15 (Genv)
	V.248–249	Psalm 66.4
	V.249–250	Psalm 66.16
	V.294	Psalm 66.5
	V.295	Psalm 66.8
	V.296–297	Psalm 66.16
	V.301–302	Psalm 145.5
	V.304–307	Psalm 145.6
	V.378–379	Gen. 9.6
	V.383–384	Luke 9.54
	V.413	Psalm 82.6
	V.460	Heb. 13.8 (Bish)
	V.481–482	Exod. 3.6
	V.532–533	Isa. 33.6

V.534	Heb. 12.28
V.536–537	Heb. 12.29
V.599–600	Rom. 5.10
V.631–632	Acts 9.4
V.635–636	Gen. 4.11
V.697–698	Psalm 81.13

II. Inexact Scriptural Citations in English (AV unless otherwise specified):

Preb	I.12–13	Luke 24.44 (Genv or Bish)
	I.101–102	Psalm 62.8
	I.150	Heb. 1.5
	I.191–192	Psalm 8.4 (all versions)
	I.229	Exod. 4.16 (Bish & AV)
	I.236–238	Heb. 4.15 (Bish & AV)
	I.239–240	Deut. 16.18
	I.252	2 Chron. 16.12
	I.385–386	Exod. 23.3
	I.386–387	Lev. 19.15
	I.408	Prov. 10.15
	I.426–427	Rom. 2.4 (Gr B, Bish, AV)
	I.427–428	Rom. 11.33
	I.630–631	Psalm 39.5 (Genv or AV)
	I.644–645	Jer. 17.5 (Genv & AV)
	I.647–648	Matt. 16.17 (Genv & AV)
	I.660	Psalm 62.11
	I.662–663	Psalm 62.6
	I.664	Psalm 62.7
	I.684–686	Mic. 7.5
	I.688–689	Mic. 7.7
Preb	II.49	Heb. 13.8 (Bish)
	II.57	Psalm 63.1
	II.76–77	2 Cor. 4.17
	II.84	Job 7.20 (Bish & AV)
	II.88–89	Matt. 20.12 (Genv & AV)
	II.89, 92, 97–98	Prov. 27.3 (Genv & AV)
	II.110–111	Eccles. 5.13

II.120	Job 1.8
II.124	1 Sam. 13.14 (all versions)
II.128–129	Matt. 4.1 (all versions)
II.147–149	Matt. 21.44
II.161–162	Ezek. 36.26 (Genv & AV)
II.170–172	Rev. 16.9
II.174	Rev. 16.11
II.177–179	Rev. 16.21 (Genv, Bish, AV)
II.232–234	Psalm 78.60, 61
II.237	Psalm 27.4
II.242–245	Psalm 84.3
II.246–247	Luke 12.7; Matt. 10.31
II.257–258	Dan. 6.10
II.273–274	Psalm 84.4
II.353–354	Heb. 11.3
II.453–454	Mark 9.24 (Genv or AV)
II.525–526	Isa. 59.17
II.597–600	Exod. 19.4
II.600–602	Ezek. 1.24 (Genv or AV)
II.602–604	Jer. 49.22
II.607–610	Dan. 3.17, 18 (Genv or AV)
II.620–621	Matt. 23.37 (Genv, Bish, AV)
II.738	John 16.24 (all versions)
II.739–740	John 16.22 (Genv)
Preb III.122	Prov. 8.31
III.123–126	Eph. 3.6, 7, 8, 10 (Genv or AV)
III.153	1 Peter 5.8 (all versions)
III.191	Gen. 1.1 (Gr B & Bish)
III.225–226	Isa. 16.9
III.226	Isa. 1.24 (Genv & AV)
III.298	Prov. 23.26 (all versions)
III.333–334	2 Sam. 7.21 (all versions)
III.345–346	Psalm 42.2 (Gr B, Bish, Genv)
III.349–350	Psalm 119.11
III.351–353	Psalm 40.10 (Genv & AV)
III.430–431	John 5.35 (all versions)
III.458–460	Prov. 22.1
III.521–523	Zeph. 3.19, 20
III.589–590	Psalm 64.10 (Gr B)

Preb IV.47   Rev. 3.20 (all versions)
      IV.52–53   Rev. 19.9
      IV.79–80, 106–107, 248–   Psalm 65.5
        249, 389–391, 466–469,
        506–509, 585, 606–608,
        640–641, 703–704,
        740–742, 843–845,
        848–849,   854,   857,
        884–885
      IV.88   Heb. 3.6 (Genv)
      IV.89   Psalm 147.2 (all versions)
      IV.97   John 4.34
      IV.132–134   Psalm 81.16 (Genv & AV)
      IV.173–174   John 1.9 (all versions)
      IV.399–401   Rom. 10.20
      IV.438–439   Isa. 53.5 (Genv & AV)
      IV.562   Psalm 49.4
      IV.604–605   Psalm 34.11 (Gr B, Bish, AV)
      IV.659–660   Mal. 1.8 (Gr B)
      IV.661–662   Psalm 47.2
      IV.668–669   Deut. 28.58 (all versions)
      IV.677–678   Hos. 7.14 (Genv)
      IV.683   James 4.3 (all versions)
      IV.685–686   James 1.6, 7
      IV.687   1 Thess. 5.17 (all versions)
      IV.690–692   Isa. 1.15
      IV.692–693   Prov. 28.9
      IV.694–695   Psalm 109.6 (Gr B, Bish, Genv)
      IV.715–716   Lam. 4.16
      IV.730–732   Matt. 7.6
      IV.773–774   1 Cor. 11.29 (Gr B & Genv)
      IV.782–783   Heb. 10.29 (Gr B, Bish, AV)
      IV.814   Matt. 26.38 (Gr B)
      IV.830–831   Psalm 130.4 (Genv & AV)
      IV.836–837   Prov. 21.15 (Genv & AV)

Preb V.41–43   Isa. 60.1
      V.47–48   Job 19.25, 26
      V.79–80, 141–142, 159,   Psalm 66.3
        622, 647, 671–672, 690

V.248–249	Psalm 66.4 (all versions)
V.297	Psalm 145.3
V.299–300	Psalm 145.4
V.373–375	Matt. 26.52 (Gr B, Bish, AV)
V.384–385	Luke 9.55 (Genv)
V.477–478	Gen. 15.12 (Bish & AV)
V.506	Psalm 66.3 (Genv & AV)
V.513–514	Mal. 2.5 (Bish & AV)
V.530–531	Psalm 2.11
V.643	Lam. 3.22 (Genv)
V.660–662	Deut. 20.4 (Gr B, Bish, Genv)
V.699–700	Psalm 81.13

III. Scriptural Allusions in English:

Preb I.171–172	1 Cor. 15.53, 54
I.176–177	Mark 12.25
I.197–199	1 John 3.1; 1 Cor. 6.20, 7.23; Zech. 11.12; 1 Cor. 6.19; Jer. 22.24; Hag. 2.23; Deut. 32.10; Psalm 17.8; Lam. 2.18; Zech. 2.8
I.245–246	Judges 7.7
I.254	1 Kings 10.15, 28; 2 Chron. 1.16; 9.14
I.254–255	1 Kings 5.6, 7.14
I.269–270	Phil. 3.8
I.270–271	Isa. 40.17
I.272	2 Cor. 12.11
I.273–274	1 Cor. 1.21
I.274–275	2 Cor. 2.16
I.275–276	1 Cor. 3.6
I.353–354	James 4.13
I.381–382	Matt. 25.34–36
I.404–405	Rev. 3.17
I.504	Matt. 21.9
I.505	Matt. 27.29; Mark 15.18; John 19.3
I.508	Matt. 12.24; Mark 3.22; Luke 11.15
I.560–562	Gen. 3.6, 7, 10
I.566–568	2 Sam. 6.6, 7
I.599	Hab. 1.16
I.646	Job 6.12

Preb	II.1–2	Wisd. of Sol. 16.20–21
	II.84–85	2 Sam. 14.26
	II.101–102	Psalm 39.5,11; Eccles. 1.2; 3.19; 12.8
	II.106–107	Sus. 1.2, 22–23, 27, 31
	II.107–108	Gen. 39
	II.109	Luke 16.19–31
	II.120–123	Job 1.12–2.13
	II.124–126	2 Sam. 13.15–18
	II.138	Psalm 22.6
	II.142–143	2 Cor. 4.17
	II.206–207	Psalm 38.2
	II.264–265	1 Kings 8.44–49
	II.512	Eph. 6.17; Heb. 4.12; Deut. 33.29; Psalm 17.13, *etc.*
	II.512	2 Sam. 22.31; Psalms 18.2,30; 91.4; Prov. 2.7, *etc.*
	II.513	Isa. 26.1; 60.18
	II.513	Psalm 61.3; Prov. 18.10
	II.513	Psalm 18.2; 1 Cor. 10.4
	II.513	Psalms 3.4; 15.1; 24.3; 99.9; Ezek. 34.26
	II.515	1 Sam. 1.11; 2 Sam. 7.27; Psalms 24.10; 59.5; 84.1, *etc.*
	II.520	1 Sam. 17.4–7
	II.527	Isa. 59.20
	II.565–566	Exod. 3.13, 14
	II.615	Exod. 25.20
	II.623–626	Psalm 17.8; 36.7; 57.1; 61.4; 91.4
	II.683	Luke 15.10
Preb	III.9–10	Jer. 33.11; Heb. 13.15
	III.127–128	Eph. 3.9
	III.140–141	Gen. 18.16
	III.141–143	Gen. 3.9
	III.167–168	1 John 3.12
	III.168–169	Matt. 10.4
	III.172–174	Lev. 26.16
	III.243	Gen. 3.14
	III.261–262	Gen. 28.12
	III.304–306	Job 1.6
	III.308–311	1 Kings 22.22

III.342–343	Psalm 35.18; 40.10
III.346–347	Psalm 51.11, 12
III.355–356	Matt. 7.6
III.494–495	Gen. 2.17
III.543–544	Matt. 7.12
III.598–600	Psalm 75.4; Isa. 44.25; Job 12.17
III.625–626	2 Peter 1.4; 1 Cor. 6.17
III.640	1 Cor. 13.12
III.641	1 John 3.2
III.652–653	Luke 23.46
III.659–671	Matt. 25.34–46
III.685	Psalm 22.14
III.687–688	Matt. 25.21
III.700, 701	Psalm 64.10
Preb IV.4–5	1 Cor. 1.21
IV.8–10	Acts 2, 4
IV.19–21	Mark 6.35–44
IV.40–42	Luke 14.16–24; Matt. 22.2–14
IV.87	Phil. 3.20
IV.91	John 14.6
IV.92	Matt. 7.13, 14
IV.94	John 10.7–9
IV.113	Rev. 19.9
IV.199–200	Rom. 1.20
IV.201	Rom. 11.33
IV.212–213	Gen. 18.23–33
IV.291–292	Deut. 34.1
IV.293	John 8.56
IV.306–307	Col. 1.2; 1 Tim. 6.12
IV.310–311	Acts 11.26
IV.333–334	John 19.19
IV.335–336	Acts 13.6
IV.349	Phil. 4.12, 13
IV.363	1 Cor. 1.12
IV.441	1 Sam 13.19
IV.444–445	Acts 12.7
IV.482–483	1 Peter 4.19
IV.501	Gen. 11.9
IV.501–502	Exod. 7–11

	IV.502	Judges 1.1–17
	IV.503	2 Kings 19.35; 2 Chron. 32.21
	IV.524	Phil. 2.12
	IV.532–533	1 Kings 18.28
	IV.534–537	Lev. 1–9, 16, 22–23
	IV.540–541	Exod. 3.8; Psalm 23.5
	IV.600–601	Psalm 5.7; Heb. 12.28
	IV.601–602	Mal. 1.6
	IV.613–616	Matt. 22.12, 13
	IV.622–623	Rom. 12.5; 1 Cor. 10.16–17, *etc.*
	IV.643	Isa. 56.7
	IV.674	Psalm 111.9
	IV.680	Matt. 20.21
	IV.696–697	Ezek. 14.14
	IV.699–700	Jer. 7.16; 11.14; 14.11
	IV.727–728	Matt. 18.18; 16.19
	IV.767	John 1.29, 34, 36
	IV.774–775	1 John 2.1, 2
	IV.781	Luke 22.63; Matt. 27.29; Mark 15.20
	IV.799–800	Gen. 3.19
	IV.819	Rev. 5.5
	IV.859	Mark 16.16
	IV.867–868	2 Cor. 2.16
	IV.873–874	Phil. 2.12
Preb	V.124	Psalm 66.3
	V.183	Isa. 43.15; Mal. 1.14; Psalm 82.6
	V.185–186	1 Cor. 15.10
	V.228–230	Exod. 20.1–17
	V.330–334	Josh. 10.12, 13
	V.336–338	Acts 2.3, 4
	V.338–339	Matt. 12.22; Mark 7.32
	V.376	Gen. 9.4
	V.406–409	Exod. 13.21, 22; Num. 14.14; Neh. 9.12, 19
	V.414–415	Exod. 33.23
	V.417–418	Deut. 34.6
	V.460	Heb. 13.8
	V.478	James 1.17
	V.479	2 Cor. 1.3

V.491	Gen. 8.8–11
V.492–493	Matt. 24.27–29; Luke 17.26–37
V.494	Gen. 6.18; 7.1; Heb. 11.7
V.495	Jon. 2; Matt. 12.40
V.502–503	James 1.17
V.530	Psalm 111.10; Prov. 9.10; 15.33
V.538	1 John 4.8
V.587–588	Rom. 5.8, 10
V.608–609	Matt. 19.6; Mark 10.9
V.626–627	Psalm 17.8
V.629–630	Isa. 53.7
V.634	Gen. 4.6, 10
V.637–638	1 Kings 13.4
V.644–666	Deut. 4.7, 8
V.680–681	Exod. 8–11

IV. Exact Scriptural Citations in Latin:

Preb	I.139–140	Gen. 3.20 (Vulg, T-J, Vatab)
	I.142	Mark 16.15 (all versions but Trem)
	I.164	Gen. 1.28 (Vulg & Pagn)
	I.191	Psalm 8.4 (Vulg, Muns, Vatab)
	I.394–395	Isa. 51.21 (Vulg only)
	I.408	Prov. 10.15 (Vulg & Muns)
	I.556	Prov. 27.7 (Vulg, Vatab, Pagn)
	I.558–559	Jer. 10.14 (Vulg only)
	I.563	Rom. 12.3 (Vulg only)
Preb	II.7	Cant. 1.2 (Vulg, Muns, Pagn)
	II.76	2 Cor. 4.17 (Vulg & Eras)
	II.81	Exod. 9.3 (Vulg & Pagn)
	II.142	2 Cor. 4.17 (Vulg & Eras)
	II.364–365	Gen. 1.26 (Vulg & T-J)
	II.437 mg.	Psalm 63.7 (Pagn only)
	II.478	Psalm 81.10 (all versions but Muns)
	II.499	Psalm 63.7 (Vulg only)
	II.535	Psalm 105.15 (Vulg only)
	II.537–538	Psalm 63.7 (Muns only)
	II.579–580	Psalm 63.7 (Muns only)
	II.667	Gen. 2.17 (Vulg & Vatab)

Preb III.43	Psalm 64.10 (Vulg & Pagn)
III.44	Psalm 64.10 (T-J & Vatab)
III.45	Psalm 64.10 (Vulg only)
III.78	Psalm 64.10 (Vulg, Vatab, Pagn)
III.91, 103	Psalm 64.10 (T-J & Vatab)
III.91, 103	Psalm 64.10 (Vulg only)
III.147	Gen. 1.27 (Vulg & T-J)
III.171	Gen. 2.17 (Vulg & Vatab)
III.227–228	Isa. 1.24 (Vulg & Pagn)
III.229	Ezek. 6.11 (Vulg & Pagn)
III.236	Psalm 64.10 (Vulg, Vatab, Pagn)
III.349	Psalm 119.11 (Muns only)
III.366	Psalm 119.19 (Vulg & T-J)
III.422	Psalm 64.10 (Vulg only)
III.555, 558–559	Psalm 64.10 (T-J & Vatab)
III.555	Psalm 64.10 (Vulg only)
III.577	Psalm 27.14 (Vulg only)
III.581	Psalm 40.1 (Vulg & Muns)
III.581–582	Psalm 52.9 (all versions but Vatab)
Preb IV.19	Mark 6.38 (all versions but Trem)
IV.200–201	Rom. 11.33 (Vulg only)
IV.240, 244–245, 246	Psalm 37.5 (Vulg & Muns)
IV.347	Cant. 1.2 (Vulg, Muns, Pagn)
IV.489	Psalm 19.8 (Vulg only)
IV.516	Psalm 65.5 (T-J only)
IV.661	Psalm 47.3 (Vulg, Muns, Pagn)
IV.662–663, 665–666	Psalm 96.4 (Vulg, Muns, Pagn)
IV.673–674	Psalm 111.9 (Vulg, Muns, Pagn)
IV.833, 837	Prov. 21.15 (Vulg only)
IV.838	Prov. 28.14 (Vulg only)
Preb V.11	Psalm 66 title (Vulg & Pagn)
V.14	Psalm 66 title (Vulg only)
V.77–79, 140–141, 160, 647	Psalm 66.3 (Vulg only)
V.90	Psalm 66.1 (Vulg, Vatab, Pagn)
V.100	Josh. 24.15 (Vulg, Vatab, Pagn)
V.247	Psalm 66.1 (Muns only)
V.248	Psalm 66.4 (Vulg only)
V.532	Isa. 33.6 (T-J only)

V. Inexact Scriptural Citations in Latin:

Preb	I.394–395	Isa. 51.21 (Vulg only)
	I.534	Isa. 58.11 (Pagn only)

Preb	II.82	Exod. 8.24 (Vulg only)
	II.86	Lam. 3.7 (Vulg only)
	II.704	Gen. 1.2 (T-J only)

Preb	III.108, 686–687	Matt. 25.21 (Vulg & Trem)
	III.297–298	Prov. 23.26 (Muns or Vulg & Pagn)

Preb	IV.366–367	Psalm 19.5 (Vulg, Muns, Pagn)
	IV.470	Psalm 65.5 (Muns & Pagn)
	IV.482	1 Peter 4.19 (Vulg, Trem, Vatab)
	IV.618, 859	Mark 16.16 (all versions but Trem)
	IV.715	Lam. 4.16 (Vulg only)
	IV.830	Psalm 130.4 (Vulg only)

Preb	V.115, 117	Psalm 115.1 (Vulg, Muns, Pagn)
	V.471–472	Psalm 66.3 (Muns & Pagn)
	V.512	Psalm 66.3 (T-J only)
	V.606	Gen. 3.15 (all versions but T-J)
	V.618	Psalm 139.22 (Vulg or T-J)

VI. Scriptural Allusions in Latin:

Preb	I.150, 151	Heb. 1.5
	I.152	Gen. 1.26
	I.181	Luke 6.35
	I.182	1 John 3.9
	I.182–183	2 Peter 1.4
	I.184	Psalm 82.6
	I.507	Mark 15.13, 14; Luke 23.21; John 19.6

Preb	II.515	1 Sam. 1.11; 2 Sam. 7.27, *etc.*
	II.679–680	Matt. 25.34
	II.688–689	Rev. 6.10

Preb III.169–170   Gen. 2.17
      III.345–346   Psalm 42.2
      III.346   Psalm 52.11, 12
      III.370   Psalm 119.11
      III.579–580   Rev. 6.10
      III.641   1 John 3.2
      III.689   1 Cor. 9.16
      III.692   Matt. 25.21

Preb IV.478   Deut. 7.9
      IV.484   1 Thess. 5.24
      IV.486   Heb. 2.17
      IV.654   Exod. 26–29
      IV.804   1 John 3.2
      IV.815   Matt. 26.39
      IV.816   Matt. 27.46
      IV.826, 828   John 19.30
      IV.828   Gen. 1.1
      IV.828   John 1.1

Preb V.324   John 1.1, etc.
      V.356   Gen. 1.3–31
      V.704   2 Cor. 12.7
      V.705   2 Cor. 12.7

VII. Literal English Translations of the Vulgate (or of Hebrew):

Preb I.394–395   Isa. 51.21
      I.534–535   Isa. 58.11 (trans. of Pagnini)
      I.556–557   Prov. 27.7
      I.559   Jer. 10.14

Preb II.668–669   Gen. 2.7 (trans. of Hebrew)

Preb III.45–46   Psalm 64.10
      III.434–435   Psalm 78.63 (trans. of Hebrew)

Preb IV.484–485   1 Thess. 5.24
      IV.489   Psalm 19.8
      IV.662–663   Psalm 96.4

IV.830–831	Psalm 130.4
IV.838–839	Prov. 28.14

Preb	V.248	Psalm 66.1
	V.415	Exod. 33.23

VIII. Literal Latin Translations of the Authorized Version:

Preb	IV.668	Deut. 28.58
	IV.830	Psalm 130.4 (or of Geneva)

Preb	V.249	Psalm 66.16

IX. Literal Latin Translations (or Amplifications) of Hebrew:

Preb	II.544–546	Gen. 1.1
	II.555	OT, *passim*
	II.668	Gen. 2.17

Preb	III.259–260	Psalm 64.10
	III.607	Psalm 112.6
	III.617	Psalm 64.10

Preb	IV.574	Num. 21.27; Psalm 49.4; 78.2, *etc.*
	IV.603–604	Psalm 34.11

Preb	V.658, 667	Psalm 66.3
	V.672–674	Psalm 66.3

Index

An asterisk following a page number indicates a marginal reference.